SUFISM
A Wayfarer's Guide to the Naqshbandi Way

Is not the time now ripe for the hearts of those who believe
a-lam ya'ni li'lladhīna āmanū
to be humbled to the Remembrance of Allāh?
an takhsha'a qulūbu-hum li-dhikri 'llāhi.
(Qur'ān 57:16)

SUFISM
A WAYFARER'S GUIDE TO THE NAQSHBANDI WAY

[*Mā huwa 't-Taṣawwuf wa-mā hiya aṭ-ṭarīqat an-Naqshbandiyya*]

Originally written in Kurdish by
Shaikh Amīn 'Alā ad-Dīn an-Naqshbandī

Translated into Arabic by
Dr. Muḥammad Sharīf Aḥmad

English Translation (from the Arabic) by
Muhtar Holland

Preface by
Shaikh Muhammad Ma'sum Naqshbandi (ra)

Forewords by
Professor Shaikh 'Abd al-Karīm
Arthur F. Buehler, and
Abdal Hakim Murad

FONS VITAE

First published in 2011 by
Fons Vitae
49 Mockingbird Valley Drive
Louisville, KY 40207
http://www.fonsvitae.com
Email: fonsvitaeky@aol.com

Special thanks and appreciation to the Naqshbandiya Foundation for Islamic Education (NFIE) for their invaluable support (http://www.nfie.com), a non-profit organization established in memory of Sayyid Jama'at 'Ali Shah Naqshbandī (r) d. 1951, and Shaykh Muḥammad Ma'sūm Naqshbandī (r) d. 2007.

Library of Congress Control Number: 2011934732

ISBN 9781891785832

This book was typeset by Neville Blakemore, Jr.

Printed by Richmond Printing, Houston TX

Dedication

This English translation of *Sufism: A Wayfarer's Guide to the Naqshbandi Way*—[*Mā huwa 't-Taṣawwuf wa-mā hiya aṭ-ṭarīqat an-Naqshbandiyya*]—is warmly dedicated to the late Shaikh Muhammad Ma'sum Naqshbandi (1917-2007), the great-grandson of Shaikh 'Uthman Sirājuddīn, Mawlānā Khālid's chief successor—may God bless their inner secrets. The current translation came about in response to persistent seekers of spiritual wisdom who repeatedly asked Shaykh Muhammad Ma'sum for a book elucidating Naqshbandi practices as they were practiced in his native Biyarah, Iraq.

Shaikh Ma'sum (ra) began his education in the Kurdish Khālidī centre of Biyara, Iraq, studying also in Mahabad, Iran, before finishing his studies with the renown scholar, 'Allāma Shaikh 'Abdulkarīm Mudarris in 1947. After obtaining an official teaching certificate to teach religious sciences, Shaikh Ma'sum (ra) received permission to teach the Qādirī and Naqshbandī-Khālidī practices from Shaikh Muhammad 'Alā'uddīn Naqshbandī. He stayed in Iran until the 1979 revolution when he moved to Iraq, finally settling in the United States in 1991. Shaikh Ma'sum (ra) passed away in 2007, on the eighth of January; his body was laid to rest in Biyara.

Shaikh Ma'sum (ra) was an exemplary spiritual teacher and leader who embodied the highest ethical and spiritual ideals, remaining patiently in exile rather than compromise his principles. Through assisting those who came to him, he exhibited a humble greatness difficult to describe. It brings to mind the Qur'anic verse, "The most noble among you are, from God's perspective, the most pious". Shaikh Ma'sum continues to inspire many who met him even though his presence no longer illuminates this world. Shaikh Muhammad Ma'sum (ra) was the Religious Advisor and Spiritual Guide of the Naqshbandiya Foundation for Islamic Education.

Table of Contents

Table of Contents, continued

Table of Contents, continued

11. The realm of Divinity [*Lāhūt*]. 211
12. The realm of Humanity [*Nāsūt*]. 211
13. The realm of Omnipotence [*Jabarūt*]. 211
14. The realm of Sovereignty [*Malakūt*]. 211
15. The four basic elements [*'anāṣir*]. 212
16. The saint [*walī*]. 212
17. The seeker [*murīd*]. 215
18. The deputy [*khalīfa*]. 219

Praiseworthy attributes: 222

1. Love of what is best for people [*ḥubb al-khair li'n-nās*]. 2. Sincerity [*ikhlāṣ*]. 3. Humility [*tawāḍu'*]. 4. Generosity [*jūd*]. 5. Truthfulness [*ṣidq*]. 6. Trustworthiness [*amāna*]. 7. Contentment [*qanā'a*]. 8. Compassion [*raḥma*]. 9. Modesty and propriety [*ḥayā' wa adab*]. 10. Affection for human beings [*maḥabbat an-nās*]. 11. Courage [*shajā'a*]. 12. Reliability [*thiqa*]. 13. Tolerance [*ḥilm*]. 14. Readiness to pardon [*'afw*]. 15. Respect for family ties [*ṣilat ar-raḥim*]. 16. Striving for what is good [*as-sa'y li'l-khair*]. 17. Thankfulness for blessing [*shukr an-ni'ma*]. 18. Self-denial and altruism [*nukrān adh-dhāt wa 'l-īthār*]. 19. Fidelity [*wafā'*].

Blameworthy attributes: 223

1. Envy [*ḥasad*]. 2. Ostentation and hypocrisy [*riyā' wa nifāq*]. 3. Arrogant pride, vain conceit and delusion [*kibr wa 'ujb wa ghurūr*]. 4. Miserliness [*bukhl*]. 5. Lying [*kadhb*]. 6. Betrayal of trust [*khiyānat al-amāna*]. 7. Greedy pursuit of wealth or prestige [*takālub 'ala 'l-māl awi 'l-jāh*]. 8. Cruelty [*qaswa*]. 9. Insolence [*waqāḥa*]. 10. Antipathy to one's fellow human beings [*karāhiyyat an-nās*]. 11. Cowardice [*jubn*]. 12. Lack of reliability [*'adam ath-thiqa*]. 13. Anger [*ghaḍab*]. 14. Vengefulness [*intiqām*]. 15. Severance of family ties [*qaṭ' ar-raḥim*]. 16. Slander [*namīma*]. 17. Ingratitude for blessing [*kufrān an-ni'ma*]. 18. Love of the self [*ḥubb adh-dhāt*].

Chapter Six: The Naqshbandī Spiritual Path [*Ṭarīqa*] 224
The Eleven Axioms of the Naqshbandī Spiritual Path 252
The Naqshbandī Chain of Transmission [*Silsila*] 265
When was this Spiritual Path called "Naqshbandī"—and why? 268
The Life of Bahā' ad-Dīn an-Naqshband 271
Sources 278
An Appendix of Photographs 281

Preface

Shaikh Muḥammad Ma'sūm Naqshbandī (ra)

In the name of Allāh, most Gracious, most Merciful.

All praises belong to Allāh. Peace and blessings be upon the blessed Prophet Muḥammad, the illuminating light, and Allāh's mercy to humankind and all of Allāh's creation.

Praise to Allāh that there are increasingly more people seeking a sacred and holistic way of life. In a world dominated by materialistic values, *taṣawwuf* balances one's spiritual life and worldly activities.

Taṣawwuf is based on the unity of Allāh (*tawḥīd*). Those who practice *taṣawwuf*, sufis, are *muslims* who strive to purify their hearts and dominate their worldly desires by following the Qur'ān and the Sunnah of the Holy Prophet under the guidance of a spiritual leader. *Taṣawwuf* is to tread along the spiritual path by applying the ethical dictates of the shariah into one's life. Spirituality is rooted in one's moral behavior, which is best done under the guidance of a spiritual master familiar with the difficulties and dangers of the path. As individual souls find their spiritual journey deepening, they approach divine Reality (*ḥaqīqat*) and reach the highest degree of spiritual excellence (*iḥsān*).

Although simple in concept, *taṣawwuf* proves to be challenging and difficult in practice. In our time, difficulty in finding qualified spiritual leaders and reliable sources of knowledge makes actualizing *taṣawwuf* difficult. As the level of difficulty increases along the path, the responsibility of each individual to the ethical dictates of the shariah rises proportionally. With this background in mind, one realizes that the purpose of creation is to serve Allāh, as it is said in the Holy Qur'ān, *I have created jinns and humankind that they may serve me* (Q. 51:56). Our deeds and all other aspects of our being is directed to fulfill this purpose. The first obstacle to overcome on the path is the "commanding ego" (*al-nafs al-ammāra*), which the Holy Prophet (PBUH) called the "greater struggle" (*jihad al-akbar*). *Yet, I do not claim that my soul was innocent. Surely a person's soul incites to evil—except in so far as my Sustainer is all forgiving, most merciful* (Q. 12:53).

The challenge to overcome one's lower nature is not easy. However, one should never lose hope because the spiritual journey is blessed by Allāh's mercy just as those who strive for Allāh's cause will have Allāh's mercy with them. *We will surely guide those who struggle in Our cause to Our path; Allāh is with those who do good* (Q. 29:69).

The shariah is the foundation of submitting to Allāh and the genuine Path to Allāh. Therefore, one is cautioned to avoid deviating from the ethical commands stemming from the Qur'ān and Sunnah of the Holy Prophet (PBUH). Deviating from the shariah, whether individually or under the auspices of a sufi lineage, would go against the dictates of submitting to Allāh, which is the practice of *islām*.

In this path one needs a pure heart, since it is the pure heart that can reflect the light of the divine. That is why the purification of the heart plays a central role in an individual's spiritual journey. As the Holy Prophet (PBUH) said, there is a polish for everything that takes away the rust and the polish of the heart is *dhikr*, i.e., the invocation of Allāh. *Truly the person who succeeds purifies it (the heart) and the person who fails corrupts it (the heart)* (Q. 91:9-10). …*and call Allāh in remembrance often so that you may prosper* (Q. 8:45).

Let us remember that guidance is only by Allāh. …*For Allāh guides whom Allāh wills to a path that is straight* (Q. 2:213). Allāh promised the Holy Prophet (PBUH) that his religion and book would be protected until the Day of Judgment. *And hold fast, all together, by the rope which Allāh (stretches out for you), and be not divided among yourselves; and remember with gratitude Allāh's favor on you. You were enemies and Allāh joined your hearts in love, so that by Allāh's grace, you became brothers. You were on the brink of the pit of fire and Allāh saved you from it. Thus Allāh makes Allāh's signs clear to you so that you are guided* (Q. 3:103). May Allāh bless us with hearts that can pray with sincerity and reflect the divine light. May we have eyes whose gaze on this world will remind us of Allāh. I pray to Allāh to bless us with the ability to practice the teachings of Islam in our daily life with excellence.

والسلام و عليكم ورحمة الله و على من اتبع الحق و الهدى و صلى الله على سيدنا و نبينا محمد و على اله الطاهرين المعصومين

Shaikh Muḥammad Ma'sūm Naqshbandī (ra)
Religious Adviser and Spiritual Guide
Naqshbandiya Foundation for Islamic Education

Foreword

by Professor Shaikh ʻAbd al-Karīm

In the Name of Allāh, the All-Merciful,
the All-Compassionate.
Bismi'llāhi 'r-Raḥmāni 'r-Raḥīm.

Praise be to Allāh and may it be sufficient! Peace be upon His servants whom He has chosen, especially our master Muḥammad, the most noble of humankind in fulfillment, his scholars, his Companions and his followers in beneficence, until the Day of Judgment.

As I discovered, this fine and noble book on the subject of Sufism was originally compiled in Kurdish by that master of the precious pen and writer of great skill, al-Ḥājj Shaikh Amīn an-Naqshbandī, for the purpose of directing Muslims to the real meaning of Sufism. It was then translated into Arabic by that splendid brother, Doctor Muḥammad Sharīf, to make it accessible to the Arabic-speaking members of the Islamic Community. I discovered both the original and the translation to be among the gems of literary composition. I was therefore delighted to have the honor of participating in that good work by contributing these concise statements about Sufism and its reality.

Sufism [*taṣawwuf*] is the management [*taṣarruf*] by the individual Muslim of his lower self [*nafs*] exercised by rousing it from states of heedlessness, restraining it from vices, and directing it toward virtues, in perfect compliance, with the Seal of the prophets and messengers (Allāh bless him and give him peace), whose innate character was the Qur'ān.

Following him depends, without a doubt, on worshipful service in practice, on account of Allāh's saying (Exalted is He).

> I did not create the jinn and humankind except to worship Me.
> *wa mā khalaqtu 'l-jinna wa 'l-insa illā li-ya'budūn.* (51:56)

It also depends on sincere devotional service, for He said (Exalted is He),

> And they have been commanded only to serve Allāh,
> *wa mā umirū illā li-ya'budu 'llāha*

devoting the religion to Him sincerely.
mukhliṣīna la-hu 'd-dīn. (98:5)

—and on conscious awareness of Him (Exalted is He), to the fullest possible extent, because of His saying (Exalted is He).

Do not be one of those who are heedless.
wa lā takun mina 'l-ghāfilīn. (7:205)

—and on keeping one's distance from people guilty of heedlessness, because of His saying (Exalted is He).

And do not obey someone
wa lā tuṭi' man
whose heart We have made heedless of Our remembrance,
aghfalnā qalba-hu 'an dhikri-nā
who follows his own lust and whose case has been abandoned.
wa 'ttaba'a hawā-hu wa kāna amru-hu furuṭā. (18:28)

—and on constant fear of the Lord (Glory be to Him and Exalted is He), on the basis of His noble saying (Exalted is He),

But as for him who feared to stand before his Lord,
wa ammā man khāfa maqāma Rabbi-hi
and forbade the lower self to follow passion,
wa naha 'n-nafsa 'ani 'l-hawā:
surely the Garden [of Paradise] will be his final place of rest.
fa-inna 'l-jannata hiya 'l-māwā. (79:40,41)

—and on intense commitment to true devotion, for He said (Exalted is He),

Practice true devotion to Allāh, and Allāh will teach you.
wa 'ttaqu 'llāh: wa yu'allimu-kumu 'llāh. (2:282)

—and on steadfast adherence to the Truth in both good times and bad.

Those who have said: "Our Lord is Allāh,"
inna 'lladhīna qālū Rabbu-na 'llāhu
and then remained steadfast, to them the angels
keep coming down
thumma 'staqāmū tatanazzalu 'alai-himu 'l-malā'ikatu
[to say]: "Do not fear and do not grieve,
allā takhāfū wa lā taḥzanū

but hear good tidings of the Garden that you
have been promised."
wa abshirū bi'l-jannati 'llatī kuntum tūʿadūn. (41:30)

—and on protecting the heart, the feelings and the senses, in active practice, against whatever Allāh has forbidden, because of His saying (Exalted is He).

Forsake the outer aspect of sin, and the inner aspect of it as well.
wa dharū ẓāhira 'l-ithmi wa bāṭinah. (6:120)

—and on right conduct in avoiding forbidden things and performing acts of worshipful obedience, in accordance with His saying (Exalted is He).

So tread the straight path as you are commanded.
fa-'staqim ka-mā umirta. (11:112)

In this clear and glorious sense, Sufism is Islam in the fullest sense. It is the guarantee of felicity in the two abodes [this world and the Hereafter]. It is nothing else, and it is absolutely nothing other than what we have said about Islam, so the Sufis at the first degree are the Muslims, and the Muslims in the fullest sense are the Ṣufīs.

If Islam is ascribed to others, it is only because of conduct in keeping with the external proprieties and actions, and on the strength of the abundance of the mercy of Allāh the Exalted.

Or do those who commit bad deeds suppose
am ḥasiba 'lladhīna 'jtaraḥu 's-sayyi āti
that We shall make them like those who believe
an najʿala-hum ka-'lladhīna āmanū
and do good works, the same in life and death?
wa ʿamilū aṣ-ṣāliḥāti sawā'an maḥyā-hum wa mamātu-hum
Bad is their judgment!
sā'a mā yaḥkumūn. (45:21)

It all depends on the enlightenment obtained by that following [of the Prophet (Allāh bless him and give him peace)], even if it be very little.

By virtue of that noble following, the Sufis became the first brigade of the Companions, who were the best Community brought forth for humankind, like the rightly guided Caliphs, the Companions of the Bench [*Aṣḥāb aṣ-Ṣuffa*], and those who chose contact with the presence of Holiness, preferring perpetuity to transitory existence.

From them spread the fragrance of the perfumes of the flowers and the roses. Their breasts have expanded with the worshipful service of the Lord of the servants, and lights have shined from them on the hearts of those who kept them company with sincere devotion. In the footsteps of the Messenger (Allāh bless him and give him peace) they became rightly guided by his guidance, mindful through his remembrance and enlightened by the light of his noble heart and its radiance. In their hearts and all their refinements, Allāh established the spiritual Prophetic Sunna, enduring within them till the Day of Meeting.

Those lights traveled from them to others, just as the light passed from [Abū Bakr] the greatest Champion of Truth [Ṣiddīq] (may Allāh be well pleased with him) to Salmān [al-Fārisī], and from him to Qāsim ibn Muḥammad, and from him to Ja'far aṣ-Ṣādiq, as well as from our master 'Alī ibn Abī Ṭālib to al-Ḥasan al-Baṣrī, and from him to al-Ḥabīb, and from him to Dāwūd aṭ-Ṭā'ī, and from him to Ma'rūf al-Karkhī, and from him to as-Sarī, and from him to Junaid ibn Muḥammad, the chief of the group. That is to say, they transmitted knowledge of the rules, knowledge of sincere devotion, and renunciation of sins (may Allāh the Exalted be well pleased with them all).

Those luminaries were all among the people of the [first] three centuries, of whom the Messenger (Allāh bless him and give him peace) testified that these centuries would be the best. They were with the genuine Truth and on the straight path?

Allāh (Exalted is He) extolled the Companions. His commendation of them is sufficiently expressed in His saying (Exalted is He).

Muḥammad is the Messenger of Allāh,
Muḥammadun Rasūlu 'llāh:
and those who are with him are hard against the unbelievers,
wa 'lladhīna ma'a-hu ashiddā'u 'ala 'l-kuffāri
merciful one to another.
ruḥamā'u baina-hum
You see them bowing and falling prostrate,
arā-hum rukka'an sujjadan yabtaghūna
seeking bounty from Allāh and good pleasure.
faḍlan mina 'llāhi wa riḍwānā:
Their mark is on their faces, the trace of prostration.
sīmā-hum fī wujūhi-him min athari 's-sujūd: (48:29)

Since the perfume spreads from flowers, whenever one of the sincerely devoted kept them company, his heart was enlightened and his breast expanded. Their followers multiplied, their hearts were illumined by the lights of Holiness, and they were far removed from self-centeredness. This led to the development of a sincere, worshipful, and mindful [Sufi] community. The mysteries were disclosed to them, so supernatural marvels and charismatic wonders manifested. People were transported from the murky darknesses of fantasies to the radiant lights of certainties, so the numbers of Muslims seeking insights and sincere devotion increased day after day and year after year.

Since they were striving in the cause of Allāh, and He said (Exalted is He):

> And as for those who strive in Our cause,
> *wa 'lladhīna jāhadū fī-nā*
> surely We shall guide them in Our ways.
> *la-nahdiyanna-hum subula-nā*
> Allāh is surely with the beneficent.
> *wa inna 'llāha la-ma'a 'l-muḥsinīn.* (29:69)

The appropriateness of certain kinds of remembrance and acts of worshipful obedience were revealed. Some of them chose practices of constant observance of seclusion, fasting and night vigil. Some of them chose the minimizing of speech about things of no benefit, and the maximizing of the remembrance of Allāh and the affirmation of Oneness. Some of them chose the remembrance practiced by the heart, vigilant awareness of its states, and its preservation from random notions. Some of them chose the maximizing of recitation of the Noble Qur'ān and of benedictions upon the owner of the splendid character, our master Muḥammad (Allāh bless him and give him peace).

All of that was included among the duties of the religion or the noble Sunna of the Prophet. It became widely known among the people as the Junaidī Spiritual Path [*Ṭarīqa*], or the Qādirī Spiritual Path, or by other names, referring to the particular practices observed in the application of the Book and the Islamic Sunna. The point is that the customary practices of religion include duties that may be individual or collective, as well as customs that are definitely established and some that are not definitely established, but are assigned to the category of voluntary observance [*taṭawwu'*]. They constitute a wide-open door to the mercy of Allāh (Exalted is He), and His mercy is wide and all-embracing. He has said (Exalted is He),

> And he who does good of his own accord—
> *wa man taṭawwa'a khairan*
> Allāh is Appreciative, All-Knowing.
> *fa-inna 'llāha Shākirun 'Alīm.* (2:158)

Nothing in them amounts to heretical innovation [*bid'a*], invented by people in contravention of what the Messenger brought or in opposition to his religion. If anyone describes them as such, he does not understand the meaning of the religion, obligatory duties [*farā'iḍ*], nor customary practices [*sunan*]. He is himself the innovator who describes as an innovation every good thing that he does not recognize. companions and the righteous predecessors [*salaf*] are far from heretical innovation, but the ignoramus is heedless!

As scholars of religion and saints of Islam have confirmed, if someone leaves the path of the religion, his consciousness is restricted, so he would have no discernment [*shu'ūr*] even if he had a thousand hallmarks [*shi'ār*], for there is no good in marks of distinction without discernment, nor in a lamp without light. However our master, the Cardinal Axis of those who know by experience, Shaikh 'Abd al-Qādir al-Gīlānī (may Allāh illuminate his spirit), expressed it exactly saying, "If you see someone walking on water or flying in the air and you find him guilty of that which contravenes the noble Sacred Law, you must know that he is a charlatan [*dajjāl*], a swindler who has missed the path of Truth and rightness."

Sufism in Islam has nothing to do with the spiritual exercises of Hinduism, nor with arts of magic and tricks of the deceivers, nor with discipline invented and developed by heretical innovators as ignorant foreigners maintain. The Sufism of Islam is the cultivation of the characteristics of the Chosen One [*al-Muṣṭafā*] (Allāh bless him and give him peace), and the illumination obtained from the lights of his noble breast and his gentle heart bestowed upon him by Allāh (Exalted is He) through the expansion of his breast. He said to him,

> Did We not cause your breast to expand for you?
> *a-lam nashraḥ la-ka ṣadrak.* (94:1)

All of his followers and his Community are among those specially favored with that expansion and that illumination. Outsiders have no justification for meddling in the significance of Sufism in Islam, for the religion belongs to Allāh (Exalted is He). The Truth is with Him and He is the Fairest of judges, the Most Merciful of the merciful, the Forgiver of sins and the Pardoner of the faults of the penitent. Careful attention must be paid to two important matters in this context, that is to say, on the subject of Sufism in Islam:

1. Early Sufis who controlled their lower selves by preserving them from corruption did not abandon lawful earning to become a burden on other people. Instead, they used to acquire lawful sustenance and live on the wealth they earned. They did not become monks, abstaining from marriage and the pleasure established as lawful by the religion, for many of those righteous men had two, three, or four wives, as did their followers in other parts of the world, in compliance with the saying of the Prophet (Allāh bless him and give him peace),

> Marry and beget offspring, for I shall take pride in you before all the communities on the Day of Resurrection, even in the miscarried fetus.

2. They were not withdrawn from the service of Islam and the sacred struggle for the religion, for the Companions of the Bench [*Aṣḥāb aṣ-Ṣuffa*], who were the first brigade, were active in sacred struggle and the defence of Islam. In addition, they were vigorously engaged in spreading Islam to distant regions. The same is true of their followers, al-Ḥasan [al-Baṣrī], al-Junaid and those who came after them. It is also true of the followers of our master, Shaikh 'Abd al-Qādir al-Jīlānī, like his venerable son, 'Abd al-'Azīz, who fought in the wars against the Crusaders and reconquered some of the Holy Lands. Then there was the distinguished Imām Abu'l-Ḥasan ash-Shādhilī, and his expedition to fight the Mongols. Many Islamic armies were augmented by men of the spirit and Islamic Sufism, and Allāh (Exalted is He) rendered them victorious in many regions. Consider the historic Imām, Shaikh Shams ad-Dīn, and how he assisted Sulṭān Muḥammad the Conqueror until Allāh enabled him to capture Constantinople. Further examples would take a very long time to recount.

Another important point is that those saints were constantly directing Muslims to expand their breasts, to encourage them to persist in acts of worshipful obedience and to help them avoid discord and confusion. This world could only degenerate by losing these holy persons. Indeed, they have provided service to knowledge, religious schools, as well as guidance to Muslims, and their ability to supply nourishment, to care for the weak, the destitute and the orphans, and to improve relations among human beings. In truth and reality, those Sufis and scholars, both exoteric and esoteric, were integral to Islam, for Sufism is Islam, and Islam is Sufism. Those who were hostile to them came to follow them. This is the truth, and Allāh confirms the truth, for He guides to the true path.

Professor 'Abd al-Karīm
Professor in the Qādirī Presence
1.22.1988

Preface of the Translator [from Kurdish into Arabiç],

Professor Dr. Muḥammad Sharīf Aḥmad

In the Name of Allāh, the All-Merciful, the All-Compassionate.
Bismi'llāhi 'r-Raḥmāni 'r-Raḥīm.

Praise be to Allāh. There is no god but Allāh. If someone seeks help from anyone but Him, he is worthy of contempt. If someone follows any path but His, he has gone astray. If Allāh does not provide a light for someone, that person has no light.

Blessing and peace be upon the Seal of the prophets and messengers, our master Muḥammad, who was sent as a mercy to all the worlds, and upon those who preceded him, those chosen to convey the Message for the guidance of humankind, and upon his family, the Companions and the Successors to their guidance until the Day when they shall be resurrected.

How strange it is—though strangeness is far from remarkable today, and strange folk are very numerous in our time!—that I should undertake the translation of a book on Sufism, a work of splendid value, when I am empty-handed and my heart is covered with rust. Sufism is the purification of the soul and the refinement of the spirit. It is the means by which to explore what lies behind nature with a radiant grace penetrating into human hearts. Ṣufis are those men who have loved to purify themselves, and have secluded themselves in the niche of loving affection, worship, and humble submission. They have tasted the flavor of that grace, so they have come to be in this world with their bodies and in the Hereafter with their hearts.

In this translation it is necessary to note that my knowledge of Kurdish, which happens to be my mother tongue, falls completely short of the lofty elegance in the style of the distinguished author, my dear friend Shaikh Amīn an-Naqshbandī. He is a Sufi man of culture, suckled from the breast of Sufism, whose upbringing flowed from its crystal-clear fountain. He experienced material and spiritual beauty in the mountains of the Kurdish region of 'Irāq, and its intellectual and spiritual school in Biyāra. He is a talented poet, whose writing exhibits charm, sweetness, and subtle refinement.

This translation began when my brother, the author, requested me to translate *What is Sufism?* from Kurdish into Arabic, the language of the inimitable Qur'ān and Islam. This proved that he had confidence in my writing, and in the brotherly connection established by sincere friendship. This book represents the juice of his life, replete with the study of Reality by a critical, philosophical mind, and by a Sufi heart overflowing with faith.

My father used to maintain that Sufism is not a science to be studied and written about, but rather a procedure in strict conformity with the modes of conduct prescribed by the Sacred Law, and an experience peculiar to its practitioners.

Sufism is consistent with the Sacred Law, with the practice of the righteous predecessors, with doctrinal adherence to the jurisprudence of scholars who exercise independent judgment, and with the jurisprudence of the traditional Sunna. These and other schools of Islamic practice and jurisprudence are included within the vast dimensions of Islam.

The original work deals with subjects relating to Kurdish society, including the influence of Sufism on Kurdish literature, as in case of the literature of Shaikh Aḥmad al-Jazīrī, Sayyid 'Abd ar-Raḥīm al-Mawlawī, Mulla Muḥammad Maḥwī, and Shaikh 'Umar Ḍiyā' ad-Dīn an-Naqshbandī, the author's outstanding grandfather and the paramount guide of the Naqshbandī Spiritual Path.

Dr. Muḥammad Sharīf Aḥmad

Foreword

by Arthur F. Buehler

The dimension of Islam specifically oriented toward inner peace, is often called Islamic mysticism or, more commonly, Sufism (technically *taṣawwuf*). Sufism has a religious justification going all the way back to the Prophet. It specializes in "acting in the full consciousness that God is witnessing your every thought and deed" (from Gabriel's Hadith). Sufism involves cultivating a continual remembrance of God and a heart that is alive with love — love of God, love of the Prophet, and love of all God's creation. Is it any coincidence that Mawlana Rūmī is the most popular poet in the United States? This perspective does not create an external other to fight. In contrast, the jihad of political ideologues in the Islamic world is external, a projection of their own denied aspects of being. The Sufis totally undercut this power-driven construction of reality. For this reason Sufis remain the ideologues' primary enemy, making the "evil West" a secondary foe. In its extremist forms like those expressed by Ibn Laden, jihad is not only external but violently inhuman. The jihad of the Sufis is internal, a struggle against one's lower, carnal nature. There is no projection of the enemy outside of oneself as one realizes that the real enemy is one's lower ego. Outer peace really manifests only when inner peace exists. Sufism brings people together, the manifestation of a universal principle that the closer one gets to God, the closer and more compassionate one feels toward one's fellow beings.

If the kernel of Islam is loving acceptance and peace, one might reasonably ask why such qualities do not manifest more throughout the Islamic world today. Instead, what one often encounters is a puritanical version of Islam, narrow in scope and tyrannical in enforcing its norms among Muslims. There are internationally powerful and well-funded organizations with an ideological, conservative, anti-Sufi stance led by political ideologues. One of their means to political power involves the control of Islamic symbols and belief systems, i.e., to define what Islam is. For them, Islam means a totalitarian "Islamic state" in opposition to all who disagree politically or theologically. Anyone who challenges their simplistic, literal Quran interpretations and their political agendas or is identified as a Sufi or non-Sunni (or non-Shi'i in the Iranian case) becomes an enemy of the "Islamic state." They have a long-term strategy of political control in majority Islamic countries and an organization with ample funding (unlike Sufis and traditional moderate Muslims). In many parts of the Islamic world these ideologues control mainstream Islam through direct or indirect state-sponsored programs. Unfortunately, the Western media focuses on this version of Islam. Such an Islam is dangerous for both Muslims and non-Muslims because it involves a hostility toward those with more inclusive interpretations of Islam (including Sufis) and almost invariably includes a hostility towards the "West." Combine this with a militant political agenda of a so-called "Islamic government," and one has a perfect environment to recruit for violent action — a closed mind, a clear goal, and a religious justification for anger. In other words, there is a creation of the Other. Regrettably, such an interpretation of Islam thrives on opposition and discord and has no patience with a perspective of loving acceptance and peace.

In this regard, the English translation of Shaykh Amīn 'Ala'uddin Naqshbandī's book on Sufism is quite timely. The author, quite well versed in Sufi literature, draws on Western works in Sufism and philosophy as well. In addition to a detailed introduction to the classical sources of Sufism, the shaykh demonstrates the Islamic basis of Sufism by citing Qur'ānic verses which undergird Sufi principles and technical terminology. Interspersed in the discussion, the author deftly addresses deniers of Sufism. To date, it details the Khalidi-Naqshbandi practices better than anything else in English translation. Although there are English translations of many classical Sufi works, it is rare that a contemporary modern treatise on Sufism is translated. It is rarer still that a book originally written in Kurdish and, through an Arabic translation, is subsequently translated into English. The translator, the late Muhtar Holland, presents the reader with a clear, nuanced rendition of the text. Readers with a desire to learn about Sufism in depth, and the Naqshbandi lineage in particular, will find this work quite worthwhile.

Arthur F. Buehler
Senior Lecturer
Victoria University
Wellington, New Zealand

Foreword

by Abdal Hakim Murad

In the name of Allah, the All-Merciful,
the All-Compassionate
Bismi'llāhi 'r-Raḥmāni 'r-Raḥīm.

At a time when the confusions of modernity seem to have intruded into so many expressions of religion, it is with relief and gratitude that one turns to a book which offers not a public discussion of one's grievances, or an exposition of 'ideology', but a healing to the soul. The Qur'an is itself a 'healing', (17:82) and books, art, and believers themselves can only claim to be truly conformed to the Revelation when they act as a source of healing for others. The Prophet himself, may peace be upon him, was a physician of bodies and of spirits, and nothing can claim to be properly Islamic unless it conforms to this fundamental Sunna.

It is one of the proofs of Islam that down the centuries its leaders should have offered not only information about doctrine and practice, but medicines for the sicknesses of the heart. Our chronicles and our graveyards bear witness to the thousands of men and women who were not content simply to absorb and convey facts, but were given a compassion so strong that it impelled them to bring the delights of His recollection to as many souls as they could reach. The truth of religion is shown in the self-giving of its adherents, those who overcome the lower possibilities of the human condition, and experience the ever-growing peace and joy that come from His remembrance. 'It is by the remembrance of Allah that hearts find peace', (13:28) the Qur'an reminds us, one of the implications of which is that religion is only truly for Him when it brings peace and ease to the heart. 'Whoever turns aside from My remembrance, his shall be a life of misery.' (20:124)

This fundamental Qur'anic wisdom has borne fruit down the Muslim centuries and in all the lands of Islam. Scholars and lay believers alike joined those who 'remember their Lord standing, sitting, and on their sides.' (3:191) The fruitfulness of Islam guaranteed the evolution of whole families of faith, each of whose brethren were accorded the grace of a special form of recollection of their Lord. As Ibn al-Banna put it: 'The ways we speak are diverse, but Your beauty is one, and all are pointing to that same Beauty.' For Islam is not totalitarian, and unity in diversity has always been its principle and its reality. Its laws form part of one Law, and its spiritual families form part of the whole spiritual family that is the brotherhood of believers. The unfolding of the Sufi Orders (*ṭuruq*) resembles the peacock opening its tail: the creature is one, and the beauty is made complete by the mutual harmony of the individual feathers.

It is a unique quality of the Muhammadan Religion that these families of lovers should have been so many and so diverse. Each has sought to capture a particular facet of the same jewel. The light shines through the jewel to them all; but they receive it from different directions, and see different aspects of its perfection. Such is the universalism of Islam.

One of the greatest signs of Divine acceptance is the manifest abundance of *baraka*, Divine blessing, in the spiritual and biological progeny of great human beings. The immense fertility of Islamic culture, and the unique brilliance of the Prophetic House, form a Divine celebration of the magnificence of the founder himself, the one to whom the Qur'an declared: 'Truly, your adversary is the one curtailed.' (108:3) As the ever-widening stream of Islamic civilisation flowed over different rocks, it took on the coloring of what lay beneath while remaining true to its essence. Some of the Sufi brotherhoods remained local, and have flourished in some Muslim provinces but not in others. But other orders proved capable of an almost universal appeal and destiny. The Qadiri and Naqshbandi orders are perhaps the most impressive testimony to this.

The wellspring of the Naqshbandi Way is the Blessed Prophet himself; and the masters of this Way have been revered down the centuries for their scrupulous adherence to his Sunna. Not contenting themselves with form alone, they have ceaselessly sought to discover something of the inner greatness of the Founder, alert to the lethal dangers posed to religion by a purely formalist approach. Literalism may satisfy children, but the mature mind and the heart have rights which Islam, as a religion grounded in the radiant heart of the Prophet himself, has proved admirably able to satisfy. The inner reality, which is Prophecy, came to an end with his death, but the Prophet's *wilāya*, his spiritual rank, remains an inspiration to which Muslim attention is constantly called. For it is the Antichrist who sees with only one eye. An unbalanced preoccupation with either the outward or the inward aspect of religion may be expected in times of ignorance and sedition. The renewer of religion, who stands against his times, is he who insists that we see with both eyes, and thus behold the world in perspective. Such has been the concern of the Naqshbandi ulama and imams down the generations to the present day.

The spirituality of the Prophet, manifesting itself as excellence (*iḥsan*) in virtues, was inherited gloriously by those of his Companions who were singled out to be the closest to him in his life and after his death. Abu Bakr, *radiya'Llahu 'anhu*, received the title *aṣ-Ṣiddiq* to indicate the superb quality of his discipleship in the cave, when the Blessed Prophet repeated to him the words, 'Do not grieve, surely Allah is with us.' (9:40) This is the station of *wilāya*, where there is no agitating grief, thanks to the stillness of the heart in God's remembrance. This stillness, or *sakīna*, is the basis and objective of the Naqshbandi practice of *dhikr*, frequently done in silence, but it also underpins the characteristically Naqshbandi virtues of humility and a contagious tranquillity of heart. There are few who can rival the Naqshbandis for their success in conveying this aspect of the Prophetic perfection to later generations in need of spiritual healing.

Among hadith scholars and imams of jurisprudence, this legacy was handed down and systematised until it reached the blessed generations known as the Khwājagān. Khwāja Yūsuf Hamadānī (d.1141) may be reckoned the first of these activist scholars, and it is with him that the Naqshbandi chain of transmission becomes definitively distinct from all others. Khwāja Yūsuf, a great Hanafi jurist who studied under the legal theorist Abū Ishāq al-Shirāzī, and spiritual associate of Shaykh 'Abd al-Qādir al-Jīlānī in Baghdad, brought his learning and sanctity to Central Asia. There, in the ancient city of Merv, he established a great college and training centre which was to uplift countless hearts.

One of Khwāja Yūsuf's four successors (*khulafā'*) was the great saint Khwāja 'Abd al-Khāliq Ghujduwānī (d.1220). A celebrated encounter with the wandering sage al-Khidr confirmed his attachment to the silent *dhikr* implied in the Qur'anic text 'And call upon your Lord in prayer and obscurity' (7:55). To Ghujduwānī, too, the order is indebted for his eightfold set of principles known as the 'Holy Words', *al-Kalimat al-Qudsiya*, whose influence is seen in later Naqshbandi manuals, including the present volume.

Shāh Bahā' al-Dīn Naqshband (d.1389) was the spiritual descendent of Khwāja 'Abd al-Khāliq in more ways than one. He received spiritual guidance in his childhood from Amīr Kulāl, himself an initiate in the chain of the Khwājagān, but in visions he also encountered the spiritual presence of Khwāja 'Abd al-Khāliq, who taught him the importance of the silent *dhikr*. With such guidance, and assisted by a naturally spiritual temperament, Shāh Bahā' al-Dīn became one of those men appointed by God to receive the pure water flowing from the Muhammadan Revelation, to drink from it, to protect it, and to speed it on its way, thereby quenching the thirst of a virtually limitless number of souls. He was a *Ghawth*, a help for thousands. But for his *baraka* and his example, tens of millions of men and women who are Muslim today would still be suffering the pains of unbelief. His is a virile, uncompromising method, calling fearlessly to Truth, challenging tyranny whether in the soul or in the palace, commanding all to submit to the commandments of the Celestial King, in whose edicts alone humanity may find liberation. This legacy continues and is being revived today, symbolised by the recent renovation of his tomb near Bukhara at the behest of the present Mufti of Uzbekistan, Mullah Yusuf Sadikov.

Hardly less celebrated was Khwāja 'Ubaydallāh Aḥrār, the disciple of Ya'kūb Charkhī, who in turn was the principal successor to Bahā' al-Dīn Naqshband. As he wrote fearlessly to a ruler, 'Every physical and spiritual delight, and all excellence, in this world and in the next, are to be achieved only by obeying the Prophet, may blessings and peace rest upon him. You must, therefore, implement his Sharī'a in every matter that comes before you.'

From Central Asia, the disciples of Shāh Bahā' al-Dīn and Khwāja Aḥrār radiated out through the lands of the Islamic world and beyond. Showing the Sufi virtue of risking all for the sake of conveying truth, they brought Islam to large areas of China, the steppelands north of the Crimea, and forested areas of Bengal. One of Aḥrār's deputies, Molla Ilāhī, settled in Macedonia, from where his pupils scattered throughout the Ottoman Balkans to spread the message of Islam to the most remote communities. Other disciples of Aḥrār voyaged to India, where the Emperor Bābur had the honour to translate one of Aḥrār's books into Turkish verse. In India, the power of Khwāja Aḥrār's spirituality and intellectuality bore fruit in the person of Shaykh Aḥmad Sirhindī (d.1624). Sirhindi, known as the Renewer (*mujaddid*) of his age, was famed for his campaign to bring Mughal law and belief into fuller conformity with Islam. He also wrote a monumental collection of letters, the *Maktūbāt*, which have been translated into many languages and lie at the living centre of many Naqshbandi teaching circles to this day.

In the same lineage was Shāh Walīullāh al-Dihlawī (d.1763), one of the greatest legal minds of Islamic history. His *Hujjat Allāh al-Bāligha* (*God's Eloquent Proof*) is a showpiece of the wisdom and comprehensiveness of the revealed law, showing how it uplifts the spiritual as well as the material and moral condition of society.

Another of the great revivers of the Way of Shāh Bahā' al-Dīn was Mawlāna Khālid al-Baghdādī (d.1827). Mawlāna Khālid was one of Kurdistan's great gifts to the wider Islamic world, a kind of Saladin of the spirit. His disciples, such as Shaykh 'Uthmān Sirāj al-Dīn, reinvigorated Sunni Islam among the Kurds in the Ottoman Empire and also in Iran. Another disciple, Mekki-zade Mustafa Asim, became Shaykh al-Islam, the presiding scholar of the entire Ottoman Caliphate. Mawlāna Khalīd's insistence on defending the Sharī'a and the Ottoman Empire against European and Persian encroachments, and his realisation that far-flung disciples could be effectively linked together through the practice known as *rābiṭa* - imaginal awareness of the Shaykh's presence - made a significant impact on Islamic history and society.

One dramatic expression of this was the war of resistance to Russian rule which erupted in the Caucasus. Shaykh Shamil was only one of the many great Khālidī imams who raised the banner of freedom and justice against Russian colonialism. The Naqshbandis were also the leaders of Central Asian resistance, and, following the collapse of Tsarist rule in 1917, provided the principal underground reservoirs of Islamic values during the seven decades of Communist rule. Thanks to practices such as *rābiṭa*, Naqshbandis have also been active in preserving Islam in republican Turkey, despite the official prohibition of the Sufi orders, and the leaders of the main Islamic party in recent years, including the former president Necmettin Erbakan, have been Naqshbandi acolytes.

Further East, the powerful impact of Mawlāna Khalīd reached Sumatra, through Shaykh Isma'il of Minangkabau (d.1857), who was initiated into the *ṭarīqa* from Mawlāna Khalīd's *khalīfa* in the Hijaz, Shaykh 'Abdallāh al-Arzinjānī. Another Khalīdī shaykh who worked to transform Sumatra was Shaykh 'Abd al-Wahhab Rokan (d.1926), who in 1883 founded Bab al-Salam, a spiritual community whose graduates soon provided the religious leadership for the major Islamic colleges of Sumatra. Both men were known as defenders of the rights of the indigenous Malays against the depradations of Dutch colonial rule. In the late 20th century the Khalidiyya spread further through the Indonesian archipelago, and are today at the forefront of the two-pronged battle against consumer nihilism and religious extremism.

Today, and despite all the odds, the vibrancy of Naqshbandi Sufism is evident across the Islamic world. The English translation of a key text such as Shaikh Amīn 'Ala' al-Dīn's treasury of spiritual instruction supplies further proof of this. It provides contemporary evidence for the Islamic claim that the Qur'an and the Hadith offer immense spiritual resources, a fact often surprising to those who have been nurtured on media stereotypes which assume that the shallow extremes are representative of the religion. It is also proof of Allah's promise that no age, however foolish and distracted, will be devoid of enlightened souls who bring peace and healing to hearts damaged by materialism, selfishness, and ignorance of God. I am sure that the book will bring solace and guidance to many, and function as an invaluable witness to the depth and beauty of the Islamic revelation.

Abdal Hakim Murad
Shaykh Zayed Lecturer
Islamic Studies
Faculty of Divinity
University of Cambridge

Author's Introduction

In the Name of Allāh, the All-Merciful,
the All-Compassionate.
Bismi'llāhi 'r-Raḥmāni 'r-Raḥīm.

O you who believe, practice true devotion to Allāh,
yā ayyuha 'lladhīna āmanu 'ttaqu 'llāha
and have faith in His Messenger.
wa āminū bi-Rasūli-hi
He will give you twofold of His mercy
yu'ti-kum kiflaini min Raḥmati-hi
and will appoint for you a light by which to walk.
wa yaj'al la-kum nūran tamshūna bi-hi. (57:28)

When an intelligent human being opens his eyes, he begins to think at length about what is happening around him, whether it is good or bad, beneficial or harmful, beautiful or ugly. He reflects with his mind and his intellect on what is most appropriate for the survival of his kind, and most favorable to his personal life.

He makes various deductions from his study of the law of nature. For instance, he concludes that life is impossible without water, and that there are several kinds of water, differing in color and flavor, including that which is bitter, that which is salty, that which is sweet to the taste, that which is pure and that which is dirty. He eventually discovers which is more beneficial and more suitable, but only after careful consideration and prolonged experience.

As is well known, the urge to survey the horizons of knowledge does not come to a halt at any boundary. This means that the inquisitive human being is faced with a very difficult problem, the problem of how to recognize the Source of Reality. He must therefore take some basic steps toward its solution. In the case of water [of which Allāh has said],

And We made every living thing from water.
wa ja'alnā mina 'l-mā'i kulla shai'in ḥayy. (21:30)

—the human being may observe that the water of the river, for example, springs from a flowing well, but he does not know the source of the well. He may fall into confusion because he does not understand the secret of the saltiness of sea-water, to give another example. Questions thus arise within his thinking, but the answers to most of them reside beyond the scope of the mind of the human being, beyond his perception and his limited experience. That is just how it is when he is all alone with his inner self and he keeps asking, "Where from? How? Where to? What is the outcome? What is the basic principle?"

A man is indeed almost baffled when he thinks about the bird that lays a solid egg, which then splits open to emit another bird, which will soon be flying in the sky. He asks himself, "Did the egg come from the bird, or the bird from the egg? Where was the spirit in the structure of the egg?"

The human being is entitled to be perplexed, since he discovers that the seed of wheat sown in the earth returns some months later, as a blessed fresh plant, and that the walnut-stone, after several years in the ground, is transformed into a big tree. He asks himself, "Why is this? Did the walnut come from the tree, or did the tree come from the walnut?"

Until the veil is lifted from us and we truly know the answer, we can only wonder, "Where did the first walnut come from? Where did the first tree come from?"

The human being is thus frozen in his bewilderment, and he is entitled to be dumbfounded, just as he is when confronted by every great mystery in the universe.

Of all the things that disturb his thinking, agitate his feelings, unsettle his composure and upset his stability, the most serious is death. By that I mean the death of everything: the death of the human being, the death of the bird, the withering of the tree and the wilting of the plant. He asks himself, "What is life? What is the spirit? Where does the spirit come from? How does it depart, and where does it go?"

By the instinctive urge to discover what nature contains and what lies behind it, the human being is constantly moved to explore the unknown. He thus becomes the prisoner of research, investigating the secret and the cause in the hope of finding a beam of light to illuminate the path to knowledge, so that he can answer such questions as: Where did he come from? How did he come and where is he going? Is there one single cause? Does every phenomenon have an independent cause?

In the vast arena that encompasses the human being, everything that exists is a source of instruction. The sun, the moon, the stars, the planets and the beautiful earth are sources of inspiration. The earth is also the home of disasters and hurricanes, which terrify the human being and cause him to flee to a place of refuge, and to investigate the mystery and the cause. What is the all-compelling force that protects the energies of existence? What is the force that has perfected the making of everything?

Since nature contains such marvelous and fascinating beauty, the human being is driven to bewilderment concerning the wisdom of its Maker, the Originator. It may occur to the human being to question the credibility of what he sees and observes: Is it a reality, or is it a fantasy?

If it has no reality, what is the reason for these strange and marvelous phenomena?

Then who is the Creator of life and the spirit?

What is the cause of fear and security?

Does the mighty protective force actually exist?

How shall I draw near to this Divine force? From where shall I find it?

How shall find my Creator? How shall I please Him if I find Him? How will He forgive my sin? How shall I draw near to Him? Is it possible that He will keep death away from me? These and other questions are likely to arise.

Yes indeed, the sharp-witted, intelligent person dearly loves to contemplate the means of knowing and understanding the Initiator, the Creator, the Lord of this vast and far-flung universe, the Mover of the celestial spheres. He strives to draw near to His exalted Essence, and to comply with the wishes of the Controller of this universe (Glory be to Him).

This ardent love of Divine contemplation drove many of the sons of Adam to seclusion in a cave, or a distant corner, or a barren desert, or on the peak of a mountain, in order to think about nature and contemplate the creation of the universe, making do with what nature provides to keep them barely alive. Some of them perceived a torch of light, so the mirror of their hearts was illumined to reflect what lies behind nature, and this is the summit of spiritual delight. Some of them died without experiencing any of that.

This represents the first seed for the growth of Sufism in the conscience of the human creature, according to my reckoning. It grew and ripened, sought guidance from the messengers and prophets, and achieved perfection and rectitude in Islam, the seal of the religions.

Some others among the sons of Adam resorted to the mind alone, without spiritual experience, in order to search for reality and knowledge of the source and the original cause, meaning knowledge of the Creator. These came to be known as the philosophers.

Despite the depth to which these philosophers probed, they still remained perplexed, differing in their views, and they did not arrive at a means of setting the soul at rest and reassuring the spirit.

Sufism was born and developed together with the development of rational thought, and of the impulse to seek real knowledge of the cause of existence and its goal; that is to say, "arrival at the oasis of certainty." But what is Islamic Sufism? What is the reality of Ṣufism? What is the difference between philosophy and Sufism? What is the difference between Sufism and the Sacred Law [*Sharī'a*]?

I have long felt an eager desire to answer these questions, and I have missed no opportunity to realize this from the spiritual training I received from the late father of Shaikh 'Alā' ad-Dīn, Shaikh 'Umar Ḍiyā' ad-Dīn, as well as from the noble Naqshbandī Order at its dervish lodge [*khānaqāh*] of Biyāra and its well-known school of spiritual knowledge, or by reading traditional and contemporary Sufi sources.

This book is the product of this desire, and the juice of this strenuous effort, through which I am endeavoring to disclose the real meaning of the knowledge of Reality. Perhaps it will enable me to supply provision and assistance for an Islamic spiritual renaissance in my homeland of 'Irāq, the homeland of the saints, the scholars and the righteous.

I have divided this book into chapters, devoting each chapter to the explanation of particular topics that stimulate our minds, and that engage the interest of those concerned with spiritual and philosophical studies.

Allāh is the Custodian of enabling grace and right guidance!

Shaikh Amīn 'Alā ad-Dīn an-Naqshbandī

Shaykh Amīn, son of Shaykh 'Ala'udin and grandson of Shaykh 'Uthman Sirajuddin, was born on 21 December 1931 in Biyara, a small Kurdish town on the Iraq-Iran border. For most of his early childhood years he attended a madrasa in Biyara with prominent teachers such as 'Abdulkarim Mudarris. In 1961 the Iraqi Kurdish revolution forced Shaykh Amīn and many other Naqshbandi families to leave Biyara and migrate to Iran. He settled in Kermanshah, Iran, where he resumed his secondary studies. Then he attended Tehran University and graduated with a B.A. in Arabic and Persian language and literature to subsequently work for radio stations in Kermanshah, Sanandaj, and Tehran. In 1979, shortly after the Iranian revolution, Shaykh Amīn and his family returned back to Iraqi Kurdistan where he began working for the Ministry of Religious Affairs as a senior consultant. During this time he compiled and published his poetry under the pen-name of "Beway" in addition to other numerous commentaries and literary work. The present book, *Sufism: A Wayfarer's Guide*, is the culmination of his life's work. Shaykh Amīn passed away on 9 April 1990 survived by his wife and five children.

Chapter One
The Reality of Sufism
[*Ḥaqīqat at-Taṣawwuf*]

Foreword

It is a well-known fact that Sufism is an ecstatic state of being in which humble spiritual travelers experience the delight of spiritual nearness to Allāh, the Necessarily Existent, the Creator of all that exists. It is a condition in which a firebrand from the light of Lordly guidance shines upon their hearts so that certainty guides them aright.

It is also known that this spiritual state is not susceptible to logical description. We must therefore resort to comparison and analogy for the understanding of Sufism. We must seek guidance in the experiences of its champions and in their sayings about the flavors of Sufism and its orientations. We shall find evidence in Imām al-Ghazālī's famous journey in search of Reality as an example of an aspect of Sufism that entranced him, thrived within his being, and caused him to forget most of this world's attachments.

We shall begin with a brief section concerning the technical term *Taṣawwuf* [Sufism]. I shall then undergo the hardship of this difficult journey, holding nothing in my hand and heart, seeking help from Allāh's mercy (Glory be to Him Alone) and appealing to Him (Glory be to Him) for my support and guidance. He is the One who hears our supplication, so I shall say, "Allāh is the Source of enabling grace!"

First Section
The Technical Term *Taṣawwuf* [Sufism]

Opinions differ as to the meaning of the technical term *Taṣawwuf* [Sufism] and its origin, just as they differ as to its application. This is the first problem that arises where Islamic Sufism is concerned.

The truth of the matter is that the word *Taṣawwuf* [Sufism] appeared in the first century of the Hijra, as evidenced by the statement of al-Ḥasan al-Baṣrī, who is considered one of the great leaders of Sufism, and who lived in the period A.H. 21–110/642–728 C.E.). He is reported as having said, "I saw a Sufi during the circumambulation [of the Ka'ba], so I gave him something, but he did not accept it and he said, 'I have with me four small coins, so what I have with me will suffice me!'[1] Sufyān ath-Thawrī (A.H. 97–161), a leading expert in the Prophetic tradition and Qur'ānic exegesis, is likewise reported as having said, "But for Abū Hāshim, the Sufi, I would not have grasped the subtle meaning of ostentation [*riyā'*]."[2] The appelation "Sufi" is therefore not a novelty invented by the Baghdādīs as is sometimes said.

It is also known that the application of a particular name to a particular concept or condition, like Sufism, is not like the application of a particular name to a newborn human child. It rather occurs in stages, following the development of the concept or what it is believed to signify, as in the case of such technical terms as *qurrā'* [reciters of the Qur'ān], *fuqahā'* [experts in Islamic jurisprudence], and *muḥaddithīn* [transmitters of the Prophetic tradition]. The point is that certain members of the early community emerged and specialized in the recitation of the Noble Qur'ān, so they were called *qurrā'*. Then there emerged a company concerned with the transmission of the Prophetic tradition [*ḥadīth*], so they were called *muḥaddithīn*. When a group of the Qur'ān-reciters became concerned with the exposition of opinion and the issuing of pronouncements on the rules of the Sacred Law, they were called *fuqahā'*. These technical terms then passed through familiar stages of development, relating to the exact significance of their meanings, as is also the case with modern inventions in areas like mechanics and electricity.

The name "Ṣūfī" was thus applied to a man who withdrew from the pleasures of life, and focused his attention on the niche of worship with a humble heart, a tongue devoted to remembrance, and a refined mode of conduct. Keeping vigil by night and fasting by day, he would seek only the good pleasure of Allāh. He would combine cleanliness of the physical limbs and organs with purity of character. He was one of those who stand ready to answer the Divine command,

> Forsake the outer aspect of sin, and the inner aspect of it as well.
> *wa dharū ẓāhira 'l-ithmi wa bāṭinah.* (6:120)

He was diligent in the remembrance, "Allāh, Allāh," with presence of the heart, until his tongue became spontaneously accustomed to

1. *al-Lumā'* of Abū 'n-Naṣr as-Sarrāj aṭ-Ṭūsī, p. 42.
2. Ibid., p.42

it. He remained constantly in the state of remembrance until his heart became accustomed to remembrance and all trace of it was erased from his tongue. He thus reached the point where the meaning of the word "Allāh" remained present in his heart alone, so the outer form and shape of expression would disappear.

The name "Sufi" was likewise applied to the following.

- The ascetics [*zuhhād*], because they abstained from what belonged to other people and preferred what belonged to them, even if it was destitution.
- The spiritual paupers [*fuqarā'*], because of their need for Allāh (Glory be to Him).
- The strangers [*ghurabā'*], because they wander on the earth for the worshipful service of Allāh (Glory be to Him).
- The recluses [*shukuftiyya*], because of their seclusion in caves.
- The ever-hungry [*jaw'iyya*], because they eat only enough to keep themselves alive, and to help them practice worshipful obedience.

Since these pure individuals most often clad themselves in garments of wool [*ṣūf*], the name "Sufi" came into common use and prevailed over other designations. This name became established as a mark of someone who followed their example, whether by wearing wool or by adopting their characteristics in good conduct and spiritual progress.

When describing the noble Messenger (Allāh bless him and give him peace), Abū Mūsā al-Ash'arī said, "He used to wear wool and ride donkeys." He also said:[3] "O my dear son, if only you had seen us when we were together with our Prophet (Allāh bless him and give him peace)! If the sky rained down upon us, you would have found us emitting the odor of sheep from our woolen clothes!"

According to al-Ḥasan al-Baṣrī, "I came to know seventy veterans of Badr, whose clothes were made of wool."[4]

Numerous sources mention that the People of the Bench [*Ahl aṣ-Ṣuffa*], a group of the Companions of the Messenger (Allāh bless him and give him peace), wore clothes of wool. They kept to a particular corner of the mosque of the noble Messenger (Allāh bless him and give him peace). The nickname was thus given, as it has been

3. *Ṭabaqāt Abī Sa'd*, vol.1, p. 80.
4. *al-Ḥilya*, vol. 1, p. 134.

said, to some of the Muslim paupers in the time of the Messenger and the Rightly Guided Caliphs. They had no houses in which to shelter, so they used to rest on a seat outside the mosque, which was built in Medina at the Messenger's command.

Wool is the symbol of humility and quiet resignation, which explains why the worshipful servants are described as wearing wool. As for those who seek to impress people with their Sufi appearance and who block the paths of goodness, they are blameworthy and ostracized in the sight of Allāh as well as in the sight of people.

According to some of the orientalists and researchers, other explanations are also possible.

1. The word "Sufi" may be derived from *ṣafā'* [purity].
2. Its origin may be traced to the Companions of the Bench [*Aṣḥāb aṣ-Ṣuffa*].
3. It may be related to the Greek word *sofia*, meaning wisdom.

The fact of the matter, however, as we have concluded after profound investigation, is that the term "Sufi" was not applied to these people except to distinguish them by the wearing of wool, a mark of propriety and humility. This view is preferred by the majority of the writers and researchers, both ancient and modern, and it is in complete conformity with linguistic principles.

Second Section
Sufism and Philosophy

It is well known, as we have mentioned in the Introduction, that the human being sought in the dawn of his creation for knowledge of what lies behind nature, looking for a way to reach it. It is also well known that the Greeks outstripped others in this pursuit and investigation of the sphere of intellectual, scientific knowledge, to which they applied the technical term "philosophy."

The Greek word philosophia is compounded from two words: *philia*, which means love, and *sophia*, which means wisdom. As a single word, it signifies "the love of wisdom." It is related that Pythagoras (600 B.C.), one of the greatest of the ancient Greek philosophers, once said, "I am not a wise man, but I do love wisdom!" He was followed in succession by the pinnacles of Greek philosophy: namely, Socrates (468–399 B.C.) and his pupil Plato (430–347 B.C.), then Aristotle (384–322 B.C.) and hundreds of thinkers and philosophers. The philosophers have not ceased to follow one another in every nation and community. Philosophy does not cease to exist. Each philosophy has its own particular method for exploring the areas that lie behind nature or for understanding the Creator of the universe and its Manager.

The fact is that many of the philosophers endured the hardship of the long journey, ardently yearning to reach the real truth until they arrived at "the knowledge of certainty [*'ilm al-yaqīn*]." At that point they came to a halt, and their travelling provision did not enable them to reach the "eye of certainty [*'ain al-yaqīn*]" or the "truth of certainty [*ḥaqq al-yaqīn*]."

I shall provide definitions of these stages in summary form to the extent that this may be useful in explaining the difference between Sufism and philosophy. We shall thereby distinguish the scope of each of the two.

Greek philosophy was concerned with all forms of knowledge, whether theoretical or practical. According to the philosopher Auguste Comte (1789–1857 C.E.), "Philosophy is the general theory of knowledge." Another French philosopher is reported as having said, "Philosophy is the knowledge of personal life and its connection with common life and with the whole universe." According to Ibn Khaldūn, "Philosophy about theological concerns is contemplation of existence."

According to one of the scholars, "The starting point of philosophy is love of the sciences. Its midpoint is understanding the realities of everything that exists to the extent of human capability. Its final stage is speaking and acting in a manner that is fully consistent with knowledge."

It is therefore clear to us that philosophy is a science with basic principles by which we acquire knowledge of existence. We derive from our knowledge a course on which we travel toward the highest goal.

Plato said, quoting Socrates, "The wise man is one whose emotion is subservient to his intellect. Someone whose intellect is subservient to his emotion is not a wise man."

Philosophy is the apex of intellectual knowledge. It is a way of thinking that illuminates the path of life for the human being. It signifies a way of thinking that is critical of the conditions of life, exploring the means by which its problems can be speedily resolved.

Numerous definitions of philosophy have been offered, from the era of the Greeks to the times of Kant, Descartes, and Hegel for philosophy is very comprehensive and very profound. We shall therefore be content with what we have set forth above for the purpose of defining philosophy.

Philosophy fails to attain the eye of certainty [*'ain al-yaqīn*] or the truth of certainty [*ḥaqq al-yaqīn*], whereas Sufism has attained to them both. We shall explain this as follows.

It is clear to us that philosophy and Sufism are the two products of thinking focused on certainty. Certainty has three degrees defined by the scholars:

1. The knowledge of certainty [*'ilm al-yaqīn*]

This means believing that something is true to a degree that falls short of complete confidence.

For example, consider the case of the hungry man who goes looking for a restaurant in a city where he is not familiar with the streets. He comes across a sign that points to a restaurant or a person directs him to the place, but it is possible that the restaurant has been converted into something else, or that the sign he noticed is old and out-of-date.

2. The eye of certainty [*'ain al-yaqīn*]

This is realized if the hungry man finds people eating and drinking in the place mentioned in the first example. His confidence then increases and his knowledge attains to the eye of certainty. He has reached the degree of witnessing, but he is still beneath the level of experiential knowledge and complete satisfaction.

3. The truth of certainty [*ḥaqq al-yaqīn*]

This is where the man reaches the peak of certainty and confidence since he actually tastes the food and experiences the satisfaction that comes with the achievement of his goal.

I can make the following statement with complete confidence:

The philosophy that depends on the human intellectual capacity for knowledge cannot attain to the truth of certainty in theological matters. That is because the human mind has a finite limit to its capability, the condition of all the senses. There are no limits to the scope of the truth of certainty in theological matters. "That which is limited and finite does not encompass that which has no limit and no end." The mind does not grasp anything except after recognizing its subjective limitation, that is, when it recognizes the limits of comprehensive understanding. It is therefore impossible for it to grasp what lies behind nature, beyond the material sphere.

For the sake of clarification, let me add:

The mind depends on material instruments and means, which it employs for the purpose of knowing and understanding things. They are the five senses: sight, hearing, taste, touch, and smell. These senses do not grasp what falls beyond their sensory power. Because of the limitation of their functions, they have nothing to do with what lies behind nature. The gist is that perception of the supernatural is a spiritual perception. It is something psychic, connected with faith and the psychic faculty. In this context, we have nothing to gain from the method of the philosophers, which is dependent on the mind and the five senses.

The path of Sufism is your means of connection, with Allāh's help, to the truth of certainty. That is because it signifies the cleansing of the mirror of the heart and the purification of the self to the point where the heart senses the existence of the Manager of the universe. It is illumined by the Divine light, which it recognizes with confidence. At the moment when the heart begins to feel the warmth of Divine emanation, it attains to "the truth of certainty."

How fortunate are those pious heroes who have grasped the truth of certainty, like the prophets, the messengers, the disciples, the Companions and the righteous ones who have followed them in active goodness!

That does not mean that knowledge of Allāh cannot be acquired except by following the Sufi path, or through Islam alone. That is because vast numbers of people have not embraced Islam, or Islam has not reached them, although they are believers. From Plato to Kant and whomever Allāh wills, intellectual reasoning has led the majority of the philosophers to faith.

The fact is that the human mind is capable of concluding, by means of deduction, that this universe has a Manager and an Almighty Lord, but it cannot go beyond the knowledge of certainty. That is because the human being possesses a natural disposition, the love of knowledge. We cannot fail to notice the persistence of children in questioning their parents about everything until they are satisfied with the response. Everything is new to them and their brains are empty of the store of knowledge.

Children ask such questions as, "What is the moon? To whom does this moon belong? Who created the moon?" It is true that we now possess a wealth of knowledge about this subject, but the ancient generations used to stand perplexed, wondering about the answer. This was the launching pad of investigation, and from it sprang philosophy and its various schools. For the purpose of helping the human being to dispel his bewilderment, Allāh sent the prophets and the messengers.

There have been two paths to knowledge of Allāh: Philosophy prevailed in the West and the Far East, while heavenly messages prevailed in the Middle East. At the time when miracles [*mu'jizāt*] became the means of inspiring belief in the messengers and the messages, the philosophers were preoccupied with intellectual evidence.

Every philosophy has a particular method of intellectual cogitation. Aristotle, for instance, based his reasoning on the principles of practicality and finality in order to arrive at knowledge of that which necessitates existence. That is to say, every effect has a cause that brings it into being, in accordance with a regular system, and nothing comes about by chance, by accident, or by supernatural occurrences. Everything in the universe is subject to this comprehensive rule, except that these causes finally reach back to a cause that exists by itself and does not result from a cause beyond itself. Aristotle calls this "the First Cause."

The same is true in the case of Muslim philosophers except that they attempted to bring philosophy close to the religion. For example, al-Fārābī focused his intellectual sight on the concept of the necessary and the possible. This pattern became clearly apparent in the thinking of Ibn Sīnā, since he arrived thereby at the reality of the necessarily existing [*wājib al-wujūd*]. According to this philosophy, the One who necessarily exists is Allāh, the Manager of the universe. Created entities are the possibilities. In the case of the philosopher al-Kindī, he studied the concept of the effect [*athar*] and that which produces effects [*mu'aththir*], the secondary cause [*sabab*] and that which produces causes [*musabbib*]. He saw that this universe is an organized system uniquely created, and that, since every effect has an effect-producer and every secondary cause has a cause-producer, the universe undoubtedly has a uniquely Creative Organizer.

This bears an intellectual resemblance to the path of faith.

In a valuable book concerning the manifestation of God in the age of science, a Western scholar has collected the opinions of forty professors and experts in contemporary human knowledge, all of whom have come to believe in God (Glory be to Him) through their intellectual contemplation of the marvels of the universe. They have all said, "This tremendous, amazing universe cannot possibly have come into existence without an eternal, everlasting Architect."

At this point I must say, There are two paths in front of us, and only two, they being the theory of chance and the theory of creation. We may either maintain that the cosmic system came into being by chance, and that no intentional purpose was involved in bringing it about—this being the opinion of the materialists—or we may maintain that it was created, this being the opinion of the believers.

It is inconceivable that blind chance should be that which has organized this wonderful system for this material cosmos, assembled its elements, arranged its rules, and brought into being such different entities as the animal, the vegetable, and the mineral.

The mind is incapable of grasping the secret of the cosmic system. Ignorance of the true nature of the Producer or of the manner of the production does not justify denial of the Producer. The intelligent person is not convinced that a material instrument like the television, for instance, is an object brought into being by chance without a producer simply because of his lack of knowledge of the producer or the manner of its production. Suppose the intelligent person finds remarkable objects in an empty building in a lonely desert, like a statue sculptured with highly artistic skill and an eloquent poem inscribed on a tablet suspended therein. He will surely concede that this statue is the work of a masterful sculptor and this poem is the work of a great poet. It would be stupid to imagine that the statue came to exist without the intervention of someone's deliberate intent, but simply by chance, or that this poem was inscribed by the action of accumulating particles of dust without the intent of an intelligent person. By the same token, if you discovered a castle in the desert without knowing to whom it belonged you would surely not deny that this castle had a builder.

Which of the two creations is more wonderful, the making of a statue and the writing of a poem or the creation of the human being who produces these things? If chance is rejected in the making of a statue, a poetic ode and a castle in the desert, how can it be accepted in the creation of the human being, who made the statute, wrote the poem, built the castle, and performed so many marvels?

It is therefore inconceivable that the system of life could be the product of blind chance when it is arranged in all its colors, its flowers, its species and its creatures from the flies to the elephant and from the ditches to the towering mountains.

Who is the One who created everything by decree?

As you must surely realize, the system of life on earth would be disordered if the established quantities of the solar rays were disordered. It is therefore unreasonable for man to deny the fact that this wonderful universe has a Creator, simply because he cannot encompass Him in knowledge and understanding. Why does the atheist believe in matter, even though he does not understand its true nature, and does not know from whence and when and how it came?

This reality is epitomized in the connection of the systematized with that which systematizes, and of the effect with the cause. If we find something arranged in order, we do not doubt that there is behind it a controlling mind. Whenever we find the effect, we do not doubt that it has a cause. There is no mere chance in the existence of a building in the desert or in the imprint of a rabbit's foot in clay or sand.

An idea occurs to me that brings this reality into sharper focus, and maybe no one else has thought of it before me, though Allāh knows best! It is the concept of "mating [*zawjiyya*]" or "the male and the female," which the noble Qur'ān has mentioned in numerous verses.

Let us assume that "natural" chance brought a male into being on the earth, millions of years ago, with all his faculties and instincts, or that the female was likewise brought into being. Is it then reasonable to ask,

- Was the genesis of the female contemporaneous with that of the male, and vice-versa?
- If they were twins, in what womb were they bred?
- If they were embryos, how did they survive?
- If they were infants, who suckled them?

Questions thus follow one another in succession, and the attentive mind finds it impossible to entertain the idea of chance in the formation of the elements of masculinity and femininity. Consider the womb, the teat, breast-feeding, and the sexual instinct experienced simultanously by both sexes. In this context, we must also consider the fecundation of various genera and species of animals and plants occurring simultaneously both in one place and in different places on the earth. If we consciously reject the idea that a gate made of timber could come into existence without someone's deliberate intent, we shall no doubt dismiss the statement that this widespread mating has come about by chance. (We shall dismiss it for the simple reason that the speaker is ignorant of the manner of creative formation.)

(The concept of evolution does not arise here, because the obvious reality is that the male is different from the female. Even if monkeys were transformed into regal beauties, the male would still be a male and the female a female, and the Creator would still be their Originator.)

The reality, of which the atheists and skeptics are ignorant, is that the mind is not endowed with the ability to grasp the essence of its Creator, for it falls short of the degree of the eye of certainty and the truth of certainty.

We are surely deficient in grasping the essence of matter, the soul, the earth and the sky, so what purpose is served by this overreaching toward that which has no limits?

The fact is that, if we contemplated the wonders of the eyes, the heart and the brain, or any organ in the animal body, we would know that the question of chance is absurd, and that faith is the reality.

This kind of understanding is the knowledge of certainty. It has been the path of faith for the scholars, philosophers, and thinkers, both before and after Islam. As for the path of Sufism, which we have examined in detail in this book of ours, with Allāh's help, it is that which enables the spiritual traveler to reach the eye of certainty or the truth of certainty. It is the path by which the believer comes to experience the taste of real faith, and acquires true conviction. It purifies the self so that it discovers reality with the eye of insight, leaving no room for doubt in the conscience. That is the eye of certainty and the truth of certainty.

From this it is clear that the path of Sufism is not the path of philosophy or theology and that each of the two paths has a scope that differs from the other in origin and procedure. Whereas philosophy or theology is dependent on the ḥuman mind for establishing what is necessary, Sufism is the preparation of the self for the experience thereof.

Neither philosophy nor theology is a starting point or basis for Sufism, because of the difference of the path and the goal peculiar to the former and the latter. It is actually impermissible to regard Indian or Chinese spiritual culture as having a fundamental influence on Islamic Sufism. That is because Islamic Sufism is an original offshoot from the Book and the Sunna. As for the contents of Greek philosophy and the reports of the sages of India, China or Persia, they were made available in Arabic in the second and third centuries of the Hijra. The books of the Greek philosophers were translated into Arabic in the reign of Hārūn ar-Rashīd (766–809 C.E.) and in the reign of the Caliph Ma'mūn (786–833 C.E.). Islamic Sufism was therefore essentially uninfluenced by ancient Greek philosophy, or by the new philosophy of Plotinus known as Alexandrian philosophy or by the new Platonic philosophy attributed to Plotinus (203–270 C.E.).

Orientalists adopted their erroneous view of this matter from the existence of a certain similarity in the utterances of some of the Sufis and philosophers, especially where the philosophy of Plotinus is concerned. In reality, however, this is a faulty induction on which no valid argument can be based. As a minimum requirement, judgment on the strength of similarity demands a scientific comparison between a number of the philosophers and a number of the great shaikhs of Sufism. There must be an objective intellectual analysis of their views regarding philosophy and Sufism rather than reliance on nothing but a few opinions or the unusual sayings of certain shaikhs. Islamic Sufism appeared before the transmission of Greek philosophy, by a long period of time.

Orientalists have clung to the sayings attributed to some Sufis in order to emphasize the supposed similarity between Sufism and philosophy. These include the saying attributed to Rābi'a al-'Adawiyya (A.H. 185), "O my Lord, I worship You for the sake of Your love and Your good pleasure, not out of fear of the Fire of Hell!" They have claimed that Rābi'a al-'Adawiyya treated love as a symbol for her Sufism, and that she thereby resembles the pious Christian nun.

Their claims have been reinforced by what they have seen as a strong similarity between the idea of illumination, meaning the manifestation of Allāh's light, and the corresponding philosophical concept. They have also noticed ideas that lead to the concept of incarnation and pantheism among some of the sayings attributed to certain great men who appeared to be Sufis.

The reality is that Sufism is a Qur'ānic procedure followed by finding guidance in the Sunna [exemplary practice] of the supreme Messenger (Allāh bless him and give him peace) and the good customs of his Companions. It appeared several centuries before the transmission of the philosophy of the Greeks and the wise teachings of Hindus.

This reality is confirmed by the fact that the aims and goals of Sufism do not coincide with with aims and goals of philosophy. That is because Islam is the basis of Sufism and its goal. In other words, Sufism is faith in the Uniqueness of Allāh (Glory be to Him), strict adherence to the Sacred Law of the Qur'ān in belief and practice, and personal and social conduct in the radiant light of the pure Prophetic Sunna. The great scholars of Sufism have unanimously agreed that Sufism is observance of the rules of Islam, but external observance is not sufficient. It must extend to the heart, so that the Sufi fulfills the teachings of the Noble Qur'ān in his spiritual journey, and arrives at the truth of certainty.

To understand the spiritual station of Sufism in Islam, let us cite the noble Prophetic tradition.

> Beneficence [*iḥsān*] means that you worship Allāh as if you see Him, for even if you do not see Him, He surely sees you!

This spiritual station, the station of beneficence, is a station in which Islamic Sufism is firmly embedded, and it is different from the station of a philosopher whom the mind has led to faith.

We have previously mentioned the fact that the human being has never ceased to reflect on what lies behind nature, and to ask himself about its real meaning. Individuals have differed in this respect, however. Some have devoted their whole lives to the investigation of this mystery, choosing isolation from people for its sake. Such a person is referred to as a "monk" in Christianity, while Islam describes the believers in the following manner.

> Those who remember Allāh,
> *alladhīna yadhkurūna 'llāha*
> standing and sitting and on their sides,
> *qiyāman wa qu'ūdan wa 'alā junūbi-him*
> and who reflect upon the creation of the heavens and the earth:
> *wa yatafakkarūna fī khalqi 's-samāwāti wa 'l-arḍ:*
> "Our Lord, You have not created this in vain.
> *Rabba-nā mā khalaqta hādhā bāṭilā:*
> Glory be to You! So guard us against the torment of the Fire."
> *subḥāna-ka fa-qi-nā 'adhāba 'n-nār.* (3:191)

We can therefore say that the human being has constantly sought knowledge and understanding of nature and what lies behind it. The resemblance of Islamic Sufism to Sufi-like inclinations before Islam does not mean that Sufism has been influenced by non-Islamic precedent, for it is a resemblance in natural disposition, not a resemblance from deliberate adoption of non-Islamic practices. Islamic Sufism is the practice of following the path of Muḥammad (Allāh bless him and give him peace) in worshipful service, in contemplation, and in life.

If we reflected on life, we would discover a remarkable similarity in many of its spheres, attributable to the likeness of instinct. These include coincidence of thought or the comparability of needs and the means of their satisfaction as well as the similarity of circumstances and their constituent elements. This does not mean, however, that what comes later is influenced by what has gone before.

By way of example, let us mention the story of the ardent love that bound Qais to Lailā, a story known in Arabic literature as "Lailā's Madman [*Majnūn Lailā*]." The same tale recurs in "Romeo and Juliet" in English literature, in "Mem and Zain" in Kurdish literature, and in "Shīrīn and Farhād" in Persian literature. In the science of the history of law, there are numerous indications of similarity in the legal statutes of countries with similar social and economic conditions.

If Islamic Sufism bears some resemblance to a tendency in human spiritual culture, as it appeared in one form or another in earlier times, this does not signify the link of continuity in practice, but simply the link of similarity in human aspiration itself.

The truth of this is confirmed by Islamic Sufism being different in its goal and procedure from the spiritual path referred to metaphorically as non-Islamic Sufism. That is from the Sufism of other religions and programs. It is a Sufism defined in the Sacred Law of Islam by the Book [of Allāh] and the Sunna [of the Prophet]. Its realities were clearly explained in valuable works compiled by the great Sufi shaikhs before the ideas of the philosophers and sages of the nations infiltrated into Islamic thinking in the spheres of ethics and morality, psychology, and philosophy.

Third Section
Islamic Sufism and the Islamic Law [*Sharī'a*]

We have epitomized Sufism in two expressions, namely, "tasting [*dhawq*]," which is seeking to experience real knowledge [*ma'rifa ḥaqīqiyya*], and "the manifestation of the Divine light in heart of the worshipful believer." These are two spiritual states that mind has no means of access. If someone chooses the mind alone as an instrument for their attainment, the roads will be blocked in front of him and his steps will lead nowhere. That does not mean that we disregard the value of intellectual knowledge [*'ilm*] and the importance of the mind. It simply means that we regard the mind as restricted to the sphere of material experience. The Sufi experience is purely spiritual, whereas the arena of the mind is matter and every product of the five senses.

Sufism transports the human being through the spheres of the spirit, the conscience, and the Divine light without transgressing the limits of the noble Sacred Law [*Sharī'a*]. That is because it does not seek guidance except in the Book and the Sunna. Its values are not inspired by anything other than the exemplary practice of the Prophet as well as the lives of those righteous predecessors, the Companions, the Successors, and the leaders of learning and religion. It is not kept apart, however, from operating within the extensive domain of the noble Sacred Law by a strictly defined framework. Islamic Law requires a Muslim to perform the ritual prayer [*ṣalāt*] as formally prescribed without obliging him to confine his breathing to a measure that diverts his heart from cogitation for a moment during the time of nearness [to the Lord]. Sufism, on the other hand, imposes the burden of vigilant awareness [*murāqaba*] so that the worshipper is always fully alive at every moment of the prayer, whether standing erect or in prostration with a constant attitude of humility and submissiveness. He will thus obtain the blessings of lights, of which he alone is aware.

> Successful indeed are the true believers
> *qad aflaḥa 'l-mu'minūn:*
> who are humble in their prayers.
> *alladhīna hum fī ṣalāti-him khāshi'ūn*. (23:1,2)

That is why we say that Sufism is adherence to the rules of the Sacred Law within a particular framework, with a strict discipline, and with a real and serious assimilation of its concepts in its nature and its procedure. It is bound by the essence of the Sacred Law and its reality. A Sufi experiences it with his inner feeling and his spirit before his physical body, and with his heart before his limbs and organs.

The connection between Sufism and the Sacred Law may be

clarified by the following statements. The Law passes judgment on the exterior so that, if a person intends to commit a sin, he is not punished for his sinful intention, as long as he does not commit the offence in practice. Sufism, on the other hand, is the training of the lower self in the avoidance of considering sin and making it accustomed to the heart's preoccupation, totally with what is good, so that the inner feeling of the Sufi becomes a nest for loving affection [*maḥabba*].

It is legally incumbent upon you to carry out the teachings of Islam concerning the ritual prayer [*ṣalāt*], the alms-due [*zakāt*] and the pilgrimage [*ḥajj*] in accordance with the rules expounded in books of jurisprudence [*fiqh*]. Sufism therefore sets you on the path of this worshipful obedience by ensuring that you do not neglect the remembrance of your Lord and that you experience spiritual delight in the constant practice of your worship and immersion in your contemplation.

When we bear witness to the illuminating examples provided by the biographies of the masters of Sufism, we acknowledge that these are the chosen *élite* among the righteous servants of Allāh. They observed a lofty mode of conduct in keeping with the rules of the Sacred Law and did not depart from them by a hair's breadth. The Noble Qur'ān contains definitive verses that clearly describe the stations of this lofty mode of conduct in worshipful service and contemplation. We shall deal with the subject in detail. What concerns us here is to explain that the path of Sufism is the path of Islam, nothing else.

Ibn Sīnā said, in his book *al-Ishārāt wa 't-Tanbīhāt* [*Indications and Instructions*],

> The ascetic [*zāhid*] is someone who abstains completely from the temptations of this world. The worshipful servant [*'ābid*] is someone who devotes his life to prayer in order to carry out the teachings of his Lord. The direct knower [*'ārif*] is someone who is totally immersed in contemplation of the splendor of his Lord begging Him (Almighty and Glorious is He) to fill his heart with the light of His direct knowledge.

These attributes may be combined in one individual so that he becomes an ascetic, a worshipful servant, and a direct knower. This individual is the Sufi.

It is thus quite clear, as we see it, that Sufism is the sacred struggle waged for the sake of attaining to direct knowledge of Allāh, on the path of the inner feeling. This kind of experience is realized by a taste in the conscience, the heart, and inner feeling, not by a taste in the tongue. It is realized by witnessing with the insight, not with the outer eye. This realization will be apparent in the sayings of the leaders of the path of Sufism, which we shall relate in the following section.

Fourth Section
Sufism in the Sayings of its Great Shaikhs

The eminent figures of Sufism and the stars of its sky are unanimously agreed that Sufism is wisdom [*ḥikma*]. Wisdom is intimate knowledge of Allāh, and it is the path of felicity in the two abodes [this world and the Hereafter]. Allāh (Glory be to Him) has said,

> And he to whom wisdom is given,
> *wa man yu'ta 'l-ḥikmata*
> he has truly received abundant good.
> *fa-qad ūtiya khairan kathīrā.* (2:269)

He has also said (Exalted is He),

> It is He who has sent among the unlettered folk
> *Huwa 'lladhī ba'atha fi 'l-ummiyyīna*
> a Messenger from among themselves,
> *Rasūlan min-hum*
> to recite to them His signs and to purify them,
> *yatlū 'alai-him āyāti-hi wa yuzakkī-him*
> and to teach them the Book and wisdom.
> *wa yu'allimu-humu 'l-Kitāba wa 'l-ḥikma.* (62:2)

If someone wishes to attain to wisdom, meaning intimate knowledge of Allāh, he must therefore adorn himself with the culture of the Sacred Law [*Sharī'a*]. He must purify his lower self and keep it away from every evil. Once his conduct has come to be in keeping with the Sacred Law, and his heart has been filled with the light of worshipful service, his state of being will deserve to receive the manifestation of the light of Truth.

This is indicated by the tradition [*ḥadīth*] related from the Prophet (Allāh bless him and give him peace).

> The heart of the believer is the Throne of Allāh.[5]

5. In one version, the wording is: "the Throne of the All-Merciful [*'Arsh ar-Raḥmān*]."

Allāh (Glory be to Him) has said,

> But as for him who feared to stand before his Lord,
> *wa ammā man khāfa maqāma Rabbi-hi*
> and forbade the lower self to follow passion,
> *wa naha 'n-nafsa 'ani 'l-hawā:*
> surely the Garden will be his final place of rest.
> *fa-inna 'l-jannata hiya 'l-māwā.* (79:40,41)

Sufi knowledge is one of the finest forms of knowledge because it is intimate knowledge [*ma'rifa*] of Allāh. There is no doubt that intimate knowledge of Allāh is the basis of every benefit. It is more noble than any other kind of knowledge, and its owner is the most noble of the children of Adam.

The Sufi is that Muslim who has traversed the stages of certainty on the path so that his heart is at peace with the truth of certainty [*ḥaqq al-yaqīn*]. As Allāh (Exalted is He) has said,

> He it is who sent down peace of reassurance
> *Huwa 'lladhī anzala 's-sakīnata*
> into the hearts of the believers
> *fī qulūbi 'l-mu'minīna*
> that they might add faith to their faith.
> *li-yazdādū īmānan ma'a īmāni-him.* (48:4)

This station is not attained except by someone who struggles and strives, as evidenced by His saying (Exalted is He),

> And that the human being has only that
> *wa an laisa li'l-insāni illā*
> for which he makes an effort, and that his effort will be seen.
> *mā sa'ā wa anna sa'ya-hu sawfa yurā.* (53:39,40)

If the human being strives sincerely for nearness to His exalted Essence, Allāh will be for him a Custodian and a Guide, as evidenced by His saying (Exalted is He),

> And as for those who strive in Our cause,
> *wa 'lladhīna jāhadū fī-nā*
> surely We shall guide them in Our ways.
> *la-nahdiyanna-hum subula-nā.* (29:69)

The Sufi seeks two inseparable forms of knowledge, intimate knowledge of his own self and intimate knowledge of Allāh. It has been said, "He who really knows his own self, knows his Lord."

Without any doubt, the scope of intimate knowledge of Allāh (Glory be to Him) is wider than any book or mind, but intimate knowledge of the self illuminates the path to intimate knowledge of Him (Glory be to Him). A man must therefore acknowledge his servitude to his Lord, call himself to account, and reconsider his earlier and later duties and responsibilities in relation to his Lord and his Creator as well as in connection with the training of his lower self and in relation to his family and his society.

By means of this educative spirit, the removal of the depravity in the Muslim's lower self, and the arousal of the awareness of truth and goodness in his conscience, he really and truly prepares his state of being for intimate knowledge of Allāh. This is the purport of, "He who really knows his own self, knows his Lord." That is because, if someone knows his own self in practice, he can deal with the temptations of sin. For the deluded fool who pays no attention to his own self, it is impossible for him to pursue this path.

The importance of the self is indicated by His saying (Exalted is He),

> We shall show them Our signs on the horizons
> *sa-nurī-him āyāti-nā fi 'l-āfāqi*
> and within themselves, until it becomes clear to them
> *wa fī anfusi-him ḥattā yatabayyana la-hum*
> that it is the Truth.
> *anna-hu 'l-Ḥaqq.* (41:53)

> As well as in your own selves. What, do you not see?
> *wa fī anfusi-kum a-fa-lā tubṣirūn.* (51:21)

According to Abū Sulaimān ad-Dārānī (may Allāh the Exalted bestow His mercy upon him), "The Sufi heart has seen Allāh. Whatever sees Allāh does not die, so he who has seen Allāh has become immortal."

According to Doctor 'Abd al-Ḥalīm Maḥmūd, in his introduction to *at-Ta'arruf li-Madhhab Ahl at-Taṣawwuf* [*Familiarity with the Doctrine of the Masters of Sufism*], by the Sufi scholar Abū Bakr Muḥammad al-Kalābādhī (d. A.H. 380),

"Every statement written by the Sufis is everlasting like the Sufi heart. It is everlasting and will never die because it is connected with Allāh, aimed at His good pleasure, inspired by His guidance, illumined by His love and radiant with His light. This is why the

Sufis believe that they are the beloved friends of Allāh, His chosen ones, His saints, the cream of His servants and the guardians of His sources and His signs."

Ma'rūf al-Karkhī was asked, "Tell us about pure affection [*maḥabba*]," so he replied, "O my brother, pure affection does not come from the teaching of people. Pure affection comes from the teaching of the Beloved."

Through this firm bond, secured by ecstasy and love, and the inspirations of intimacy and nearness, the Sufi comes to be such that whichever way he turns, there is the Face of Allāh, so he sees nothing apart from Him,

> So whichever way you turn, there is the Face of Allāh.
> *fa-aina-mā tuwallū fa-thamma wajhu 'llāh.* (2:115)

Everything in existence is like a mirror in which the Sufi sees the Face of Allāh, His signs, His power and His mercy.[6]

According to Dhū 'n-Nūn al-Miṣrī,[7] "My God, I have not listened to the sound of animals, nor to the rustling of trees, nor the rippling of water, nor the singing of a bird, nor the murmur of rain, nor the drone of a wind, nor the rattle of thunder, without finding it a witness to Your Uniqueness, proving that there is nothing like unto Him."[8]

The method of Sufism is the annihilation of the lower self. [As Allāh (Exalted is He) has said],

> Surely the self is always inciting to evil.
> *inna 'n-nafsa la-ammāratun bi's-sū'i.* (12:53)

May Allāh be well pleased with those who have curbed the defiance of their lower selves, for He has said,

> And forbade the lower self to follow passion.
> *wa naha 'n-nafsa 'ani 'l-hawā.* (79:40)

The Sufi causes the passion of the lower self and its lustful desires to be annihilated in that which Allāh loves, wishes, and commands. He thus comes to be like the servant addressed in the Sacred Tradition [*Ḥadīth Qudsī*],

---

6. See *at-Ta'arruf li-madhhab ahl at-taṣawwuf* [*Familiarity with the Doctrine of the Masters of Sufism*], by al-Kalābādhī, p. 5.
7. Dhū 'n-Nūn al-Miṣrī (d. A.H. 245) is one of the great elders of Sufism.
8. See *Ḥilyat al-adab* [*Adornment of Propriety*] by Abū Nu'aim, pt. 9, p. 20.

> O My servant, be lordly! Say to the thing, "Be!" and it will come to be.

As Imām al-Junaid, the shaikh of the shaikhs, once said, "All of his movements come to be in conformity with the Truth, to the exclusion of its contradictions. So he becomes extinct to contradictions, permanent in conformities."[9]

This amounts to the replacement of human nature by the Lordly nature, a condition which this world ascribes to none but the Islamic Sufis. Sufi annihilation is not the annihilation of a body in a body nor the annihilation of a spirit in a spirit. It is the annihilation of a will in a Will, the annihilation of characteristics in Characteristics, and of attributes in Attributes. As the Sufis say, "Extinct to his own qualities, permanently endowed with the qualities of the Truth."

Sufism is a peak of perfection, which ascends until its wings flap from the horizon of the highest holiness, then flap as they ascend till they reach the lofty height of assuming the characteristics of the Divine attributes. This is referred to in the Sacred Tradition [*Ḥadīth Qudsī*],

> I become his hearing by which he hears, and his sight by which he sees.

According to al-Kalābādhī, one of the great shaikhs of Sufism,[10] "The annihilation of worldly interests is referred to in the tradition of Ibn Mas'ūd, who said, 'I did not know that there was anyone among the Companions of Allāh's Messenger (Allāh bless him and give him peace) who desired this world until Allāh (Exalted is He) said,

> There are some of you who desire this world,
> *min-kum man yurīdu 'd-dunyā*
> and there are some of you who desire the hereafter.
> *wa min-kum man yurīdu 'l-ākhira.* (3:152)'

> "'Abdu'llāh ibn Mas'ūd was at this station, extinct to the desire of this world."

Sufis have been annihilated in the love of their Master. They have assumed His characteristics, adopted His proper modes of conduct, been educated in His prayer niches, and devoted their lives to His

9. See *at-Ta'arruf li-madhhab ahl at-taṣawwuf*, p. 125.
10. See the introduction to his book *at-Taṣawwuf al-Islāmī* [*Islamic Sufism*], p. 16.

remembrance and intimate converse with Him. So He has taught them, cleansed, and purified them, chosen, and selected them, loved them and been well pleased with them. He has opened to their hearts the dominion of the heavens and the earth, showing them the marvels of His being, the wonders of His power, and the secrets of His creation. He has bestowed upon them His presents and His gifts, in knowledge and experience. As He has said (Exalted is He),

> Practice true devotion to Allāh, and Allāh will teach you.
> *wa 'ttaqu 'llāh: wa yu'allimu-kumu 'llāh.* (2:282)

Even though the Sufi is well aware of the bliss of the Garden of Paradise, he strives to gain nearness to the Owner of the Garden. One of the great shaikhs of Sufism said to one of his disciples, "If you wish for the Garden, go to Ibn Madyan. He is a scholar of the Sacred Law. If you wish for the Owner of the Garden, come here to me [for I can show you the way]."

As we read in the book *Nafḥ aṭ-Ṭīb* [*Fragrance of Perfume*], "The Sacred Law is the path of the Garden, while Sufism is the path of Allāh," meaning Reality [*Ḥaqīqa*].

It was Rābi'a al-'Adawiyya, she being the wounded bird on the path of true affection, who said, "My God, I do not worship You in fear of Your Fire, nor in search of Your Garden, but I love You, so I prostrate myself before Your Glory!"

According to Doctor Zakī Mubārak,[11] "Sufism requires denial of the self." He also said, "I used to study Sufism by observing indications, ceremonies, and formalities, but only in the heart and the spirit did I come to know its true meaning."

According to Abū Naṣr as-Sarrāj (d. A.H. 378), the author of the book entitled *al-Luma'* [*Radiances*],[12] "Many different responses have been given to questions about the meaning of Sufism. Ibrāhīm ibn al-Muwallad ar-Raqqī mentioned one hundred answers. In the book *Nashr al-Maḥāsin al-Ghāliya* [*Publication of Precious Benefits*], al-Yāfi'ī has listed one thousand answers concerning the technical term *Taṣawwuf* [Sufism]."

According to Shaikh Aḥmad ash-Shirbāṣī,[13] "Sufism is a doctrine

11. See the introduction to his book *at-Taṣawwuf al-Islāmī* [*Islamic Sufism*], p. 16.

12. See *al-Lumā'* [*Radiances*] by Abū Naṣr as-Sirāj aṭ-Ṭūsī, p. 47.

13. In his study published in *Silsilat ath-thaqāfa al-Islamiyya* [*Chain of Transmission of Islamic Culture*], 1961.

that is moral and ethical, social, and psychological. It has its point of origin, its history and its process, its method, its proof, its signposts, its men and its heroes, its books and its sources, its advantages and its drawbacks."

The fact of the matter, as I have mentioned previously, is that if someone wishes to understand Sufism, he must travel in the regions of its wide world, wandering on its horizons as an explorer in order to discover its ways. It is just like someone who wishes to explore an unknown world.

Access to the world of Sufism is not easily attained, for it is a matter of vision, taste, and the radiation of Allāh's light in the heart. It has stations [*maqāmāt*] and states [*aḥwāl*]. Its stations are like the stations of this world, as when it is said, for example, "So-and-so is *mudīr* [manager; director; governor]." They are stations conferred by Allāh (Glory be to Him) upon the truly devout among His servants. The state [*ḥāl*] is different, for it is a fleeting condition that comes and goes. As for the station [*maqām*], its occupant is established in his ascending progress unless he is deprived of his Lord's blessing because of a sin he has committed.[14]

To provide an exact definition of Sufism is just as difficult, therefore, as trying to define the flavor of a fruit, like a pear or a fig, for a person who has never tasted it in his life. One may describe it as sweet to the taste, but sugar is also sweet to the taste, and so are honey and dates. Each has its own peculiar flavor. Is the acidity in a pomegranate comparable to that in vinegar, for instance?

If the subject is psychological, or a case of Divine illumination and a spiritual station, how can it be defined for someone who has not tasted anything of the kind, and has not entered this domain?

One of the seekers came to Shaikh Muḥyi'd-Dīn ibn al-'Arabī (1165–1240 C.E.) and said to him, "People do not believe our Spiritual Path to be true." The shaikh replied, "If someone asks you for evidence to prove the true nature of this path, you must ask him, 'How do you know that honey is sweet to the taste?' If he says, 'I have tasted it, and by the taste it is known,' then tell him, 'The same applies to Sufism. You do not know it until you taste it.'"

As a matter of fact, those who are inebriated by the taste of the

14. The station [*maqām*] is a position that, once earned, is firm and established. It involves effort and striving, for it is conferred on the aspirant in accordance with his effort and his striving. As for the states [*aḥwāl*], they are mystic presents, bestowals, and gifts.

bliss of Sufism, addicted to the fruits of its luxuriant gardens and immersed in the oceans of His grace and His noble generosity (Glory be to Him), are cognizant of Allāh's might (Glory be to Him) and His compassion for His creatures. They will not find an opportunity to define what they discover in themselves. If they did describe it, they would say, "This realm is pleasant to the taste. It fruits are tasty. If anyone among you is rightly guided, let him come here so that he may enjoy a share in this permanent bliss and constant joy." They would not do anything other than that.

It also adds to the difficulty that the masters of Sufism speak in a peculiar language in which the meaning is expressed in metaphor and symbolism, and that they may speak in the language of their spiritual states and stations. For that reason, whatever one of these luminaries is experiencing and expressing is in his own peculiar language and represents only one aspect of Sufism. Sufism therefore has various definitions, in accordance with the state and station of each person. Nevertheless, they all aspire to a single goal. Numerous definitions are attributed to the great men of this domain.

1. According to Shaikh Ma'rūf al-Karkhī (d. A.H. 200),[15] "Sufism is acceptance of the realities and despairing of what is in the hands of creatures."

2. According to Shaikh Abū Sulaimān ad-Dārānī,[16] "The Sufi experiences moments known only to Allāh, and he is with Allāh in states known only to Allāh."

3. According to Abū Turāb an-Nakhshabī (d. A.H. 245),[17] "Nothing troubles the Sufi, and everything is made serene by him."

4. According to Bishr al-Ḥāfī (A.H. 150–225), "The Sufi is someone whose heart is pure and serene."

5. According to Shaikh Bāyazīd al-Bisṭāmī (A.H. 188–266), "The Sufis are children in the lap of the Truth."

6. According to Abū Ya'qūb as-Sūsī, "The Sufi is someone who is never sad, even if he loses everything and who never wearies on the path that leads to the goal."

7. According to Shaikh Abu 'l-Ḥasan an-Nūrī (d. A.H. 295), "The Sufis are a people whose hearts are pure, free from the troubles of humanity and the vices of the lower self. They have been liberated

15. See *'Awārif al-ma'ārif* by as-Suhrawardī, p. 41.
16. *at-Tadhkira*, pt. 1, p. 233. See also: "*The Origin of Islamic Sufism*" by Dr. Ibrāhīm al-Basyūnī, p. 21.
17. *'Awārif al-ma'ārif.*

from their lustful desires so they have come to be in the first rank and the highest degree in the presence of the Truth. Since they have abandoned everything apart from Allāh, they have come to be owners and not slaves."

8. According to Shaikh Junaid al-Baghdādī (d. A.H. 297), "Sufism means that the Lord of Truth makes you die to yourself and makes you live through Him."[18]

9. He also said, "[Sufism means] that you are with Allāh without any attachment." "The Sufi is like the earth on which everything unpleasant is dumped, and from which nothing emerges except every pleasant thing."[19] "The Sufis are those who are with Allāh Alone, and whom none but He knows." "Sufism is purification of the heart from conformity with creatures, separation from natural characteristics, extinction of human attributes, avoidance of selfish instincts, adoption of spiritual attributes, attachment to the sciences of reality, engagement in what is best suited to eternity, good advice to the Community, fidelity to Allāh in accordance with Reality, and following the Messenger (Allāh bless him and give him peace) in the Sacred Law."[20]

10. According to Ḥusain al-Ḥallāj (d. A.H. 309), "The Sufi is solitary by nature. No one accepts him, and he accepts no one."[21]

11. According to Shaikh Abū Bakr ash-Shiblī (d. 945 C.E.), "Sufism is sitting in the presence of Allāh without a care."[22]

12. It was also ash-Shiblī who said, "The Sufi is detached from creatures, linked to the Lord of Truth, as in His saying (Exalted is He),

> And I have reared you for Myself.
> *wa 'ṣṭana'tu-ka li-Nafsī*. (20:41)

—for He has detached him from every other, then said to him,

> You will not see Me.
> *lan tarā-nī*. (7:143)"

13. According to Abū 'l-Ḥasan al-Ḥaṣrī, "The Sufi is someone who does not revert to a sin he has abandoned. His heart is not con-

18. *'Awārif al-ma'ārif*, p. 43.
19. *'Awārif al-ma'ārif*, p. 43.
20. *al-Kalābādhī*, p. 25.
21. *ar-Risāla al-Qushairiyya*, p. 129.
22. *ar-Risāla al-Qushairiyya*, p. 129.

tent with any but his Lord and he places all his trust in his Lord who knows what He has foreordained for him."

14. According to Abū Sa'īd Abū 'l-Khair (d. A.H. 440), "The Sufi is someone who discharges his obligation and gives what is in his hands."

15. According to Shaikh 'Abd al-Qādir al-Jīlānī (A.H. 470–561), "You must earn the wealth of this world by lawful means, but set it on the palms of your hands, not in the core of your heart!"

16. Shaikh Muḥammad ibn 'Alī al-Qaṣṣāb, the Shaikh of al-Junaid, was asked, "What is Sufism?" He replied, "Noble ethics and morality. It appeared in a noble time from a noble man, together with a noble set of people."

17. Saḥnūn, a contemporary of al-Junaid, was asked, "What is Sufism?" He replied, "That you possess nothing and nothing possesses you."[23]

18. According to Shaikh 'Amr ibn 'Uthmān al-Makkī (d. A.H. 298), "Sufism means that the servant [of the Lord] is engaged at every moment in what is most appropriate to the moment."

19. According to Shaikh Abū 'n-Naṣr as-Sarrāj (d. A.H. 378),[24] "The Sufis are those endowed with knowledge of Allāh and of Allāh's rules who practice what Allāh (Exalted is He) has taught them, who realize what Allāh (Almighty and Glorious is He) requires them to do, who love what they come to realize, and who are annihilated by what they love, because everyone is annihilated by what he loves."

20. According to Dhū 'n-Nūn al-Miṣrī (d. A.H. 245), "The signs of intimate knowledge of Allāh are three: (1) The light of intimate knowledge of Allāh does not extinguish the light of the servant's pious restraint. (2) He does not speak in secret of a knowledge at variance with the obvious meaning of the Book and the Sunna. (3) He is not moved by charismatic talents to uncover the veils of Allāh's sanctuaries."

21. According to Sahl ibn 'Abdullāh at-Tustarī (d. A.H. 896),[25] "The Sufi is someone who is free from distress and filled with contemplation. He is detached from human beings in his devotion to Allāh and gold and clay are one and the same to him."

22. According to Dhū 'n-Nūn al-Miṣrī, "I saw a woman on one

---

23. For these definitions, see *ar-Risāla al-Qushairiyya*, p. 127, and other Sufi reference works.

24. *al-Luma'*, p. 26.

25. See *'Awārif al-ma'ārif*, p. 43, and *Tadhkirat al-awliyā'*, p. 264.

of the beaches of Syria, so I said to her, 'Where have you come from? May Allāh bestow His mercy upon you!' She replied, 'From the presence of people whose sides shun their couches, as they call to their Lord in fear and hope.' I said, 'And where do you intend to go?' She said, 'To men whom neither commerce nor trade distracts from the remembrance of Allāh.' I said, 'Describe them for me,' so she broke into poetry, saying,

They are folk whose aspirations are focused on Allāh,
so they have no interest in aspiring to anyone else.
The goal of their quest is their Patron and their Master.
How fine is their quest for the One, the Everlasting!
They are not tempted by worldly interest or nobility,
in the form of ambitions and pleasures and children,
nor the wearing of splendid and elegant clothing,
nor enjoyment of the delight of settling in a town.
They wish only to make haste in search of a site
to step wherein brings the distant near to eternity,
for they are the pledges of rivers and valleys,
and in the heights you will meet them at the ready.'"

23. According to Yūsuf ibn al-Ḥusain, "Every religious community has an *élite* [*ṣafwa*], they being Allāh's deposit whom He has concealed from His creatures. If some of them are in this Community, they are the Sufis."

24. According to Sa'īd al-Jarrāz (d. A.H. 268), "The Sufi is someone whose heart his Lord has purified [*ṣaffā*], so it is filled with light. He is someone who alights in the source of delight through his remembrance of Allāh."[26]

25. According to Ja'far al-Khuldī (d. A.H. 348), "Sufism is subjecting the lower self to servitude, departing from human nature, and looking to the Lord of Truth entirely."

26. According to ash-Shiblī, "The starting point of Sufism is intimate knowledge of Allāh, and its final point is the realization and affirmation of His Oneness."

27. According to Abū Bakr al-Kattānī (d. A.H. 322), "Sufism is morality. If someone surpasses you in morality, he surpasses you in purity [*ṣafā'*]."

28. According to Shaikh Muḥammad Bahā' ad-Dīn an-Naqshband (A.H. 717–791), "Our Spiritual Path is proper conduct."

26. *Nashāt at-taṣawwuf al-Islāmī*, p. 22.

29. Abū Muḥammad al-Jarīrī was asked, "What is Sufism?" He replied, "Entering into every superior characteristic, and departing from every inferior characteristic."

30. According to Abu 'l-Ḥasan an-Nūrī (d. A.H. 295),[27] "Sufism is neither a formal practice nor a science, but rather a development of character. If it were a formal practice, it would be achieved by vigorous effort, and if it were a science, it would be achieved by teaching. It is actually the cultivation of the characteristics of Allāh, and you can never approach the Divine characteristics by means of a science or a formal practice."

31. It was also an-Nūrī who said, "Sufism is freedom, nobility, and the abandonment of affectation and pretentiousness."

32. According to Shaikh Muḥammad Amīn al-Kurdī al-Irbilī (d. 1913 C.E.),[28] "The Sacred Law [*Sharī'a*] is a tree; the Spiritual Path [*Ṭarīqa*] is its branches; and Reality [*Ḥaqīqa*] is its fruits."

33. According to Abū Bakr al-Kattānī, "Sufism is a purification [*ṣafā'*] and a visionary experience [*mushāhada*]." This concise definition combines the two basic principle of the means and the aim. The means is purification and the aim is visionary experience.[29]

The learned Professor Nicholson collected approximately two hundred definitions arranging them in chronological order with the purpose of arriving at a comprehensive definition of Sufism. He could not achieve that purpose, however, and he decided—as the shaikhs had decided before him—that it is impossible to define the essence and reality of Sufism. [30]

Fifth Section
Sufism in the Experience of Imām al-Ghazālī
(A.H. 450–505/1059–1114 C.E.)

Imām al-Ghazālī, the Proof of Islam [*Ḥujjat al-Islam*], is the best of those who have experienced Sufism and explained its meaning. He was sure that the Sacred Law [*Sharī'a*] and the Spiritual Path [*ṭarīqa*] are one, but the Sacred Law is concerned with the external aspect of matters while the Spiritual Path is concerned with what is

27. *Tadhkirat al-awliyā'*.
28. *Tanwīr al-qulūb*, p. 409.
29. *Nashāt at-taṣawwuf al-Islāmī*, p. 21.
30. See the special section on the definition of Sufism, in *Nashāt al-falsafat aṣ-ṣūfiyya* [*Origin of Sufi Philosophy*] by Dr. 'Irfān 'Abd al-Ḥamīd.

in the hearts. He believed that Sufism is not attainable by learning, but rather by taste, spiritual state, and the transformation of attributes. In his book *Iḥyā' 'ulūm ad-dīn* [*Revival of the Religious Sciences*], al-Ghazālī said,

> The Path is dedication to earnest endeavor, the eradication of blameworthy attributes, the severance of all attachments, and commitment to Allāh (Exalted is He) with the utmost degree of aspiration. Whenever that is attained, Allāh becomes the Custodian of His servant's heart and the Guarantor of its illumination with the lights of knowledge. When Allāh takes charge of the business of the heart, mercy showers upon it. Light shines in the heart, the breast expands, and the secret of Sovereignty [*Malakūt*] is disclosed to it. The veil of might and glory is removed from the face of the heart by the grace of mercy and in it gleam the realities of the Divine affairs.

Sufism means following the Sacred Law with the heart and the physical limbs and organs, not with the tongue alone. We may refer to the principal sources of the knowledge of Sufism, including: *Iḥyā' 'ulūm ad-dīn* by al-Ghazālī, *ar-Risāla al-Qushairiyya* by Shaikh 'Abd al-Karīm ibn Hawāzin, *at-Ta'arruf li-madhhab ahl at-taṣawwuf* by Shaikh Muḥammad al-Kalābādhī, *Qūt al-qulūb* by Shaikh Abū Ṭālib al-Makkī (d. A.H. 386), *al-Luma'* by Shaikh Abū Naṣr as-Sarrāj, the *Maktūbāt* of Imām ar-Rabbānī, *Tadhkirat al-awliyā'* by al-'Aṭṭār, and *al-Mawāhib as-sarmadiyya wa tanwīr al-qulūb* by Shaikh Muḥammad Amīn al-Kurdī.

In order to extend the horizons of knowledge and understanding within the vast expanses of Sufism, I propose to shed light on the Sufi experience of Imām al-Ghazālī, that flier in the sky of direct knowledge and insight as he wrote about it himself in his book *al-Munqidh mina 'ḍ-ḍalāl* [*Deliverance from Error*]. In that work, the Imām relates the story of his contemplative life as it moved from exhaustive study to doubt, then on to certitude. The substance of this journey is expressed in his words,

> You have asked me, O my brother in religion, to unfold to you the ultimate aim of the sciences and their secrets. You have asked me to tell you what I have gone through in discovering the Truth from the midst of the confusion associated with the disparity of the courses of action, and how I dared to ascend from the lowland

> of convention to the hill of direct perception. I have therefore made haste to respond to your request.

He then went on to say,

> In the prime of my youth, since I approached maturity before the age of twenty, and until now when I am more than fifty years old, I have never stopped diving to the very bottom of this deep sea. I plunge into its flood with the plunge of a daring diver, not with the plunge of a cautious coward. I penetrate into every dark corner. I tackle every difficult problem. I invade every dilemma. I investigate the creed of every sect and I explore the secrets of the doctrine of every faction in order to distinguish between those who tell the truth and those who lie, between those who follow the Sunna and those who are guilty of heretical innovation. I do not leave an esotericist without wishing to observe his inner lining, nor a exotericist without seeking to know the content of his outer lining, nor a philosopher without trying to ascertain the essence of his philosophy, nor a theologian without striving to grasp the purpose of his speech and his argument, nor a Sufi without endeavoring to detect the secret of his purity [*ṣafwa*], nor a worshipper without observing what the content of his worship relates to, nor an atheistic freethinker without probing to disclose the reasons for his insolent profession of atheism and freethinking.
>
> A thirst to pursue true facts has always been my habit and my custom. From the start of my career and the prime of my life, it has been a disposition and a temperament received from Allāh and implanted in my nature, not by my own choice and design. As a result, the bond of convention fell from me, and I lost confidence in hereditary doctrines around the age of early youth.

He added,

> I said to myself, first of all, 'All that I seek is knowledge of the true facts, so there is no alternative to seeking the reality of knowledge. What is it, I wonder?'
>
> It then became clear to me that truly certain knowledge is that in which what is known by spiritual disclosure has no doubt clinging to it, and is not associated with the possibility of error and illusion. The heart is not capable of evaluating that. Security from error requires knowledge so close to certainty that, even if

> someone tried to demonstrate its falsehood—for instance, someone who transforms a stone into gold, or a staff into a snake—that would not give rise to doubt and denial. Since I know that ten is more than three, even if someone told me, 'Oh no, three is more, as evidenced by the fact that I can transform this staff into a snake,' and he did transform it before my very eyes, he would not cause me to doubt my knowledge. I would simply experience amazement at his ability to perform such a feat. As for doubting what I know, that would not happen.
>
> I then understood that whatever I do not know in this sense, and of which I am not certain with this kind of certitude, is knowledge that cannot be trusted and has no reliability. Any knowledge that has no reliability is not a truly certain knowledge.
>
> I then examined my items of knowledge and I found myself devoid of any knowledge matching this description except in sensory matters and basic necessities.

He then went on to say,

> When these ideas occurred to me (casting doubt on every thought and perception), and impressed themselves upon me, I attempted to apply a remedy. It was no easy task, however, since there can be no cure without proof, and proof cannot be established without assembling the fundamental elements of knowledge. If these are not set in good order, the proof cannot be assembled. This sickness was therefore difficult to treat and it lasted for almost three months. During that time I was engaged in sophistry by virtue of my spiritual state, not on the strength of verbal utterance and speech until Allāh (Exalted is He) cured me of that sickness. I was then restored to health and normality. Intellectual stresses became acceptable and reliable on the basis of a Divine commandment and certainty.

That was not due to a formulation of proof and reasoned argument, but to a light cast into the breast by Allāh (Exalted is He). When Allāh's Messenger (Allāh bless him and give him peace) was asked about expansion and its meaning in His saying (Exalted is He),

> Whoever it is Allāh's will to guide,
> *fa-man yuridi 'llāhu an yahdiya-hu*
> He expands his breast to Islam [Surrender to His Will].
> *yashraḥ ṣadra-hu li'l-Islam.* (6:125)

—he said, "It is a light that Allāh (Exalted is He) casts into the heart."

According to al-Ghazālī, "The purpose of these stories is that he [the seeker] should work in the quest with perfect earnestness, until he finally arrives at the point of seeking what is not sought." He enlarged on his splendid explanation, saying,

> When Allāh (Exalted is He) cured me of this sickness, by His gracious favor and the abundance of His generosity, seekers of various types assembled in my presence in four groups:
>
> 1. The scholastic theologians [*mutakallimūn*] who claim to be the masters of informed opinion and discernment.
>
> 2. The esotericists [*bāṭiniyya*] who claim to be the masters of teaching, specially endowed with enlightenment from their infallible leader.
>
> 3. The philosophers [*falāsifa*] who claim to be the masters of logic and proof.
>
> 4. The Sufis who claim to be the *élite* of the Spiritual Presence and the masters of direct vision and disclosure.
>
> I said to myself, 'The Lord of Truth will not abandon these four types for they are the wayfarers in search of the Truth. If the Truth eludes them, there is no longer any hope of attaining to the Truth.' I therefore made haste to pursue these paths, and to investigate what these four groups have to offer. I began with the science of theology, which I mastered and thoroughly understood. I studied the books of its qualified experts, and compiled what I wished to compile on the subject. I found it to be a science sufficient for its purpose, but insufficient for my own purpose. Its purpose is simply to safeguard the doctrine of the upholders of the Sunna and to preserve it from the derangement of the promoters of heretical innovation. As far as I was concerned, scholastic theology was therefore not sufficient nor was it a cure for the sickness of which I complained. Next, I started on the science of philosophy.

He then went on to say,

> I devoted serious effort to the books [of the philosophers], studying on my own without the assistance of a professor, and I attended to that in my moments of leisure from compiling and giving instruction on the sciences of Sacred Law. I was allotted

> the task of teaching and informing three hundred souls among the students in Baghdād. Allāh (Glory be to Him and Exalted is He) enabled me, by private study in those few spare moments to acquire full knowledge of their sciences in less than two years.

He also said,

> I noticed that, regardless of the multitude of their groups and the variation of their doctrines, they can be divided into three categories: the materialists [*dahriyyūn*], the naturalists [*ṭabī'iyyūn*], and the theists [*ilāhiyyūn*].
>
> 1. In the first category, the materialists [*dahriyyūn*] are a party of the ancients who rejected belief in the Creator, the Controller, the All-Knowing and the All-Powerful. They claimed that the universe has never ceased to exist by itself without a Creator, and that the animal has never ceased to come from the sperm, and the sperm from the animal. That is how it has been, according to them, and that is how it will always be. They are also known as *zanādiqa* [infidels; atheists].
>
> 2. The second category the naturalists [*ṭabī'iyyūn*] who are a set of people whose research is mostly concerned with the world of nature and the marvels of animal and vegetable life. They have frequently delved into the science of dissecting the bodies of animals. In the process, they have seen such marvels of the work of Allāh (Exalted is He) and so many wonders of His wisdom that they have been compelled to acknowledge a Wise Creator, an Overseer of the aims and purposes of things. No one studies dissection and the wondrous benefits of physical organs, without acquiring this necessary knowledge of the perfection of the management of Constructor of the structure of the animal, and especially the structure of the human being.
>
> Nevertheless, on account of their considerable study of nature, they have assigned to the balance of the physical constitution a tremendous influence on the maintenance of the animal's strengths and energies. They have also supposed that the intellectual strength of the human being results from his physical constitution, and that it is nullified by the nullification of his physical constitution, so he ceases to exist. Then, once he has ceased to exist, the restoration of what is nonexistent is inconceivable, or so they claim. They have therefore espoused the doctrine that the soul dies and does not return. They have rejected belief in the Hereafter, and denied

the Garden of Paradise, the Fire of Hell, the Resurrection and the Reckoning. So there is no reward for obedience, in their view, and no punishment for disobedience. The bridle of restraint has thus fallen from them, and they have become engrossed like cattle in the satisfaction of carnal desires.

These are also classed as infidels [*zanādiqa*], because the root of faith is belief in Allāh and the Last Day. These have rejected belief in the Last Day, even though they believe in Allāh and His attributes.

3. The third category are the theists [*ilāhiyyūn*] who are more recent, like Socrates, who was the teacher of Plato. Plato was the teacher of Aristotle and Aristotle was the one who systematized logic and developed the sciences for them.

Imām al-Ghazālī then classified their sciences, and he said, "You should know that their sciences are of six types: experimental, logical, natural, theistic, political, and ethical."

After discussing them, he said, "Then, when I had finished studying the science of philosophy, summarizing its import and making sense of it and eliminating its spurious content, I realized that it was also insufficient for complete achievement of the goal. I realized that the intellect is not independently capable of comprehending all problems nor of removing the veil from all enigmas. The geniuses of academia had been remarkably impressive and public attention had been drawn to their account of understanding the true meaning of things from the perspective of the infallible leader, the upholder of the Truth. It occurred to me that I should investigate what they had to say so that I would be thoroughly acquainted with the contents of their books."

Imām al-Ghazālī studied their views in detail, and came to the conclusion that they have no saving remedy from the darkness of speculative opinions.

He then discussed his experience with Sufism, about which he said,

> Then, when I had finished with these sciences, I focused my attention on the method of the Sufis. I learned that their Spiritual Path is completed only by knowledge and practice. The gist of their knowledge is about surmounting the hurdles of the lower self, and abstinence from its blameworthy characteristics and its noxious attributes to the point of arriving at the purification of

the heart from everything other than Allāh (Exalted is He) and adorning it with the remembrance of Allāh.

Knowledge was easier for me than practice, so I began by acquiring their knowledge from the perusal of their books like *Qūt al-qulūb* [*Food of Hearts*] by Abū Ṭālib al-Makkī, the books of al-Ḥārith al-Muḥāsibī, the miscellanies transmitted from al-Junaid, ash-Shiblī and Abū Yazīd al-Bisṭāmī (may Allāh sanctify their spirits), and other examples of the speech of their shaikhs. I eventually grasped the essence of their scientific purposes and came to know as much as can possibly be known about their method through learning and listening. It thus became clear to me that the most special of their special properties cannot be reached through study, but only by the experience of taste, the spiritual state, and the transformation of attributes.

There is such a great difference between knowing the definition of health and repletion and the causes and prerequisites thereof, and actually being healthy and replete. There is likewise a great difference between knowing the definition of drunkenness and that it signifies a state resulting from the overwhelming effect of vapors that ascend from the stomach to the faculties of thought, and actually being drunk. The drunkard does not know the definition of drunkenness and its scientific meaning, yet he is drunk without having any such knowledge. The sober person knows the definition of drunkenness and its elements, yet he has no experience of drunkenness. The physician in the state of sickness knows the definition of health and its causes and remedies, yet he is suffering the loss of health. There is likewise a difference between your knowing the real meaning of abstinence and its causes and prerequisites, and your spiritual state being that of abstinence and detachment from this world.

I thus came to know for certain that they [the Sufis] are the masters of spiritual states, not the masters of verbal pronouncements, and that I had acquired whatever can be acquired by means of knowledge. All that remained was that to which there is no means of access by listening and learning, but only by taste and practice. It had become quite clear to me that there is no prospect of bliss in the Hereafter except through true devotion and restraining the lower self from passionate desire. I realized that the main part of all that is severing the heart from attachment to this world, by shunning the abode of illusion and turning in repentance to

> the abode of immortality, and by approaching Allāh (Exalted is He) with the utmost degree of aspiration. As I also realized, that can only be completed by forsaking prestige and material wealth and by fleeing from preoccupations and attachments.
>
> I then examined my spiritual states only to find myself immersed in attachments that surrounded me from all sides. I also examined my actions, the best of them being lecturing and teaching, only to find that I was dealing with sciences of no importance and no benefit on the path of the Hereafter.
>
> Then I considered my intention in lecturing, only to find that is was not purely devoted to Allāh (Exalted is He), but that its motive was the pursuit of prestige and the spreading of good repute. I thus became convinced that I was on the edge of a perilous cliff. I was on the brink of the Fire of Hell if I did not attend to the correction of my conditions. I reflected on this for some time, considering on a daily basis whether I should decide to leave Baghdād and those conditions. I would make that decision one day and take a step toward it, then step back from it another day. I would feel a keen urge to seek the Hereafter in the early morning, but it would be attacked by the army of carnal desire, so that it faded by the evening. The desires of this world were binding me to the spot with their chains, while the herald of faith was calling, 'Make the move! Make the move! What is left of your lifetime is very little and a long journey lies in front of you. All the knowledge and practice that you are involved in is ostentation and play acting, so if you do not prepare now for the Hereafter, when will you prepare?'

Imām al-Ghazālī then shifted in his story to explaining how he contrived his disappearance and his departure [from Baghdād], in fear of opposition from the Caliph and the senior scholars. Then he said,

> I left Baghdād and parted with all the wealth I possessed, keeping only the means of bare survival and the sustenance of children.... Then I entered Syria and stayed there for almost two years, preoccupied with nothing but isolation, seclusion, spiritual exercise and earnest endeavor. I was dedicated to the purification of the lower self, the training of character and the devotion of the heart to the remembrance of Allāh (Exalted is He) as I had learned it from the knowledge of the Sufis. I stayed for some time in seclusion in the mosque of Damascus where I spent the whole daytime up

in the minaret, closing its door on my lower self.

Then I traveled to Jerusalem where I entered the desert every day, closing its door on my lower self. Then in me stirred the summons to perform the duty of Pilgrimage [*Ḥajj*], to seek support from the blessings of Mecca and Medina, and to visit the [tomb of] Allāh's Messenger (Allāh bless him and give him peace) after visiting the [tomb of Abraham] the Bosom Friend [*al-Khalīl*] (may Allāh's blessings be upon him), so I traveled to the Hijāz. I was then drawn to the homeland by the aspirations and appeals of the children, so I went back to it after becoming the most unlikely of creatures to return there. I preferred isolation there too, eager for seclusion and devotion of the heart to the remembrance [of Allāh]. I continued like that for as long as ten years. Disclosed to me during these times of seclusion were matters impossible to count and relate in detail, but the amount I shall mention will be beneficial.

I came to know for certain that the Sufis in particular are the travelers on the path of Allāh (Exalted is He). Their journey is the finest of journeys; their path is the straightest of paths; and their characters are the purest of characters. Indeed, even if the intelligence of the intelligent, the wisdom of the wise and the knowledge of those scholars who grasp the secrets of the Sacred Law—even if all these combined to make some change in their journey and their characters and to substitute something better, they would not find any means to do so. That is because all their movements and pauses, in both their outer and their inner life, are illumined by the light of the lamp of prophethood, and beyond prophethood there is no source of illumination on the face of the earth.

In short, according to those who speak of the Spiritual Path, its state of purity—the first of its preconditions—is the purification of the heart by which it is cleansed entirely of everything apart from Allāh (Exalted is He). Its key—the source of the sanctification that flows from the ritual prayer—is the total immersion of the heart in the remembrance of Allāh. Its final stage is total annihilation in Allāh.

From the outset of the Spiritual Path, its followers begin to receive disclosures and visionary experiences so that in their wakefulness they witness the angels and the spirits of the prophets from whom they hear voices and from whom they obtain benefits.

> Then their spiritual state progresses from the witnessing of forms and likenesses to degrees that can hardly be described in words so that no one can express them without uttering a patent error that he cannot guard against.
>
> In short, the matter results in a nearness [to the Truth], from which imaginary conclusions are drawn by the heretical faction of *ḥulūl* [incarnation of the Deity], the faction of *ittiḥād* [pantheism], and the faction of *wuṣūl* [union with the Deity]. All of that is erroneous. We have explained the nature of the error in the book *al-Maqṣid al-Asnā* [*The Highest Goal*]. In actual fact, if someone experiences that condition, he should do no more than say,
>
> Whatever happened, it was something I shall not describe, so hold a good opinion and do not question what is good.

At this point, I shall cite explanations by Shaikh Muḥammad Bahā' ad-Dīn an-Naqshband (may Allāh sanctify his innermost being), in order to clarify what al-Ghazālī said. According to an-Naqshband,

> In the time when I become calm, I find myself being addressed by a voice and being spoken to. My likeness therein is that of the written line, which speaks although it is silent and speechless. In the time when I am neither working nor actively useful, I am still of benefit to others like the marks of addition and subtraction by which the reckoning is known even though they are not included in the account.

He then went on to say, "I have no idea how to make you understand the meaning of nearness, O ascetic among the exotericists, except that I may liken it to the rose-water in the roses." By that he means that his nearness to Him is like the nearness of the rose-water in the roses.

I shall now return to the Sufi experience of al-Ghazālī, since he went on to say, "In short, if someone does not experience any of this by taste, he will not perceive the reality of prophethood apart from the name. The charismatic talents of the saints are really the elementary stages of the prophets." He then addressed the purification of the heart, for he said, "Those of whom Allāh (Glory be to Him) says,

> In their hearts there is a disease.
> *fī qulūbi-him maraḍun.* (2:10)

These people are those who have not purified their hearts. By the heart He means the reality of the spirit, which is the location of intimate knowledge of Allāh unlike the flesh and blood." As al-Ghazālī has said, "The physical body has a state of health by which it flourishes, and a state of sickness in which its destruction lies. The heart likewise has a state of health and well-being."

The contemplative Sufi, al-Ghazālī, concludes the account of his experience by saying, "As for real knowledge, its owner increases in fear and dread, and also in hope. That prevents him from committing sinful acts of disobedience, except those slips that the human being cannot avoid from time to time, and that do not imply weakness of faith. The believer is tested but is always ready to repent. He refrains from persistence and perseverance [in sin]."

Chapter Two
Responses to questions about Sufism and its problems

1. When did Islamic Sufism originate?

From what has already been said, it is clear that Islamic Sufism is essentially the same as Islamic Law [*Sharī'a*], meaning compliance with the Noble Qur'ān and the pure Prophetic Sunna. The Sufi, however, is concerned with the struggle to control the lower self and he turns toward the prayer niche of worship not only to fulfill a religious duty but motivated by an ardent feeling of love. He may even rejoice in the being he suffers on his path, repeating Allāh's saying (Exalted is He),

> Say, "Nothing will befall us except what Allāh has decreed for us."
> *qul lan yuṣība-nā illā mā kataba 'llāhu la-nā.* (9:51)

Since metaphorical ardor impels the lover to sacrifice for the sake of his beloved, how will it be in the case of genuine ardor? Rābi'a al-'Adawiyya is describing this condition when she says:[1] "I have not served Him from fear of His Fire, not from love of His Garden, for then I would be like the bad employee. I have served Him from love of Him and yearning for Him."

Sufism originated with the appearance of the dawn of Islam and its shining in the heart of the noble Prophet Muḥammad (Allāh bless him and give him peace). The light of Reality then beamed from the treasury of prophethood into the hearts of his rightly guided Caliphs and his Companions, with whom Allāh is well pleased and who are well pleased with Him.

Some of them were especially prominent in the Muḥammadan Radiance, like the splendid Companion Ḥudhaifa ibn al-Yamān al-'Abbāsī and Ḥāritha ibn Mālik about whom the Messenger (Allāh bless him and give him peace) once said,

> If it pleases someone to look at a person whose heart
> Allāh has illumined, let him look at Ḥāritha ibn Mālik!

---

1. *Tanwīr al-qulūb*, vol. 2, p. 113; *Nashāt at-taṣawwuf al-Islāmī*, p. 189.

According to al-Qushairī in his *Risāla*, "The Companions of the noble Prophet acquired every virtue through the honor of companionship, and since there is no excellence more noble than that, they were called 'the Companions,' while those who joined their company were called 'the Successors [*at-Tābi'īn*].'"

In the time of the Successors, worldly ambitions gradually intruded, but certain people resented this state of affairs and found it distressing. They opted for seclusion, rescuing their religion from temptations and contenting themselves with giving sound advice to their brethren. These people came to be known by various appelations, including 'Sufi' and 'ascetic.' As a matter of fact, the term 'ascetic [*zāhid*]' was familiar to the Arabs both before and after the advent Islam, whereas the term 'Sufi' became familiar in the time of the Successors when it was applied to someone who withdrew from the temptations of this world, such as palatial mansions, maidservants, and material possessions, and immersed himself in the worshipful service of Allāh and His remembrance. I shall mention two proofs of that:

> 1. Imām al-Ḥasan al-Baṣrī (A.H. 61–110) said, "I noticed a Sufi during the circumambulation [around the Ka'ba], so I offered him something, but he did not accept it. He said, 'I have four small coins with me, so what I have with me will suffice me.'"
>
> 2. According to Imām Sufyān ath-Thawrī (A.H. 97–161), "But for Abū Hāshim, the Sufi, I would not have understood the subtle nature of ostentation."

When describing the noble Prophet, our master 'Umar (may Allāh be well pleased with him) said, "Let my father and my mother be your ransom, O Messenger of Allāh! You have dressed in wool [*ṣūf*] and taken to riding the donkey!"

Islamic Sufism is what is exemplified in the Sunna of the Messenger (Allāh bless him and give him peace) and this is clearly apparent in the conduct of the most excellent Companions, who were distinguished by insightful knowledge. It then becomes evident in the conduct of men like al-Ḥasan al-Baṣrī, Dāwūd aṭ-Ṭā'ī, Ma'rūf al-Karkhī, as-Sarī as-Saqaṭī and al-Junaid al-Baghdādī. Since then it has spread and became widely known as a name and a description, as a title and a nickname. For the sake of comparison, the term *ḥawārī* used to mean "white shirt," but then it was applied to a group of devoted followers, like the disciples of our master Jesus (peace be upon him).

2. How can we establish the compatibility of Islamic Sufism with Islamic Law [*Sharī'a*]?

It is well known that a number of doubts are raised concerning the correctness of this compatibility, the most important of them being the following,

1. It is said that Sufism is a heretical innovation [*bid'a*] and the most striking evidence of that is what is associated with certain great Sufi shaikhs like Shaikh Bāyazīd al-Bisṭāmī, Muḥyi'd-Dīn ibn al-'Arabī, Dhū'n-Nūn al-Miṣrī, al-Ḥallāj, and Shaikh as-Suhrawardī who was killed in Aleppo (not as-Suhrawardī who is buried in Baghdād, the author of the book *'Awārif al-ma'ārif* and the chief of the Suhrawardī Order).
2. Following the shaikhs may reach the boundary of polytheism [*shirk*] and unbelief [*kufr*] through the sanctification of their shaikhs [by the Sufis], especially after their demise.
3. Some groups among the Sufis tread the paths of error, and mislead the people in the name of Sufism for the sake of their own special interests. They are highway robbers. Some of them have strange ideas that clash with the realities of Islam like existential monism [*waḥdat al-wujūd*], incarnation of the Deity [*ḥulūl*], and pantheism [*ittiḥād*].

In order to dispel these doubts, let me state the following,

Ecstatic utterances [*shaṭaḥāt*] are sayings that are not compatible with the teachings of the true Islamic religion. It may happen, however, that the Sufi experiences an unnatural state because of his immersion in the remembrance of Allāh (Glory be to Him), so he becomes like the drunkard who is not usually held responsible for his delirious raving. As a matter of fact, these ecstatic utterances are a metaphorical expression of what they experience in the form of mystic disclosure and they return to their normal rectitude after the disappearance of this state. It is related that many of the jurists [*fuqahā'*] have pronounced in favor of their legality, including Shaikh ash-Sha'rānī, who validated the ecstatic utterances of Shaikh Muḥyi'd-Dīn ibn al-'Arabī as being compatible with the teachings of Islam. Examples of ecstatic utterance include the saying attributed to Shaikh Bāyazīd al-Bisṭāmī, "There is nothing under my cloak except Allāh!" On the face of it, this statement amounts

> to unbelief [*kufr*], but they interpret it in the sense that when the Sufi reaches the station of "Sultan of the remembrances," or the station of "annihilation in Allāh," his heart and all his limbs and organs become totally immersed in the remembrance of Allāh so he sees nothing but Him (Glory be to Him). He is therefore not lying when he utters that saying, even though it is superficially at odds with the Sacred Law.

To prove that Islamic Sufism is essentially identical with the Islamic religion, the clearest evidence is provided by the conduct and sayings of the men of this Spiritual Path, since they are bound by the rules of the Sacred Law, distinguished by their piety, and treat the purification of the lower self as the emblem of their life. We have not found Sufism to contain anything contrary to Islam, for it is all about repentance and the pure heart, remembrance, earnest endeavor and other spiritual stations and qualities, concerning all of which explicit Qur'ānic verses have been revealed.

The first step in Sufism is repentance, which is the renunciation of every bad deed and remorse for having committed it. As for those who persist in going astray, the Noble Qur'ān has described them as,

> Deaf, dumb, and blind, so they do not return.
> *ṣummun bukmun 'umyun fa-hum lā yarji'ūn.* (2:18)

The Noble Qur'ān has mentioned the heart is numerous verses, which we shall be citing in various contexts. It is enough at this point for us to quote the noble verse alluding to blame,

> No indeed; but what they have been earning has rusted upon their hearts.
> *kallā bal rāna 'alā qulūbi-him mā kānū yaksibūn.* (83:14)

—and the noble verses alluding to praise,

> And he comes with a penitent heart.
> *wa jā'a bi-qalbin munīb.* (50:33)

> Except one who comes to Allāh with a whole heart.
> *illā man ata 'llāha bi-qalbin salīm.* (26:89)

The Noble Qur'ān contains more than one hundred and fifty references to the heart from which it is understood that the heart may be a location for faith and true devotion. It may also be a location for evil.

Repentance comes after the feeling of remorse, but how does

remorse become a real experience? Is it through Divine guidance, through contemplation, or through the fellowship of the truthful?

The lower self is always instigating evil, as Allāh (Exalted is He) has said on the tongue of Joseph,

> "I do not exculpate myself.
> *wa mā ubarri'u nafsī:*
> Surely the self is always instigating evil."
> *inna 'n-nafsa la-ammāratun bi's-sū'i.* (12:53)

When the sense of remorse is felt, the lower self becomes censorious [*lawwāma*]. Allāh (Exalted is He) has said,

> But as for him who feared to stand before his Lord,
> *wa ammā man khāfa maqāma Rabbi-hi*
> and forbade the lower self to follow passion,
> *wa naha 'n-nafsa 'ani 'l-hawā:*
> surely the Garden [of Paradise] will be his final place of rest.
> *fa-inna 'l-jannata hiya 'l-māwā.* (79:40,41)

In this state the lower self turns toward repentance. Repentance is the first stage in Islamic Sufism. Allāh (Exalted is He) has said,

> And repent unto Allāh all together, O believers,
> *wa tūbū ila 'llāhi jamī'an ayyuha 'l-mu'minūna*
> for then you may be able to succeed.
> *la'alla-kum tufliḥūn.* (24:31)

It has thus become clear that repentance, which is the first step on the threshold of Sufism, is compatible with the statutes of the Sacred Law and its teachings. The subject will be discussed in greater detail in the chapter on the stages of progress in Sufism.

Likewise in need of clarification is *mujāhada* [dedicated striving to control the lower self], for certain people dismiss this idea and consider it contrary to Islam arguing that this world was created to be enjoyed, as indicated by His sayings (Exalted is He),

> O Children of Adam, attend to your adornment
> *yā Banī Ādama khudhū zīnata-kum*
> at every place of worship, and eat and drink,
> *'inda kulli masjidin wa kulū wa 'shrabū*
> and do not be prodigal. He does not love the prodigals.
> *wa lā tusrifū: inna-hu lā yuḥibbu 'l-musrifīn.* (7:31)

Say, "Who has forbidden the adornment of Allāh
qul man ḥarrama zīnata 'llāhi 'llatī
which He has brought forth for His servants,
akhraja li-'ibādi-hi
and the good things of His providing?"
wa 'ṭ-ṭayyibāti mina 'r-rizq. (7:32)

O you who believe, do not forbid the good things
yā ayyuha 'lladhīna āmanū lā tuḥarrimū ṭayyibāti
that Allāh has made lawful for you, and do not transgress.
mā aḥalla 'llāhu la-kum wa lā ta'tadū,
Allāh does not love the transgressors.
inna 'llāha lā yuḥibbu 'l-mu'tadīn. (5:87)

These people have failed, however, to comprehend the full import of these Qur'ānic verses. The verses do not call for total absorption in pleasures, but simply admonish those who declare the good things unlawful, as happened with some of the noble Companions. When some women wished to perform the circumambulation around the Ka'ba in a state of nakedness, His saying (Exalted is He) down came,

Attend to your adornment at every place of worship.
khudhū zīnata-kum 'inda kulli masjidin. (7:31)

—and "adornment" means clothing.

Dedicated striving [*mujāhada*] means the effort to purify the lower self by ridding it of blameworthy attributes like arrogant pride, the accumulation of material wealth, tyranny, envy, boastfulness, backbiting, and other such vices. The eradication of these attributes is not realized by mere wishes. It can only be accomplished by dedicated striving and by weaning the lower self from its unruly impulses and its lustful desires in order to facilitate the substitution of attributes of virtue in place of those of vice, like truthfulness in place of lying and contentment in place of greed.

The purification of the lower self is realized by discarding blameworthy attitudes. Sufism does not treat what is lawful as unlawful. What it does prescribe for us in the form of mental and physical exercises is comparable to the medication prescribed by the physician for his patient until the latter is cured. As al-Būṣīrī (d. A.H. 696) expressed it in poetry,

The lower self is like a child who grows. If you neglect him,
[he continues] to suck the breast, but if you wean him he is weaned.

The seeker of knowledge likewise persists in training, effort, and study, until knowledge becomes a talent. He needs no extra readings.

The purification of the lower self is an important branch of the tree of Sufism, and dedicated striving for its sake is one of the teachings of true Islam. If the lower self is neglected, it becomes unruly and recalcitrant and leads its owner to destruction. Allāh has said (Glory be to Him and Exalted is He),

Say, "I take refuge with the Lord of humankind,
qul a'ūdhu bi-Rabbi 'n-nās,
the King of humankind, the God of humankind,
Maliki 'n-nās: Ilāhi 'n-nās,
from the evil of the slinking whisperer,
min sharri 'l-waswāsi 'l-khannās,
who whispers in the breasts of humankind,
alladhī yuwaswisu fī ṣudūri 'n-nāsi
of the jinn and of humankind."
mina 'l-jinnati wa 'n-nās. (114:1–6)

It is clear that the lower self is destructive if you do not wean it from lustful desires and if you do not accustom it to training and exercise. The Noble Qur'ān has commanded us to struggle with the lower self and its blameworthy attributes. It has plainly shown us the ways to take permissible advantage of the properties and good things of this world. Sufism definitely does not overstep the limits set by the Noble Qur'ān in that regard. Allāh (Exalted is He) has said,

And do not let your eyes overlook them,
wa lā ta'du 'ainā-ka 'an-hum
desiring the pomp of the life of this world.
turīdu zīnata 'l-ḥayāti 'd-dunyā.
And do not obey someone whose heart We have made heedless
wa lā tuṭi' man aghfalnā qalba-hu
of Our remembrance, who follows his own lust
'an dhikri-nā wa 'ttaba'a hawā-hu
and whose case has been abandoned.
wa kāna amru-hu furuṭā. (18:28)

You must therefore struggle with your lower self, and subject it to constant restraint and reprimand so that you may obtain the reward. Allāh (Glory be to Him) has said,

> Wealth and children are the adornment of the life of this world,
> *al-mālu wa 'l-banūna zīnatu 'l-ḥayāti 'd-dunyā*
> but the abiding deeds of righteousness are better
> *wa 'l-bāqiyātu 'ṣ-ṣāliḥātu khairun*
> in your Lord's sight for reward, and better in respect of hope.
> *'inda Rabbi-ka thawāban wa khairun amalā.* (18:46)
>
> The life of this world is but comfort of illusion.
> *wa ma 'l-ḥayātu 'd-dunyā illā matā'u 'l-ghurūr.* (3:185)
>
> This worldly life is nothing but a diversion and a sport.
> *wa mā hādhihi 'l-ḥayātu 'd-dunyā illā lahwun wa la'ib,*
> Surely the Last Abode is Life, if they did but know.
> *wa inna 'd-dāra 'l-ākhirata la-hiya 'l-ḥayawān,*
> *law kānū ya'lamūn.* (29:64)

In a nutshell, Sufism is directed solely toward the firm establishment of the values of Islam and it is not in conflict with the earning of lawful sustenance and the building of the good family. It does say, however, "You must not follow your religion and your interest in the Hereafter for the sake of your worldly interests. You must not cultivate your modesty for the sake of accumulating material wealth. You must not overstuff your belly with food, so that it weighs your body down. Material wealth must not be your constant concern by night and day, but you must not forget your fair share of this world. You must work for your interest in this world on the basis of your temporary sojourn therein, not on the strength of the endless succession of your descendants and descendants' descendants. You must not mix the lawful with the unlawful."

As for true devotion [*taqwā*], it is a Sufi emblem, for its source is the Noble Qur'ān and Sufism has not introduced any heretical innovation concerning it into Islam. It is said to have three stages,

1. The Sufi must be truly devoted to guarding himself against unbelief.
2. He must be truly devoted to guarding himself against sinful acts of disobedience.
3. He must be truly devoted to guarding himself against total absorption in the acquisition of material wealth.

In his definition of the saint, the Sufi poet Mawlawi said,

> If his conduct were to be measured,
> along with his true devotion in its three stages,
> it would not differ by a hair's breadth from the Sacred Law.

The Noble Qur'ān has criticized those who are totally absorbed in this world, by His saying (Glory be to Him),

> And you devour the inheritance greedily,
> *wa ta'kulūna 't-turātha aklan lammā*
> and you love wealth with an ardent love.
> *wa tuḥibbūna 'l-māla ḥubban jammā.* (89:19,20)

> Those who hoard up gold and silver
> *wa 'lladhīna yaknizūna 'dh-dhahaba wa 'l-fiḍḍata*
> and do not spend it in the way of Allāh,
> *wa lā yunfiqūna-hā fī sabīli 'llāhi*
> to them give tidings of a painful torment.
> *fa-bashshir-hum bi-'adhābin alīm.* (9:34)

Remembrance [*dhikr*] is mentioned in the Qur'ān in a number of senses. It sometimes means the Noble Qur'ān, as in His saying (Exalted is He),

> Surely We have revealed the Remembrance,
> *innā Naḥnu nazzalna 'dh-dhikra*
> and We assuredly watch over it.
> *wa innā la-hu la-Ḥāfiẓūn.* (15:9)

—and it sometimes means the ritual prayer [*ṣalāt*],

> O you who truly believe! When the call is proclaimed
> *yā ayyuha 'lladhīna āmanū idhā nūdiya*
> for the prayer on the Day of Congregation,
> *li'ṣ-ṣalāti min yawmi 'l-jumu'ati*
> hasten to the remembrance of Allāh and leave trading aside.
> *fa-'s'aw ilā dhikri 'llāhi wa dharu 'l-bai'.* (62:9)

Its most usual meanings, however, are *tasbīḥ* [glorification], *tahlīl* [the assertion that there is no god but Allāh] and *takbīr* [the assertion that Allāh is Supremely Great]. Allāh (Exalted is He) has said,

> Those who believe and whose hearts are at rest
> *alladhīna āmanū wa taṭma'innu qulūbu-hum*

in the remembrance of Allāh,
bi-dhikri 'llāh,
it is truly in the remembrance of Allāh
a-lā bi-dhikri 'llāhi
that hearts feel comfortably at rest.
taṭma'innu 'l-qulūb. (13:28)

To emphasize the importance of remembrance in the purification of the lower self, the Noble Qur'ān has cautioned the heedless, for Allāh (Exalted is He) has said,

But woe unto those hearts are hardened
fa-wailun li'l-qāsiyati qulūbu-hum
against the remembrance of Allāh.
min dhikri 'llāh.
Those are in manifest error.
ulā'ika fī ḍalālin mubīn. (39:22)

And do not obey someone whose heart We have made heedless
wa lā tuṭi' man aghfalnā qalba-hu
of Our remembrance, and who follows his own lust.
'an dhikri-nā wa 'ttaba'a hawā-hu. (18:28)

It is therefore quite clear that Sufism, since it guides us toward constant remembrance, is guided only by the Noble Qur'ān and the teachings of true Islam. We shall treat the subject of remembrance in detail.

It is also clear that true devotion [*taqwā*], which signifies the path of Sufism to the attainment of hope, has the Noble Qur'ān as its source. It is mentioned approximately two hundred times in various forms in the Noble Qur'ān. Allāh (Exalted is He) has said,

Practice true devotion to Allāh, and Allāh will teach you.
wa 'ttaqu 'llāh: wa yu'allimu-kumu 'llāh. (2:282)

True devotion is therefore the means of obtaining the light of intimate knowledge [*ma'rifa*], and intimate knowledge of Allāh is the basic principle. As He has said (Exalted is He),

O you who believe, practice true devotion to Allāh,
yā ayyuha 'lladhīna āmanu 'ttaqu 'llāha
and be with the truthful.
wa kūnū ma'a 'ṣ-ṣādiqīn. (9:119)

The best provision is true devotion.
fa-inna khaira 'z-zādi 't-taqwā. (2:197)

It is understood from these Qur'ānic verses that superficial devoutness is not sufficient, but there must also be true devotion within the inner being. This is indicated by His saying (Exalted is He),

Those are they whose hearts Allāh has tested for true devotion.
ulā'ika 'lladhīna 'mtaḥana 'llāhu qulūba-hum li't-taqwā
Theirs will be forgiveness and immense reward.
la-hum maghfiratun wa ajrun 'aẓīm. (49:3)

And whoever magnifies the offerings consecrated to Allāh,
wa man yu'aẓẓim sha ā'ira 'llāhi
it is surely from the true devotion of the hearts.
fa-inna-hu min taqwa 'l-qulūb. (22:32)

After the explanation of this real fact, let us focus our attention on the heart, which may be the resting place of His mercy (Glory be to Him) and a station for His light (Majestic and Exalted is He), just as it is possible for it to be perverted by the action of passion and desire. In the context of Sufism, the heart is the motor of the mechanism of life, the source of feelings and sensations both good and bad. It is the proof of the servant's station in the realm of the spirit, and the first stage reached by the Sufi in the process of purification. What is expressed in the language of the Sufis on the subject of the heart, far from contradicting the teachings of the religion, actually confirms them.

As is well known, "the heart [*qalb*]" has numerous meanings, including the pine-shaped gland in the left side of the breast. The term is also applied to the center of emotional human feeling as well as signifying the inclination toward good or evil in the human being. In the usage of the Sufis, "the heart" conveys the meaning intended in the Noble Qur'ān in the sense that it may be sick or sound. Allāh (Glory be to Him) has said,

Lest he with a diseased heart be moved to desire.
fa-yaṭma'a 'lladhī fī qalbi-hi maraḍun (33:32)

That He may make that which Satan suggested a temptation
li-yaj'ala mā yulqi 'sh-shaiṭānu fitnatan
to those in whose hearts is a disease and whose hearts are hardened.
li'lladhīna fī qulūbi-him maraḍun wa 'l-qāsiyati qulūbu-hum. (22:53)

The statement,

> In their hearts is a disease.
> *fī qulūbi-him maraḍun.*

—occurs in seven places in the Noble Qur'ān [2:10; 5:52; 8:49; 9:125; 22:53; 24:50; 33:60].

All of these sicknesses are spiritual, not natural in the biological sense. Allāh (Glory be to Him) has said,

> No indeed; but what they have been earning has rusted upon their hearts.
> *kallā bal rāna 'alā qulūbi-him mā kānū yaksibūn.* (83:14)

The rusting of the heart is likewise a spiritual corrosion, for He has said (Glory be to Him),

> His heart is surely sinful.
> *fa-inna-hu āthimun qalbu-h.* (2:283)

The heart may also be blind in error or able to see through guidance, as Allāh (Exalted is He) has said,

> Have they not traveled in the land, and have they hearts
> *a-fa-lam yasīrū fi 'l-arḍi fa-takūna la-hum qulūbun*
> wherewith to feel and ears wherewith to hear?
> *ya'qilūna bi-hā aw ādhānun yasma'ūna bi-hā:*
> For indeed it is not the eyes that are blind,
> *fa-inna-hā lā ta'ma 'l-abṣāru*
> but blind are the hearts within the breasts.
> *wa lākin ta'ma 'l-qulūbu 'llatī fi 'ṣ-ṣudūr.* (22:46)

This refers to the sphere of spiritual concepts, not physical perceptions, as indicated by His saying (Exalted is He),

> What, do they not ponder the Qur'ān?
> *a-fa-lā yatadabbarūna 'l-Qur'āna*
> Or are there locks upon their hearts?
> *am 'alā qulūbin aqfālu-hā.* (47:24)

> Their hearts refuse to know.
> *qulūbu-hum munkiratun.* (16:22)

> Their hearts are preoccupied.
> *lāhiyatan qulūbu-hum.* (21:3)

Allāh has sealed their hearts.
khatama 'llāhu 'alā qulūbi-him. (2:7)

"My Lord! Expand my breast for me."
Rabbi 'shraḥ lī ṣadrī. (20:25)

It thus becomes clear, beyond any doubt, that what is conveyed in the sayings of the scholars and masters of Sufism concerning the heart and the breast is derived from the Noble Qur'ān. It is clear that the spiritual stations of Sufism and the practices of the Sufi are derived from the Noble Qur'ān, in which the believers are described in such terms as the following,

Men who speak the truth and women who speak the truth.
aṣ-ṣādiqīna wa 'ṣ-ṣādiqāti. (33:35)

Men who obey and women who obey.
al-qānitīna wa 'l-qānitāti. (33:35)

Men who repent.
at-tā'ibūna. (9:112)

Women who repent.
tā'ibātin. (66:5)

Men who are submissive and women who are submissive.
al-khāshi'īna wa 'l-khāshi āti. (33:35)

Men who fast.
as-sā'iḥūna. (9:112)

Women who fast.
as-sā'iḥāti. (66:5)

Those who have sure faith.
al-mūqinīn. (51:20)

Those who are sincerely devoted.
al-mukhlaṣīn. (12:24)

The benefactors.
al-muḥsinīn. (2:58)

The humble.
al-mukhbitīn. (22:34)

The worshipful servants.
al-'ābidūna. (9:112)

Those who put their trust [in Allāh].
al-mutawakkilīn. (3:159)

The truly devout.
al-muttaqīn. (2:2)

The righteous.
al-abrār. (3:193)

The ones brought near.
al-muqarrabūn. (56:11)

The chosen, the excellent.
al-muṣṭafaina 'l-akhyār. (38:47)

This is no heretical innovation! As related in the noble Prophetic tradition [*ḥadīth*],

The heart of the believer is the Throne of the All-Merciful.

3. What is the method [*minhāj*] of Sufism?

The discussion from now on will be with the believers in Islam. It will be about Sufism as a Spiritual Path [*ṭarīqa*] and a method [*minhāj*].

We have already explained a great deal about Sufism and its numerous definitions that relate to the variety of the spiritual states and stations peculiar to the great men of Sufism. It has been said that any definition that represents a particular experience or "taste [*madhāq*]" is peculiar to its author. All of them maintain that Sufism is the dedicated striving of a Muslim in a Sufi course of training for the purpose of realizing the commandments of Allāh (Glory be to Him) with a perfect realization. It is also applying the Noble Qur'ān and the Prophetic Sunna in private and in public, in spirit and in body, outwardly and inwardly, which is the Spiritual Path of the *élite*. They maintain that this tremendous effort is aimed at two goals.

1. The good pleasure of Allāh (Glory be to Him).
2. The attainment of the truth of certainty [*ḥaqq al-yaqīn*] and the eye of certainty [*'ain al-yaqīn*], meaning perfect faith, through vision or taste and spiritual experience. This is achieved through the purification of the heart by cleansing it of corrupt desires. One adorns of the heart with every fine virtue, until the heart becomes a repository for the light of Allāh. The heart of the Sufi is illumined by the light of His countenance (Glory be to Him). When his heart comes to be like that, he attains to certainty. When someone's heart is illumined by the light of Allāh, Allāh is well pleased with him, and when Allāh is well pleased with someone, Allāh lays open to him the gates of His mercy. When someone's heart is polished by intimate knowledge of Allāh, he worships no one other than Him, and he attains to the degree of active goodness [*iḥsān*], which is one of the degrees of Sufism. The Messenger (Allāh bless him and give him peace) once said,

> Active goodness means that you worship Allāh as if you could see Him, for even if you do not see Him, He surely sees you!

It is well known that the genuine Sufi does not neglect the remembrance of his Lord for the twinkling of an eye. That is what the degree of active goodness signifies in the understanding of the Sufis.

We must make it really clear that we do not intend, when we speak of "the Sufi," to refer to any particular group among the followers of the Sufi paths. We use the term in a wider sense, embracing the servants of Allāh in general, be they Qādirīs or Naqshbandīs or others among the servants of Allāh, whether they belong or do not belong to other Sufi lineages.

It is also well known that "Sufism [*Taṣawwuf*]" is a term for the application of both the outer and inner aspects of the Sacred Law. It is a special discipline, which has its own scholars and its own guidelines, which is the case with every discipline and science. It does not make sense to plunge into it without knowledge of its method. Just as knowledge of the exoteric sciences of the Sacred Law requires study with a teacher and education in the company of the scholars, a guide is likewise needed in the case of Sufi knowledge, which is relevant to the heart as well as to the mind. If a person studies medical science without the help of an expert teacher, does he become a qualified physician in the practical arena? The science of Sufism likewise needs a guide. We do not believe that you will reach your goal in the field of practice without seeking assistance from the necessary guide. That is why it is said,

> Islamic Sufism is the application of a particular program and procedure, and it also requires adherence to the method of Sufism as a spiritual path and course of development. If you do not discover a guide, will you abandon your aim, which is the good pleasure of Allāh (Glory be to Him) and the essence of certainty? Will you seek help from the pretenders of the Spiritual Path, and many they indeed are! Will you take the blind man as your guide on this hard and fear-inspiring road? The answer must be no!

I shall now draw attention to the two subjects of the saint [*walī*] and the spiritual guide [*murshid*]. The best way of checking the quality of the guide is to examine, first of all, the extent to which his whole conduct is consistent with the Sacred Law of Islam. Then secondly, the extent of his knowledge and understanding of the Sacred Law and its sciences. The point is that if someone does not apply the Sacred Law completely, it is not permissible to follow him and the ignoramus is not capable of guiding others. Allāh (Exalted is He) has said,

> Do you enjoin righteousness on other people,
> *a-ta'murūna 'n-nāsa*

> while you forget [to practice it] yourselves?
> *bi'l-birri wa tansawna anfusa-kum.* (2:44)

It is therefore incumbent on the seeker to examine the actions of those who claim to be shaikhs of the Sufi orders, who adopt their style of dress, and who seclude themselves in their lodges, *tekkes* or *khānqāhs*. If their conduct is consistent with the Sacred Law, and they are scholars, they may possibly be leaders capable of providing spiritual guidance. If not, there is no good in them. "Allāh does not accept an ignoramus as a saint." If someone reaches the degree of sainthood, Allāh (Glory be to Him) will teach him,

> Practice true devotion to Allāh, and Allāh will teach you.
> *wa 'ttaqu 'llāh: wa yu'allimu-kumu 'llāh.* (2:282)

If we suppose that a seeker does not find someone to guide him, what should he do? We must have recourse to the Noble Qur'ān,

> Practice true devotion to Allāh, and Allāh will teach you.
> *wa 'ttaqu 'llāh: wa yu'allimu-kumu 'llāh.* (2:282)

It is therefore incumbent upon him to practice true devotion to Allāh in his religion, and to concentrate on His remembrance (Glory be to Him), for He is the Guarantor of His mercy and He is the Most Merciful of the merciful. If the servant says with the fullness of his heart,

> You alone do we worship, and of You alone do we seek help.
> *iyyā-ka na'budu wa iyyā-ka nasta'īn.*
> Guide us in the straight path.
> *ihdi-na 'ṣ-ṣirāṭa 'l-mustaqīm.* (1:4,5)

—Allāh will undoubtedly guide him, and that will be realized by striving to control the lower self.

> As for those who strive in Our cause,
> *wa 'lladhīna jāhadū fī-nā*
> We surely guide them in Our ways.
> *la-nahdiyanna-hum subula-nā.* (29:69)

For those who work on the path of His knowledge and His love, there are splendid good tidings in the Noble Qur'ān, where Allāh says (Glory be to Him),

> Say, "If you love Allāh, follow me;
> *qul in kuntum tuḥibbūna 'llāha fa-'ttabi'ū-nī*

> Allāh will love you and forgive you your sins.
> *yuḥbib-kumu 'llāhu wa yaghfir la-kum dhunūba-kum,*
> Allāh is All-Forgiving, All-Compassionate."
> *wa 'llāhu Ghafūrun Raḥīm.* (3:31)

—and in the Sacred Tradition [*Ḥadīth Qudsī*], where He says (Exalted is He),

> I am the Close Companion [*Jalīs*] of him who remembers Me.

There is no doubt that constant commitment to worshipful service brings the worshipful servant near to Allāh (Glory be to Him). In the words of the Sacred Tradition [*Ḥadīth Qudsī*],

> My servant does not cease to draw near to Me through supererogatory acts of worship until I love him. Then, when I love him, I become his hearing by which he hears, his sight by which he sees, and his hand with which he strikes.

Allāh (Glory be to Him) has explained to us the way of drawing near to Him, for He said to His Prophet,

> And prostrate yourself and draw near.
> *wa 'sjud wa 'qtarib.* (96:19)

—and prostration signifies worship in its various forms. Allāh (Glory be to Him) will answer the supplication of the supplicants,

> Call upon Me and I will answer you.
> [*u*] *'d'ū-nī astajib la-kum.* (40:60)

> Our Lord, in You we put our trust, and to You we repent,
> *Rabba-nā 'alai-ka tawakkalnā wa ilai-ka anabnā*
> and to You is the homeward journey."
> *wa ilai-ka 'l-maṣīr.* (60:4)

> Praise be to Allāh, who has guided us to this.
> [*u*] *'l-ḥamdu li'llāhi 'lladhī hadā-nā li-hādhā,*
> We could not have been led aright if Allāh had not guided us.
> *wa mā kunnā li-nahtadiya law lā an hadā-na 'llāh.* (7:43)

Nevertheless, it is incumbent on the man to be regular in his worshipful obedience, attentive to his actions, alert to the whispering of the Devil, wary of slipping into the chasms of delusion and heedlessness, and together with Allāh's rightly guided servants in repeating,

> Our Lord! Do not cause our hearts to stray
> *Rabba-nā lā tuzigh qulūba-nā*
> after You have guided us aright,
> *ba'da idh hadaita-nā.*
> and bestow on us mercy from Your Presence.
> *wa hab la-nā min ladun-ka raḥma,*
> You, only You are the Bestower.
> *inna-ka Anta 'l-Wahhāb.* (3:8)

It is thus quite clear that Sufism is realized through the guidance of spiritual guides and through strict adherence to the teachings of the Noble Qur'ān and the pure Sunna. By practicing true devotion, dedicated striving, remembrance, supererogatory acts of worship, and appealing for guidance, Allāh (Glory be to Him) may then guide the servant to the path of His love and His worshipful service, and to spending the night in prayer. He has said (Exalted is He),

> Their sides shun their couches,
> *tatajāfā junūbu-hum 'ani 'l-maḍāji'i*
> as they call on their Lord in fear and hope,
> *yad'ūna Rabba-hum khawfan wa ṭama'ā.*
> and spend of what We have bestowed on them.
> *wa mim-mā razaqnā-hum yunfiqūn.* (32:16)

The method of Sufism is submission to the individual who will teach the servant the method of Sufism. That person is called "the spiritual director [*murshid*]," "the Shaikh," or "the guide [*dalīl*]." The one who aspires to the path is called "the spiritual traveler [*sālik*]," "the seeker [*murīd*]," "the Sufi," or "the dervish."

But how shall we attain to Allāh (Glory be to Him) by means of the spiritual director? We must first examine the director's attributes, for it is necessary to ascertain the following.

1. His procedure conforms to the standard of the Sacred Law.
2. He is learned in the Sacred Law of Islam. That is because the Spiritual Path is its essence. If someone does not understand the Sacred Law, how can he understand its essence?
3. He is truly familiar with the procedures of the path.
4. He has been trained at the hand of a perfect spiritual director in a circle linked to the Chieftain of the Universe, our master Muḥammad (Allāh bless him and give him peace).

5. He has reached the degree of perpetuity after annihilation [*al-baqā' ba'da 'l-fanā'*], and that his heart has been illumined by the truth of certainty [*ḥaqq al-yaqīn*].

6. He is the physician of the heart, expert in the remedial treatment of spiritual sicknesses. His pupils feel sure of him.

As we read in the book entitled *Na't al-bidāyāt wa tawṣīf an-nihāyāt* [*Account of the Initial Stages and Description of the Final Stages*],

> The Shaikh is someone who instructs you with his speech [*qāl*] and inspires you with his spiritual state [*ḥāl*]. The Shaikh is someone who benefits the seeker and opens up the objects sought. The Shaikh is someone who is perfect in his essence and perfect in his attributes. The Shaikh is someone in whom, when you join his company, you will find independence from people other than him. The Shaikh is someone who benefits you in the visible world and the unseen, and who cleanses your innermost being from faults with his innermost being.

This means that the seeker must not submit himself to every would-be Shaikh and would-be Sufi, for Allāh has honored the human being, endowed him with intelligence, and guided him with the heavenly messages,

> Surely We created the human being in the fairest stature.
> *la-qad khalaqna 'l-insāna fī aḥsani taqwīm.* (95:4)

> And We have surely honored the Children of Adam,
> *wa la-qad karramnā banī Ādam.*
> and We have carried them on land and sea,
> *wa ḥamalnā-hum fi 'l-barri wa 'l-baḥri*
> and have provided them with good things,
> *wa razaqnā-hum mina 'ṭ-ṭayyibāti*
> and preferred them greatly over many of those We created.
> *wa faḍḍalnā-hum 'alā kathīrin mim-man khalaqnā tafḍīlā.* (17:70)

> And He has made the sun and the moon
> constant in their courses, to be of service to you.
> *wa sakhkhara la-kumu 'sh-shamsa wa 'l-qamara dā'ibain.* (14:33)

And He has constrained the night and the day
and the sun and the moon to be of service to you.
wa sakhkhara la-kumu 'l-laila wa 'n-nahāra
wa 'sh-shamsa wa 'l-qamar. (16:12)

And He has made of service to you
wa sakhkhara la-kum
whatever is in the heavens and whatever is in the earth.
mā fi 's-samāwāti wa mā fi 'l-arḍi jamī'an. (45:13)

Since this is the honorable status of the human being in the sight of his Lord, how can someone like him reasonably accept humiliation and abasement in front of another individual? He must therefore make a profound investigation concerning the perfect spiritual guide so that his life is not wasted like scattered dust.

The seeker is someone who is searching for Sufism on the lookout for a spiritual guide who is perfect and endowed with true knowledge. When his heart becomes tranquil and he feels the warmth of faith in his breast, and when the guide makes a good impression on this heart, it is incumbent on him to submit himelf to his direction and to act in accordance with his advice and counsel. It is also incumbent on him, however, not to be deluded by the charismatic talents and mystic disclosures of the shaikh. If his conduct were to contravene the Sacred Law, even by a hair's breadth, he would not qualify as a spiritual director, but would actually be a highway robber. If someone does not adhere to the Prophetic Sunna, he is not a spiritual director, and his charismatic talent is akin to the spell-binding of Satan and the witchcraft of the Hindus or something that happens by chance.

As we read in the books of Sufism, Bāyazīd al-Bisṭāmī (may Allāh be well pleased with him) once went to visit an individual who had the reputation of a perfect saint. On meeting him, he noticed that the spiritual director was spitting toward the Qibla [the direction of prayer], so he went away without giving him the greeting of peace, saying, "His conduct is contrary to the Sunna, so he is not a spiritual director!" The spiritual director is obliged to practice true devotion, more than any other human being. It is not permissible for him to speak badly, to laugh loudly, to accumulate material wealth, to be guilty of arrogance, to behave in a vulgar fashion, to indulge in backbiting, and to approve of hatred toward others without respect for justice. The truth of the matter is the following,

1. The genuine spiritual director is one who wishes right guidance for all and who works hard for that without weariness and without personal interest.

2. The non-genuine spiritual director is one who works hard to gather simple folk around him to present him with gifts and sacrificial offerings. He comes in two types,

• The exoteric scholar who knows about Sufism through reading. It is difficult to recognize this type because they conceal their true nature, but the criterion is their inability to influence the hearts.

• The group of the ignoramuses, especially those who have inherited Shaikhdom from their ancestors and have not earned it themselves.

3. The middle group, whose members enjoin what is right and proper [*ma'rūf*] and forbid what is wrong and improper [*munkar*], but do not bring anyone to the stage of certainty. It is useful to hear their advice and counsel, since they are scholars, but they do not benefit the seekers of certainty.

The Noble Qur'ān and the Prophetic Sunna will always be the standard by which to assess the spiritual director and to determine his truthfulness or his falsehood. We can also point to a rational standard for the assessment of spiritual directors. If the spiritual director applies his advice and counsel to himself as well as drawing people close to him, he is truthful in his directorship. Otherwise he is not. Allāh (Glory be to Him) has said,

> O you who believe, why do you say what you do not do?
> *yā ayyuha 'lladhīna āmanū li-ma taqūlūna mā lā taf'alūn,*
> It is most hateful in the sight of Allāh
> *kabura maqtan 'inda 'llāhi*
> that you say what you do not do.
> *an taqūlū mā lā taf'alūn.* (61:2)

The son of Noah and the wife of Lot are two examples indicating that nearness is not beneficial if the work is not righteous.

In this connection, you have heard the story of how, for the sake of Allāh's religion, 'Umar (may Allāh be well pleased with him) applied the penalty of the Sacred Law to his son until he died without taking pity on him. This is the truth of certainty.

(I am acting here as a writer, not as a counsellor, and I need someone to counsel me. I am simply transmitting the views of the people of remembrance. May Allāh include me among them, and may He guide me to the straight path!)

After having discovered the genuine spiritual director, what should we do then? If someone wishes to arrive at his destination, he must seek the path from the spiritual director as is the case of any pupil or student of a craft. He must aim for the oasis of certainty, walking step by step, stage by stage, treading the perils of the path by the grace of his spiritual director until he alights at the intended destination, beginning with repentance and ending at the stage of perpetuity after annihilation [*al-baqā' ba'da 'l-fanā'*].

But how shall we attain to Allāh by the path of Sufism? Is it permissible to submit to the spiritual director? Does the spiritual director represent an intermediary, a secondary cause, or a means of access? What is it that the spiritual director can actually do?

The seeker must be in the presence of his spiritual director like the corpse in front of the ritual washer of the dead. He must repent at his hands and be designated by "commitment [*tamassuk*]," meaning admission to the circle of Sufism. Every chain of Sufi transmission [*silsila*] is linked to a great spiritual director, and the circles ascend until they reach the noble Prophet Muḥammad (Allāh bless him and give him peace). Hence the expression "chain of the Spiritual Path [*silsilat aṭ-ṭarīqa*]."

The first lesson in the texts is called "the teaching of the Spiritual Path [*talqīn aṭ-ṭarīqa*]." It is a lesson delivered by the spiritual director himself or by one of his deputies and its subject is repentance. He then teaches the practice of remembrance [*dhikr*]. In the Naqshbandī lineage, he also teaches, in addition to remembrance, the process of "bonding [*rābiṭa*]," which is the mode of spiritual connection with the director. After that, the seeker becomes a disciple.

One point that must be made very clear is that the genuine spiritual director should not teach anyone until he is convinced of the seeker's strict observance of religious duties, unlike the common practice in this time of ours.

The seeker is like a student of academic knowledge who studies its sciences stage by stage until he becomes a physician, or an engineer, or a teacher. One seeker may be distinguished from another by the difference of his earnest endeavor or by the difference of his director's status and his ability to advance of his pupils, like with jurists. Some jurists reach the degree of absolute independent judgment [*ijtihād muṭlaq*] while some of them reach a lesser degree.

On certain occasions, the spiritual director will take his disciple by the hand in order to lead him to a higher degree that he himself has reached. It is thereby acknowledged that this is his limit, and that the disciple must study without a director or transfer to a director of higher realization. Such was the case in the life of an-Naqshband, as we shall explain. Likewise, in the sciences of the Sacred Law, the student may come to the end of a particular stage in the company of a certain professor, then advance to another and higher stage for which a more learned professor is needed. Repentance is comparable to a solemn pledge in the presence of the spiritual director, and is called "the pledge of allegiance [*bai'a*]."

The Sufi pledge of allegiance begins with Shaikh 'Abd al-Qādir al-Jīlānī, to whom people used to throng in large numbers in order to pledge allegiance to him for repentance. Qur'ānic verses also point to the pledge of allegiance of the Companions in the presence of the noble Messenger (Allāh bless him and give him peace), including Allāh's saying (Exalted is He),

> Allāh was well pleased with the believers
> *la-qad raḍiya 'llāhu 'ani 'l-mu'minīna*
> when they swore allegiance to you beneath the tree.
> *idh yubāyi'ūna-ka taḥta 'sh-shajarati.* (48:18)

—and His saying (Exalted is He),

> Those who swear allegiance to you,
> *inna 'lladhīna yubāyi'ūna-ka*
> swear allegiance only to Allāh.
> *inna-mā yubāyi'ūna 'llāh,*
> The Hand of Allāh is above their hands.
> *Yadu 'llāhi fawqa aidī-him.* (48:10)

As we have already mentioned, the spiritual director is someone who has graduated from the school of another spiritual director, and has attained to the stage of perpetuity after annihilation.

The Sufi poet Mawlawī produced an ode which he sent to his spiritual director, Shaikh 'Uthmān Sarrāj ad-Dīn an-Naqshbandī. In it he said,

O Shaikh, rich in a mighty and lasting fortune
in the core of the Aḥmadī reality,
you have passed the stage of annihilation
and are now at the peak of the mountain of perpetuity!

Since the perfect spiritual director is a physician who treats spiritual diseases like envy and pride, spiritual directors have been described as "the wise who know by experience [*al-ḥukamā' al-'ārifīn*]."

As for *tawajjuh*, meaning the Shaikh's focusing of his attention on his disciple in order to treat the contents of his heart, it may also occur between the disciple and the Shaikh from a distance. It does not depend their being in the same place together. The form of this *tawajjuh* is described below.

The Shaikh sits in the circle of remembrance turning toward his disciple and focusing with his heart on his heart so that his left side encounters his left side, while keeping his eyes closed. The disciple expects blessed grace from the Shaikh or his deputy, and in this spiritual session he feels a spiritual warmth. This spiritual process is comparable to a physical activity. The disciple is affected by it and he may not be able to bear the effect, so he may utter a shout. He may then lose consciousness in some instances. Since the Shaikh's *tawajjuh* is aimed at bringing his disciple in contact with a higher station, the disciple may collapse like a drunkard and not recover for several hours, or a whole day. He may laugh with joy because of what he has experienced and he may also dance about. It should be noted, however, that these manifestations are sometimes practiced as a dramatic performance, not a real experience, on the part of those who deceive the ingenuous.

Does the secondary cause and the means of access have any legal basis in Islam? Everything has a secondary cause, whether it be a human being or something manufactured by a human being in the form of tools and machines. The human being needs a means of access to the realization of his desires and he needs a teacher. This does not conflict with the necessity of believing in the assistance of Allāh and His Will, just as the invalid needs a physician. It is not permissible for him to deny this need. We must have recourse to the physician and adhere to his directions on the condition that we believe that the real Healer is Allāh (Glory be to Him). We must do whatever is subject to our limited human power. What is subject only to His unlimited Divine power, we must appeal to Him in hope.

That is why He is described (Glory be to Him) as "the Original Cause of causes [*Musabbib al-asbāb*]."

He has said (Glory be to Him) in the Sūra of the Table [al-Mā'ida],

> O you who believe, practice true devotion to Allāh,
> *yā ayyuha 'lladhīna āmanu 'ttaqu 'llāha*
> and seek the means of access to Him,
> *wa 'btaghū ilai-hi 'l-wasīlata*
> and strive in His way, so that you may succeed.
> *wa jāhidū fī sabīli-hi la'alla-kum tufliḥūn.* (5:35)

It is clear that the means of access is true devotion and righteous work, as indicated by His saying (Exalted is He), "Practice true devotion to Allāh..., and strive in His way." The Muslim must therefore seek the means of access to contact with His good pleasure (Glory be to Him).

We have never ceased to need the teacher in connection with the problems of Islamic jurisprudence [*fiqh*]. We need this teacher in connection with deeper problems, being the lessons by which we arrive at the essence of certainty. The means of access is not a purpose in itself, however. The purpose is only Allāh (Glory be to Him). Do we not prostrate ourselves in worship before Allāh (Glory be to Him), and do we not turn toward the ennobled Ka'ba? Do we direct our worship to the Ka'ba itself?

Allāh (Glory be to Him) has said, in the story of Dhū'l-Qarnain,

> We made him strong in the land,
> *innā makkannā la-hu*
> and gave him unto everything a means.
> *fi 'l-arḍi wa ātainā-hu min kulli shai'in sababā.* (18:84)

The secondary cause and the means of access are not at odds with the method prescribed by the Noble Qur'ān as long as we do not believe them to be [independently] effective in reality.

Allāh (Glory be to Him) has also commanded the Muslim to draw near to the righteous, since He has said,

> O you who believe, practice true devotion to Allāh,
> *yā ayyuha 'lladhīna āmanu 'ttaqu 'llāha*

and be with the truthful.
wa kūnū ma'a 'ṣ-ṣādiqīn. (9:119)

The custom of Allāh (Glory be to Him) is that the human being is born from two parents so should the child be expected without two parents, on the ground that Allāh (Glory be to Him) is the Creator? But for the Will of Allāh (Glory be to Him), the child will not be born,

And that He creates the two spouses, the male
wa anna-hu khalaqa 'z-zawjaini 'dh-dhakara
and the female.
wa 'l-unthā. (53:45)

Likewise in the case of death, He has said (Glory be to Him),

Say, "The Angel of Death, who has charge
concerning you, will gather you."
qul yatawaffā-kum Malaku 'l-Mawti 'lladhī
wukkila bi-kum. (32:11)

—but it is not permissible to say, "Death is at the disposal of the Angel of Death."

Another example is the search for provision, since it needs a secondary cause and a means of access despite His saying (Exalted is He),

Allāh is indeed the All-Provider,
inna 'llāha Huwa 'r-Razzāqu
the Lord of Mighty Strength, the Ever-Firm.
Dhū 'l-Quwwati 'l-Matīn. (51:58)

He has also said (Glory be to Him),

And We appointed from among them leaders
wa ja'alnā min-hum a'immatan
guiding by Our command, when they endured patiently,
yahdūna bi-amri-nā lammā ṣabarū ,
and had sure faith in Our signs.
wa kānū bi-āyati-nā yūqinūn. (32:24)

—and this is a reference to the spiritual directors, scholars, and jurists.

From all that has gone before, we may reach this conclusion: It is strictly necessary to have recourse to the external causes and means of access in order to manage the affairs of daily life. Jurists and scholars are also important in order to learn about the religion and this world. It is likewise strictly necessary to have recourse to the perfect spiritual guide in order to reach the desired goal in spiritual concerns. The aim in every case is Allāh (Glory be to Him).

The seeker will never reach his goal, as long as he does not truly rever his spiritual director. According to what is related from Abū Yazīd al-Bisṭāmī, "If someone has no Shaikh, his Shaikh is the Devil!" In other words, if someone pursues the path of intimate knowledge of Allāh in the Sacred Law or in Sufism, he is obliged to seek help from a spiritual director or a teacher without whom he will be exposed to the Devil's misguidance.

As proof that the genuine Sufi is one who adheres to the teachings of the Qur'ān and the Prophetic Sunna, both in private and in public, the evidence is that the character of the Sufi is the character of the Noble Qur'ān, and that he is guided by the *sunna* of the most splendid Messenger, our master Muḥammad (Allāh bless him and give him peace) whose splendid character is celebrated in the Noble Qur'ān,

> And you are indeed of a splendid character.
> *wa inna-ka la-'alā khuluqin 'aẓīm.* (68:4)

The Noble Qur'ān contains several clear verses concerning the splendid character, including,

> Keep to forgiveness, and enjoin kindness,
> *khudhi 'l-'afwa wa amur bi'l-'urfi*
> and turn away from the ignorant.
> *wa a'riḍ 'ani 'l-jāhilīn.* (7:199)

> It was by the mercy of Allāh that you were lenient with them,
> *fa-bi-mā raḥmatin mina 'llāhi linta la-hum:*
> for if you had been harsh and hard of heart,
> *wa law kunta faẓẓan ghalīẓa 'l-qalbi*
> they would have scattered from all around you.
> *la-'nfaḍḍū min ḥawli-k:*
> So pardon them and ask forgiveness for them,
> *fa-'fu 'an-hum wa 'staghfir la-hum*
> and consult with them about the conduct of affairs.
> *wa shāwir-hum fi 'l-amr.*
> And when you are resolved, then put your trust in Allāh.

fa-idhā 'azamta fa-tawakkal 'ala 'llāh,
Allāh loves those who put their trust in Him.
inna 'llāha yuḥibbu 'l-mutawakkilīn. (3:159)

And when they hear vanity they withdraw from it
wa idhā sami'u 'l-laghwa a'raḍū 'an-hu
and say, "To us our works and to you your works.
wa qālū la-nā a'mālu-nā wa la-kum a'mālu-kum,
Peace be unto you! We do not desire the ignorant."
salāmun 'alai-kum: lā nabtaghi 'l-jāhilīn. (28:55)

Someone asked Dhū'n-Nūn al-Miṣrī, one of the greatest of the Sufis, "Of all people, who has the most to worry about?" He replied, "Someone whose character is bad."

According to Shaikh Bahā' ad-Dīn an-Naqshbandī, "Our path is proper conduct, all of it!"

The Sufis are the poorest of people and the most truly devout among them. The Sufi is someone who immerses himself in the love of his Lord, who does not slacken for an instant from the remembrance of his Lord, and of whom nothing can be imagined except good conduct. That is because he is trained in the school of Islamic characteristics, and he controls the willfulness of his lower self. It is true that the virtuous are many; but the Sufis are at the summit of virtue.

The Sufi poet said, in comparing our master Moses and our master Muḥammad (Allāh bless him and give him peace), "Muḥammad saw his Lord, and Moses heard the voice of his Lord." How does hearing compare with seeing?

The faith of the Sufi is the faith of direct witnessing, whereas the faith of others is a rational faith. Throughout Islamic history, the great shaikhs of Sufism have been characterized by chivalry, humility, helpfulness to people, and all praiseworthy attributes. They are not damaged by what is associated with the pretender-shaikhs. That is because,

Every soul is a pledge for that which it has earned.
kullu nafsin bi-mā kasabat rahīna. (74:38)

Is it correct to say that Islam is not beneficial on the ground that some Muslim people have deviated from its highway? Muslims are in one valley and Islam is in another?

The most advanced degree of training is the heart-centered spiritual training. If the source is pure the water is pure, but if it is murky nothing will purify it. The source is the heart and the conscience. If the heart is pure the actions are pure. This is Sufism, which strives to cleanse the heart of every vice "to the point where the heart becomes fit to be a resting place for the light of Allāh (Glory be to Him)." A heart like this, which is illumined by the light of His intimate knowledge (Glory be to Him), becomes a compassionate heart, which causes no harm to anyone at all.

Consider the world that embraces the purity of the likes of these. Is anyone afraid in their company of theft, treachery, lying, or bad intention? They are all brothers in Allāh's religion prepared to serve the human being and humanity. This is the world of Sufism. If someone does not tread this genuine path, he is not a Sufi. If someone desires to make people subject to his own will by laying claim to shaikhdom, he is neither a Sufi nor a shaikh nor an Axis [*Quṭb*]. He is merely a pretender to Sufism, nothing else. The term *mutaṣawwif* [would-be Sufi] is applied to those pretenders who affect the style of the shaikhs, or those seekers who imitate them in their outward appearances. The fact is that they are putting on a show and acting.

The Sacred Law is the standard of authenticity. Some of them may appear to be enraptured, but they are really escaping from work out of laziness. Some are relieving themselves of their legal obligations, although they are not lunatics confined to mental sanatoria, nor healthy people going to the workplace, nor servants of Allāh in the mosque. Simple-minded folk may weave stories about their charismatic talents, for which there is no basis. The would-be Sufi and the would-be Shaikh are people who neglect the teachings of the Sacred Law and who deceive other people with their outward appearances.

How does the Sufi arrive at the stage of certainty?

There is only one way, and that is purification of the lower self. That stage is reached by sincere devotion to His service (Glory be to Him), and to His remembrance with the tongue and the heart under the guidance of a spiritual director. Without this guidance one can genuinely repent, which makes the Sufi constant in his worshipful obedience and in remembering Allāh (Glory be to Him) until He is well pleased with him. When Allāh is well pleased with someone, Allāh will expand his breast with His light and his heart will become perceptive. When Allāh opens the eye of perception within the Muslim's heart, the veils are removed from the secrets and the "eye of certainty [*'ain al-yaqīn*]" bears witness to faith.

How does the Muslim's character develop after his arrival at the degree of certainty? If someone is firmly convinced, with the eye of certainty, that Allāh sees him, not an atom of hypocritical display will remain in his worshipful service and he will completely avoid any action contrary to Allāh's Sacred Law. An intelligent person will not commit theft when he knows that the owner of the property is watching him.

Inasmuch as he does not neglect the remembrance of Allāh and because his breast is expanded by the spiritual blessing, his conduct is transformed into Muḥammadan conduct in strict adherence to Allāh's Sacred Law and the Sunna of His Prophet (Allāh bless him and give him peace). It is a degree above which there is no station, apart from the station of prophethood. If someone achieves it, he migrates from the realm of humanity [*Nāsūt*] to the realm of Sovereignty [*Malakūt*]. [In the words of the Sacred Tradition],

> O My servant, be lordly! Tell the thing, "Be!" and it will come to be.

When he reaches this degree, he does not worship Him (Glory be to Him) out of fear of the Fire, nor out of longing for the Garden, but out of love for Allāh (Glory be to Him).

Shaikh 'Umar Ḍiyā' ad-Dīn an-Naqshandī is among those who have attained to these degrees since he says in a Sufi ode,

> I am today a jurist, professor of the affirmation of Oneness,
> and an expert in the sphere of the affirmation of Singularity.
> I have overtaken others in the affirmation
> of Divine Incomparability,
> and I am today the lamp of the caravan on the road
> of Glorification,
> and I am the guide of the army of the affirmation
> of Uniqueness.

It is possible for a man to be a Sufi as a disciple to a spiritual director, a Sufi who has no spiritual director, or a Sufi who is directed but does not reach these degrees, let alone the degrees of Ghawthiyya, Quṭbiyya, or those of the Abdāl and the Awtād. These degrees resemble the positions of government officers and each one has his responsibility in the realm of spiritual affairs.

How should we apply the teachings of the Sacred Law, both outwardly and inwardly? We notice that someone who is born into a Muslim family is registered as a Muslim, while someone who is born into a Christian family is registered as a Christian. When someone reaches the age of fifteen years, however, he is qualified to bear religious responsibility. So if he discharges it he is righteous, but if he disobeys it he is clearly in error.

If someone applies the Sacred Law outwardly, he becomes a Muslim, but he does not become a true believer [*mu'min*] except after his inner conviction, and inner conviction does not come about through compulsion,

> There is no compulsion in religion.
> *lā ikrāha fi 'd-dīn*. (2:256)

> Say [to them, O Muḥammad], "You do not believe,
> *qul lam tu'minū*
> but rather say, 'We surrender,'
> *wa lākin qūlū aslamnā*
> for the faith has not yet entered into your hearts."
> *wa lammā yadkhuli 'l-īmānu fī qulūbi-kum*. (49:14)

A man may be both a Muslim and a true believer, yet he may be afflicted by temptation, hypocritical ostentation and vain conceit that he is neglectful of this worshipful service.

If a person intends to commit a sin, he will be not called to account for his intention, since he may regret it or not carry it out, but the Sufi worshipper "is one who does not intend the commission of sins, because he is pure in his heart and his conscience."

Allāh (Glory be to Him) has said,

> Forsake the outer aspect of sin, and the inner aspect of it as well.
> *wa dharū ẓāhira 'l-ithmi wa bāṭinah*. (6:120)

He has also said (Magnificent is His Majesty),

> And whether you publish what is inside yourselves,
> *wa in tubdū mā fī anfusi-kum*
> or keep it hidden, Allāh will call you to account for it.
> *aw tukhfū-hu yuḥāsib-kum bi-hi 'llāh*. (2:284)

We did indeed create the human being,
wa la-qad khalaqna 'l-insāna
and We know what his lower self whispers within him,
wa na'lamu mā tuwaswisu bi-hi nafsu-h:
and We are nearer to him than the jugular vein.
wa Naḥnu aqrabu ilai-hi min ḥabli 'l-warīd. (50:16)

Say, "My Lord forbids only indecencies,
qul inna-mā ḥarrama Rabbiya 'l-fawāḥisha
such of them as are apparent and such as are within."
mā ẓahara min-hā wa mā baṭana. (7:33)

And do not draw near to lewd things,
wa lā taqrabu 'l-fawāḥisha
whether they be open or concealed.
mā ẓahara min-hā wa mā baṭan. (6:151)

All of these Qur'ānic verses emphasize sincerity of purpose and intention, and the purification of the lower selves from sinful inclinations. A man derives no benefit from formal work devoid of the sincerity of purpose. Feelings of the heart and conscience are matters that cannot be kept hidden from other people. If someone seeks to purify them, that is evidence of his faith.

One of the most important attributes of Sufism is readiness to sacrifice personal interest. We shall draw attention here to the struggle waged by Shaikh Muḥyi'd-Dīn ibn al-'Arabī against the invading crusaders, and by Shaikh Najm ad-Dīn al-Kubrā, the founder of the Kubrawiyya Order, against the Mongols.

It is said that Genghiz laid siege to Khwarizm, and that he negotiated with Shaikh Najm ad-Dīn, the chief of Kubrawiyya lineage, inviting him to refrain from opposition and leave the city in exchange for pardon for [the Shaikh] himself and for thousands to be designated by the Shaikh. The Shaikh, however, who was then eighty years of age, refused to accept his offer. He said, "We are not more worthy of favor than others." He fought with the warriors in defence of their city until he was killed in the year A.H. 618.

Scholars of Sufism were always fine examples of altruism, knowledge, and proper conduct. Learned propriety is evidence of their superiority in good conduct. One can sense the blessed grace of their speech in poetry and prose. Those endowed with delicate hearts are thrilled to hear about their refined behavior.

(The pages of history contain many specimens and examples of how they worked to improve relations between people. My ancestors—may Allāh bestow His mercy upon them—played a great part in reconciling differences, and, were it not for the suspicion that I intend to boast, I would relate some rare stories of their services in this arena.)

The record of the great masters of Sufism is a precious treasure in the Islamic inheritance and its loss would be an irreparable misfortune. "It is well known that the respected leaders of the schools [of Islamic jurisprudence] are also among the great scholars of Sufism."

Chapter Three
The Spiritual Stations [*Maqāmāt*] of Sufism

The spiritual station [*maqām*] is mentioned a number of times in the Noble Qur'ān, including Allāh's saying (Exalted is He),

> It may be that your Lord will raise you up
> *'asā an yab'atha-ka Rabbu-ka*
> to a praiseworthy station.
> *maqāman maḥmūdā.* (17:79)

> Surely the righteous will dwell amid gardens and a river,
> *inna 'l-muttaqīna fī jannātin wa nahar:*
> in a sure abode, in the presence of a King All-Powerful.
> *fī maq'adi ṣidqin 'inda Malīkin Muqtadir.* (54:54,55)

In the same sense, mention is also made of "degrees," which are synonymous with stations, as in His saying (Exalted is He),

> We raise by degrees whomever We will.
> *narfa'u darajātin man nashā'* (12:76)

> They have degrees with their Lord,
> *la-hum darajātun 'inda Rabbi-him*
> and forgiveness, and generous provision.
> *wa maghfiratun wa rizqun karīm.* (8:4)

> Some of those messengers We have caused to excel others,
> *tilka 'r-Rusulu faḍḍalnā ba'ḍa-hum 'alā ba'ḍ:*
> and there are some of them to whom Allāh spoke,
> *min-hum man kallama 'llāhu*
> and He exalted some of them by degrees.
> *wa rafa'a ba'ḍa-hum darajāt.* (2:253)

From this it is understood that the degrees of nearness to Him are various, even between the prophets, but the term *maqām* [station] is used in the technical vocabulary of Sufism in the sense of *daraja* [degree], meaning the stage of progress attained by the spiritual traveler of the path of Sufism.

According to some, these degrees are ten in number, but some authorities assign ten stages to each degree, so the total is one hundred stations and degrees.

Nevertheless, each spiritual station does have a special meaning, which is not recognized except by one who has actually experienced it. We shall seek guidance for its explanation in the noble Qur'ānic verses as well as in the views of the great scholars of Sufism. We shall discuss the following spiritual stations:

1. Repentance [*tawba*].
2. [Confirmed] repentance [*ināba*].
3. Abstinence [*zuhd*].
4. Pious caution [*wara'*].
5. Contentment [*qanā'a*].
6. Patience [*ṣabr*].
7. Thankfulness [*shukr*].
8. Absolute trust [*tawakkul*].
9. Submission [*taslīm*].
10. Good pleasure [*riḍā*].
11. Reckoning [*muḥāsaba*].
12. Fear and hope [*khawf wa rajā'*].
13. Poverty [*faqr*].
14. Truthfulness [*ṣidq*].
15. Vigilant awareness [*murāqaba*].
16. Beneficence [*iḥsān*].
17. Nearness [*qurb*].
18. Sincerity [*ikhlāṣ*].
19. Annihilation [*fanā'*].
20. Perpetuity [*baqā'*].
21. Affirmation of Oneness [*tawḥīd*].
22. Disengagement [*tajrīd*].
23. Segregation [*tafrīd*].
24. Deanthropomorphism [*tanzīh*].
25. Worshipful servitude [*'ubūdiyya*].

Repentance [*tawba*] represents a first station for those who dedicate themselves to Allāh (Glory be to Him), so it is appropriate to begin therewith:

1. Repentance [*Tawba*]

Repentance is a duty incumbent upon every Muslim, as Allāh (Glory be to Him) has said,

> And repent unto Allāh all together, O believers,
> *wa tūbū ila 'llāhi jamī'an ayyuha 'l-mu'minūna*
> for then you may be able to succeed.
> *la'alla-kum tufliḥūn.* (24:31)

> O you who believe, turn to Allāh in repentance—
> *yā ayyuha 'lladhīna āmanū tūbū ila 'llāhi*
> in sincere repentance!
> *tawbatan naṣūḥā.* (66:8)

The meaning of sincere repentance is the repentance that settles firmly in the heart, and leads to a change in conduct toward acts of worshipful obedience and the model of goodness. Allāh (Exalted is He) has said,

> Allāh does not change what is in a people,
> *inna 'llāha lā yughayyiru mā bi-qawmin*
> until they change what is in themselves.
> *ḥattā yughayyirū mā bi-anfusi-him.* (13:11)

The proof that the matter here is one of strict obligation is that Allāh (Glory be to Him) describes those who do not repent as being wrong-doers: He has said (Glory be to Him),

> And those who do not repent, such are the wrongdoers.
> *wa man lam yatub fa-ulā'ika humu 'ẓ-ẓālimūn.* (49:11)

He describes those who repent as being loved by Allāh, for He says (Exalted is He),

> Truly, Allāh loves those who repent.
> *inna 'llāha yuḥibbu 't-tawwābīna.* (2:222)

It is related on the authority of the scholars of Sufism that repentance is the root of every spiritual state and station in Sufism, so no one reaches a spiritual station or state except someone whose repentance has gone before.

Repentance has three degrees:

1. That which is called *tawba.* [Using the corresponding verb *tāba*], Allāh (Glory be to Him) has said,

> And I am indeed All-Forgiving toward anyone
> *wa innī la-Ghaffārun li-man*

who repents and believes, and does righteous work.
tāba wa āmana wa 'amila ṣāliḥan. (20:82)

2. That which is called *ināba*. [Using the corresponding participle *munīb*], Allāh (Exalted is He) has said,

Anyone who fears the All-Merciful in secret,
man khashiya 'r-Raḥmāna bi'l-ghaibi
and comes with a penitent heart.
wa jā'a bi-qalbin munīb. (50:33)

3. That which is called *awba*. [Using the corresponding adjective *awwāb*], Allāh (Glory be to Him) has said,

How excellent a servant!
ni'ma 'l-'abd:
He was ever turning in repentance.
inna-hu awwāb. (38:30)

Whenever someone repents out of fear of the torment and desire for the reward, he is credited with the repentance called *tawba*. Whenever someone repents from a sense of shame before his Lord, he is credited with the repentance called *ināba*. Whenever someone repents in obedience and submission to His Might and Majesty (Glory be to Him), he is *awwāb* [and he is credited with the repentance called *awba*].

According to Dhū'n-Nūn al-Miṣrī,[1] "The repentance of the common folk is of sins, and the repentance of the élite is of heedlessness." According to 'Abdu'llāh at-Tamīmī, "What a difference there is between the penitent who repents of indulgence in lustful pleasures, the penitent who repents of acts of heedlessness, and the penitent who repents of taking pride in (his own) virtues."

According to Sahl ibn 'Abdullāh, "Repentance means that you do not forget your sin." According to Shaikh Junaid al-Baghdādī, "Repentance means that you forget your sin." Each of them was referring to a spiritual state. Sahl was referring to the states of the seekers, while Junaid al-Baghdādī was referring to the repentance of those who have real experience. They do not remember their sins because their hearts have been overwhelmed by constant remembrance of Him (Glory be to Him).

It is related that Shaikh Ruwaim ibn Aḥmad used to say, "Incumbent upon you is repentance of repentance!" This saying may be

1. See *ar-Risāla al-Qushairiyya*, p.48.

interpreted to mean that the penitent is obliged to immerse himself in worshipful service, not to preoccupy his mind and his heart with his repentance and forget the remembrance of his Lord.

We maintain that repentance is a demarcation line and a preventive barrier separating the penitent's conduct before his repentance from his conduct after his repentance. Some authorities have assigned the following preconditions to it: (1) remorse over what the penitent has committed in the way of contraventions, (2) determination not to revert to the like of what he has committed, and (3) application of the teachings of the Sacred Law.

According to Shaikh al-Islam 'Abdu'llāh al-Anṣārī al-Harawī (A.H. 396–481) in his *Manāzil as-sā'irīn* [*Stages of the Travelers*], "The station of repentance is not completed except by finally arriving at the repentance of whatever is less than the Truth, then recognizing the deficiency of that repentance, then repenting the recognition of that deficiency."

The meaning of that is that the station of repentance is realized for someone who forgets everything except Allāh (Glory be to Him). Repentance is not merely separation from vices and connection with virtues.

According to Ibn Qayyim al-Jawzī (A.H. 691–751), with reference to this station,[2] "What guides them to that is traversing the valley of annihilation in direct witnessing so that they do not witness together with the Truth any secondary cause, any means of access, or any formality whatsoever." He then went on to say, "We do not deny the taste of this station nor that when the spiritual traveler finally reaches it. He discovers that it has a sweetness, an ecstasy, and a delight that he does not find in anything else. Anyone who experiences it and works for it must recognize something behind it, namely that it is perfection. It is more perfect than the state of someone who witnesses his own deeds and contemplates them and their details. He must recognize that they emerge from him by the will and wish of Allāh and with His help. He must recognize his servitude at the same time as recognizing the One he serves. He must not become absent in witnessing servitude from the One who is served nor from servitude in witnessing the One who is served. Each of these is deficient. Perfection means that you witness servitude as resulting from the favor of the One who is served by His grace and by His will. The two acknowledgments must therefore be combined. If you are absent in one of them you are absent in the

2. *Madārij as-sālikīn*, commentary on *Manāzil as-sā'irīn*, p. 278.

other. The station is one of repentance so an absence from servitude is also an absence of repentence."

Such is the significance of the concept of repentance of repentance, that is to say, annihilation of the servant in the essence of the Truth and survival for the sake of the Truth alone. What makes the Ṣūfi pursue this path is the hope of attaining direct witnessing and the vision of the Truth with the eye of insight and the heart, "so he does not witness any secondary cause together with the Truth." He then needs no guide because he has reached the object of guidance. He needs no means of access because that is needed only before direct witnessing and the essence of certainty.

Ibn Qayyim al-Jawzī then went on to say, "The spiritual travelers do not stop at this point nor does their aspiration settle there. They raise their sights toward a loftier horizon, which is perfection in the intimate knowledge of Allāh (Glory be to Him) because that is a higher stage. Perfection is realized when the servant recognizes servitude as the result of His grace and favor (Glory be to Him). He has said (Exalted is He),

> Say, 'Do not consider your surrender a favor to me.
> *qul lā tamunnū 'alayya islāma-kum*
> It is rather that Allāh is treating you with gracious favor,
> *bali 'llāhu yamunnu 'alai-kum*
> inasmuch as He has guided you to faith, if you are honest.'
> *an hadā-kum li'l-īmāni in kuntum ṣādiqīn*. (49:17)

> And He it is who accepts repentance from His servants,
> *wa Huwa 'lladhī yaqbalu 't-tawbata 'an 'ibādi-hi*
> and pardons evil deeds.
> *wa ya'fū 'ani 's-sayyi āti*. (42:25)

"When the servant's love for his Lord reaches an extreme that makes him forget himself and at which he remembers only his Lord, he has arrived at the station of repentance [*tawba*]."

2. Reversion [*Ināba*]

According to Shaikh 'Abdullāh ad-Dihlawī, in his book *Īḍāḥ aṭ-ṭarīq* [*Clarification of the Path*], "Reversion [*ināba*] is the second spiritual station after the station of repentance [tawba]." There are some authorities, however, who do not count it among the spiritual stations.

Reversion [*ināba*] is reverting from heedlessness to remembrance.[3] It is also said to mean reverting to Allāh from everything. The reverting penitent [*munīb*] is someone who has no recourse apart from Him, so he reverts to Him.

In the language of ordinary people, the expression "so-and-so is a *rāji'* [reverter]" means that he has reverted from his misdeeds to good behavior and from the creation to the Creator. In the context of Sufism, this reversion is realized when the reverting penitent forgets himself and becomes immersed in the remembrance of his Lord.

The servant's reversion [*ināba*] is subdivided into three types: (1) The reversion of the lower self, which means that he devotes it exclusively to worshipful obedience to Allāh. (2) Reversion with the heart, which means emptying it of everything apart from Him. (3) Reversion with the spirit, which means persisting in remembrance until he remembers nothing but Him and feels no satisfaction except with Him.

According to Shaikh 'Umar as-Suhrawardī (A.H. 539–632), "The reverting penitent [*munīb*] is one who reverts to Allāh from everything that distracts him from Allāh. The reverting penitent is also one who has no recourse apart from Him."

He also said, "Reversion [*ināba*] is invalid except for someone who really achieves the station of repentance [*tawba*]. The station of repentance is not accessible except through genuine commitment to the sacred struggle. The servant is not truly committed to the sacred struggle without the existence of patience."

Shaikh 'Abdullāh al-Harawī cites the noble Qur'ānic verse as evidence.

> And revert to your Lord in repentance, and surrender to Him,
> *wa anībū ilā Rabbi-kum wa aslimū la-hu*
> before the torment comes to you, for then you will not be helped.
> *min qabli an ya'tiya-kum 'l-'adhābu thumma lā tunṣarūn.* (39:54)

He also says that reversion [*ināba*] consists of three things.

1. Reverting to Allāh for the sake of good conduct and with a sense of remorse for the wrong one has done.
2. Reverting to Allāh in fidelity to His Lordship and adhering strictly to this fidelity.
3. My heart's reversion to Allāh, in response to His command

3. See *Mu'jam muṣṭalaḥāt aṣ-ṣūfiyya*, p. 26.

(Exalted is He), "And revert… [*wa anībū*]…."

3. Abstinence [*Zuhd*]

The word zuhd does not occur in the Noble Qur'ān though the related word *zāhidīn* occurs in the Sūra of Joseph [Yūsuf], where Allāh (Exalted is He) has said,

> And they sold him for a paltry price,
> *wa sharaw-hu bi-thamanin bakhsin*
> a handful of counted silver coins,
> *darāhima ma'dūda:*
> for they were among those who set small store by him.
> *wa kānū fī-hi mina 'z-zāhidīn.* (12:20)

This [setting small store by someone] hardly corresponds to abstinence [*zuhd*] as the term is applied to one of the spiritual stations of Sufism.

Abstinence [*zuhd*] is being content with little and being satisfied with what exists. It also means aversion to the temptations of this world such as wealth and prestige. It is one of the attributes of the Sufi spiritual traveler.

Abstinence in this sense is not peculiar to Islam for there were abstainers among the Arabs before Islam. We find such ascetics [*zuhhād*] as Waraqa ibn Nawfal and Saṭīḥ Waqs ibn Sā'ida as well as some of the followers of other religions. There were also some among the believers among the Arabs who followed the teachings of Abraham (blessing and peace be upon him).

Some of the Companions of the noble Messenger (Allāh bless him and give him peace) were also known for abstinence including Bilāl, Abū Dharr, Salmān, and the Companions of the Bench [*Aṣḥāb aṣ-Ṣuffa*].

Abstinence is encouraged by the Noble Qur'ān, in Allāh's saying (Exalted is He),

> O humankind, Allāh's promise is true,
> *yā ayyuha 'n-nāsu inna wa'da 'llāhi ḥaqqun*
> so do not let the life of this world beguile you,
> *fa-lā taghurrana-kumu 'l-ḥayātu 'd-dunyā:*
> and do not let the Beguiler beguile you concerning Allāh.
> *wa lā yaghuranna-kum bi'llāhi 'l-Gharūr.* (35:5)

> This worldly life is nothing but a diversion and a sport.

wa mā hādhihi 'l-ḥayātu 'd-dunyā illā lahwun wa la'ib:
Surely the Last Abode is Life,
wa inna 'd-dāra 'l-ākhirata la-hiya 'l-ḥayawān:
if they did but know.
law kānū ya'lamūn. (29:64)

Wealth and children are the adornment
al-mālu wa 'l-banūna
of the life of this world.
zīnatu 'l-ḥayāti 'd-dunyā
But the abiding deeds of righteousness are better
wa 'l-bāqiyātu 'ṣ-ṣāliḥātu khairun
in your Lord's sight for reward, and better in respect of hope.
'inda Rabbi-ka thawāban wa khairun amalā. (18:46)

Numerous Qur'ānic verses and authentic Prophetic traditions encourage the practice of abstinence.

Abstinence does not mean laziness and idleness. It means being content with little, being satisfied with what is lawful, and being averse to what is unlawful.

Some Muslim scholars are well known for abstinence, like Shaikh al-Ḥasan al-Baṣrī (d. A.H. 110), Shaikh Ibrāhīm ibn Adham (d. A.H. 161), Shaikh Dāwūd aṭ-Ṭā'ī (d. A.H. 165), Fuḍail ibn 'Iyāḍ (d. A.H. 187), Shaqīq al-Balkhī (d. A.H. 194), as well as many others.

As related by Ibn Māja, the Prophet (Allāh bless him and give him peace) once said,

> Abstain from this world, for then Allāh will love you, and abstain from what is in the hands of other people, for then they will love you.

According to Imām 'Alī, "Abstinence means that you do not care who consumes this world, whether he be a believer or an unbeliever."

According to al-Junaid al-Baghdādī, "Abstinence means thinking little of this world and erasing its traces from the heart."

According to Abū Sulaimān ad-Dārānī, "Abstinence means abandoning whatever distracts you from Allāh."

According to as-Sarī as-Saqaṭī, "Life is not pleasant for the abstainer is when he is distracted from himself, and life is not pleasant for the master of intimate knowledge when he is preoccupied with himself."

According to Yaḥyā ibn Mu'ādh, "No one reaches the reality of abstinence until he has three qualities: work without attachment, speech without desire, and dignity without leadership."

According to Bishr al-Ḥāfī, "Abstinence is a property that does not settle except in an emptied heart."

According to as-Saqaṭī, "Abstinence means that you must not take anything from anyone, that you must not ask anyone for anything, and that you must not keep anything that you could give to someone."

Junaid al-Baghdādī also said, "Abstinence means that hands are empty of possessions and hearts of attachment."

All the sayings about abstinence could only be collected in a separate book.

According to Imām al-Ghazālī in his book *Iḥyā' 'ulūm ad-dīn* [*Revival of the Religious Sciences*], "When a man dislikes this world, he thinks about this dislike. As for one who loves this world, his heart is attached to this love. Abstinence means that your thinking is about Him (Glory be to Him)." (This is comparable to repentance of repentance.)

From all that has gone before, it is clear to us that abstinence means cleansing the heart of attachment to this world and its temptations, such as wealth and prestige, because the heart, according to Sufis, is the site of the love of Allāh Alone. If someone wishes His light to settle in his heart, he must therefore banish from it everything apart from Him.[4]

The meaning of that is not that earning is unlawful, but that you may earn lawful wealth without attaching your heart to it, or feeling humiliation because of poverty. Poverty is one of the degrees of abstinence, and abstinence is one of the stations of Sufism after repentance.

According to Ibn 'Ajība, one of the great scholars of Sufism,

> The abstinence of the Muslims is contentment with barely enough to ensure survival. As for the abstinence of the righteous among them, it is distancing yourself from everything that keeps you at a distance from Allāh. As for the abstinence of the masters of intimate knowledge, it is the removal from your heart of everything apart from Allāh. It is also remembering Him (Glory be to Him) by night and day without heedlessness. This kind of abstinence enables the servant to reach his goal.

4. See *'Awārif al-ma'ārif* by as-Suhrawardī, *Qūt al-qulūb* by Abū Ṭālib al-Makkī, and *ar-Risāla al-Qushairiyya*, under the subject of abstinence [*zuhd*].

4. Pious Caution [*Wara'*]

Pious caution [*wara'*] is the avoidance of every sinful act of disobedience and care in ascertaining what is lawful and unlawful. This not only is in order to guard against the lawful, but to guard against everything in which there is any suspicion of unlawfulness.

Its sphere is not restricted to the affairs of daily life, but includes interference in what does not concern you, or issuing legal opinions without jurisprudence or scholarship. In the words of Prophetic tradition,

> Part of the excellence of a man's Islam is his forsaking what does not concern him. The basis of your religion is pious caution.[5]
>
> Be piously cautious, for then you will be the most worshipful of people.[6]
>
> Leave what makes you suspicious in favor of that which does not make you suspicious.

According to Abū Bakr, the Champion of Truth [*aṣ-Ṣiddīq*], "We used to leave aside seventy types of lawful sustenance for fear of lapsing into a category of the unlawful."[7]

As we read in *at-Ta'rīfāt* [*Definitions*] by al-Jurjānī, "Pious caution means abandoning things that are doubtful, for fear of lapsing into the unlawful."[8]

It has also been said,

> Pious caution means that the servant speaks nothing but the truth, whether he is angry or contented, and that his concern is for what will please Allāh. The practitioners of pious caution are on three levels: (1) Some of them are cautiously wary of dubious things, meaning what is between the clearly lawful and the clearly unlawful. (2) Some of them are cautiously wary of that from which the heart holds back, and which causes a disturbance in the breast when it is approached. This is familiar only to masters of the heart and those who have real experience. (3) As for the third level of pious caution, it belongs to those endowed with intimate knowledge and to the ecstatics.

---

5. *al-Luma'*, p. 70.
6. *ar-Risāla al-Qushairiyya*, p. 53.
7. *ar-Risāla al-Qushairiyya*, p. 53.
8. See *Mu'jam muṣṭalaḥāt aṣ-ṣūfiyya*, p. 266.

According to Ibrāhīm ibn Adham, "Pious caution means abandoning dubious things and everything that does not concern you."

According to Shaikh Ma'rūf al-Karkhī, "You must keep your tongue from praise, just as you keep it from blame."[9]

In the words of the authentic Prophetic tradition recorded in the Ṣaḥīḥ of al-Bukhārī,

> That which is lawful [*ḥalāl*] is clear and that which is unlawful [*ḥarām*] is clear, and between them are dubious matters [*mutashabbihāt*], which many people do not know. If someone guards against dubious matters, he keeps his religion and his honor free from blame. If someone lapses into dubious matters, he lapses into the unlawful, like the shepherd who herds around the forbidden zone and is likely to pasture his flock inside it. Every king has a forbidden zone, and Allāh's forbidden zone consists of the areas that He has declared unlawful.

According to Sufyān ath-Thawrī, "There is nothing easier than pious caution, which means that you abandon every matter about which you feel uncertain."

It is clear from the foregoing that Sufi pious caution is derived from the authentic Prophetic Sunna. The men of Sufism adhere to it strictly, until it becomes a characteristic firmly rooted in their mode of conduct, and a station among their spiritual stations. As practiced by them, pious caution may reach a point where they use it to conceal their charismatic talents and their spiritual discoveries, for fear of letting Satanic delusion intrude into their natures. This is the purport of their saying, "No charismatic exploit except for a wise reason [*lā karāma illā li-ḥikma*]." In other words, it is not permissible to display miracles except for a wise reason.

According to Abū Ṭālib al-Makkī, "Some of the Sufis have said:,'If someone loves to have his pious caution recognized by anyone other than Allāh (Glory be to Him), it has nothing to do with Allāh.'"

5. Contentment [*Qanā'a*]

Contentment [*qanā'a*] is satisfaction with the sustenance that is absolutely necessary, restricting oneself to the basic essentials of clothing, furniture, and food, and preferring little to much. According to Abū Huraira, Allāh's Messenger (Allāh bless him and give him peace) said one day,

9. *ar-Risāla al-Qushairiyya*, p. 54.

> O Abū Huraira, when hunger afflicts you severely, you must take a loaf of bread and a small jug of water, and let this world go to ruin![10]

The Prophet (Allāh bless him and give him peace) is also reported as having said,

> Contentment is a treasure that is never exhausted.

According to Abū 'Abdiullāh ibn Khafīf, "Contentment means refraining from looking for what is unavailable, and being satisfied with what is available." According to Muḥammad ibn 'Alī at-Tirmidhī, "Contentment is the satisfaction of the self with the provision that has been allotted to it by destiny."[11]

Contentment is not a separate station, according to some of the experts, but rather an introduction to the station of good pleasure [*riḍā*], just as pious caution [*wara'*] is an introduction to the station of abstinence [*zuhd*].

They have also said that "Contentment is the opposite of greedy desire, and greedy desire is addiction to the accumulation of wealth from every container, by night and by day. Contentment is complete satisfaction with whatever Allāh has graciously bestowed, and working with whatever Allāh has made easy in order to lead a good life."

If someone is not content with what he has at his disposal, he is not following the Sunna of the Prophet (Allāh bless him and give him peace). If someone does not follow the Prophetic Sunna, he will not reach the station of sainthood.

Contentment is a relaxation for the lower self. If a man possesses it, he feels at ease in this world from a first step, and he does not pay attention to what other people have, whatever he may own and they may own. If a man does not possess it, cares weary him until he dies and leaves everything behind. That is why it has been said, "A pauper is everyone filled with greedy desire, and a rich man is everyone who is content."

6. Patience [*Ṣab*r]

Patience [*ṣabr*] is being well pleased with the adversities and misfortunes of this world and restraining the lower self from complaining

10. See *Mu'jam muṣṭalaḥāt aṣ-ṣūfiyya*, p. 219.
11. *ar-Risāla al-Qushairiyya*, p. 75.

about them. It is no easy matter for a man to be well pleased with affliction in the state of trial and tribulation, and for him to say, "Whatever comes from Allāh, it is good!" Nevertheless, the men of Sufism surpass this concept [of patience], for they do not distinguish between the trial and the blessing. Both of them are from Allāh (Glory be to Him), so they accept them both with equal willingness and gladness, and they thank Allāh (Glory be to Him) for every blessing, small or great. Allāh has commended those who are patient, and He has mentioned them in His Noble Book, for He has said,

> Surely those who are patient will be paid their wages in full
> *innamā yuwaffa 'ṣ-ṣābirūna ajra-hum*
> without reckoning."
> *bi-ghairi ḥisāb*. (39:10)

> These will be given their reward twice over,
> *ulā'ika yu'tawna ajra-hum marrataini*
> because they have been patient.
> *bi-mā ṣabarū*. (28:54)

> And be patient. Allāh is with those who are patient.
> *wa 'ṣbirū: inna 'llāha ma'a 'ṣ-ṣābirīn*. (8:46)

> By the Time! The human being is surely at a loss;
> *wa 'l-'aṣr: inna 'l-insāna la-fī khusr:*
> except for those who believe and do good works,
> *illa 'lladhīna āmanū wa 'amilu 'ṣ-ṣāliḥāti*
> commending truth and patience to one another.
> *wa tawāṣaw bi'l-ḥaqqi wa tawāṣaw bi'ṣ-ṣabr*. (103:1–3)

Patience and true devotion often come together in the Noble Qur'ān,

> But if you are patient and practice true devotion,
> *wa in taṣbirū wa tattaqū*
> then that is of the steadfast heart of things.
> *fa-inna dhālika min 'azmi 'l-umūr*. (3:186)

> And those who are patient in tribulation and adversity
> *wa 'ṣ-ṣābirīna fi 'l-ba'sā'i wa ḥīna 'l-ba's:*
> and in time of stress, such are they who are sincere
> *wa 'ḍ-ḍarrā'i ulā'ika 'lladhīna ṣadaqū:*
> and such are the truly devout.
> *wa ulā'ika humu 'l-muttaqūn*. (2:177)

The majesty of the station of patience is due to the fact that it is practiced for the sake of Allāh Alone, not for any other than Him, as well as entailing the endurance of adversities. The majority of the great men of Sufism consider the station of patience to be higher than the station of thankfulness [*shukr*]. That is because patience is the state of trial, whereas thankfulness is the state of blessing, and there is no doubt that the endurance of adversities is harder than the realization of thankfulness in response to blessings. That is why Allāh (Glory be to Him) has said,

> These will be given their reward twice over,
> *ulā'ika yu'tawna ajra-hum marrataini*
> because they have been patient.
> *bi-mā ṣabarū*. (28:54)

The degree of thankfulness has not advanced to the point of "twice over," and He has likewise said (Glory be to Him),

> Surely those who are patient will be paid their wages in full
> *innamā yuwaffa 'ṣ-ṣābirūna ajra-hum*
> without reckoning."
> *bi-ghairi ḥisāb*. (39:10)

Furthermore, we see that Allāh (Glory be to Him and Exalted is He) shares thankfulness with those servants of His who are parents, for He has said,

> Give thanks to Me and to your parents.
> *ani 'shkur lī wa li-wālidaik*. (31:14)

As for patience, on the other hand, He has said,

> For your Lord's sake be patient!
> *wa li-Rabbi-ka fa-'ṣbir*. (74:7)

> So wait patiently for your Lord's decree.
> *wa 'ṣbir li-ḥukmi Rabbi-ka*. (52:48)

One of the signs of the majesty of the station of patience is that it is the station of the messengers endowed with constancy. Allāh (Glory be to Him and Exalted is He) has said,

> So be patient [O Muḥammad],
> *fa-'ṣbir*
> as the messengers endowed with constancy were patient.
> *ka-mā ṣabara ulu 'l-'azmi mina 'r-Rusuli*

The description of those who are patient and the virtue of patience comes in more than ninety places in the Noble Qur'ān, as a teaching for His servants and a practice for them to observe. As related by 'Aṭā', it was Ibn 'Abbās who said that "The Messenger (Allāh bless him and give him peace) once passed by a group of his Companions, one of them being 'Umar (may Allāh be well pleased with him), so he said to them, 'Are you truly believers?' 'Umar said, 'Yes, O Messenger of Allāh!' He asked (Allāh bless him and give him peace), 'What is the sign of that?' 'Umar replied, 'We thank Allāh for blessings, we are patient with trials, and we are well pleased with Allāh's judgment and His decree.' Allāh's Messenger (Allāh bless him and give him peace) then said, 'By Allāh, you truly are believers!'"

According to Abū Ṭālib al-Makkī in *Qūt al-qulūb* (vol. 1, p. 405), "Patience and thankfulness may be two spiritual states, and they may also be two spiritual stations. If someone's station is patience, his state is thankfulness for it. He is therefore more meritorious, because he is the owner of a station. If someone's station is thankfulness, his state is patience with it, so his state is an addition to his station. Patience thus becomes an addition to the thankful in his station." That is the gracious favor of Allāh, which He bestows upon whomever He will.

Abū Ṭālib al-Makkī also said that "The patient person endowed with intimate knowledge is more meritorious than the thankful person endowed with intimate knowledge because patience is the state of poverty, whereas thankfulness is the state of wealth. If someone considers thankfulness superior to patience in spiritual merit, it is as if he considers wealth superior to poverty, and this is not the doctrine of anyone among the ancients."

There is no doubt that the great men of Sufism pass through this great station, for the disasters of this world do not vanquish them, even if they are very hard to bear. The temptations of life do not weaken their resolve, since patience becomes a lasting virtue and a property for them, so they do not alter with the changing conditions of this world.

According to Dhū'n-Nūn al-Miṣrī, "Patience is keeping one's distance from misdemeanors, swallowing the agonies of tribulation, and manifesting independence when poverty descends in the sphere of daily life." According to al-Jurjānī, in the commentary on *Riyāḍ aṣ-Ṣāliḥīn* [Gardens of the Righteous], "Patience is refraining from complaining about the agony of tribulation to anyone other than Allāh."

7. Thankfulness [*Shukr*]

Thankfulness [*shukr*] is the expression of good pleasure with His blessings (Glory be to Him) and the employment of the tongue in remembrance and praise of Him (Glory be to Him).

Thankfulness is another station among the spiritual stations of Sufism. These stations are derived from the Qur'ānic verses of Allāh (Glory be to Him), or from the pure Sunna [of the Prophet (Allāh bless him and give him peace)], and they are signposts for the progress of the believers. They ascend to a special position in Sufism, inasmuch as these qualities and stations become permanent traits, characteristics, and properties, enjoyed by the heart of the believing Sufi.

Several noble Qur'ānic verses have been revealed on the subject of thankfulness, and Allāh (Glory be to Him) has decribed Himself as the One who is Thankful [*Shākir*] for the righteous deeds of His servants, for He has said (Exalted is He),

> And he who does good of his own accord—
> *wa man taṭawwa'a khairan*
> Allāh is Thankful, All-Knowing.
> *fa-inna 'llāha Shākirun 'Alīm.* (2:158)

> Allāh is Thankful, All-Knowing.
> *wa kāna 'llāhu Shākiran 'Alīmā.* (4:147)

He has also (Glory be to Him) sought thankfulness to Him from His servants, for He has said (Exalted is He),

> Give thanks, O House of David!
> *i'malū Āla Dāwūda shukrā:*
> And few of My servants are very thankful.
> *wa qalīlun min 'ibādiya 'sh-shakūr.* (34:13)

> So remember Me, and I will remember you.
> *fa-'dhkurū-nī adhkur-kum*
> Be thankful to Me, and be not ungrateful toward Me.
> *wa 'shkurū lī wa lā takfurūn.* (2:152)

He has also (Glory be to Him and Exalted is He) singled out those who are thankful as the recipients of an abundant reward, for He has said,

> We shall reward the thankful.
> *wa sa-najzi 'sh-shākirīn.* (3:145)

> If you are thankful, I will surely give you more;
> *la-in shakartum la-azīdanna-kum*
> but if you are ungrateful,
> *wa la-in kafartum*
> My punishment is terrible indeed.
> *inna 'adhābī la-shadīd.* (14:7)

> And whoever gives thanks, he gives thanks on his own behalf.
> *wa man yashkur fa-inna-mā yashkuru li-nafsi-h.* (31:12)

Allāh (Glory be to Him) then informs us that all blessings are a gracious favor from Him (Glory be to Him), especially the blessing of faith and Islam, for He says (Glory be to Him),

> But Allāh has endeared the faith to you
> *wa lākinna 'llāha ḥabbaba ilai-kumu 'l-īmāna*
> and He has beautified it in your hearts.
> *wa zayyana-hu fī qulūbi-kum.* (49:7)

This is a great blessing, as He has said (Glory be to Him),

> A gracious favor and a blessing from Allāh.
> *faḍlan mina 'llāhi wa ni'ma.* (49:8)

Then He has said (Glory be to Him),

> They make it a favor to you that they have surrendered [to Him].
> *yamunnūna 'alai-ka an aslamū*
> Say, "Do not consider your surrender a favor to me.
> *qul lā tamunnū 'alayya islāma-kum*
> It is rather that Allāh is treating you with gracious favor,
> *bali 'llāhu yamunnu 'alai-kum*
> inasmuch as He has guided you to faith, if you are honest."
> *an hadā-kum li'l-īmāni in kuntum ṣādiqīn.* (49:17)

> But for the grace of Allāh and His mercy to you,
> *wa law lā faḍlu 'llāhi 'alai-kum wa raḥmatu-hu*
> not one of you would ever have grown pure.
> *mā zakā min-kum min aḥadin abadan.* (24:21)

> And whatever blessing you enjoy, it is from Allāh.
> *wa mā bi-kum min ni'matin fa-mina 'llāhi.* (16:53)

And as for the blessing of your Lord, tell of it!
wa ammā bi-ni'mati Rabbi-ka fa-ḥaddith. (93:11)

You must therefore acknowledge the blessings bestowed upon you by Allāh, and give thanks to Him (Glory be to Him) for them. You must not turn your face away and hold your tongue silent, for Allāh (Glory be to Him) has commanded you to praise Him and thank Him for His blessings, and He has extolled those of His servants who are thankful. He has said (Glory be to Him) concerning our master Abraham,

And he was not one of the idolaters.
wa lam yaku mina 'l-mushrikīn:
[He was] thankful for His bounties.
shākiran li-an'umi-h. (16:120,121)

He has also said, concerning Noah,

He was a very thankful servant.
inna-hu kāna 'abdan shakūrā. (17:3)

What, then, is the meaning of *shukr* in the ordinary [Arabic] language, and what is *shukr* in the vocabulary of the Ṣūfis?

In the ordinary [Arabic] language, *shukr* is extolling what is beautiful, or "acknowledgment of the beautiful."

As used by the Sufis, the term *shukr* has a deeper meaning: namely, thankfulness of the tongue, thankfulness of the limbs, and thankfulness of the inner core. For each blessing there is a special thankfulness, according to those who practice Sufism. As they see it, thankfulness is not merely a matter of saying, "I thank you, O Lord!" Thankfulness of the tongue is that by which we remember Allāh, and it means that you say only what is good. Thankfulness of the limbs means that you employ them in order to earn what is lawful and to worship Allāh (Glory be to Him), and that you do not use them to take a single step toward that which Allāh has forbidden. Thankfulness of the inner core means that you remember Allāh with your heart, and that it contains nothing other than Him (Glory be to Him). As for thankfulness for wealth, it is expressed by spending it on His path (Glory be to Him).

According to the masters of Sufism, "The first sentence in the Noble Qur'ān is, 'Praise be to Allāh [*al-ḥamdu li'llāh*],' in order to teach us how to praise Him (Glory be to Him) and to extol His attributes,

The All-Merciful, the All-Compassionate,
ar-Raḥmāni 'r-Raḥīm :
Master of the Day of Doom.
Māliki yawmi 'd-dīn. (1:2,3)"

One of the most excellent of blessings, according to the scholars, is the blessing of Islam, because it is a guidance from Allāh (Glory be to Him) and a gracious favor from Him.

The outstanding leaders of Sufism likewise consider that thankfulness itself is in need of thankfulness. That is because thankfulness necessitates goodness and grace,

If you are thankful, I will surely give you more.
la-in shakartum la-azīdanna-kum. (14:7)

—and thankfulness for this goodness and blessing is rightfully deserved.

It is related that "the most excellent remembrance is, 'There is no god but Allāh [*lā ilāha illa 'llāh*],' and the most excellent supplication is, 'Praise be to Allāh [*al-ḥamdu li'llāh*].'"

According to al-Qushairī, "Thankfulness of the body is employing the limbs and organs for the sake of pleasing Him Alone (Glory be to Him), immersing the heart in the remembrance of Allāh (Glory be to Him) Alone, employing the tongue in praising and extolling Him Alone (Glory be to Him), and spending wealth for the sake of goodness and the best interests of the Muslims."

According to Abū Ṭālib al-Makkī, "Thankfulness means acknowledging that all blessings are from Allāh (Glory be to Him)."

According to Abū 'Uthmān, who is one of the outstanding figures of Sufism, "The thankfulness of the common folk is for food and clothing, while the thankfulness of the élite is for the spiritual concepts that are received in their hearts."

8. Absolute Trust [*Tawakkul*]

Absolute trust [*tawakkul*] is another station among the spiritual stations of Sufism, and it occupies a particularly great position in their view. Someone asked Ibrāhīm al-Khawwāṣ, one of the outstanding figures of Sufism, "To what has Sufism led you?" He replied, "To absolute trust!"

Absolute trust means delegating full authority in the matter concerned to a certain individual. What it signifies here is that a man attains, through his worshipful service, his love for his Lord, and his intimate knowledge of Him (Glory be to Him), to a contentment that makes him surrender his religious and his worldly business to his Lord. He relies on no one but Him. It is well known that a man does not easily attain to this contentment, which sets him before his Lord like the corpse in front of the ritual washer of the dead, or like the invalid in the presence of his physician.

Allāh (Glory be to Him) has said,

> And whoever puts all his trust in Allāh, He will suffice him.
> *wa man yatawakkal ʻala 'llāhi fa-Huwa ḥasbu-h.* (65:3)

Allāh (Glory be to Him) has also explained that absolute trust is one of the attributes of the believers, for He has said in His Mighty Book,

> And put all your trust in Allāh, if you are indeed believers.
> *wa ʻala 'llāhi fa-tawakkalū in kuntum mu'minīn.* (5:23)

Part of the fruit of absolute trust is that the man who is absolutely trusting becomes the beloved friend of Allāh (Glory be to Him),

> Allāh loves those who are absolutely trusting [in Him].
> *inna 'llāha yuḥibbu 'l-mutawakkilīn.* (3:159)

But what exactly is absolute trust? Does it mean detachment from the pursuit of secondary causes, as when the invalid withdraws from consulting the physician, for instance, relying on Allāh Alone for the remedy?

Certainly not! Islam contains no Book or Sunna or record of the righteous predecessors that assigns such a meaning to absolute trust. If the Muslim falls sick, he is obliged to search for the secondary causes of his healing, they being the physician and the medicine. At the same time, however, it is necessary for him to believe that the healing is by the Hand of Allāh (Glory be to Him), not by the hand of the physician. The Muslim must likewise work on his farm, but he must believe that the Provider is Allāh (Glory be to Him). Once such faith has become established in your heart, you will surrender your business to His control, putting all your trust in Him (Glory be to Him), so you will not despair because of any problem that arises, nor be deluded by any gains that accrue. You will often say, "In the Name of Allāh! I have put all my trust in Allāh. There is no might nor any power except with Allāh."

If we contemplate the meanings of those expressions and affirm the truth that they contain, that will be sufficient to ensure that we are believers endowed with intimate knowledge and that we are among the people of Sufism. The expression "In the Name of Allāh" means, "I begin my work by invoking Allāh's Name." It implies an acknowledgment of the servant's servitude and an affirmation of the Lordship of his Creator, as do the assertions, "I have put all my trust in Allāh. There is no might nor any power except with Allāh."

Some of the truly wise have counted three levels of absolute trust,

1. At the first and lowest level, you are with Allāh like a mandator with a polite and compliant agent.
2. At the second and middle level, you are with Allāh like an infant with his mother, to whom alone he refers all his concerns.
3. At the third and highest level, you are with Allāh (Exalted is He) like an invalid in the presence of the physician.

Absolute trust is thus an expression signifying the acceptance of secondary causes, together with the conviction that they will produce neither harm nor benefit except with His permission (Glory be to Him).

According to Ibn 'Ajība (may Allāh be well pleased with him), who was endowed with intimate knowledge of Allāh, "Absolute trust is the heart's reliance on Allāh, to the point where you rely on nothing apart from Him. One has attachment to Allāh and dependence on Him in everything in the knowledge that He is All-Knowing, and that being in the Hand of Allāh is more reliable than reliance on what is in your own hand."

According to al-Qushairī (may Allāh bestow His mercy upon him), "The location of absolute trust is the heart. Movement with the outer being does not conflict with absolute trust with heart, provided the servant realizes that decision-making rests with Allāh (Exalted is He). If something proves to be difficult, it is by His decree; and if something proves to be convenient, it is by His facilitation."

As related by at-Tirmidhī, a man once came to Allāh's Messenger on a she-camel and said, "O Messenger of Allāh, shall I set my camel free and have absolute trust?" He replied (Allāh bless him and give him peace), "Hobble her first, then have absolute trust."

According to al-Qushairī, "Absolute trust is reliance on what is at Allāh's disposal and despairing of what is at the disposal of human beings."

According to Abū 'Alī ad-Daqqāq, "Trust has three degrees: trust, then surrender, then delegation. Trust is the attribute of the believers; surrender is the attribute of the saints; and delegation is the attribute of those who affirm Divine Oneness."

According to Sahl ibn 'Abdullāh, "Three duties are incumbent on someone who is absolutely trusting: (1) He must not seek anything from anyone. (2) He must refuse to accept anything from anyone. (3) He must not keep anything for his tomorrow."

Summarizing, the fruit of absolute trust is tranquillity and happiness, since the person who is absolutely trusting believes that Allāh (Glory be to Him) is Aware of his condition, that He is the Healing Provider, and that He is the Most Merciful of the merciful. He believes that whatever Allāh wills comes to be and whatever He does not will does not come to be. He therefore resorts to secondary causes, but without believing that they are really effective, for Allāh is the Creator of the secondary causes. Absolute trust is the source of happiness, good pleasure, courage, and heroism, so it does not make anyone subject to abasement and humiliation. If someone has absolute trust, he does not seek help except from his Lord. While he does make use of secondary causes in the outer sphere, his heart is attached to his Lord Alone. He does not seek anything for himself from his Lord, because he believes that Allāh is Aware of his condition.

I would like to cite two verses from an ode of mine, for they are samples of this fruit, in order to conclude the subject of absolute trust.

For Your grace I yearn, not for treasure and pearls.
'Tis the same in Your grace that I be in poverty or wealth.

What should I seek, if it is not obvious what is finest?
Let me have, my Lord, what is best and so shall I be, my Lord.

9. Submission [*Taslīm*]

Submission [*taslīm*] is compliance with the commandment of Allāh (Exalted is He) and refraining from indulgence in what is improper. It is also said to mean steadfastness in the face of tribulation without alteration in the outer and inner being.

Allāh (Glory be to Him and Exalted is He) has said,

And when the true believers saw the clans, they said:

wa lammā ra'a 'l-mu'minūna 'l-aḥzāba qālū
"This is what Allāh and His Messenger promised us.
hādhā mā wa'ada-na 'llāhu wa Rasūlu-hu
Allāh and His Messenger are true."
wa ṣadaqa 'llāhu wa Rasūlu-h:
It did but confirm them in their faith and submission.
wa mā zāda-hum illā īmānan wa taslīmā. (33:22)

Submission thus comes after faith, and it means that you submit yourself to someone you believe in. For instance, in the case of someone who is satisfied with the skill of a physician, he submits himself to him so that when he takes his scalpel and cuts into his stomach after anesthetizing him, he does not voice any complaint against him, but thanks him for the excellence of his operation.

According to as-Sarī as-Saqaṭī, "There are three things by which certitude becomes clear: (1) sticking to the truth in dangerous situations; (2) submitting to Allāh's commandment at the advent of tribulation, and (3) being well pleased with destiny's decree when the blessing passes away."

The author of *Qūt al-qulūb* has linked absolute trust and submission closely together.[12] According to him, absolute trust [*tawakkul*] has three degrees: (1) The highest degree is that of someone who puts all his trust in Allāh because of glorification and veneration. (2) The middle degree is that of someone who puts all his trust in Him because of love and fear. (3) The lowest degree is that of someone who puts all his trust in Him as a way of submitting to Him and endearing himself to Him. He also said, "The best may reside in what the servant does not know, and it may reside in what he dislikes, although Allāh (Glory be to Him) knows the goodness of its outcome. It is therefore incumbent upon him to submit to the judgment of the Judge, and to be well pleased with the distribution of the Distributor." Allāh (Exalted is He) has said,

Fighting is prescribed for you, though it be hateful to you.
kutiba 'alai-kumu 'l-qitālu wa huwa kurhun la-kum:
But it may happen that you hate a thing that is good for you,
wa 'asā an takrahū shai ān wa huwa khairun la-kum:
and it may happen that you love a thing which is bad for you.
wa 'asā an tuḥibbū shai'an wa huwa sharrun la-kum:

12. *Qūt al-qulūb*, vol. 2., p. 73.

Allāh knows, and you know not.
wa 'llāhu ya'lamu wa antum lā ta'lamūn. (2:216)

Submission is a spiritual station included by Abū Ṭālib al-Makkī in the station of absolute trust, and likewise by Shaikh Abū Naṣr as-Sarrāj. As for Shaikh Aḥmad al-Fārūqī (A.H. 971–1034), known as the Renewer [*Mujaddid*] of the second [*hijrī*] millenium, and Shaikh 'Abdullāh ad-Dihlawī,[13] the spiritual guide of our master, Khālid an-Naqshbandī, they mention ten spiritual stations, including submission. Mullah Ḥāmid al-Bīsārānī (A.H. 1225–1310) does likewise. As we read in the book entitled *al-Qudsiyya*, by Shaikh Muḥammad Bahā' ad-Dīn al-Bukhārī, surnamed an-Naqshband, "Submission is the proper conduct of the Sufi with his spiritual guide, before everything, in the sense that he must submit his business to the control of his spiritual guide, until he learns his path. Then he will reach the station of submission to his Lord, and at that point he will attain to the station of worshipful service and submission."

10. Good Pleasure [*Riḍā*]

According to the author of *al-Luma'*, "Good pleasure [*riḍā*] is a noble spiritual station."

According to al-Qushairī in his book *ar-Risāla al-Qushairiyya*, "The 'Irāqīs and the Khurāsānīs have held different opinions with regard to good pleasure, as to whether it is one of the spiritual states [*aḥwāl*] or one of the spiritual stations [*maqāmāt*]. The people of Khurāsān have said, 'Good pleasure is included among the spiritual stations, and it is the final result of absolute trust.' This means that it is attributed to what the servant attains by his earning. As for the 'Irāqīs, they have said, 'Good pleasure is included among the spiritual states.' That is not something earned by the servant, but a receiving that alights in the heart, like the rest of the spiritual states. It is possible to combine the two statements, for it may be said, 'The initial stage of good pleasure is earned by the servant, so it is one of the spiritual stations, while its final stage is included among the spiritual states, and it is not an earned acquisition.'"

Summarizing, good pleasure is happiness, and the heart's good pleasure is its happiness with what it receives. The good pleasure of Allāh is His good pleasure with the work of His servant, so light settles in his heart and blessings descend upon him. As for the ser-

13. *Īḍāḥ aṭ-Ṭarīq.*

vant's good pleasure, it is tranquillity and calm contentment with whatever befalls him.

Nothing in this is at odds with the Sacred Law, for Allāh (Glory be to Him) rewards His servants by His saying,

Allāh is well pleased with them,
raḍiya 'llāhu 'an-hum
and they are well pleased with Him.
wa raḍū 'an-hu
That is the mighty triumph.
dhālika 'l-fawzu 'l-'aẓīm. (5:119)

That means that this believing and worshipful servant has won the station of good pleasure, and that is a mighty triumph. This reward is in the Garden of Paradise, yet it belongs to the work of this world.

Allāh (Glory be to Him) has also said,

But there is also the sort of man
wa mina 'n-nāsi
who would sell himself, desiring Allāh's good pleasure.
man yashrī nafsahu 'btighā'a marḍāti 'llāh:
And Allāh is Kind to servants.
wa 'llāhu Ra'ūfun bi'l-'ibād. (2:207)

All of that is intended to confirm the reality of Allāh's good pleasure (Glory be to Him).

Good pleasure also means that the servant's heart is calmly resigned to the judgment of Allāh (Almighty and Glorious is He).[14] When al-Junaid (may Allāh bestow His mercy upon him) was asked about good pleasure, he said, "Good pleasure is the renunciation of free choice."

According to al-Qannād (may Allāh bestow His mercy upon him), "Good pleasure is the heart's calm acceptance of the bitterness of destiny's decree."

As we read in *ar-Risāla al-Qushairiyya*, "Good pleasure is the eviction of displeasure from the heart, so that it contains nothing but joy and happiness."

According to Ibn Khafīf, "Good pleasure is the heart's calm acceptance of His judgments, and the heart's compliance with whatever Allāh is well pleased with and prefers."

According to Ibn 'Aṭā' (may Allāh bestow His mercy upon him),

14. *al-Luma'*, p. 80.

"Good pleasure is the heart's regard for the eternal choice of Allāh (Exalted is He) for the servant, because it knows that He has chosen the very best for him, so it is well pleased with Him and abandons displeasure."

Allāh (Exalted is He) has said,

> But it may happen that you hate a thing that is good for you,
> *wa 'asā an takrahū shai'ān wa huwa khairun la-kum:*
> and it may happen that you love a thing which is bad for you.
> *wa 'asā an tuḥibbū shai'an wa huwa sharrun la-kum.* (2:216)

> For it may happen that you hate a thing
> *fa-'asā an takrahū shai'an*
> wherein Allāh has placed much good.
> *wa yaj'ala 'llāhu fī-hi khairan kathīrā.* (4:19)

That is why we consider the station of good pleasure to be one of the lofty stations related to the heart. Provided the body and the spirit are trained by acts of worship, and the heart is cleansed of psychological and physical impurities, the servant's heart will be adorned with praiseworthy qualities, so he will sit in the station of good pleasure, well pleased and tranquil.

According to the majority of the outstanding figures of Sufism, like as-Sarrāj, al-Qushairī and as-Suhrawardī al-Baghdādī, the station of good pleasure is the last degree of the spiritual stations. That is why they conclude their studies with it, and then move on to studies of the spiritual states. They say, "The station of good pleasure is greater than the station of patience, for the following reason: When a man reaches the station of good pleasure, he accepts everything unpleasant with happiness, and regards it as a benefit that has come to him from his Lord, even death. Consider how Bilāl al-Ḥabashī (may Allāh be well pleased with him) laughed at the approach of death, and said, 'I am going to meet my beloved friend Muḥammad (Allāh bless him and give him peace) and all the loved ones in the Garden of Paradise!'"

The Messenger (Allāh bless him and give him peace) advised his Companions, many times, to be well pleased with Allāh's decree.

According to Abū 'Alī ad-Daqqāq, "Good pleasure does not mean that you do not feel adversity. Good pleasure simply means that you do not object to the judgment of destiny's decree."

The fact of the matter is that if the love of Allāh possesses the ardor of someone's heart, he cannot fail to be well pleased with whatever Allāh has decreed and foreordained. This does not mean that the servant should not work, or should not look to his Lord in hope, appealing for relief from tribulation, for Allāh (Glory be to Him) has said,

> Call upon Me and I will answer you.
> *ud'ū-nī astajib la-kum.* (40:60)
>
> He is the One who made the earth subservient to you,
> *Huwa 'lladhī ja'ala la-kumu 'l-arḍa dhalūlan*
> so walk in its paths and eat of His providence.
> *fa-'mshū fī manākibi-hā wa kulū min rizqi-h.* (67:15)

You therefore have the right to beseech your Lord to send His mercy down upon you, and to remove misfortune from your path. You have the right to earn, to labor and to work within the limits of the Sacred Law. You also have the right to protect your earning and your honor.

The life of the glorious Messenger (Allāh bless him and give him peace) is the example and the fine model for us in every work and every undertaking, for he strove hard to spread the message of Islam, to the point where he was pelted with stones in the battle of aṭ-Ṭā'if, and his noble foot was caused to bleed. His sons al-Qāsim and Ibrāhīm died young, and his paternal uncle Ḥamza was martyred at the hand of the polytheists. In spite of that, he used to say in his prayer of supplication (Allāh bless him and give him peace),

> If You are not displeased with me, I shall not worry.

Let me also say that good pleasure is one of the greatest stations of Sufism, for it is the station of the greatest sainthood and the last of the degrees of the purified self. It is well known that the self becomes censorious [*lawwāma*], then inspired [*mulhama*], then tranquil [*muṭma'inna*], then well pleased [*rāḍiya*], and finally well pleasing [*marḍiyya*].

Allāh (Exalted is He) has said,

> O self now at peace,
> *yā ayyatuha 'n-nafsu 'l-muṭma'inna :*
> return unto your Lord, well pleased, well pleasing!
> *irji'ī ilā Rabbi-ki rāḍiyatan marḍiyya.* (89:27,28)

11. Reckoning [*Muḥāsaba*]

Reckoning [*muḥāsaba*] means subjecting the lower self to censure and rebuke, weighing actions and words in the balance of the Sacred Law, and engaging in self-examination by questioning what one is doing, so that the spiritual traveler may be on the right track. That is because the lower self is always instigating evil, and if he did not curb its defiance, a man would go astray and his business would be finished.

That is indicated by Allāh's saying (Exalted is He),

> O you who believe, practice true devotion to Allāh.
> *yā ayyuha 'lladhīna āmanu 'ttaqu 'llāha*
> And let every self consider what it has forwarded
> *wa 'l-tanẓur nafsun mā qaddamat*
> for the day ahead. And practice true devotion to Allāh.
> *li-ghad: wa 'ttaqu 'llāh:*
> Allāh is indeed Aware of what you do.
> *inna 'llāha Khabīrun bi-mā ta'malūn.* (59:18)

It is clear that training the lower self, by examining his character and his daily activities, accustoms a man to noble dignity. The Sufis have an eminent method of teaching in this connection, and their earnest endeavor in combat with passionate desire is a mark of the spiritual position they occupy in the sight of their Lord.

12. Fear and Hope [*Khawf wa Rajā'*]

The combination of fear and hope fluctuates between the spiritual state and the spiritual station in the science of Sufism. Some place it among the spiritual stations, while others place it among the spiritual states. One thing that is established in Sufism is that the spiritual state may sometimes turn into a permanent spiritual station.

The concept of fear is firmly rooted in the Noble Qur'ān and the Prophetic Sunna. Allāh (Glory be to Him) has said,

> They hope for His mercy and they fear His torment.
> *wa yarjūna rahmata-hu wa yakhāfūna 'adhāba-h.* (17:57)

> They call on their Lord in fear and hope.
> *yad'ūna Rabba-hum khawfan wa ṭama'ā.* (32:16)

> They used to vie one with the other in good deeds,
> *inna-hum kānū yusāri'ūna*

and they cried to Us in longing and in fear,
fi 'l-khairāti wa yad'ūna-nā raghaban wa rahabā:
and they were submissive unto Us.
wa kānū la-nā khāshi'īn. (21:90)

It is therefore incumbent on the Muslim to dread his Lord, at the same time as it is impermissible for him to despair of His mercy. Allāh (Glory be to Him and Exalted is He) has said,

Do not despair of the mercy of Allāh!
lā taqnaṭū min raḥmati 'llāh:
Surely Allāh forgives sins altogether.
inna 'llāha yaghfiru 'dh-dhunūba jamī'ā:
He is indeed the All-Forgiving, the All-Compassionate.
inna-hu Huwa 'l-Ghafūru 'r-Raḥīm. (39:53)

Hope does not eliminate fear, however. Indeed, it is necessary for it to be several times as much as hope. The fear of the Sufi, is even more intense, because he knows the religion with the essence of certainty. Allāh (Exalted is He) has said,

Only those of His servants fear Allāh who have knowledge.
inna-mā yakhsha 'llāha min 'ibādi-hi 'l-'ulamā'. (35:28)

It is well known that the Messenger (Allāh bless him and give him peace) was more afraid of his Lord than any of them, because he was the one of them who knew Him best (Glorious and Exalted is He). He said (Allāh bless him and give him peace),

[The Sūra of] Hūd and its sisters have turned my hair gray, because so much of the [Divine] threat is contained in these Sūras.

A far removal for Thamūd!
a-lā bu'dan li-Thamūd. (11:68)

A far removal for 'Ād, the folk of Hūd!
a-lā bu'dan li-'Ādin qawmi Hūd. (11:60)

A far removal for Midian,
a-lā bu'dan li-Madyana
even as Thamūd had been removed afar!
ka-mā ba'idat Thamūd. (11:95)

The two states are therefore necessary, both fear and hope.

According to Sahl ibn 'Abdullāh, "Fear and hope are like the male and the female, which do not bear fruit except through their meeting. The meeting [of fear and hope] is true devotion, and true devotion yields the fruit of certainty."

The Noble Qur'ān contains several verses with particular reference to fear. Allāh (Exalted is He) has said,

> Fear Me, if you are true believers.
> *wa khāfū-ni in kuntum mu'minīn.* (3:175)

> And treat Me with reverent fear.
> *wa iyyā-ya fa-'rhabū-n.* (2:40)

> He took up the tablets, and in their inscription
> *akhadha 'l-alwāḥa wa fī nuskhati-hā*
> there was guidance and mercy for those who fear their Lord.
> *hudan wa raḥmatun li'lladhīna hum li-Rabbi-him yarhabūn.* (7:154)

It is related that the Messenger (Allāh bless him and give him peace) once said,

> I am the one of you who is most afraid of Allāh (Exalted is He).

It has also been said that fear is being ashamed of committing sinful acts of disobedience and things that are forbidden, and feeling pain because of them.

The following is one of the sayings of the distinguished figures of Sufism, "It is incumbent on a man to be on his guard against his own lower self more than against his enemy. It is also incumbent on him to fear his Lord Alone, for He has said (Exalted is He),

> Do not fear them, but fear Me, if you are true believers.
> *fa-lā takhāfū-hum wa khāfū-ni in kuntum mu'minīn.* (3:175)"

Fear is not a matter of speech, nor of shedding tears. As the outstanding figures of Sufism have said, it is rather compliance with the commandments of Allāh and avoidance of His prohibitions. If someone fears his Lord, he will follow the Sacred Law. He will be marked by pious caution and he will among the truly devout. Fear is one of the characteristics and dispositions of the Sufis.

According to Abū Sulaimān ad-Dārānī, "Fear does not desert a heart without its being ruined."

According to Ibn 'Ajība, "Fear has three degrees: (1) The first belongs to those Muslims who fear His punishment (Glory be to

Him). (2) The second belongs to those Muslims who fear His reproach (Glory be to Him) and being deprived of His nearness. (3) The third belongs to the special few, who fear being deprived of the sight of Him on the Day of Resurrection, and who fear that they may be counted among those who have behaved badly."

This fear is mixed with hope, and its spiritual effects are experienced only by those who follow the example of the dedicated striving of the saints, who hope for His mercy and fear His torment.

For extensive treatment of this spiritual station, one should refer to *Qūt al-qulūb*, *ar-Risāla al-Qushairiyya*, *Iḥyā' 'ulūm ad-dīn*, and other major books of Sufism.

Hope is also mentioned in the Noble Qur'ān where Allāh (Glory be to Him) has said,

> Say, "O my servants who have transgressed against themselves,
> *qul yā 'ibādiya 'lladhīna asrafū 'alā anfusi-him*
> do not despair of the mercy of Allāh;
> *lā taqnaṭū min raḥmati 'llāh:*
> surely Allāh forgives sins altogether;
> *inna 'llāha yaghfiru 'dh-dhunūba jamī'ā:*
> He is indeed the All-Forgiving, the All-Compassionate."
> *inna-hu Huwa 'l-Ghafūru 'r-Raḥīm.* (39:53)

> Those who believe and those who emigrate
> *inna 'lladhīna āmanū wa 'lladhīna hājarū*
> and strive in Allāh's cause, these have hope of Allāh's mercy.
> *wa jāhadū fī sabīli 'llāhi ulā'ika yarjūna raḥmata 'llāh:*
> Allāh is All-Forgiving, All-Compassionate.
> *wa 'llāhu Ghafūrun Raḥīm.* (2:218)

Hope is different from wishing, since the hopeful person is one who uses the means of worshipful obedience, seeking good pleasure and acceptance from Allāh, whereas the wishful person neglects the means and the efforts of striving, then expects from Allāh the reward and the recompense. This is understood from His saying (Exalted is He):

> So whoever hopes for the meeting with his Lord,
> *fa-man kāna yarjū liqā'a Rabbi-hi*
> let him do righteous work,
> *fa-'l-ya'mal 'amalan ṣāliḥan*

> and let him give no one any share at all
> in the worship due unto his Lord.
> *wa lā yushrik bi-'ibādati Rabbi-hi aḥadā.* (18:110)

This also explains why the men of Sufism pay much attention to fear and hope until they become firmly established traits of character.[15]

Their sayings include the following, "If someone wishes to follow this path of ours, he must be endowed with fear and hope, in such a manner that his fear does not crush his hope so that he despairs, and his hope does not lead him to the point where his lower self steers him into the pitfalls of passionate desire. He must circle aloft with the wing of fear and hope until he reaches the peak of the mountain of certainty and gains His good pleasure (Glory be to Him)."[16]

13. Poverty [*Faqr*]

Poverty [*faqr*] is another spiritual station of Sufism. It does not mean material poverty only, but that the servant is poor in relation to Allāh (Glory be to Him), even if he has much wealth. Just as the needy person looks to the rich man for assistance in his penury, the spiritual pauper, who is in need of Allāh, raises the palms of supplication toward Him, seeking His mercy and His help. Allāh (Glory be to Him and Exalted is He) has said,

> O human beings, you are the poor in your relation to Allāh,
> *yā ayyuha 'n-nāsu antumu 'l-fuqarā'u ila 'llāh:*
> and Allāh, He is the All-Sufficient, the Praiseworthy.
> *wa 'llāhu Huwa 'l-Ghaniyyu 'l-Ḥamīd.* (35:15)
>
> Allāh is All-Sufficient and you are the needy ones.
> *wa 'llāhu Ghaniyyun wa antumu 'l-fuqarā'.* (47:38)

If the Muslim does not regard himself as poor in relation to Him, he has contradicted the teachings of his religion. It is incumbent on the Muslim to take pride in poverty while not feeling ashamed of his poverty. He must seek sufficiency because of it. He must also strive to keep his life safe without exceeding the proper bounds in his striving. He must develop this character by approving of logic and intelligence and by promoting the standards of this age. This process is distinguished by the supremacy of concern for social welfare and with regard to the fair distribution of wealth and provision of equal

15. *Qūt al-qulūb*, p. 465.
16. *ar-Risāla al-Qushairiyya*, p. 60.

opportunities for workers in the community. In reality and actual fact, we are all servants of Allāh, none of whom is superior to another except by virtue of his true devotion. As Allāh (Glory be to Him and Exalted is He) has said,

> Surely the noblest among you in the sight of Allāh
> *inna akrama-kum 'inda 'llāhi*
> is the one of you who is most truly devout.
> *atqā-kum.* (49:13)

Wealth has no influence on the measure of nobility and superiority, so it is possible for one of us to be richer in property, to have more children, and to speak with greater eloquence. It is not permissible for him to be conceited or arrogantly proud. He must rather give thanks to his Lord for His blessings, so that his wealth will be adorned by his true devotion and people will love him. That is why the men of Sufism do not strive for riches. Even if Allāh bestows wealth and properties upon them, they remain paupers within themselves. They earn lawful sustenance with one hand and spend it with the other hand on things of benefit to Muslims such that they consider poverty superior to wealth. In the words attributed to the Messenger (Allāh bless him and give him peace),

> My poverty is my pride.

The Sufis were originally called the "paupers [*fuqarā'*]," because they did not strive for material property. If something good came their way, they spent it and did not cling to it.

As we read in the book entitled *Mu'jam muṣṭalaḥāt aṣ-ṣūfiyya*, "Poverty is a noble station. Sufis were called paupers because of their detachment from possessions. Its real meaning is that the servant is in need of nothing but Allāh, and its mark is the nonexistence of all material means. The attribute of the pauper is tranquillity in face of his nonexistence, and sacrifice and altruism in face of his existence."

According to *ar-Risāla al-Qushairiyya* (p. 123), "The spiritual pauper is qualified by three things: (1) keeping his secret, (2) the performance of his religious duty, and (3) the preservation of his poverty." When Abū Bakr al-Miṣrī was asked about the genuine spiritual pauper, he said that "He is the one who takes possession and does not deviate."

According to Abū 'Abdullāh al-Ḥaṣrī, "Abū Ja'far al-Ḥaddād spent twenty years working every day for one gold coin, which he spent on the poor while he was fasting." The fact is that the history of the men of Sufism is replete with illuminating examples of this kind of altruism. They were not opposed to lawful earning, but only to the accumulation and amassing of material wealth. Whenever someone is endowed with this attribute, this spiritual station belongs to him. This is based on the teachings of the Qur'ān and the pure Sunna. Allāh (Glory be to Him and Exalted is He) has said,

> Those who hoard up gold and silver and do not spend it
> *wa 'lladhīna yaknizūna 'dh-dhahaba wa 'l-fiḍḍata wa lā yunfiqūna-hā*
> in the way of Allāh, to them give tidings of a painful torment,
> *fī sabīli 'llāhi fa-bashshir-hum bi-'adhābin alīm.*
> on the Day when it will be heated in the Fire of Hell,
> *yawma yuḥmā 'alai-hā fī nāri Jahannama*
> and their foreheads and their flanks and their backs will be branded therewith,
> *fa-tukwā bi-hā jibāhu-hum wa junūbu-hum wa ẓuhūru-hum:*
> "Here is what you hoarded for yourselves.
> *hādhā mā kanaztum li-anfusi-kum*
> Now taste of what you used to hoard!"
> *fa-dhūqū mā kuntum taknizūn.* (9:34,35)

> As for that Ultimate Abode, We shall assign it to those
> *tilka 'd-dāru 'l-ākhiratu naj'alu-hā li'lladhīna*
> who are neither intent on high-and-mighty status in the earth,
> *lā yurīdūna 'uluwwan fī 'l-arḍi*
> nor on corruption.
> *wa lā fasādā:*
> The sequel is for those who practice true devotion.
> *wa 'l- āqibatu li'l-muttaqīn.* (28:83)

The Messenger (Allāh bless him and give him peace) once said,

> O Allāh, let the sustenance of the family of Muḥammad be a supply of nourishment.

He also said (Allāh bless him and give him peace):

> The love of this world is the source of every error.

These wise counsels are the starting point of the Sufi path, for they regard poverty as more pleasant and more noble [than wealth]. If Allāh

(Glory be to Him) gives them some property or it comes to them from inheritance or work, their heart will not become attached to it. They will not make the accumulation of wealth their aim but will spend it in the way of Allāh, on the welfare of the family and children, and on assistance for the poor. If they are deprived of wealth, they will not beg from other people.

We shall now conclude our discussion of poverty with a piece of good advice which the Prophet gave to his Companions.

> Congratulations are due to someone whose own fault distracts him from the faults of other people, someone who spends the surplus of his wealth and keeps the surplus of his speech to himself!

14. Truthfulness [*Ṣidq*]

Truthfulness [*ṣidq*] is the equality of what is said in private and what is said in public, and that is maintained by being honest with Allāh (Exalted is He) both outwardly and inwardly. That honesty depends on one's having no concern except Allāh. If someone matches this description, in the sense that public and private are one and the same to him, and he refrains from noticing creatures by constantly witnessing the Truth, he is called a "champion of the Truth [*ṣiddīq*]."[17]

Championship of the Truth is a lofty degree, which comes after prophethood and belongs to the saints. This spiritual station is based on six degrees: (1) Islam, (2) faith, (3) righteousness, (4) beneficence, (5) testimony, and (6) intimate knowledge. It is the quintessence of the station of, "If someone truly knows himself, he truly knows his Lord [*man 'arafa nafsa-hu 'arafa Rabba-h*]." If someone attains to this station, he has arrived at the knowledge of certainty, the essence of certainty and the truth of certainty, and the veils of certainty disappear in front of him.

Truthfulness is the opposite of lying. It is essential for truthfulness to be realized in action, in conscience and in speech. If you promise something, you are therefore obliged to fulfill what you have promised, otherwise you are not truthful but a liar. The Qur'ān has mentioned truthfulness in many places, and it has also mentioned "the entry of truthfulness," "the exit of truthfulness," "the abode of truthfulness," "the tongue of truthfulness," and "the footing of truthfulness." Allāh (Exalted is He) has said,

> And say, "My Lord, cause me to enter with an entry of truthfulness,
> *wa qul Rabbi adkhil-nī mudkhala ṣidqin*

17. See *Ḥaqā'iq 'ani 't-taṣawwuf.*

and cause me to go out with an exit of truthfulness."
wa akhrij-nī mukhraja ṣidqin. (17:80)

And grant me a tongue of truthfulness in later generations.
wa 'j'al lī lisāna ṣidqin fī 'l-ākhirīn. (26:84)

Warn humankind and bring to those who believe the good news
an andhiri 'n-nāsa wa bashshiri 'lladhīna āmanū
that they have a footing of truthfulness with their Lord.
anna la-hum qadama ṣidqin 'inda Rabbi-him. (10:2)

Surely the righteous will dwell amid gardens and a river,
inna 'l-muttaqīna fī jannātin wa nahar:
in an abode of truthfulness, in the presence of a King All-Powerful.
fī maq'adi ṣidqin 'inda Malīkin Muqtadir. (54:54,55)

Allāh (Glory be to Him) has also included truthfulness among the qualities of His righteous servants, for He has said (Exalted is He),

Such are those who are truthful. Such are the truly devout.
ulā'ika 'lladhīna ṣadaqū: ulā'ika humu 'l-muttaqūn. (2:177)

And whoever brings truthfulness and believes therein,
wa 'lladhī jā'a bi'ṣ-ṣidqi wa ṣaddaqa bi-hi
such are the truly devout.
ulā'ika humu 'l-muttaqūn. (39:33)

The true believers are only those who believe
inna-ma 'l-mu'minūna 'lladhīna āmanū
in Allāh and His Messenger and then do not doubt,
bi'llāhi wa Rasūli-hi thumma lam yartābū
but strive with their wealth and their own lives
wa jāhadū bi-amwāli-him wa anfusi-him
for the cause of Allāh. Such are the truthful.
fī sabīli 'llāh: ulā'ika humu 'ṣ-ṣādiqūn. (49:15)

And they help Allāh and His Messenger.
wa yanṣurūna 'llāha wa Rasūla-h:
Those are the truthful ones.
ulā'ika humu 'ṣ-ṣādiqūn. (59:8)

The beloved friends of Allāh (Glory be to Him) are described as,

Those who are patient, those who are truthful,

> *aṣ-ṣābirīna wa 'ṣ-ṣādiqīna*
> those who are obedient, those who are charitable spenders,
> *wa 'l-qānitīna wa 'l-munfiqīna*
> and those who seek forgiveness in the watches of the night.
> *wa 'l-mustaghfirīna bi'l-asḥār.* (3:17)

Our master Abū Bakr attained to the station of Championship of the Truth [*ṣiddīqiyya*], so he came to be known as the Champion of the Truth [*aṣ-Ṣiddīq*]. The prophets attained to this station, over and above their Propethood, for Allāh (Glory be to Him) has said,

> And make mention in the Book of Abraham.
> *wa 'dhkur fi 'l-Kitābi Ibrāhīm:*
> He was a Champion of the Truth, a Prophet.
> *inna-hu kāna Ṣiddīqan Nabiyyā.* (19:41)

> And make mention in the Book of Idrīs.
> *wa 'dhkur fi 'l-Kitābi Idrīs:*
> He was a Champion of the Truth, a Prophet.
> *inna-hu kāna Ṣiddīqan Nabiyyā.* (19:56)

> Joseph, O Champion of the Truth!
> *Yūsufu ayyuha 'ṣ-Ṣiddīqu.* (12:46)

> This is what the All-Merciful had promised,
> *hādhā mā wa'ada 'r-Raḥmānu*
> and the messengers spoke the truth.
> *wa ṣadaqa 'l-Mursalūn.* (36:52)

Referring to Mary, the mother of Jesus, Allāh (Glory be to Him) has said,

> And his mother was a Champion of the Truth.
> *wa ummu-hu ṣiddīqa.* (5:75)

He has also said, in the Sūra of Women [*an-Nisā'*],

> And whoever obeys Allāh and the Messenger,
> *wa man yuṭi'i 'llāha wa 'r-Rasūla*
> they are in the company of those
> *fa-ulā'ika ma'a 'lladhīna*
> to whom Allāh has granted gracious favor—
> *an'ama 'llāhu 'alai-him*
> the prophets, the Champions of Truth, the martyrs
> *mina 'n-nabiyyīna wa 'ṣ-ṣiddīqīna wa 'sh-shuhadā'i*

> and the righteous—and the best of company are they!
> *wa 'ṣ-ṣāliḥīn: wa ḥasuna ulā'ika rafīqā.* (4:69)

The point made here is that the station of truthfulness is a great and noble station, which is realized through truthful worship and after the endurance of difficult trials in life. That is because truthfulness in speech alone is not enough, for there must also be truthfulness of conscience, of the heart, and of the feelings. The outward appearance of truthfulness is not sufficient if it is not confirmed by action and if it is not established in the heart. Allāh (Glory be to Him and Exalted is He) has said,

> When the hypocrites come to you, they say:
> *idhā jā'a-ka 'l-munāfiqūna qālū*
> "We bear witness that you are indeed Allāh's Messenger."
> *nashhadu inna-ka la-Rasūlu 'llāh:*
> And Allāh knows that you are indeed His Messenger,
> *wa 'llạhu ya'lamu inna-ka la-Rasūlu-h:*
> and Allāh bears witness that the hypocrites are liars indeed.
> *wa 'llāhu yashhadu inna 'l-munāfiqīna la-kādhibūn.* (63:1)

This is praiseworthy attribute is one of the attributes of Allāh (Glory be to Him), for He has said (Glory be to Him),

> Who is more true in statement than Allāh?
> *wa man aṣdaqu mina 'llāhi ḥadīthā.* (4:87)

> And who is more truthful than Allāh in telling?
> *wa man aṣdaqu mina 'llāhi qīlā.* (4:122)

He also says (Glory be to Him),

> They said, "This is what Allāh and His Messenger promised us,
> *qālū hādhā mā wa'ada-na 'llāhu wa Rasūlu-hu*
> and Allāh and His Messenger tell the truth."
> *wa ṣadaqa 'llāhu wa Rasūlu-h.* (33:22)

> O you who believe, practice true devotion to Allāh
> *yā ayyuha 'lladhīna āmanu 'ttaqu 'llāha*
> and be with the truthful.
> *wa kūnū ma'a 'ṣ-ṣādiqīn.* (9:119)

According to the distinguished scholar Ibn Abī Sharīf, in *Ḥawāshi 'l-'aqā'id*,

> As used by the Sufis, the term *ṣidq* [truthfulness] means the equality of private and public and of the outer and the inner in the sense that the spiritual states of the servant do not give the lie to his actions, nor his actions to his spiritual states. In other words, it is essential for the seeker endowed with truthfulness to be the same where purity and truthfulness are concerned in both his private and his public life. He will thereby make rapid progress in ascending the degrees of faith, for truthfulness is a motivating force that propels the truthful person toward the highest heights. It is an obligatory qualification for every station leading to His intimate knowledge (Glory be to Him).
>
> The Muslim must therefore be truthful in fighting his passionate desire, and truthful in his struggle to correct his conduct. He must be truthful in every step he treads, and he must be truthful with his Lord. He will then be recorded among the Champions of Truth.

According to Shaikh Ma'rūf al-Karkhī, "How many are the righteous, and how few are the truthful among the righteous!"

The Prophet (Allāh bless him and give him peace) once said,

> You must leave what makes you doubt in favor of that which does not make you doubt, for truthfulness is a state of tranquillity and lying is a state of doubt.

He also said (Allāh bless him and give him peace),

> The sign of the hypocrite is threefold: when he talks he tells lies, when he promises he breaks his promise, and when he is trusted he betrays.

Truthfulness is one of the most important virtues of those who follow the path of the Sufis, for they are truthful in their words, their deeds and their spiritual states.

In concluding the subject of truthfulness, let me mention a saying of Junaid al-Baghdādī, "The real meaning of truthfulness is that you are truthful in situations from which nothing will deliver you except telling lies."

15. Vigilant awareness [*Murāqaba*]

Vigilant awareness [*murāqaba*] is one of the technical terms in common use among the Sufis, and some of them count it among the spiritual states. According to Shaikh as-Sarrāj, in his book *al-Luma'*,

"Vigilant awareness [*murāqaba*] is a noble spiritual state."

Abu 'l-Qāsim al-Qushairī opened the subject of vigilant awareness in his book with this noble Qur'ānic verse.

> And Allāh is Watchful over all things.
> *wa kāna 'llāhu bi-kulli shai'in Raqībā.* (33:52)

Vigilant awareness means that the Sufi constantly remembers that Allāh (Glory be to Him) is watching over him. He has said (Exalted is He),

> Do they not know that Allāh knows
> *a-lam ya'lamū anna 'llāha ya'lamu*
> both their secret and the thought that they confide,
> *sirra-hum wa najwā-hum*
> and that Allāh is the Knower of things hidden?
> *wa anna 'llāha 'Allāmu 'l-ghuyūb.* (9:78)

Vigilant awareness is mentioned in numerous places in the Noble Qur'ān. It is the duty of the angels who are seated on the right and on the left, but it is hard for us to grasp the meaning of the vigilant awareness of the angels. We are accustomed to interpret everything with the logic of the mind and materialistic knowledge. If we were told that the artificial satellites are watching from the heights of the sky over everything on the earth, we would be ready to believe it even though we do not know them. That is because they are tangible material objects. The same is true of the electronic observations and investigations that are stored by the computer system, consisting of ideational matters of extreme subtlety. They are produced by human craftsmanship, so we believe them. For some, however, it is difficult to believe in the angels' supervision of the actions of the servant, and that Allāh is Watchful over everything.

The people of Sufism are not heedless of the state of vigilant awareness and they do believe that Allāh is Watchful over them. If someone has this kind of faith, he does not go astray in his course of action or his way of life. Allāh (Glory be to Him) has said,

> Or do they reckon that We cannot hear
> *am yaḥsabūna annā lā nasma'u*
> their secret thoughts and their private confidences?
> *sirra-hum wa najwā-hum.*
> Nay, but Our messengers, present with them, do record.
> *balā wa Rusulu-nā ladai-him yaktubūn.* (43:80)

> Keep your words private or speak openly;
> *wa asirrū qawla-kum awi 'jharū bih*:
> He knows what the breasts contain. (67:13)
> *inna-hu 'Alīmun bi-dhāti 'ṣ-ṣudūr*.
>
> And know that Allāh knows what is in your own selves,
> *wa' 'lamū anna 'llāha ya'lamu mā fī anfusi-kum*
> so beware of Him, and know that Allāh is All-Forgiving, All-Forbearing.
> *fa-'ḥdharūh: wa' 'lamū anna 'llāha Ghafūrun Ḥalīm*. (2:235)
>
> Is he not aware that Allāh sees?
> *a-lam ya'lam bi-anna 'llāha yarā*. (96:14)

Allāh (Glory be to Him and Exalted is He) told Abraham and Moses,

> Fear not, for I am with you both. I hear and I see.
> *lā takhāfā innī ma'a-kumā: asma'u wa arā*. (20:46)

He has also said (Glory be to Him),

> And yet over you there are watchers,
> *wa inna 'alai-kum la-ḥāfiẓīn:*
> Noble Recorders, who know whatever you do.
> *Kirāman Kātibīn: ya'lamūna mā taf'alūn*. (82:10–12)

There are many Qur'ānic verses like this, so it is incumbent upon us to contemplate their meanings and to assimilate their guidance. Sufis are constantly in the state of vigilant awareness, never deviating by a hair's breadth from their proper modes of conduct and being humbly submissive to the commandments of their Lord. By matching this description they attain to the state of nearness to Allāh (Glory be to Him). According to some of the distinguished figures of Sufism, vigilant awareness comes after the station of good pleasure [*riḍā*], while some of them maintain that it comes after the station of beneficence [*iḥsān*]. Each of them has referred to the state through which he passed in his spiritual experience, especially if we include vigilant awareness among the spiritual states, for the spiritual state is a Divine gift that accompanies every spiritual station.

But how is vigilant awareness perfected, and what is its result?

In the Naqshbandī Order, vigilant awareness is the path trodden by the seeker in order to reach his goal by following the direction of his spiritual guide. The likeness of his spiritual guide is that of the physician, who identifies the medicine required to treat his patient or that of the professor who teaches in accordance with the preparedness of his student. The spiritual guide instructs his disciple in the knowledge of the path to the extent of his ability to understand it and instills in his heart the spiritual enthusiasm that will prompt him to make further progress. He may also be likened to the engineer who puts everything in its place where it fits.

If the seeker has no spiritual guide, he must still travel on the path, for perhaps Allāh will guide him in the right direction. The penitent and worshipful servant must seclude himself in a clean and empty place, performing the ritual ablution and turning toward the *qibla* [direction of prayer]. In this condition, he must implore his Lord to send down His mercy upon him and to fill his heart with the light of His guidance. He will also do well to recite the Qur'ān in his secluded retreat. Many have reached their goals by means of vigilant awareness.

The distinguished figures of Sufism have treated the subject of vigilant awareness in their books. If someone recognizes that Allāh is Aware of him, Watchful over his deeds, he will never turn toward any action that contravenes the teachings of his Lord. Is it conceivable that an intelligent person would engage in a wicked act, like theft for example, in front of the owner of the house? How then, if I know that Allāh is watching me, can I commit an act that contravenes the commandment of my Lord?

If this vigilant awareness is really and truly experienced, private and public will be the same for the servant, and he will apply the teachings of the Sacred Law. Then will come the fruit—and what a fruit that will be!

16. Beneficence [*Iḥsān*]

Beneficence [*iḥsān*] is another station among the spiritual stations of Sufism. The term *iḥsān* has numerous meanings, which are defined according to the context. It may signify drawing near to Allāh (Glory be to Him) by worshipful service. It may also signify the bestowal of gifts and charitable donations, or other forms of beneficence. Allāh (Glory be to Him and Exalted is He) has said,

> If someone produces a good deed,
> *man jā'a bi'l-ḥasanati*

he shall have ten just like it.
fa-la-hu ʿashru amthāli-hā. (6:160)

And do good. Allāh surely loves the beneficent.
wa aḥsinū inna ʾllāha yuḥibbu ʾl-muḥsinīn. (2:195)

And be good to parents.
wa biʾl-wālidaini iḥsānan. (2:83)

And as for those who strive in Our cause,
wa ʾlladhīna jāhadū fī-nā
surely We shall guide them in Our ways.
la-nahdiyanna-hum subula-nā:
Allāh is surely with the beneficent.
wa inna ʾllāha la-maʿa ʾl-muḥsinīn. (29:69)

And be kind, even as Allāh has been kind to you.
wa aḥsin ka-mā aḥsana ʾllāhu ilai-ka. (28:77)

Surely Allāh commands the implementation of justice,
inna ʾllāha yaʾmuru bi-ʾl-ʿadli
and charitable conduct, and giving to close relatives.
wa ʾl-iḥsāni wa ītāʾi dhī ʾl-qurbā. (16:90)

Is the reward of beneficence anything but beneficence?
hal jazāʾu ʾl-iḥsāni illa ʾl-iḥsān. (55:60)

The various meanings and nuances of beneficence all indicate that it is the opposite of wickedness. Allāh (Exalted is He) has said,

In their case, Allāh will change their evil deeds into good deeds.
fa-ulāʾika yubaddilu ʾllāhu sayyiāti-him ḥasanāt. (25:70)

And perform the ritual prayer
wa aqimi ʾṣ-ṣalāta
at the two ends of the day and in some watches of the night.
ṭarafayi ʾn-nahāri wa zulafan mina ʾl-lail.
Surely the good deeds will drive away the evil deeds.
inna ʾl-ḥasanāti yudhhibna ʾs-sayyiāt. (11:114)

It is clear from these Qurʾānic verses that beneficence may convey the meaning of worship (the ritual prayer), and that it may signify the opposite of evil.

And what is beneficence [*iḥsān*] in the view of Sufism?

Beneficence refers, in the view of Sufism, to the noble Prophetic tradition in which it is related that Gabriel (peace be upon him) comes to the Prophet in the shape of a human being, and asks him about faith, Islam, and beneficence, in order to teach people their religion. At the end of his questioning, he said, "O Messenger of Allāh, what is beneficence?" He replied,

> Beneficence means that you worship Allāh as if you could see Him, for even if you do not see Him, He surely sees you!

Gabriel said, "You have spoken the truth." The Companions were puzzled by this, since the man who had asked the question showed no signs of having traveled, asked a question, and then had told the Prophet (Allāh bless him and give him peace) that he had spoken the truth. They asked him (Allāh bless him and give him peace), "Who was the questioner?" Allāh's Messenger (Allāh bless him and give him peace) replied,

> It was Gabriel. He came to you in order to teach you your religion.

Let us return to the well-known Prophetic tradition,

> Beneficence means that you worship Allāh as if you could see Him, for even if you do not see Him, He surely sees you!

—so that we may see that Islam is a matter of external actions, like ritual prayer, fasting, pilgrimage, payment of the alms-due, and so on, while faith is a belief within the heart and actions that verify it. Beneficence is the very core of faith and Islam, for it means that you fulfill your Islam and your faith with the most excellent fulfillment by the body and the spirit. Beneficence is realized when the servant is convinced that Allāh is Watchful over all his movements and pauses. When he is engaged in ritual prayer, for instance, he feels as if he is actually standing before his Lord, calm and humbly submissive, without being distracted by the cares of worldly life or being in a hurry to perform the external movements. There is no doubt that real ritual prayer is that in which you are at the degree of beneficence, "as if you could see Him, for even if you do not see Him, He surely sees you." This is the meaning of the humility referred to in the Noble Qur'ān, where Allāh (Glory be to Him) has described such humble worshippers as those who are successful. He has said (Exalted is He),

Successful indeed are the true believers
qad aflaḥa 'l-mu'minūn.
who are humble in their prayers.
alladhīna hum fī ṣalāti-him khāshi'ūn. (23:1,2)

Is not the time now ripe for the hearts of those who believe
a-lam ya'ni li'lladhīna āmanū
to be humbled to the Remembrance of Allāh
an takhsha'a qulūbu-hum li-dhikri 'llāhi
and to the Truth which has been revealed?
wa mā nazala mina 'l-Ḥaqqi. (57:16)

Humility is realized when the servant performing the prayer is convinced that Allāh is Present and Watching him. That is the station of beneficence, which is a station that requires humility in the heart of the believing worshipper. Beneficence in the acts of worship is realized through humility and through humility success is realized,

Successful indeed are the true believers
qad aflaḥa 'l-mu'minūn.
who are humble in their prayers.
alladhīna hum fī ṣalāti-him khāshi'ūn. (23:1,2)

This spiritual station becomes clearly apparent when we consider its opposite in which the act of worship is empty of content and substance, mixed with hypocritical display and close to polytheism (may Allāh grant us refuge!), for it is not sincerely devoted to Allāh (Glory be to Him). He has said (Glory be to Him and Exalted is He),

So woe to those who pray, but are heedless of their prayers,
fa-wailun li'l-muṣallīn: alladhīna hum 'an ṣalāti-him sāhūn:
and to those who make a show.
alladhīna hum yurā'ūna. (107:4–6)

There is no humility in this kind of prayer and it does not compare in degree to the humble prayer of the people of the station of beneficence.

If someone wishes for Allāh to accept his worship and to bestow His good pleasure upon him on the Day of Resurrection, he must worship Allāh Alone. He has said (Glory be to Him and Exalted is He),

So whoever hopes for the meeting with his Lord,
fa-man kāna yarjū liqā'a Rabbi-hi

let him do righteous work,
fa-'l-ya'mal 'amalan ṣāliḥan
and let him give no one any share at all
wa lā yushrik
in the worship due unto his Lord.
bi-'ibādati Rabbi-hi aḥadā. (18:110)

I should also say that this is a station reached by someone who passes through the stations of repentance, reversion, abstinence, absolute trust, sincere devotion, thankfulness, and good pleasure. According to the great leaders of Sufism, it is the introduction to the degree of vigilant awareness.

17. Nearness [*Qurb*]

Nearness [*qurb*] is one of the states peculiar to the spiritual wayfarers. It is realized for them after they cleanse their hearts and their lower selves of every bad characteristic, and prepare themselves for this lofty position.

According to the author of *al-Luma'*, "The state of nearness belongs to the servant who witnesses with his heart the nearness of Allāh to him, so he draws near to Allāh (Exalted is He) through his worshipful service. His entire aspiration is set before Allāh (Exalted is He), through constant remembrance of Him in both his public and his private life.

We all know that Allāh (Exalted is He) is Near to us, and the Noble Qurān contains verses to make that clear. This nearness is of two kinds: (1) The nearness of those servants who fear Allāh in private and in public, and who worship Him by devoting the religion sincerely to Him. (2) The nearness of those servants who indulge their lower selves, so that their conduct is not correct. In this general sense comes His saying (Exalted is He),

We did indeed create the human being,
wa la-qad khalaqna 'l-insāna
and We know what his lower self whispers within him,
wa na'lamu mā tuwaswisu bi-hi nafsuh:
and We are Nearer to him than the jugular vein.
wa Naḥnu Aqrabu ilai-hi min ḥabli 'l-warīd. (50:16)

He has also said (Exalted is He), with reference to someone approached by death,

And We are Nearer to him than you are,
wa Naḥnu Aqrabu ilai-hi min-kum
but you do not see.
wa lākin lā tubṣirūn. (56:85)

Sufi nearness is the servant's state of nearness to Allāh by virtue of what he has invested in the struggle with the lower self. Worshipping Allāh in such a manner that he forgets himself and remembers only his Lord, he reaches the degree of "annihilation of the self [*fanā' an-nafs*]" and "the perpetuity of Allāh [*baqā' Allāh*]." This state is also the subject of suspicion, since there are some who suspect the Sufis of heresies like *ḥulūl* [incarnation of the Deity], *ittiḥād* [pantheism] and *waḥdat al-wujūd* [existential monism]. It may indeed happen that the Sufi in this state of "the state of nearness" departs from his normal condition because of the blessing of nearness that he feels within his being, so that he utters expressions foreign to the Sacred Law. The fact is that he is experiencing a state in which he is unconscious of what he is saying. He would not say these words in his normal state of consciousness. He would consider these words contrary to the Sacred Law in his state of mindfulness.

Shaikh an-Naqshband, Muḥammad Bahā' ad-Dīn composed a verse of poetry to this effect.

O abstinent worshipper, who sees only the exterior,
what are you asking me about the state of nearness?
I am near to Him and He is Near, like the nearness
of the water of the rose to its fragrant perfume.

There is no doubt that the fragrant perfume is something different from the water, and the water is something else different from the fragrant perfume, so they mingle together and come near to each other, but there is no question of incarnation or pantheism.

This, as we see it, is how the Qur'ān speaks of Allāh's nearness to His servant, comparing it to the nearness of the jugular vein,

And We are Nearer to him than the jugular vein.
wa Naḥnu Aqrabu ilai-hi min ḥabli 'l-warīd. (50:16)

What is the nature of this nearness? Is it the nearness of the Essence to the essence? Certainly not! That would amount to unbelief [*kufr*]. It is rather the nearness of the knowledge of Allāh (Glory be to Him). This feeling of nearness enters the sphere of insight, not the five senses. It resembles the nearness of the child to the parents' heart, for the child does not enter [physically] into the heart of the parents, yet the parents feel as near to him as if he were an inseparable part of them. If a finger of the child suffers pain, the parents lose their comfort and their sense of security.

The Qur'ān provides us with evidence and proofs, for Allāh (Glory be to Him and Exalted is He) has said,

> And prostrate yourself and draw near.
> *wa 'sjud wa 'qtarib*. (96:19)

> We called to him from the right slope of the Mount,
> *wa nādainā-hu min jānibi 'ṭ-Ṭūri 'l-aimani*
> and We brought him near in communion.
> *wa qarrabnā-hu najiyyā.* (19:52)

> And the frontrunners, the frontrunners,
> *wa 's-sābiqūna 's-sābiqūn:*
> those will be the ones brought near.
> *ulā'ika 'l-muqarrabūn*. (56:10–12)

But how do we draw near to Him (Glory be to Him)? We have already cited the noble Qur'ānic verse.

> And prostrate yourself and draw near.
> *wa 'sjud wa 'qtarib*. (96:19)

He has also said (Glory be to Him),

> And part of the night; bow down before Him
> *wa mina 'l-laili fa-'sjud la-hu*
> and glorify Him through the long night.
> *wa sabbiḥ-hu lailan ṭawīlā*. (76:26)

> And it is not your wealth nor your children that will bring you near
> *wa mā amwālu-kum wa lā awlādu-kum bi'llatī tuqarribu-kum*
> to Us, but he who believes and does good [will draw near].
> *'inda-nā zulfā: illā man āmana wa 'amila ṣāliḥā:*
> As for such, theirs will be a double reward for what they have done,
> *fa-ulā'ika la-hum jazā'u 'ḍ-ḍi'fi bi-ma 'amilu*
> and they will dwell secure in lofty halls.
> *wa hum fi 'l-ghurufāti āminūn*. (34:37)

The import of the commentary on this Qur'ānic verse is that faith and work contribute to bringing the Muslim near to his Lord. It is well known that a most exalted station in the Hereafter in the presence of Allāh is the praiseworthy station which Allāh has promised to His Prophet (Allāh bless him and give him peace). When his Lord gives him the glad tidings of this station, he commands him to perform the prayer during the night while keeping vigil so that he may be awarded this station. He has said (Exalted is He),

> And as for the night, keep vigil during a part of it,
> *wa mina 'l-laili fa-tahajjad*
> as a supererogatory work of devotion for you;
> *bi-hi nāfilatan lak:*
> it may be that your Lord will raise you up
> *'asā an yab'atha-ka Rabbu-ka*
> to a praiseworthy station.
> *maqāman maḥmūdā.* (17:79)

As we learn from the Sacred Tradition [*Ḥadīth Qudsī*],

> If someone is hostile toward a saintly friend of Mine, I have permitted him to wage war [against that enemy]. My servant does not draw near to Me through anything dearer to Me than what I have enjoined upon him. My servant does not cease to draw near to Me by means of supererogatory devotions, until I love him, and when I love him I become his hearing by which he hears, his sight by which he sees, and his hand with which he strikes....

What is referred to here is the nearness that results from frequent prayer and worship, whereby the servant becomes the beloved friend of Allāh (Exalted is He), so that He becomes his hearing, his sight and his hand. It also seems that Allāh (Glory be to Him) endows him with a new strength, which enables him to perform wondrous marvels.

18. Sincere Devotion [*Ikhlāṣ*]

Sincere devotion [*ikhlāṣ*] is another station among the spiritual stations of Sufism.

As we have mentioned, the aim in Sufism is that the spiritual state and the spiritual station become properties and dispositions rooted in what the servant has accomplished in the way of spiritual exercise, namely, struggle with the lower self, and constant commitment to worshipful service. He will then be endowed with spiritual blessings known only to Allāh and understood by none but their owner.

We shall now discuss the station of sincere devotion [*ikhlāṣ*], which is worship devoted purely to Allāh, containing no ostentation and no conceit, and performed for the sake of the good pleasure of Allāh (Glory be to Him) Alone. As Rābi'a al-'Adawiyya expressed it, "I do not worship You out of fear of Your Fire, not from desire for Your Garden...." That does not mean that the shaikhs of Sufism are not afraid of the Fire of Hell, and do not long for the Garden of Paradise. What they mean by it is, "Even if there were no Fire or Garden, we would still worship You out of love for Your Essence."

According to Abū 'l-Qāsim al-Qushairī, "Sincere devotion means singling out the Lord of Truth (Glory be to Him) for worshipful obedience, by deliberate intent. By his worshipful obedience, the servant seeks to draw near to Him (Glory be to Him), to the exclusion of anything else, whether it be impressing a fellow creature, or earning praise in people's sight, or the love of applause from creatures, or any purpose other than drawing near to Allāh (Exalted is He)."[18]

In the Sūra of the Troops [*az-Zumar*], Allāh (Glory be to Him) advises His Prophet three times to practice sincere devotion in his worshipful service, for He says,

> Say, "I am commanded to worship Allāh,
> *qul innī umirtu an a'buda 'llāha*
> devoting the religion sincerely to Him."
> *mukhliṣan la-hu 'd-dīn*. (39:11)

> Say, "Allāh I worship, devoting my religion sincerely to Him."
> *quli 'llāha a'budu mukhliṣan la-hu dīnī*. (39:14)

> So worship Allāh, devoting the religion sincerely to Him.
> *fa-''budi 'llāha mukhliṣan la-hu 'd-dīn.*
> Surely pure religion is only for Allāh.
> *a-lā li'llahi 'd-dīnu 'l-khāliṣ*. (39:2,3)

As we are told in the Sūra of the Clear Proof [al-Bayyina],

> And they have been commanded only to serve Allāh,
> *wa mā umirū illā li-ya'budu 'llāha*
> devoting the religion to Him sincerely.
> *mukhliṣīna la-hu 'd-dīn*. (98:5)

Hypocritical display is regarded as tantamount to polytheism in the Noble Qur'ān. In the Sūra of the Cave [*al-Kahf*], Allāh (Exalted is

18. *ar-Risāla al-Qushairiyya*, p. 95.

He) has said,

> So whoever hopes for the meeting with his Lord,
> *fa-man kāna yarjū liqā'a Rabbi-hi*
> let him do righteous work,
> *fa-'l-ya'mal 'amalan ṣāliḥan*
> and let him give no one any share at all in the worship due unto his Lord.
> *wa lā yushrik bi-'ibādati Rabbi-hi aḥadā.* (18:110)

As reported by Muslim, the Prophet (Allāh bless him and give him peace) once said,

> Allāh does not look at your bodies nor at your outer forms, but He does look at your hearts.

This refers implicitly to the acts of worship that are performed by the limbs of the body like the ritual prayer and the pilgrimage. The noble Prophetic tradition confirms that sincere devotion of the heart is the standard of acceptance and good pleasure on the servant's part.

According to Ibn 'Ajība (may Allāh the Exalted bestow His mercy upon him),

> Sincere devotion is on three levels: the sincere devotion of the common folk, that of the *élite*, and that of the *élite* of the *élite*:
>
> 1. The sincere devotion of the common folk is the exclusion of creatures from relations with the Lord of Truth, together with the pursuit of worldly and Otherworldly interests like the preservation of the body and property, the abundance of sustenance, and the palaces and *houris* [of Paradise].
>
> 2. The sincere devotion of the *élite* is the pursuit of Otherworldly interests to the exclusion of worldly interests.
>
> 3. The sincere devotion of the *élite* of the *élite* is the exclusion of self interests entirely for their worship is the realization of servitude and the performance of Lordly duties out of love and ardent longing for the sight of Him.

The shaikhs of Sufism pin their hopes on the attainment of the ultimate degree of servitude in their sincere devotion in order to reach the Truth. They have no other aspiration. If they do not proceed in accordance with this spirituality, they will never reach the station of sincere devotion.

The path of the seekers is fraught with perils. They must be warned against these dangers, so that the actions of the spiritual traveler will be purely for the sake of Allāh (Exalted is He). These perils are obstacles that impede his progress toward Allāh (Exalted is He). The most important of them are outlined below,

1. The first obstacle is his interest in his own work, his admiration of it, his being screened by it from the One for whom the work is done and his being screened by his worship from the One who is worshipped. What will deliver him from interest in his own work is his acknowledgment of the favor and enabling grace bestowed on him by Allāh (Exalted is He). He also needs to realize that he is a creature of His and his work is for Allāh (Exalted is He). He must therefore give thanks to Him (Glory be to Him) for His guidance, since everything good that issues from him is sheer favor and bounty from Allāh.

> But for the grace of Allāh and His mercy to you,
> *wa law lā faḍlu 'llāhi 'alai-kum wa raḥmatu-hu*
> not one of you would ever have grown pure.
> *mā zakā min-kum min aḥadin abadan.* (24:21)

If the seeker adheres to this and is rescued from the noose of ostentation, he will be saved and attain to the station of sincere devotion.

2. The second obstacle is his pursuit of compensation for his work, especially worldly compensation like the pursuit of reputation and fame and the love of outward display as well as his pursuit of spiritual states and stations, mystic disclosures and insights, so that his worship is not purely for the sake of his Lord.

This is why the great and truly wise Shaikh Arslān (may Allāh bestow His mercy upon him) gives this sound advice to everyone who pays attention to anything other than the object of his quest, his love and his purpose, "O captive of carnal desires and acts of worship, O captive of spiritual stations and mystic disclosures, you are deluded!"

Let me add that the captive of worship is someone who greatly admires his worship, his ritual prayer and his performance of duty. He expects illumination for himself and takes pride in his worship.

According to certain authorities, the dangers of expecting illumination reside in the fact that it sometimes happens when a seeker attains to a spiritual station his heart becomes deluded. It seems that he worships Allāh (Glory be to Him) for the sake of reaching the station, not for the love of Allāh, so the station becomes the aim and the goal. That is why some see the need for the presence of the perfect spiritual director to take the spiritual traveler by the hand, step by step, so that he may reach the stations without mistakes or afflictions.

It is incumbent on the spiritual traveler, whether or not he has a director, to cultivate two matters with care: (1) vigilant awareness of his faults in the course of his journey, so that his mistake is not repeated, and (2) his knowledge of what is owed to the Lord (Magnificent is His Majesty), like the duties of servitude and its proprieties, both external and internal.

19, 20. Annihilation [*Fanā'*] and Perpetuity [*Baqā'*]

These two are an ocean that has no shore and no limit to its profundity among the degrees of the men of Sufism, who are the only ones who know them by experience and speak about them.

According to Imām ar-Rabbānī in his *Maktūbāt* [Letters], "Annihilation [*fanā'*] is filled with false steps and exposed to accidents and changes, for it is, after all, an ocean that has no end." That is why some authorities do not accept all that has been claimed for annihilation, "The author of these sayings has not reached the ultimate degree of this station, and it is doubtful whether annihilation is really like that."

As we read in the book entitled *al-Qudsiyya*, by Shaikh Muḥammad al-Pārsā, which also contains the sayings of Shaikh an-Naqshband, "Shaikh Abū Sa'īd Aḥmad ibn 'Īsā al-Kharrāz (d. A.H. 277 or 279) was the first of those who spoke about perpetuity and annihilation." I have not found any indication of this in the other sources, but the contemporary researcher, Doctor 'Irfān 'Abd al-Ḥamīd, maintains that Abū Yazīd al-Bisṭāmī preceded him in the discussion of annihilation. My own view is that Abū Yazīd experienced the spiritual station himself, but did not speak about it, whereas al-Kharrāz did write about it.

According to Ibn al-'Arabī, "Perpetuity [*baqā'*] is close in meaning to *abadiyya* [eternity without end]." It is not opposite, however, to *azaliyya* [eternity without beginning]. It is opposite to the term *nafād* [dwindling away; coming to an end]. Allāh (Exalted is He) has said,

What is with you dwindles away,
mā 'inda-kum yanfadu
but what is with Allāh is permanent.
wa mā 'inda 'llāhi bāq. (16:96)[19]

It is clear to me that annihilation [*fanā'*] is of two kinds,

1. The first relates to the servant's own spiritual progress and it occurs as the result of his persistence in curbing the defiance of his lower self and purifying it by acts of worshipful obedience, and by eliminating serious flaws in his psychological and physical conduct. In similar fashion, the experience of perpetuity becomes manifest as the result of his ability to establish the praiseworthy qualities in place of the blameworthy attributes. It also appears as the result of his ability to adopt virtues, to avoid vices, to dispel the darkness from his heart, and to admit light into his breast. It depends on the extent to which he keeps his distance from Satan and draws near to the All-Merciful by forsaking this world and its pleasures while focusing entirely on the Truth to the point where love of the essence of the Truth distracts him completely from himself so that he sees nothing but his Lord.

When a man reaches this extreme and is cleansed of every evil, he has attained to the station of annihilation. By virtue of the righteousness and true devotion established in his heart, he has attained to the station of perpetuity. To put it another way, he has reached perpetuity through goodness, and he has reached annihilation through the abandonment of this world. He has also reached perfect contentment, which is the perpetuity of contentment and the annihilation of greedy desire. He has obtained a morsel of the bread of life, more nourishing than he had ever imagined.

2. The second kind of annihilation is a spiritual station and it is a Divine gift that is not earned by any number of remembrances and spiritual exercises practiced over a very long period of time. Someone may spend years of his life on this path without acquiring any part of it. There are some, according to the men of Sufism, who remain in the state of annihilation and do not pass beyond it to perpetuity.

---

19. *Ḥaqā'iq 'ani 't-taṣawwuf*, p. 321.

As we read in *ar-Risāla al-Qushairiyya*, "If someone abstains from this world with his heart, he is said to have become extinct to his desire. Then, when he has become extinct to his worldly desire, he survives in perpetuity through the truthfulness of his penitent reversion [*ināba*]." Where is the like of this person in whose heart remains nothing but the remembrance of his Lord? It is related that an individual once came to Abū Yazīd. Abū Yazīd asked him, "What are you seeking?" He said, "I am seeking Abū Yazīd." The latter replied, "Abū Yazīd! Who is Abū Yazīd? I am looking for him." That means that Abū Yazīd was in the state of annihilation.

No one can understand some of the ecstatic utterances that issue from the Sufi in this state, and they may be contrary to the Sacred Law. This irregularity gives rise to the suspicion that Sufi thought is incarnationist [*ḥulūlī*], or that it supports [the heretical doctrines of] existential monism [*waḥdat al-wujūd*] or pantheism [*ittiḥād*]. These shaikhs are quick to repent, however, as soon as they regain consciousness after their experience of the state of annihilation. That is why they ask of Allāh (Glory be to Him) that their experience of annihilation may be short and experience of perpetuity may be long-lasting. The fact is that annihilation is a stage not a dwelling as indicated by Mawlawī, the Kurdish Sufi poet, in his address to his Shaikh, Sarrāj ad-Dīn,

> O you who have passed beyond the stage of annihilation,
> and journeyed to an abode of yours in the land of perpetuity!

According to an-Naqshband, "They have said, 'Annihilation is the final stage on "the journey to Allāh," meaning the journey to contact with the Truth. As for perpetuity, it is the first stage in "the journey in Allāh," which means the attainment of the goal and the experience of the perfections of nearness.'" He then goes on to say, "The journey to Allāh cannot be completed unless the seeker rids himself of the interests of humanity, concentrates entirely on his Lord, and traverses the desert of life with the gait of sincerity and truthfulness until he reaches the intended Ka'ba." In other words, the seeker must rid his inner being of material and physical values so that he does not feel the pressure of natural existence in his life and his likeness is that of the drunkard or the sleeper. The poet says,

> Toward You, O my object of desire, is my pilgrimage and my visitation,
> while the pilgrimage of some folk is toward dust and stones.

Shaikh an-Naqshband also said, "The stage of the journey in Allāh with help from Allāh's light is realized after absolute annihilation, which is an expression for the annihilation of the attributes and the essence. That is, when Allāh blesses the seeker with real existence by which he will progress to the realm of the Divine qualities in the sense that he will be as Allāh loves him to be, in conduct and attributes. He will realize the Sacred Tradition,

> By Me he will hear,
> by Me he will speak,
> by Me he will see,
> by Me he will walk,
> and by Me he will comprehend.

"At this point he will be extinct to his attributes and his essence, and in this state he will enter into the sphere of Sufi attraction, for his heart will be attracted toward his Lord. The light of the Truth will shine in his breast and his likeness will be that of iron in the crucible of fire. For even though it does not lose the quality of iron, it acquires the quality of fire. The same applies to a stick of wood that is thrown into the fire. It turns into fire and then, after the extinction of the fire, the wood is no longer wood and the fire is no longer fire. The cause of that is the nearness of the fire, but the difference is that nearness here is not material, but means that there is an ineffable connection of the substance to the substance. It is a spiritual nearness, and its likeness is that of the annihilation of the parents in the love of their children. There is another difference here in that the transformation of iron into fire is a natural rather than a volitional action. The human being possesses volition and consciousness, so he wishes to obey his Lord and to be near to Him while seeking His good pleasure. Allāh (Exalted is He) has said,

> And prostrate yourself and draw near.
> *wa 'sjud wa 'qtarib.* (96:19)

> And We are nearer to him than the jugular vein.
> *wa Naḥnu aqrabu ilai-hi min ḥabli 'l-warīd.* (50.16)

"Material nearness is inconceivable here, because Allāh (Glory be to Him) is utterly devoid of physicality and spaciality.

> There is nothing like unto Him.
> *laisa ka-mithli-hi shai'.* (42:11)

"When they speak of annihilation and nearness they do not mean the material condition. I compare this state to the case of fire and iron and to the annihilation of the lover in his love. I also compare it to the nearness of the moon to the sun inasmuch as the result is realized if no obstacle like the earth comes between them. The same applies to spiritual connections.

"Whenever the servant contravenes the commandments of his Lord, separation enters his heart and distances him from the light of his Lord, so annihilation is not the annihilation of substance in substance, and the nearness is not the nearness of body to body. It is a spiritual nearness, not a physical bond."

Bahā' ad-Dīn an-Naqshband also had this to say, "Sufi attraction spreads its wings over the carpet of the servant's heart. It cleanses the seeker's heart of all temptations, so material sensitivities are annihilated and incinerated. Divine qualities alight in it, so he is left with no power over the affairs of his heart. He functions only in the radiance of the qualities that have settled in the abode of his heart. The sign of his truthfulness is that he applies the teachings of his Lord, so He keeps him safe (Exalted is He). If he contravenes those teachings, he has not experienced genuine annihilation."

That is indicated by the saying of Abū Sa'īd al-Kharrāz, "Whenever an inner state is contradicted by its outer state, it is false."

Bahā' ad-Dīn an-Naqshband then went on to say, "Those who truly experience perpetuity and annihilation enjoy the comfort of ecstasy and the delight of the meeting [with the Lord]. This is the ultimate aim, so they are left with no other aim. They do not seek spiritual status or charismatic talents, but consider them part of what intervenes between the servant and his Lord. They lose all physical appetites. This means that annihilation is a sign of the reality of love of the Essence and annihilation is an irreversible gift for the servant. It has been said in this context that 'He who experiences annihilation is one who does not return to his natural characteristics.'"

This means that the servant to whom Allāh has granted this station, and whose heart He has filled with these qualities will always be blissfully happy in both his worldly and his Otherworldly life. According to Dhū'n-Nūn al-Miṣrī, "He who turns back does not turn back except from [somewhere along] the path. Whatever point someone has reached [short of his destination], he may turn back therefrom. If someone is able to surmount the difficulties of the path, and he traverses the deserts and the valleys and reaches the destination, he becomes settled there, then he does not return." The noble Qur'ānic verse applies here.

> My servants, over them you have no power.
> *inna 'ibādī laisa la-ka 'alai-him sulṭān.* (17:65)

They are thereby delivered from the wiles of Satan. Otherwise, we are all servants of Allāh, whether we are willing or unwilling. Yet Satan deceives us in spite of that.

An-Naqshband refers to this in his saying, "When the servant's existence is annihilated, he does not return to human existence. Even though absolute annihilation is a Divine gift, it is realized gradually in keeping with his actions. This includes the servant's concentration on his Lord with all his energies with a concentration of the heart that keeps him at a distance from blameworthy attributes."

The purpose of this annihilation is the removal of the human aspect in the spiritual traveler, and the emergence within him of the real and spiritual aspects. Let us point once again to the iron that is heated by the fire so that it acquires certain attributes but does not lose its essential nature. As one expert has said, "You are a servant and you will never be like Him, but if you were to make a dedicated effort, you would become something for yourself."

He also said that "The intellect reaches its limit on the shores of the ocean of annihilation. On these shores and what lies beyond them, there are secrets perceptible only to the spiritual travelers in this domain among those whom Allāh has graciously favored." He also said, "This degree, called 'annihilation in Allāh and perpetuity with Allāh,' does not exempt the seeker from responsibility under the Sacred Law."

According to Ibrāhīm ash-Shaibānī, "The sign of annihilation and perpetuity is centered on the sincere affirmation of Divine Oneness and the genuineness of servitude. Everything apart from that consists of errors and atheism."

Some of them have spoken of "the annihilation of annihilation [*fanā' al-fanā'*]." This means that the spiritual traveler annihilates spiritual desire, just as he annihilates physical desire. He does not crave for a spiritual station or an Otherworldly reward. He becomes totally immersed in the Majesty of Allāh (Glory be to Him), so his mind and his lower self are annihilated, and his annihilation is annihilated.

When asked about the various kinds of annihilation, an-Naqshband said, "It has two kinds only, one of them being annihilation in the gloomy natural existence and the other being annihilation in the radiant spiritual existence. This is an allusion to the Prophetic tradition:

> Allāh has seventy thousand veils of light and darkness.

"In the sense that even though they number seventy thousand, they are still limited to two kinds only: light and darkness."

These two kinds are also indicated by the saying of one of the great figures of Sufism, "Two steps and you have arrived!"

According to an-Naqsband, "The veil is your existence. Leave yourself and come forth!" He also said, "The lover's meeting with the Beloved is realized after annihilation and perpetuity. When the meeting is achieved after annihilation and perpetuity, he will approach the Divine manifestation with ardent longing."

At this stage nothing affects him. Witnessing the Truth does not keep him away from creatures nor does mingling with people screen him from the Truth, for he is perpetual in annihilation and annihilated in perpetuity. At this point the spiritual traveler is in the station of "the journey in Allāh."

Shaikh Farīd ad-Dīn al-'Aṭṭār (d. A.H. 600) referred to this station in this sense, when he said, "You must adorn yourself with proper conduct, in order to traverse the path of the Lord of Truth and you must strive in His cause without weariness or boredom and without limit so that you may finally reach Him. Even if you drink an ocean, you will not quench your thirst and you will look for more."

Shaikh 'Abd ar-Raḥmān an-Naqshbandī composed an ode about this spiritual station,[20] which reads,

> I am astonished by a lover who said of the ardor of love,
> "It beginning is sweet and its end is bitter, hard to bear."
> Though I have become like the purity of wine, I cry,
> "O cupbearer, hand a glass around and let it circulate!"

As we read in the book *at-Ta'ārruf*, by Tāj al-Islam al-Kalābādhī,

> Annihilation means that the servant becomes extinct to all interests and preference departs from him. The perpetuity that follows in its wake means that he becomes extinct to what belongs to him

---

20. The descendant of Shaikh 'Uthmān Sarrāj ad-Dīn, one of the great scholars of Sufism.

> and survives perpetually with what belongs to Allāh.

He also said,

> According to some, "If all his movements are compatible with the Truth without confict, he is extinct to habitual contraventions and to his own qualities. He is perpetually surviving with the qualities of the Truth."

According to al-Kalābādhī, "The annihilation of annihilation is becoming extinct to the veneration of everything apart from Allāh, and perpetuity in the veneration of Allāh." According to Abū Sa'īd al-Kharrāz, "The sign of someone who experiences annihilation is the loss of his interest in this world and the Hereafter apart from his interest in Allāh (Exalted is He)." He then goes on to say, "There are some who class these spiritual states as one, even though their acts of worship are different. They consider annihilation to be the same as perpetuity and integration." The real experts, including al-Junaid, al-Kharrāz, an-Nūrī and an-Naqshband, do not hold that view. According to al-Qushairī, "Annihilation is the shedding of blameworthy qualities, while perpetuity is the maintenance of praiseworthy qualities."

The following is the gist of what the scholars of Sufism have mentioned on the subject of annihilation and perpetuity.[21] For the saint and anyone endowed with intimate knowledge of Allāh, it is important to recognize both distinction and integration, along with singularity and multiplicity, all four being Sufi technical terms. It is essential to distinguish between that which Allāh loves and has therefore commanded and what He does not love and has therefore prohibited. This is the meaning of distinction. The meaning of singularity signifies the Uniqueness of Allāh (Glory be to Him). Multiplicity signifies the plurality of His attributes (Glory be to Him). If someone has true knowledge, he believes in Allāh, the Unique, the One, and His attributes. This is the meaning of multiplicity in singularity. Integration is believing that everything that happens does so by the decree of Allāh and His foreordainment.

As we read in the book *Madārij as-sālikīn*, "The highest of the degrees of love is the union of the will of the lover with the will of

---

21. See the relevant sections in: *Madārij as-sālikīn wa Manāzil as-sā'irīn*, *Mu'jam muṣṭalaḥāt aṣ-ṣūfiyya* and *Alfāẓ aṣ-ṣūfiyya*.

the Beloved and the annihilation of the will of the lover in the will of the Beloved. None advance to that degree except the special few. These are people who are annihilated in worshipful obedience to Allāh (Glory be to Him), who love for the sake of Allāh and hate for His sake, who pin their hopes on their Lord Alone, and who fear none other than Him."

The reality of this annihilation is the annihilation of the self for the sake of His good pleasure (Glory be to Him). Its fruit is the realization of the meaning of, "There is no god but Allāh [*lā ilāha illa 'llāh*]."

The meaning of annihilation and perpetuity is implicit in the negation and affirmation of, "There is no god but Allāh [*lā ilāha illa 'llāh*]." That is because the expression "There is no god [*lā ilāha*]" annihilates the worship of anything, while the expression "but Allāh [*illa 'llāh*]" signifies the perpetuity of worship for Allāh Alone.

As we read in the book *Alfāẓ aṣ-ṣūfiyya*, "Annihilation and perpetuity are inseparable. Each of them perfects the other. If someone forsakes the interests of this world, he has annihilated his worldly existence. He lives by honesty and the Truth and this is perpetuity. If someone is controlled by reality, he will always be honest with his Lord. He is extinct to creatures, perpetually devoted to the Truth."

As we read in *Mu'jam muṣṭalaḥāt aṣ-ṣūfiyya*, "Annihilation is the replacement of human attributes by the Divine attributes, so that a man becomes such that 'the Truth is his hearing and his sight,' as stated in the Prophetic tradition."

The sign of the genuineness of this annihilation is the abandonment of reliance on people for the sake of this world, and placing absolute trust in Allāh Alone.

Annihilation, as we have mentioned, is of two kinds: (1) The first kind is a gracious favor from Allāh and a gift which He grants to whomever He will. (2) The second kind is the earnest endeavor of the servant to reach this spiritual station. It is completed by the adoption of praiseworthy qualities and by abandonment of all blameworthy attributes. The servant thus alights as a guest in the stopping place of annihilation. Then his Lord sets him down in the abode of perpetuity. He enters among the saintly friends of Allāh upon whom there is no fear and who do not grieve. That is a gracious favor from Allāh, which He grants to whomever He will.

21. The Affirmation of Oneness [*Tawḥīd*]

That is to say, the belief that Allāh is Single [*Wāḥid*], One [*Aḥad*], Unique [*Fard*], Eternally Self-Sustaining [*Ṣamad*], and there is nothing like Him.

The noble Messenger (Allāh bless him and give him peace) was asked about the attributes of his Lord, so the following Qur'ānic verse was revealed.

> Say, "He is Allāh, One!
> *qul Huwa 'llāhu Aḥad:*
> Allāh, the Eternally Self-Sustaining!
> *Allāhu 'ṣ-Ṣamad:*
> He does not beget, nor was He begotten;
> *lam yalid wa lam yūlad:*
> and there is none comparable unto Him."
> *wa lam yakun la-hu kufuwan aḥad.* (112:1–4)

The affirmation of Oneness is made by saying, "There is no god but Allāh [*lā ilāha illa 'llāh*]," while truly believing it in your heart. It is contradicted by polytheism [*shirk*], unbelief [*kufr*] and atheism [*ilḥād*].

The term *kufr* has several meanings, including concealment [*satr*] and ingratitude [*kufrān an-ni'ma*]. The term shirk means treating someone or an idol as a partner with Allāh in worship. It likewise signifies belief in the ability of the intermediary per se to assist the human being in this world or in the Hereafter. It also applies to hypocritical ostentation [*riyā'*] in worship, as when someone's worship is performed for the sake of acquiring good reputation [*sum'a*].

Frequently would-be Sufis and claimants to the Spiritual Path repeat supplications in which help is sought from the righteous. They say, for example, "O Shaikh…, O resting place of the Shaikh…, grant me a son," or "Deliver me!" This appears on the surface to be a flagrant form of unbelief and a case of attributing partners to Allāh. The supplicant is exonerated, however, since he has turned to him [the Shaikh] because he is one of the righteous servants of Allāh, so his supplication will be answered in the presence of Allāh. Nevertheless, this is a very serious slip, for the Muslim is obliged to be extremely careful of his faith, devoting his complete attention to it when visiting the righteous, be they among the living or the dead. He must be on his guard against the notion of idolatry, so that the feeling of love for his Shaikh does not lead him into the realm of polytheism and deviation.

As for atheism [*ilḥād*], it is the denial of the existence of Allāh the Creator (Glory be to Him). Some of the children of Adam still suppose that this universe came into being by chance, without an intelligent purpose, and that it has no Mover but simply moves by its own nature. At the same time as finding it incomprehensible that a nail or a peg could be produced without a craftsman, they accept the idea that the wondrous and marvelous human being is created by chance, without a Maker in charge. Humankind would be astonished and amazed, saying, "How could television or airplanes be produced without a maker or a factory?" Yet they refuse to believe that the maker of the television or the airplane has a Creator, and they say that the human being was produced by chance, without a Creator!

The affirmation of Oneness [*Tawḥīd*] is the assertion with the tongue and the attestation with the heart's core that Allāh is Single [*Wāḥid*]—"There is no god but Allāh [*lā ilāha illa'llāh*]." It is also belief in His Names, for He has ninety-nine Names, and it is likewise belief in His attributes. Some of these are peculiar to Allāh alone, like *al-Khāliq* [the Creator], *al-Muḥyī wa 'l-Mumīt* [the Giver of Life and the Cause of Death], *al-Mubdi' wa 'l-Mu'īd* [the Initiator and the Restorer], and *'Ālim al-Ghaib* [the Knower of the Unseen]. Some of them are attributes of which the meanings are realized in the human being, within the context of their human significance. There is an important distinction to be drawn here with regard to an expression like "the Lord of the thing [*Rabb ash-shai'*]," since the Lordship of Allāh has a meaning that is entirely different from what is meant by the statement that the human being is "a lord of his house [*rabban li-dārih*]," for Allāh is Everlasting, Ever-Living, whereas the human being is impermanent and sure to die. The same applies to the attributes *as-Sakhī/sakhī* [the Generous/generous] and *al-Karīm/karīm* [the Noble/noble].

The affirmation of Oneness [*tawḥīd*] therefore has an extensive meaning, which includes the confirmation of the existence of the Creator, the Lord of All the Worlds, the assertion that He is Single, One, and the attestation that there is nothing like Him in His Essence and His attributes.

The Noble Qur'ān contains numerous verses [*āyāt*] on the subject of the affirmation of Oneness, of which thirty-six are mentioned in the Sufi Lexicon [*al-Mu'jam aṣ-Sufi*], by transmission from Shaikh Muḥyi'd-dīn ibn al-'Arabī. These noble verses are the following,

1. And your God is One God.
   wa Ilāhu-kum Ilāhun Wāḥid:
   There is no god but He, the All Merciful, the All-Compassionate.
   lā ilāha illā Huwa 'r-Raḥmānu 'r-Raḥīm. (2:163)

2. Allāh! There is no god but He, the Ever-Living, the Eternal.
   Allāhu lā ilāha illā Huwa 'l-Ḥayyu 'l-Qayyūm. (2:255)

3. *Alif Lām Mīm.*
   Alif–Lām–Mīm:
   Allāh! There is no god but He, the Ever-Living, the Eternal.
   Allāhu lā ilāha illā Huwa 'l-Ḥayyu 'l-Qayyūm. (3:1,2)

4. There is no god but He, the Almighty, the All-Wise.
   lā ilāha illā Huwa 'l-'Azīzu 'l-Ḥakīm. (3:6)

5. Allāh bears witness that there is no god but He—and [so do]
   shahida 'llāhu anna-hu lā ilāha illā Huwa
   the angels and the men of learning—upholding justice.
   wa 'l-malā'ikatu wa ulū 'l-'ilmi qā'iman bi'l-qisṭ. (3:18)

6. Allāh, there is no god but He.
   Allāhu lā ilāha illā Hū:
   He will surely gather you all to the Day of Resurrection.
   la-yajma'anna-kum ilā Yawmi 'l-Qiyāmati. (4:87)

7. Follow what is inspired in you from your Lord;
   ittabi' mā ūḥiya ilai-ka min Rabbi-k:
   there is no god but He;
   lā ilāha illā Hū:
   and turn away from the idolaters.
   wa a'riḍ 'ani 'l-mushrikīn. (6:106)

8. There is no god but He. He quickens and He causes death.
   lā ilāha illā Huwa yuḥyī wa yumīt. (7:158)

9. And they were commanded to worship only One God.
   wa mā umirū illā li-ya'budū Ilāhan Wāḥidā:
   There is no god but He. Glory be to Him
   lā ilāha illā Hū: subḥāna-hu
   above what they ascribe as partners!
   'ammā yushrikūn. (9:31)

10. So if they turn their backs, say, "Allāh is enough for me.
fa-in tawallaw fa-qul ḥasbiya 'llāhu
There is no god but He. In Him I have put my trust,
lā ilāha illā Hū, 'alai-hi tawakkaltu
and He is the Lord of the Mighty Throne."
wa Huwa Rabbu 'l-'arshi 'l-'aẓīm. (9:129)

11. Till, when the drowning overtook them, he exclaimed,
Ḥattā idhā adraka-hu 'l-gharaqu qāla
"I believe that there is no god
āmantu anna-hu lā Ilāha
but He in whom the Children of Israel believe."
ila 'lladhī āmanat bi-hi Banū Isrā'īla. (10:90)

12. Then know that it is revealed only in the knowledge of Allāh;
fa-''lamū anna-mā unzila bi-'ilmi 'llāh
and that there is no god but He.
wa allā ilāha illā Hū:
So will you be of those who surrender?
fa-hal antum muslimūn. (11:14)

13. And they are disbelievers in the All-Merciful.
wa hum yakfurūna bi'r-Raḥmān:
Say, "He is my Lord; there is no god but He.
qul Huwa Rabbī lā ilāha illā Hū:
In Him I have put my trust, and unto Him I must turn."
'alai-hi tawakkaltu wa ilai-hi matāb. (13:30)

14. Warn that there is no god but I,
an andhirū anna-hu lā ilāha illā Ana
so practice true devotion to Me.
fa-'ttaqūn. (16:2)

15. He surely knows the secret and that which is more deeply hidden.
fa-inna-hu ya'lamu 's-sirra wa akhfā.
Allāh! There is no god but He.
Allāhu lā ilāha illā Hū.
His are the Most Beautiful Names.
la-hu 'l-asmā'u 'l-ḥusnā. (20:7,8)

16. And I have chosen you, so listen to what is inspired.
wa Ana 'khtartu-ka fa-'stami' li-mā yuwḥā.
I am indeed Allāh; there is no god but I;
innī Ana 'llāhu lā ilāha illā Ana

therefore worship Me,
fa-'bud-nī. (20:13,14)

17. Your God is only Allāh, other than Whom there is no god.
inna-mā Ilāhu-kumu 'llāhu 'lladhī lā ilāha illā Hū:
He embraces all things in His knowledge.
wasi'a kulla shai'in 'ilmā. (20:98)

18. And We sent no Messenger before you but We inspired him,
wa mā arsalnā min qabli-ka min Rasūlin illā nūḥī ilai-hi
"There is no god but I, so worship Me.'
anna-hu lā ilāha illā Ana fa-'budū-n. (21:25)

19. And Dhū 'n-Nūn—when he went forth enraged
wa Dhā 'n-Nūni idh dhahaba mughāḍiban
and thought that We would have no power over him;
fa-ẓanna an lan naqdira 'alai-hi
then he called out in the darkness, "There is no god but You.
fa-nādā fi 'ẓ-ẓulumāti an lā ilāha illā Anta
Glory be to You! I have been an evildoer."
subḥāna-ka innī kuntu mina 'ẓ-ẓālimīn. (21:87)

20. Now Allāh be Exalted, the True King!
fa-ta'āla 'llāhu Maliku 'l-Ḥaqq:
There is no god but He, the Lord of the Noble Throne.
lā ilāha illā Hū: Rabbu 'l-'Arshi 'l-Karīm. (23:116)

21. Allāh, there is no god but He,
Allāhu lā ilāha illā Huwa
the Lord of the Mighty Throne.
Rabbu 'l-'Arshi 'l-'Aẓīm. (27:26)

22. And He is Allāh; there is no god but He.
wa Huwa 'llāhu lā ilāha illā Hū:
His is all praise in the former and the latter,
la-hu 'l-ḥamdu fi 'l-ūlā wa 'l-ākhira:
and His is the command, and to Him you will be returned.
wa la-hu 'l-ḥukmu wa ilai-hi turja'ūn. (28:70)

23. And do not cry to any other god along with Allāh.
wa lā tad'u ma'a 'llāhi ilāhan ākhar:
There is no god but He. Everything will perish
lā ilāha illā Hū: kullu shai'in hālikun

but His countenance.
illā Wajhah. (28:88)

24. Is there any creator, apart from Allāh,
hal min khāliqin ghairu 'llāhi
who provides for you from the heaven and earth?
yarzuqu-kum mina 's-samā'i wa 'l-arḍ.
There is no god but He.
lā ilāha illā Hū. (35:3)

25. When it was said to them,
inna-hum kānū idhā qīla la-hum
"There is no god but Allāh," they were scornful.
lā ilāha illa 'llāhu yastakbirūn. (37:35)

26. Such is Allāh, your Lord. His is the Sovereignty.
dhālikumu 'llāhu Rabbu-kum la-hu 'l-mulk:
There is no god but He.
lā ilāha illā Hū. (39:6)

27. The Stern in punishment, the Bountiful.
Shadīdi 'l-'iqābi Dhī 'ṭ-Ṭawl:
There is no god but He. Unto Him is the homeward journey.
lā ilāha illā Hū: ilai-hi 'l-maṣīr. (40:3)

28. Such is Allāh, your Lord, the Creator of all things.
dhālikumu 'llāhu Rabbu-kum Khāliqu kulli shai':
There is no god but He. How then are you perverted?
lā ilāha illā Hū: fa-annā tu'fakūn. (40:62)

29. He is the Ever-Living One. There is no god but He,
Huwa 'l-Ḥayyu lā ilāha illā Huwa
so pray to Him, making religion pure for Him.
fa-'d'ū-hu mukhliṣīna la-hu 'd-dīn:
Praise be to Allāh, the Lord of the Worlds!
al-ḥamdu li'llāhi Rabbi 'l-'Ālamīn. (40:65)

30. There is no god but He. He quickens and He causes death;
lā ilāha illā Huwa yuḥyī wa yumīt:
your Lord and the Lord of your forefathers.
Rabbu-kum wa Rabbu ābā'i-kumu 'l-awwalīn. (44:8)

31. So know that there is no god but Allāh,
fa-''lam anna-hu lā ilāha illa 'llāhu

and ask forgiveness for your sin,
wa 'staghfir li-dhanbi-ka
and for the believing men and the believing women.
wa li'l-mu'minīna wa 'l-mu'mināt. (47:19)

32. He is Allāh; there is no god but He, the King, the Holy One.
Huwa 'llāhu 'lladhī lā ilāha illā Hū: al-Maliku 'l-Quddūsu. (59:23)

33. Allāh! There is no god but He.
Allāhu lā ilāha illā Hū:
In Allāh, therefore, let the believers put their trust.
wa 'ala 'llāhi fa-yatawakkali 'l-mu'minūn. (64:13)

34. Lord of the East and the West;
Rabbu 'l-mashriqi wa 'l-maghribi lā ilāha
there is no god but He, so choose Him as a Guardian.
illā Huwa fa-'ttakhidh-hu Wakīlā. (73:9)

35. Such is Allāh, your Lord. There is no god but He,
dhālikumu 'llāhu Rabbu-kum: lā ilāha illā Hū:
the Creator of all things, so worship Him.
Khāliqu kulli shai'in fa-''budū-h. (6:102)

36. He is Allāh, other than Whom there is no god,
Huwa 'llāhu 'lladhī lā ilāha illā Hū:
the Knower of the Unseen and the Visible.
'Ālimu 'l-ghaibi wa 'sh-shahāda:
He is the All-Merciful, the All-Compassionate.
Huwa 'r-Raḥmānu 'r-Raḥīm. (59:22)

The Noble Qur'ān is the book of the affirmation of Divine Oneness [*at-tawḥīd al-Ilāhī*], and that affirmation is the hallmark of the true Islamic religion. Jurists, the leaders of the schools of legal doctrine [*madhāhib*] and theologians have endeavored to explain the Names of Allāh and His attributes in order to ascertain the meaning of Singularity [*Waḥdāniyya*] and to dispel all doubts concerning this Qur'ānic Reality.

The signal of this hallmark is, "There is no god but Allāh [*lā ilāha illa 'llāh*]." This statement has a very great impact, both spiritual and faith-related, on the personalities of the Muslims. In the domain of Sufism, this momentous statement has a special taste.

As we have explained, the basis of Sufism is constant commitment to the remembrance of Allāh (Glory be to Him), by which we mean [the recollection expressed by declaring] "Allāh!" or "*lā ilāha illa 'llāh!*" The term "remembrance [*dhikr*]" has come to be used in the sense of reciting the Qur'ān, performing the ritual prayer, engaging in contemplation, and so on. The meaning here, in the sphere of Sufism, is "Allāh!" or "*lā ilāha illa 'llāh!*" in the sense of the affirmation of Oneness. Remembrance as the affirmation of Oneness is called "the remembrance of negation and affirmation [*dhikr an-nafy wa'l-ithbāt*]," in the sense that the expression "*lā ilāha* [There is no god]" signifies negation, whereas the expression "*illa 'llāh* [but Allāh]" signifies affirmation.

The matter is not exhausted by this simple explanation. It involves a special procedure, which we shall deal with fully under the heading "Remembrance [*Dhikr*]."

In short, when the servant says, "*lā ilāha* [There is no god]," it is essential for him to focus his attention, his mind and his feelings entirely on the fact that there is none worthy of worship, and no one whose existence is eternal [*azalī*] and everlasting [*abadī*] except Allāh. He must continue to repeat "Allāh!" millions of times until the spiritual traveler and seeker becomes annihilated. This annihilation [*fanā'*] is called "annihilation in negation and affirmation." In this state, since everything is annihilated apart from Allāh [*siwa 'llāh*], certain secrets of the Unseen become manifest in presence of the servant. Blessings are showered upon him from the gracious favor of Allāh.

It may happen that someone loses consciousness in this state. Then he says things beyond the scope of reason and the Sacred Law and is therefore suspected of heresies like *ḥulūl* [incarnation of the Deity], *ittiḥād* [pantheism] and *waḥdat al-wujūd* [existential monism]. Nothing of this kind is inherent in this spiritual state, which is properly described as the state of annihilation [*ḥāl al-fanā'*]. The servant will soon return to his consciousness, to present awareness, and to the state of perpetuity in Allāh [*al-baqā' bi'llāh*].

The lordly Imām Shaikh Aḥmad al-Fārūqī, whose lofty station in Sufism comes after that of Shaikh Muḥammad Bahā' ad-Dīn Naqshband in the Naqshbandī Spiritual Path, is known as the Renewer of the Second [*Hijrī*] Millenium. He is the author of a Sufi treatise on the state of annihilation in the affirmation of Oneness and his writings contain appropriate advice for those who experience this state or who seek to pursue it. We are interested in knowing what Sufism is, not in learning how we may become Sufis. The affirmation of Oneness is the highest of the stations of Sufism. All spiritual stations and blessings are derived from the affirmation of Oneness.

There are some who speak of *tawḥīd al-Ulūhiyya* [affirmation of the Oneness of Divinity], *tawḥīd ar-Rubūbiyya* [affirmation of the Oneness of Lordship], and *tawḥīd al-'ubūdiyya* [affirmation of the Oneness of servitude]. *Tawḥīd al-Ulūhiyya* means the affirmation of the Singularity of the Essence of Allāh (Glory be to Him). *Tawḥīd ar-Rubūbiyya* means the belief that there is no Creator, no Provider, no Giver of Life and no Cause of Death, except Allāh. *Tawḥīd al-'ubūdiyya* means the worshipful service of Allāh Alone, surrender to Him Alone, and trust in Him Alone.

The shaikhs of Sufism have numerous sayings about the meaning of the affirmation of Oneness. Each of them has described the spiritual state that he knew from his own experience.

22, 23 Disengagement [*Tajrīd*] and Segregation [*Tafrīd*]

The term *tajrīd* [disengagement] signifies the expulsion of nonessentials. The term *tafrīd* [segregation] is derived from *fard* [separate, alone], which occurs in the Qur'ānic verse,

> "My Lord, do not leave me alone [without offspring],
> *Rabbi lā tadhar-nī fardan*
> though You are the Best of inheritors."
> *wa Anta Khairu 'l-wārithīn.* (21:89)

In the technical language of Sufism, these are two special terms for certain modalities experienced by the traveler on the path of Sufism comparable to *tawḥīd* [affirmation of Divine Oneness] and *tanzīh* [incomparability]. They represent the spiritual stations of the saints who have passed beyond the stage of annihilation [*fanā'*], and whose journey has brought them to rest in the harbor of perpetuity [*baqā'*]. Blessings descend upon them by gracious favor from Allāh (Glory be to Him) and through earnest endeavor on their part in the prayer-niche of servitude to Him.

According to the author of the book entitled *Madārij as-sālikīn*, disengagement [*tajrīd*] and segregation [*tafrīd*] belong in the category of annihilation and perpetuity. He has said, "Annihilation and perpetuity constitute the reality of the affirmation of Oneness, innocence and sainthood, elimination and verification, disengagement and segregation." He has also said, "[When the spiritual traveler has experienced annihilation and perpetuity] he is abstracted from the worship of anything apart from Him, and he segregates Him Alone for worshipful service. Disengagement is a negation and segregation is an affirmation.The two combined are the affirmation of Oneness." He has then gone on to say, "The people worthiest of Allāh, His messengers, His Books and His religion are those who can reconcile distinction with integration. They uphold the distinction between what Allāh loves and what He hates, between what He commands and what He forbids, and between those He treats as friends and those He treats as foes. They do so in knowledge and testimony, intention and action, while bearing witness to the integration of all in His decree, His foreordainment, and His all-comprehensive will. They believe in reality, both religious and existential, and they give each reality its due share of worshipful service. The due share of religious reality is compliance with His commandment and His prohibition, love of what He loves and hatred of what He hates, friendship for those He befriends and hostility toward those He treats with hostility. The basis is love for His sake and hatred for His sake. The due share of existential reality is segregating Him by needing Him exclusively, seeking help from Him exclusively, trusting Him exclusively, and taking refuge with Him exclusively. This means begging and asking of Him exclusively and humbly submitting to Him exclusively. It means acknowledging that whatever He wills comes to be, whatever He does not will does not come to be, and no one apart from Him has any power to cause harm or benefit or death or life or resurrection."

As we read in *al-Mu'jam aṣ-ṣūfī*, "Segregation [*tafrīd*] is a stage reached by the spiritual traveler after disengagement [*tajrīd*]. When the spiritual traveler disengages from the cosmos and everything else from his heart and his innermost being, he segregates the One."

As we read in *al-Luma'*, "Segregation [*tafrīd*] means singling out the singular [*ifrād al-mufrad*] by removing the incidental, and singling out the eternal by discovering the realities of singularity [*fardāniyya*]. According to some, 'Among the believers, those who affirm the Oneness of Allāh are many. Among those who affirm His Oneness, however, there are few who segregate Him for exclusive devotion.' As for disengagement [*tajrīd*], it signifies the Divine disclosures that are disengaged for the heart, once it is purified and free from human turbidity."[22]

As defined by one of the experts,[23] "Disengagement [*tajrīd*] is the freedom of the servant's heart and innermost being from everything apart from Allāh, in the sense that he is outwardly detached from nonessentials and inwardly detached from compensations. In other words, he does not take anything from the triviality of this world nor does he seek any immediate or future recompense for what he has abandoned. His conduct is in accordance with his duty to Allāh (Exalted is He), not for any other cause or reason. He is detached in his innermost being from paying attention to the stations at which he arrives and the spiritual states he experiences. He does not settle in or cling to them. Segregation [*tafrīd*] means that his actions are for the sake of Allāh Alone without any hypocritical display or desire for good reputation. He is not afraid of anyone but Allāh and he rejoices only in His nearness (Glory be to Him). According to a well-known definition, "Segregation [*tafrīd*] means that you are not possessed and disengagement [*tajrīd*] means that you do not possess."

As we read in the book *Alfāẓ aṣ-ṣūfiyya*, "Segregation [*tafrīd*] means that the servant is with his Lord, trusting in Him Alone. Disengagement [*tajrīd*] means complete detachment from this world. Righteous conduct is not for the sake of reward or recompense, neither in the present nor in the future. It is the absence of the heart's preoccupation with spiritual states and stations or with the quest for more of them. It is cleansing the lower self of these concerns and making it content with whatever state or station Allāh wishes for the servant." The author has then gone on to say, "Segregation [*tafrīd*] is the affirmation of Allāh's Singularity (Glory be to Him), and disengagement [*tajrīd*] means that the human being is detached from seeking anything."

As we also read in that same book, "Segregation [*tafrīd*], disengagement [*tajrīd*] and the affirmation of Oneness [*tawḥīd*] are synonyms with only one meaning. Whatever fine and subtle difference there may be between them, it is known only by someone who has tasted the delicious fruits of these spiritual stations and has experienced the nourishment peculiar to each one of them.

---

22. *al-Luma'*, p. 425.
23. *Mu'jam muṣṭalaḥāt aṣ-ṣūfiyya*, p. 41.

24. Affirmation of Divine Incomparability [*Tanzīh*]

The term *tanzīh* has a subtle meaning in Sufism, different from its meaning in the ordinary Arabic language. It stands in contrast to *tashbīh* [attribution of similarity]. Allāh (Exalted is He) has said,

> There is nothing like unto Him.
> *laisa ka-mithli-hi shai'*. (42:11)

Tanzīh [affirmation of Divine Incomparability] bears a close resemblance to *tawḥīd* [affirmation of Divine Oneness], *tajrīd* [disengagement] and *tafrīd* [segregation]. *Tanzīh* does not have only one form, just like there is a difference between the *tawḥīd* of a righteous servant and that of an unrighteous servant.

In the present context, the meaning of *tanzīh* is the belief that Allāh (Glory be to Him) is Incomparable [*Munazzah*] to phenomena, for He is Eternal [*Qadīm*] and Necessarily Existing [*Wājib al-wujūd*], Eternal-without-beginning [*Azalī*] and Eternal-without-end [*Abadī*]:

> He is the First and the Last, the Outer and the Inner.
> *Huwa 'l-Awwalu wa 'l-Ākhiru wa 'ẓ-Ẓāhiru wa 'l-Bāṭin*. (57:3)

> There is nothing like unto Him,
> *laisa ka-mithli-hi shai'*
> and He is the All-Hearing, the All-Seeing.
> *wa Huwa 's-Samī'u 'l-Baṣīr*. (42:11)

Allāh is a Living Being who never dies, whereas we are transitory, so we come as communities and individuals, then away we go and not one of us will remain after a century from now.

Several noble Qur'ānic verses have been revealed concerning the affirmation of Allāh's Incomparability, for He has said (Glory be to Him):

> Glory be to your Lord, the Lord of Majesty,
> *subḥāna Rabbi-ka Rabbi 'l-'Izzati*
> far from what they attribute!
> *'ammā yaṣifūn*. (37:180)

> He does not beget, nor was He begotten,
> *lam yalid wa lam yūlad*:
> and there is none comparable unto Him.
> *wa lam yakun la-hu kufuwan aḥad*. (112:3,4)

The Noble Qur'ān has clearly stated that Allāh (Glory be to Him) is All-Knowing, All-Hearing, All-Seeing, but we do not comprehend the true significance of these Divine attributes. We must therefore profess these convictions with the meaning appropriate to His Essence (Glory be to Him). That is the meaning of *tanzīh*, because it is the affirmation of these convictions in the heart of the spiritual traveler, and the conviction that Allāh (Glory be to Him) is Incomparable to human attributes. It is absurd for us comprehend the meanings of His Divine attributes within the limits of human experience, not in their Divine reality.

25. Servitude [*'Ubūdiyya*]

In its ordinary linguistic meaning, servitude [*'ubūdiyya*] applies to the righteous [*ṣāliḥ*] and the unrighteous [*āliḥ*], to the believer [*mu'min*] and the unbeliever [*kāfir*]. The believer is someone who adopts the path of faith, and the Muslim is someone who embraces the true religion. As for the servant, his servitude is realized by his very existence, whether he is willing or unwilling to accept the fact.

In Sufism, however, servitude ascends to the rank of a great spiritual station. That is because, according to the Sufis, the true meaning of servitude is realized by the fulfillment of Allāh's commandments (Glory be to Him). The nouns "servant [*'abd*]" and "servants [*'ibād*]" and the imperative verb "serve/worship [*u'bud*]" occur in more than two hundred places in the Noble Qur'ān.

Sufi servitude embraces all the spiritual states and stations because it is realized in every aspect of servitude to Allāh (Glory be to Him) like abstinence, absolute trust, contentment, and so on.

Proofs of the loftiness of this station include the fact that Allāh (Glory be to Him) ascribes it to His Prophets and His Messengers. He describes them as,

> How excellent a servant!
> *ni'ma 'l-'abd.* (38:30)

With reference to our master Muḥammad (Allāh bless him and give him peace), He has said (Glory be to Him),

> Glory be to the One who carried His servant by night
> *subḥāna 'lladhī asrā bi-'abdi-hi lailan.* (17:1)

> And He revealed to His servant that which He revealed.
> *fa-awḥā ilā 'abdi-hi mā awḥā.* (53:10)

> He has revealed the Book to His servant.
> *anzala 'alā 'abdi-hi 'l-Kitāba.* (18:1)

Whenever Satan threatens the human being with delusion and error, Allāh (Glory be to Him) says to the Devil,

> My servants, over them you have no power.
> *inna 'ibādī laisa la-ka 'alai-him sulṭān.* (17:65)

He has also said (Glory be to Him), when describing the righteous:

> Those who turn in repentance, those who serve.
> *at-tā'ibūna 'l-'ābidūna.* (9:112)

> The earth shall be the inheritance of My righteous servants.
> *anna 'l-arḍa yarithu-hā 'ibādiya 'ṣ-ṣāliḥūn.* (21:105)

From this it is clear that there is a vast difference between one kind of servitude and another. In his *Risāla*,[24] Imām al-Qushairī has transmitted the sayings of prominent figures of Sufism on the subject of servitude. He has said, "I heard the professor, Abū 'Alī ad-Daqqāq (may Allāh bestow His mercy upon him), say, 'Servitude [*'ubūdiyya*] is more complete than service [*'ibāda*]. First comes service [*'ibāda*], then servitude [*'ubūdiyya*], then servanthood [*'ubūda*]. Service is practiced by the common folk among the believers, while servitude is peculiar to the *élite*, and servanthood is peculiar to the *élite* of the *élite*.' I also heard him say, 'Service is peculiar to someone who has the knowledge of certainty, while servitude is peculiar to someone who has the essence of certainty. Servanthood is peculiar to someone who has the truth of certainty.' He also said, 'Servanthood is forsaking the freedom of choice.'"

According to Dhū 'n-Nūn al-Miṣrī, "Servitude means that you are His servant in every situation, just as He is your Lord in every situation." According to al-Jarīrī, "The servants of benefits are many in number, but servants of the Benefactor are rarely to be found." Allāh's Messenger (Allāh bless him and give him peace) once said:

> Perish the servant of the gold coin!
> Perish the servant of the fancy gown!

According to 'Abdullāh ibn Manāzil, "The servant is a servant as long as he does not seek a servant for himself. If he seeks a servant for himself, he has fallen from the category of servitude and abandoned

24. *ar-Risāla al-Qushairiyya*, p. 91.

his proper modes of conduct." As it has also been said, "Servitude is the acknowledgment of Lordship."

As we read in the book *Alfāẓ aṣ-ṣūfiyya*, "The men of Sufism use the word 'servant [*'abd*]' with reference to the station of servitude [*'ubūdiyya*], and the word 'Lord [*Rabb*]' with reference to the station of Lordship [*Rubūbiyya*]. Servitude is peculiar to the righteous servants of Allāh. If Allāh (Glory be to Him) wishes to endow His servant with the blessing of servitude, he raises him toward Himself and frees him from the clutches of his carnal desires. The servant is then transported to blessings and spiritual delights, the likes of which no human heart can imagine, so he forgets himself and remembers only his Lord." This is what is meant by His saying (Exalted is He):

> How excellent a servant! He was ever turning in repentance.
> *ni'ma 'l-'abd: inna-hu awwāb.* (38:30)

The genuine servant is one whose heart is free from everything apart from Allāh (Almighty and Glorious is He). Someone like that is worthy of being a servant to Allāh, as we are told in the Noble Qur'ān in connection with Jesus (peace be upon him),

> He said, "I am the servant of Allāh.
> *qāla innī 'abdu 'llāh:*
> He has given me the Book and has appointed me a prophet."
> *ātā-niya 'l-Kitāba wa ja'ala-nī Nabiyyā.* (19:30)

Allāh (Exalted is He) has not called the believers by any finer name than "servant," for He says,

> Nay, but they are honored servants.
> *bal 'ibādun mukramūn.* (21:26)

He has also called His prophets and His messengers (peace be upon them) by that name, for He says,

> And mention Our servants Abraham, Isaac, and Jacob.
> *wa 'dhkur 'ibāda-nā Ibrāhīma wa Isḥāqa wa Ya'qūba.* (38:45)

> And remember Our servant David.
> *wa 'dhkur 'abda-na Dawuda.* (38:17)

The feet of Allāh's Messenger used to become swollen from standing so often at night, so he was asked (Allāh bless him and give him peace), "O Messenger of Allāh, is it not sure that Allāh has forgiven you for both your former and your later sins?" He replied,

> Should I not be a very thankful servant?

He also said (Allāh bless him and give him peace),

> I was given the choice between being a prophet-king and a prophet-servant, so I chose to be a prophet-servant.[25]

As we read in *Mu'jam muṣṭalaḥāt aṣ-ṣūfiyya*, "Servanthood [*'ubūda*] is service [*'ibāda*] to Him (Exalted is He) inspired by reverence, awe, a sense of shame before Him and love for Him. It ranks higher than servitude [*'ubūdiyya*], which ranks higher than service. The location of service is the body and it signifies the performance of the commandment. The location of servitude is the spirit and it signifies good pleasure with the judgment. The location of servanthood is service with the innermost being."

I shall treat the subject in detail in my account of the Naqshbandī Spiritual Path. Let me say here and now that the innermost being is one of the spiritual faculties, which are the heart, the spirit, the innermost being, that which is hidden, and that which is most deeply concealed. As we read in the *Mu'jam* itself, "Our master Abū Bakr was in this spiritual station." In the words of the noble Prophetic tradition,

> Abū Bakr has not surpassed you all through frequency of fasting or prayer. He has surpassed you only through something that has lodged in his heart, and that something is the Might of Allāh and His Majesty.

In the Arabic language, as stated in the dictionary, servanthood [*'ubūda*] is "the final stage of servitude [*'ubūdiyya*]."

---

25. *Mu'jam muṣṭalaḥāt aṣ-ṣūfiyya*, p. 182.

Chapter Four
Spiritual States [*Aḥwāl*]

1. Constriction [*qabḍ*]. 2. Expansion [*basṭ*]. 3. Obliteration and establishment [*maḥw wa ithbāt*]. 4. Sobriety and inebriation [*ṣaḥw wa sukr*]. 5. Absence and presence [*ghaiba wa shuhūd*]. 6. Ardent yearning [*shawq*]. 7. Intimacy [*uns*]. 8. Ecstasy [*wajd*]. 9. Majesty [*jalāl*]. 10. Beauty [*jamāl*]. 11. Perfection [*kamāl*]. 12. Pure affection [*maḥabba*]. 13. Gleams, dawnings, and sparkles [*lawā'iḥ wa ṭawāli' wa lawāmi'*]. 14. Attraction [*jadhb*]. 15. Receiving [*wārid*].

1,2. Constriction [*Qabḍ*] and Expansion [*Basṭ*]

These are two states experienced by the spiritual traveler. In the state of constriction the human being feels distress and in the state of expansion he feels comfort and joy.

As we read in the book *Alfāẓ aṣ-ṣūfiyya*, "Constriction results from the dominance of fear, while expansion results from the dominance of hope. Constriction comes about in the states of reflection on the Qur'ānic verses concerning torment and threat. In the states of contemplation of the verses concerning hope and forgiveness, expansion enters the heart of the spiritual traveler. Some maintain that constriction comes about whenever the attribute of Divine Majesty [*Jalāl*] becomes manifest, while expansion arises whenever the attribute of Divine Beauty [*Jamāl*] becomes manifest. At certain times, constriction results from fear of the loss of the heart-centered blessings felt only by the spiritual traveler and known only by Allāh. Expansion sometimes arises from hope of attaining to the heart-centered talents.

According to Shaikh Abu'l-Ḥasan ash-Shādhilī (C.E. 1196–1258), "Constriction is a darkness that appears underneath the light. Expansion is a Divine light that covers the heart of the spiritual traveler. In other words, expansion is a light upon a light, whereas constriction is a darkness beneath a light."

According to Imām al-Qushairī,[1] "Constriction and expansion are two spiritual states experienced after the servant has progressed beyond the state of fear and hope. For one endowed with intimate knowledge,

1. *ar-Risāla al-Qushairiyya*, p. 32.

constriction is in the position of hope for the novice." He has also said, "The two states of awe [*haiba*] and intimacy [*uns*] are above constriction and expansion. Just as constriction is above the level of fear, and expansion is above the position of hope, awe ranks higher than constriction, and intimacy is more complete than hope." He has also said, "When someone is at the stage of fear and hope, his heart is attached to his future prospect. That is to say, he is either afraid or hopeful. When someone is at the stage of constriction and expansion, however, he is captivated by a receiving that overwhelms him in his immediate present. That is to say, he is either happy in his state or depressed therein."

According to Shaikh 'Umar as-Suhrawardī,[2] "Constriction and expansion are two noble spiritual states." He has also said, "The shaikhs have spoken about them and they have provided indications that are the signs of constriction and expansion. I have not found any disclosure of their real meaning. That is because the shaikhs have been content with intimation, and intimation satisfies the experts. I would like to discuss them both in greater detail." He has also said,

"Constriction and expansion have a known season and a determined time, before which they do not occur and after which they do not occur. Their time and their season are in the early stages of the state of special affection [*maḥabba*], not in its final stage and not prior to special affection. If someone is in the station of common affection established by virtue of faith, he does not experience constriction and expansion, but only fear and hope. He may discover the semblance of the state of constriction and the semblance of the state of expansion, supposing that to be constriction and expansion. That is not so. It is merely an anxiety that befalls him so he supposes it to be a constriction and an agitation or a self-centered pleasure and a natural cheerfulness, that he supposes to be an expansion."

The master of the Suhrawardī Order has then gone on to say, "Anxiety and cheerfulness emerge from the location and the essential nature of the lower self, because of the survival of its attributes. So long as the attribute of "instigating [*ammāra*]" remains applicable to the lower self, it will be the source of agitation and cheerfulness. Anxiety and agitation are the dog-collar of the lower self and cheerfulness is the rising of the billows of the lower self in the collision of the sea of nature. When the spiritual traveler progresses from the state of common affection to the early stages of special affection, he becomes the owner

2. *'Awārif al-ma'ārif*, p. 360.

of a spiritual state, the owner of a heart, and the owner of a censorious self [*nafs lawwāma*]. Constriction and expansion then alternate within him because he has advanced from the rank of faith to the rank of certainty, and to the state of special affection. The Truth will sometimes constrict him and sometimes cause him to expand."

He has then gone on to say, "The experience of constriction is due to the manifestation of the quality of the lower self and its dominating influence, while the emergence of expansion is due to the manifestation of the quality of the heart and its dominating influence. So long as the self continues to be censorious, it will sometimes be overwhelmed and sometimes overwhelming. Constriction and expansion are due only to the manifestation of the two qualities. The owner of the heart is beneath a radiant veil because of the existence of his heart. The owner of the lower self is beneath a gloomy veil because of the existence of his lower self. Once he has progressed beyond the heart and emerged from his veil, the spiritual state is no longer useful to him and he cannot function within it. Then he departs at that point from the influence of constriction and expansion. He is neither constricted nor expanded as long as he is free from the radiant entity that is the heart while experiencing the reality of nearness without the veil of the lower self and the heart. Then, when he returns to normal existence from the experience of annihilation and perpetuity, he will return to the radiant entity that is the heart, so constriction and expansion will return to him at that point. Whenever he is released into annihilation and perpetuity, there is no constriction and expansion."

He has also said, citing one of the experts, "First comes constriction, then expansion, then neither constriction nor expansion. This is because constriction and expansion fall within existence, but not in conjunction with annihilation and perpetuity." Our purpose here is to explain that constriction and expansion are two states pertaining to the Sufi spiritual traveler. The first he experiences as a state of utter dejection. In the second he feels the delight of abundant happiness.

3. Obliteration and Establishment [*Maḥw wa Ithbāt*]
4. Sobriety and Inebriation [*Ṣaḥw wa Sukr*]
5. Absence and Presence [*Ghaiba wa Shuhūd*]

According to as-Suhrawardī in his book *'Awārif al-ma'ārif,*

Obliteration [*maḥw*] is the removal of the attributes of the lower

> selves to be replaced by the establishment [*ithbāt*] of the effects of love, which they [the spiritual travelers] drink from cups that are circulated among them. Obliteration is also the obliteration of the formalities of conduct due to the annihilation of the self and the consequences thereof. Establishment is the establishment of conduct based on what the Truth has brought into being. It is the product of the Lord of Truth, not of the lower self. It is established anew by the Lord of Truth after He has obliterated its previous attributes.

On the subject of sobriety [*ṣaḥw*] and inebriation [*sukr*], as-Suhrawardī has said,

> Inebriation is the overwhelming effect of the power of the spiritual state, while sobriety is reversion to setting deeds in order and using words correctly.

According to Muḥammad ibn Khafīf, "Inebriation is the fermentation of the heart in reaction to the remembrance of the Beloved." He also said, "The stations of ecstasy are four: distraction, then bewilderment, then inebriation, then sobriety."

In connection with absence [*ghaiba*] and presence [*shuhūd*], as-Suhrawardī has said,

> The term *shuhūd* means presence, sometimes in the sense of vigilant awareness [*murāqaba*] and sometimes in the sense of witnessing [*mushāhada*]. As long as the servant is characterized by *shuhūd* and attentiveness, he is present [*ḥāḍir*]. When he loses the state of witnessing and vigilant awareness, he departs from the sphere of presence, and is absent [*ghā'ib*]. By absence [*ghaiba*] they sometimes mean absence from things in the presence of the Truth. It refers in this sense to the station of annihilation [*fanā'*].

According to al-Qushairī, "Obliteration is the removal of the attributes of custom, and establishment is the performance of the rules of worshipful service. If someone rids his spiritual states of blameworthy attributes and replaces them with praiseworthy actions and states, he is a master of obliteration and establishment." He has then gone on to say, "The reality of obliteration and establishment result from the Divine power. Obliteration refers to what the Lord of Truth conceals and negates, while establishment refers to what the Lord of Truth manifests and discloses. Allāh (Exalted is He) has said,

> Allāh obliterates what He will, and establishes [what He will].
> *yamḥu 'llāhu mā yashā'u wa yuthbitu.* (13:39)"

On the subject of sobriety and inebriation, al-Qushairī has said, "Sobriety means returning to consciousness after absence, while inebriation is absence due to a powerful receiving (of blessings). Absence results from a blessing and a light. Inebriation is stronger than absence in terms of blessing."

"Absence is the absence of the heart from knowledge of what is happening among creatures due to preoccupation with what the servant has received. He then becomes absent from his awareness of himself and others due to recollecting the reward or contemplation of the punishment." He thereby reaches a limit where he forgets himself and thinks only of a reward or a punishment. In this state, he may even touch fire without feeling the flame and the heat. It once happened that ash-Shiblī came to al-Junaid, both of them being among the distinguished figures of Sufism. Al-Junaid's wife wished to conceal herself, so al-Junaid said to her, "Ash-Shiblī is quite unaware of you, so sit still!" Al-Junaid then went on talking to him, until ash-Shiblī burst into tears. As soon as ash-Shiblī started to weep, al-Junaid said to his wife, "Hide yourself now, for ash-Shiblī has recovered consciousness from his absence."

According to as-Suhrawardī, "Abū Naṣr, the muezzin in Nishapur, was a righteous man. I once heard him say, 'I used to recite the Qur'ān at the meeting held by Abū 'Alī ad-Daqqāq in Nishapur, during the time he was there. He had a great deal to say about the Pilgrimage. His speech touched my heart, so I set out on the Pilgrimage that same year, leaving the shop and my occupation. Abū 'Alī (may Allāh bestow His mercy upon him) also set out on the Pilgrimage that year. I served him throughout the time he spent in Nishapur, and I devoted myself assiduously to reciting the Qur'ān at his meeting. When I saw him one day in the desert, he had performed his ablution and forgotten a water-bottle, so I carried it to him. He took it and set it on his camel saddle. Then he said, 'May Allāh (Exalted is He) reward you well for having brought this to me!' Then he looked at me for a long time, as if he had never seen me before, and said, 'I have seen you once. Who are you?' I replied, 'Allāh is the One from whom we seek help! I spent some time in your company. I left my home and my property because of you, and joined you out here in the desert, yet now you say, "I have seen you once before"!'"

Such is the state of absence. Presence means that when the servant becomes absent from creatures, he is present with the Lord of Truth. He seems to be present because of the overwhelming impact on his heart of remembrance of the Lord of Truth for he is present with his heart before his Lord. His nearness to the Creator is in proportion to his absence from creatures. If he is absent entirely, his presence is in proportion to his absence. If it is said that so-and-so is present, this means that he is present for his Lord with his heart, not heedless of Him. Then, in accordance with the level of his presence, he will discover spiritual concepts disclosed by the Lord of Truth (Glory be to Him and Exalted is He) as a special favor to him.

There are differences among those who experience the spiritual state of absence. There are some whose absence is not prolonged and some whose absence is long-lasting.

It is related that Dhū 'n-Nūn al-Miṣrī sent one of his Companions to Abū Yazīd. When the man came to Bisṭām, he asked for directions to the home of Abū Yazīd. He entered his presence and Abū Yazīd asked, "What are you seeking?" He replied, "I am seeking Abū Yazīd." The latter said, "Who is Abū Yazīd? Where is Abū Yazīd? I am in search of Abū Yazīd!" The man went out, saying, "This is a lunatic!" Then he went back to Dhū 'n-Nūn and told him what he had witnessed. Dhū 'n-Nūn wept and said, "My brother Abū Yazīd has gone to join those who are going to Allāh!"[3]

On the subject of inebriation and sobriety, in *Mu'jam muṣṭalaḥāt aṣ-ṣūfiyya*, it says "Inebriation is a noble station among the spiritual stations of the saints. It is not followed by annihilation, and knowledge does not reach it. Sobriety is a station above inebriation and it resembles expansion [*basṭ*]. It is a station that is neither sought nor expected, a station cleansed of turbidities."

It is also stated that absence has three degrees: (1) The absence of the seeker for he becomes absent from his property and his children. His heart is not attached to anything belonging to this world nor is he afraid of anything. (2) The absence of the spiritual traveler for he forgets the knowledge and opportunities of life. (3) The absence of one who is endowed with intimate knowledge for he becomes absent from spiritual states and degrees, and enters "integration [*jam'*]," so he draws near to His grace (Glory be to Him).

3. *'Awārif al-ma'ārif*, p. 38.

According to *Mu'jam muṣṭalaḥāt aṣ-ṣūfiyya*, "Obliteration is the removal of the attributes of custom, since the servant then becomes absent from from his mind and becomes the source of deeds and words that would never enter his mind like someone drunk on wine. The obliteration of plurality, the real obliteration, is the annihilation of multiplicity in singularity. Establishment, the opposite of obliteration, is performance according to the rules of worshipful service. Sobriety is the return to consciousness of one endowed with intimate knowledge after his absence and his loss of consciousness. Its opposite is inebriation. The meaning of these terms is close to that of presence and absence. The difference between presence and sobriety is that becoming sober is a sudden occurrence, whereas being present is a long-lasting condition. Sobriety and inebriation are more complete and more compelling than presence and absence."

According to the same source, "Absence is the absence of the heart from knowledge of what is happening among creatures due to the preoccupation of the inner feeling with what it has received. It is also said that the servant is absent from the interests of his lower self so he does not notice them because he is absent from them in the presence of what belongs to the Lord of Truth." According to the same source, "Presence means that he notices the interests of his lower self, so it stands as the exact opposite of absence."

According to Shaikh Muḥyi'd-Dīn ibn al-'Arabī, "Obliteration and establishment are among the paired terms of Sufism, like annihilation and perpetuity. When obliteration causes the servant to lose consciousness of himself, he is in the most intense of the states of presence. That signifies that he is absent here and present over there."

As for effacement [*saḥq*], according to Shaikh Muḥyi'd-Dīn ibn al-'Arabī, "It is the servant's awareness of the annihilation of his body, because of the manifestation of the light of Allāh (Glory be to Him). Eradication [*maḥq*] is stronger than effacement [*saḥq*], for it means that the spiritual traveler is unaware of his own existence, and does not sense anything in the universe apart from His Power (Glory be to Him). He believes that everything comes about through His Will and His Power."

6. Ardent Yearning [*Shawq*]

According to some of the distinguished figures of Sufism, ardent yearning [*shawq*] is a spiritual state that follows in the wake of pure affection [*maḥabba*].

As we read in *Mu'jam muṣṭalaḥāt aṣ-ṣūfiyya*, "Ardent yearning [*shawq*] is the excitement of the heart in response to remembrance of the Beloved. The difference between ardent yearning [*shawq*] and craving [*ishtiyāq*] is that ardent yearning becomes calm at the meeting. Whereas craving does not cease at the meeting, it increases and multiplies."

In this context, what is meant by ardent yearning is that which is experienced by spiritual travelers on the Sufi path. It is a special state with a special significance, and we cannot fully explain what has been said about the spiritual states and stations experienced by the masters of the path. Shaikh as-Suhrawardī has mentioned his own opinion about ardent yearning, as well as the opinions of some of the distinguished figures of Sufism. According to one of them, "Ardent yearning is for the absent, so, as long as Allāh (Glory be to Him) is Present, there is no ardent yearning." Since it is a state that arises before direct witnessing, as-Suhrawardī regards ardent yearning as one of the states of loving affection. If someone loves Allāh (Glory be to Him), he will long for Him and the state of ardent yearning and love will not depart from him.

Shaikh as-Suhrawardī has also said, "These are the states of certain people among the lovers who occupy the station of ardent yearning. Ardent yearning results from loving affection just as abstinence results from repentance. When repentance is firmly established, abstinence appears; and when loving affection is firmly established, ardent yearning appears."

Ibn al-'Aṭā' was asked about ardent yearning and said, "It is the inflammation of intestines, the burning of hearts and the dismemberment of livers." He was also asked, "Is ardent yearning higher in degree or loving affection?" To this he replied, "Loving affection is because ardent yearning is engendered by it."

As we read in the book *Manāzil as-sā'irīn*, "Ardent yearning has three degrees: (1) The ardent yearning of the worshipful servants for the Garden of Paradise and deliverance from the Fire of Hell, (2) Ardent yearning for contact with Allāh (Glory be to Him), (3) The fire of loving affection in the heart, which blazes and cannot be extinguished by anything apart from meeting the Lord (Glory be to Him) with insight." As we read in the book *al-Luma'*, "Ardent yearning demands intimacy."

As an introduction to his treatment of the subject of ardent yearning, al-Qushairī quotes the saying of Allāh (Exalted is He),

> Whoever looks forward to the meeting with Allāh,
> *man kāna yarjū liqā'a 'llāhi*
> Allāh's appointed term is surely coming.
> *and fa-inna ajala 'llāhi la-āt.* (29:5)

According to Yaḥyā ibn Mu'ādh (d. A.H. 258), "The symptom of ardent yearning is the weaning of the limbs and organs from lustful desires."

In his *Risāla*, al-Qushairī also says, "I heard as-Sarī say, 'Ardent yearning is a most splendid station for one endowed with intimate knowledge when he truly attains to it.'"

As we notice here, each of them speaks about what he has personally experienced, witnessed with his insight, and tasted in his spiritual states.

7. Intimacy [*Uns*]

Intimacy [*uns*] is one of the spiritual states of Sufism. It signifies the lowliness of the heart of the spiritual traveler who is attached to the love of his Lord and whose heart is intimate with none but Allāh (Glory be to Him). In this state, the Sufi is fond of seclusion from people and he wishes for no one to be close to him. When he meets a congregation he is with them physically, but he is with his Lord where his heart is concerned. He is happy and delighted with his intimacy with his Lord regardless of how life's troubles assail him for he does not wish to let anyone disturb the happiness he enjoys. In this state, the thing that is dearest to him is the remembrance of his Lord.

In the view of the great Sufi shaikhs, intimacy sometimes reaches the point of mystic disclosure and witnessing. This degree is one of the ecstatic states, which linguistic definitions are incapable of describing and accounting for completely. Due to the inability of language to grasp the meanings of these Sufi states and stations, many of the purposes of Sufism remain in our hearts without our finding how to express them. Each of them has a peculiar significance different from any other. This resembles the case of someone who invites people to attend his wedding feast and prepares for each of them a special pavilion containing a special meal. All of the guests are invited, but the state of each one is different from the state of the other in terms of the position and food provided for him. There is no doubt that each one of them will have a different story to tell about this invitation. Language is simply inadequate when it comes to describing this state.

These are spiritual matters, perceived by the eye of insight, and our understanding of them is based only on what is apparent from the sayings related about them.

As we read in *Mu'jam muṣṭalaḥāt aṣ-ṣūfiyya*, "Intimacy is the spirit's enjoyment of the perfection of Beauty. It is the effect of witnessing the Divine Presence in the heart and it is the Beauty of Majesty. Some say that intimacy is the opposite of awe and some say that it comes together with awe."

According to another source,[4] "The people of intimacy experience intimacy in three states: (1) There is one who is on intimate terms with remembrance and estranged from heedlessness, and who is on intimate terms with obedience and estranged from sin. (2) The second state of intimacy belongs to the servant who becomes intimate with Allāh and who is alienated from everything apart from Him such as trivial events and distracting notions. (3) The third state is departure from concentration on intimacy through the presence of awe, nearness, and reverence together with intimacy."

It is related on the authority of Dāwūd aṭ-Ṭā'ī (d. A.H. 165) that a Sufi once approached him and asked, "O Abū Sulaimān, what is this joyfulness that is obviously yours?" He told him, "At the dawn of day I was given a draught of intimacy to drink."

Intimacy is indeed a state of joy and happiness, which results from the sense of nearness to Allāh (Glory be to Him), and when His light (Glory be to Him) shines in the heart of the believer. The heart of the Sufi is thus filled with an abundant happiness, which makes him wish for no one else to draw near to him and disturb his happiness.

8. Ecstasy [*Wajd*]

Ecstasy [*wajd*] is a Sufi spiritual state.

In one of the reference works it says,[5] "The term *wajd* applies to that which comes unexpectedly upon the heart in the form of joy or sorrow or fear, or recognition of the significance of one of the states of the Hereafter, or disclosure of a relationship between the servant and Allāh (Almighty and Glorious is He)."

According to Shaikh as-Suhrawardī,[6] "The term *wajd* applies to that which is received from Allāh by the inner being of the servant causing him to feel joy or sorrow and altering his condition. The term

4. *al-Luma'*, p. 96.
5. *at-Ta'arruf li-madhhab at-taṣawwuf*, p. 112.
6. *'Awārif al-ma'ārif*, p. 367.

tawājud signifies the procurement of ecstasy [*wajd*] by means of remembrance and contemplation. The term rapture [*wujūd*] signifies expansion of the joy of ecstasy [*wajd*] by moving into the vastness of exaltation [*wijdān*]. Ecstasy is subject to the risk of evanescence while rapture is stable with the stability of the mountains."

He has also said, "The term *ghalaba* signifies successively repeated ecstasy for ecstasy is like the flash of lightning. *Ghalaba* is like the uninterrupted succession and repetition of lightning."

He has then added, "The stations of ecstasy are four: distraction, then bewilderment, then inebriation, then sobriety. Compare the situation of someone who hears about the ocean, then approaches it, then enters into it, and is then seized by the waves. On this basis, if someone continues to bear an effect from the impact of the state upon him, he bears a trace of inebriation. As for someone from whom everything returns to its source, he is sober. Inebriation is for the masters of hearts, while sobriety is for those who discover the realities of the unseen realms."

As we have said, ecstasy is one of the spiritual states experienced by the Sufi. It may also happen to any Muslim during the recitation of the Noble Qur'ān, or on hearing something very moving so that he cries out or bursts into tears. This is ecstasy, meaning the excitement of the heart, as indicated by His saying (Glory be to Him),

> Those only are believers
> *innama 'l-mu'minūna 'lladhīna*
> whose hearts quake when Allāh is mentioned.
> *idhā dhukira 'llāhu wajilat qulūbu-hum.* (8:2)

In the view of some distinguished figures of Sufism, the degree of the spiritual traveler progresses when he controls himself in the states of ecstasy and does not utter a shout or cry. Some of them consider this correct, but others maintain that unrestrained behavior is more appropriate to the states of ecstasy. Each has supporting evidence, but the prevailing opinion is that restraint is preferable in these states.

It is important for us to understand that ecstasy is among the states of the novices, that is to say, among the states of those who are still in the station of variegation [*talwīn*], and this state is not experienced by someone who has reached the station of consolidation [*tamkīn*].

The fact is that the Noble Qur'ān has pointed to the alteration of states, and has praised those hearts that are humble and blamed those hearts that are hard. We should therefore reflect on these noble verses:

Allāh has revealed the fairest of statements, a consistent Book,
Allāhu nazzala aḥsana 'l-ḥadīthi Kitāban mutashābihan
paired, whereat creeps the flesh of those who fear their Lord,
mathāniya taqsha'irru min-hu julūdu 'lladhīna yakhshawna Rabba-hum:
so that their flesh and their hearts soften at Allāh's reminder.
thumma talīnu julūdu-hum wa qulūbu-hum ilā dhikri 'llāh. (39:23)

When the signs of the All-Merciful were recited to them,
idhā tutlā 'alai-him āyātu 'r-Raḥmāni
they fell down, adoring and weeping.
kharrū sujjadan wa bukiyyā. (19:58)

When they listen to what has been revealed to the Messenger,
wa idhā sami'ū mā unzila ila 'r-Rasūli
you see their eyes overflow with tears
tarā a'yuna-hum tafīḍu mina 'd-dam'i
because of their recognition of the Truth.
mimmā 'arafū mina 'l-Ḥaqq. (5:83)

They fall down on their faces, weeping,
wa yakhirrūna li'l-adhqāni yabkūna
and it increases humility in them.
wa yazīdu-hum khushū'ā. (17:109)

From these noble Qur'ānic verses, it is clearly understood that Allāh (Glory be to Him) is speaking of the owners of quaking hearts and tearful eyes, of shivering skins and foreheads bowing low, when He says (Exalted is He),

Their hearts quake.
wajilat qulūbu-hum. (8:2)

These are states in which the righteous servants feel afraid of Allāh (Glory be to Him), so their hearts tremble with loving affection and their eyes overflow with tears at the remembrance of Allāh and the recitation of the Noble Qur'ān.

In other verses, the Qur'ān blames the owners of hard hearts coated with rust, for He has said (Exalted is He) on the subject of the Children of Israel,

Then your hearts were hardened, even after that,
thumma qasat qulūbu-kum min ba'di dhālika

> and became like rocks or even harder still.
> *fa-hiya ka-'l-ḥijārati aw ashaddu qaswa*:
> For indeed there are rocks whence rivers gush,
> *wa inna mina 'l-ḥijārati la-mā yatafajjaru min-hu 'l-anhār*:
> and indeed there are rocks which split asunder
> *wa inna min-hā la-mā yashaqqaqu*
> so that water flows from them.
> *fa-yakhruju min-hu 'l-mā'*:
> And indeed there are rocks which fall down for fear of Allāh.
> *wa inna la-mā yahbiṭu min khashyati 'llāh*:
> Allāh is not unaware of what you do.
> *wa ma 'llāhu bi-ghāfilin 'ammā ta'malūn*. (2:74)

He has also said (Exalted is He):

> Is not the time now ripe for the hearts of those who believe
> *a-lam ya'ni li'lladhīna āmanū*
> to be humbled to the remembrance of Allāh?
> *an takhsha'a qulūbu-hum li-dhikri 'llāhi*. (57:16)
>
> And that they do not become like those who received the Book
> *wa lā yakūna ka-'lladhīna ūtu 'l-Kitāba*
> of old, but the term was prolonged for them,
> *min qablu fa-ṭāla'alai-himu 'l-amadu*
> and so their hearts were hardened,
> *fa-qasat qulūbu-hum:*
> and many of them are profligates.
> *wa kathīrun min-hum fāsiqūn*. (57:16)
>
> But woe unto those hearts are hardened
> *fa-wailun li'l-qāsiyati qulūbu-hum*
> against the remembrance of Allāh.
> *min dhikri 'llāh*. (39:22)

By what we have mentioned and cited as evidence, we intend to prove that the state of ecstasy—of weeping and shivering at the recitation of the Noble Qur'ān and the remembrance of Allāh (Glory be to Him)—is experienced by worshipful believers, and that spiritual travelers of Sufism are really and truly believing servants. The hardness of heart at remembrance of Allāh and recitation of the Noble Qur'ān it is the sign of rust and darkness. We take refuge therefrom with Allāh!

9,10. Majesty [*Jalāl*] and Beauty [*Jamāl*]

These two terms are linked together in the books of Sufism. The first means might and glory, and the second refers to what is fine and beautiful.

In this context, they are among the attributes of Allāh (Glory be to Him), and the traveler on the Sufi path may experience them. He has said (Glory be to Him),

> Everyone who dwells upon the earth must pass away,
> *kullu man 'alai-hā fān*:
> yet the Face of your Lord still abides, in Majesty and Honor.
> *wa yabqā wajhu Rabbi-ka Dhū 'l-Jalāli wa 'l-Ikrām.* (55:26,27)
>
> Blessed be the Name of your Lord,
> *tabāraka 'smu Rabbi-ka*
> the Owner of Majesty and Honor.
> *Dhī 'l-Jalāli wa 'l-Ikrām.* (55:78)

The spiritual traveler may taste some of the Majesty of the Almighty or some of His Beauty in the state of spiritual traveling. If Allāh (Glory be to Him) bestows a manifestation of His attribute of Majesty on the heart of His servant the spiritual traveler, astonishment will fill his heart. If Allāh (Glory be to Him) bestows a manifestation of His attribute of Beauty on the heart of His servant, a state of eager longing will fill his heart. The spiritual traveler is annihilated in the manifestation of Majesty and he is revived in the manifestation of Beauty. This annihilation and revival are spiritual matters that cannot be measured by the material balance. They are states that cannot be comprehended except by someone who experiences them.

From what has been said above, it is understood that the disclosure of Majesty leads to obliteration and absence, which we have already discussed in detail. The disclosure of Beauty leads to sobriety and nearness to Allāh (Glory be to Him). According to Shaikh Muḥyi'd-Dīn ibn al-'Arabī, "When Allāh discloses His Majesty to those who truly know Him, they become absent. When He discloses His Beauty to lovers, they are overjoyed.... If someone becomes absent, he is enchanted; and if someone is overjoyed, he is enthralled.... Majesty is the attribute of Omnipotence peculiar to Allāh (Glory be to Him), while Beauty is one of the attributes of kindness and mercy."

As we read in the book *Mu'jam muṣṭalaḥāt aṣ-ṣūfiyya*, "Majesty is the attribute of compelling force, and it signifies the attributes of might and grandeur, glory and splendor. Every beauty has a majesty, for the intensity of its appearance is called a majesty just as every majesty has a beauty, for it is called a beauty when it first becomes apparent to creatures. That is why it has been said that every beauty has a majesty and every majesty has a beauty. Absolute majesty and absolute beauty can only be witnessed by Allāh Alone because Majesty is His property. By virtue of its manifestation from His Names, just as His attributes are ascribed to Him, Majesty and Beauty belong to Him by right. The Name 'Allāh' contains the meaning of Majesty and Beauty."

According to the same source, "The term beauty [*jamāl*] is used in two senses: (1) The beauty that is familiar to all and sundry, like purity of color, softness to the touch, and loveliness of appearance. (2) Real Beauty, which is an eternal attribute peculiar to Allāh (Glory be to Him)." According to al-Jurjānī, "Beauty is one of the attributes connected with good pleasure and kindness." According to al-Kāshānī, "Beauty signifies the qualities of Allāh's Grace and Mercy." According to Ibn ad-Dabbāgh, "Beauty is absolute and strictly defined. Full treatment of the subject is beyond the scope of our study."

According to the author of *Mu'jam muṣṭalaḥāt aṣ-ṣūfiyya*, "In the view of the perfect human being, the Beauty of Allāh (Exalted is He) is an expression signifying His loftiest attributes and His finest Names. This applies to the common folk. As it relates to the *élite*, it is the attribute of Mercy, the attribute of Knowledge, the attribute of Grace and Favor, the attribute of Generosity, Providership, and Creatorship, and the attribute of Benefit. All of these are attributes of Beauty. There are also collective attributes sharing an aspect of Beauty and an aspect of Majesty like the Name ar-Rabb [the Lord]. It is a Name of Beauty with reference to instruction and development and a Name of Majesty with reference to Lordship and power."

On the subject of awe and intimacy, Shaikh Muḥyi'd-Dīn ibn al-'Arabī said, "They are two states of the spiritual traveler arising from the attributes of Majesty and Beauty. Awe results from the witnessing of Majesty in the heart and it may also result from the witnessing of a Beauty resulting from Majesty. Intimacy results from the witnessing of Allāh's Beauty (Glory be to Him)."

The subject of Majesty and Beauty is discussed in the book *al-Qudsiyya*, by Shaikh Muḥammad Pārsā (A.H. 749–866), a book containing the sayings of Shaikh Bahā' ad-Dīn an-Naqshband, the founder of the Naqshbandī lineage.

"Inasmuch as the spiritual traveler develops the attributes of Majesty and Beauty, his majesty is a form of beauty and his beauty is a form of majesty. Whenever fear prevails upon him, he takes refuge in hope. Whenever hope predominates, he returns to the state of fear."

At the moment when he becomes a point of manifestation for the attribute of Majesty, he can concentrate on the attribute of Beauty. According to an-Naqshband, "The masters of reality have said, 'It is necessary for the spiritual traveler to have reached the reality of essential loving affection before he encounters the lessons of training in the attributes of Majesty and Beauty. The sign of arrival at the reality of this loving affection is that the opposite attributes of the Exalter and the Abaser and Cause of harm and the Benefactor become unified in front of him. This means that this loving affection makes him well pleased with everything that befalls him without distinguishing between what is harmful and what is beneficial. In this spiritual station he becomes lordly. In the words of the Sacred Tradition [*Ḥadīth Qudsī*],

> O My servant, be lordly! Tell the thing, "Be!" and it will come to be.

If the human being is delivered from the animal attributes and adorned with the Divine characteristics, Allāh (Glory be to Him) will grant him the reality of what he seeks. What is most important, however, is that the spiritual traveler, when he reaches this station, seeks only the good pleasure of Allāh (Glory be to Him). They are human beings in body and angels in spirit, so they wish for nothing but His worshipful service, and there is no room in their hearts for anything else. An-Naqshband said in a poetic verse,

> The saintly friends of Allāh have a power from Allāh,
> by which to return the arrow to its bow despite its being shot.

Shaikh an-Naqshband also had this to say on the subject of sainthood in the book *al-Qudsiyya*, "There are two kinds of perfect seekers who reach their goal. The first are people who have drawn near to Majesty, and who have been granted some manifestation of its attribute. They have reached perfection, so they have been immersed in the ocean of integration and have walked to the desert of annihilation. They are in a state peculiar to themselves, so they are not responsible for the training and perfecting of others. They have alighted in the shrines of solicitude and settled in the abodes of bewilderment. If someone is in bewilderment and has lost consciousness of himself and others, it is not possible for him to work at bringing others to the goal. The likes of these are prevented from emulating the work of the prophets (in promulgating a *sharī'a*).

"The second group consists of people whose hearts, even if they lost them, would return to them through the power of the eternal Beauty. This delivers them from the desert of annihilation and grants them the strength to judge between people. By the grace of eternal Providence, having drowned in the ocean of the affirmation of Oneness, they return to the realm of perpetuity, to discharge the duty of spiritual guidance and training, and to summon people to salvation and spiritual triumph.

"These are the 'perfect perfecters,' and they have reached this high rank by virtue of following the Sunna of the noble Prophet Muḥammad (Allāh bless him and give him peace). They have been permitted to convey his summons and his message, as Allāh (Glory be to Him) has said:

> Say: 'This is my way: I call on Allāh with sure knowledge,
> *qul hādhihi sabīlī ad'ū ila 'llāhi 'alā baṣīratin*
> I and whoever follows me.'
> *ana wa mani 'ttaba'a-nī.* (12:108)
>
> Who speaks better than one who summons to Allāh
> *wa man aḥsanu qawlan mim-man da'ā ila 'llāhi*
> and acts righteously, and says:
> *wa 'amila ṣāliḥan wa qāla*
> 'I am among those who surrender.'
> *inna-nī mina 'l-muslimīn.* (41:33)
>
> And We appointed from among them leaders
> *wa ja'alnā min-hum a'immatan*
> guiding by Our command, when they endured patiently,
> *yahdūna bi-amri-nā lammā ṣabarū:*
> and had sure faith in Our signs.
> *wa kānū bi-āyati-nā yūqinūn.* (32:24)"

Let me add that these are the great men who perceive the radiance of Beauty, so they are blissfully happy, compassionate, and expansive in feeling. They do not worry about those who hurt them, or by what means they hurt them, for they are preoccupied with their blissful happiness, not with anything else. As for those who are encompassed by the radiance of Majesty, even if a bird flew by them without their wishing it to do so, they would cut off its wings. It would keep its distance from them, knowing that they are in this state. How are we to recognize them? Congratulations are due to someone whom Allāh has provided with a share of these exalted gifts!

11. Perfection [*Kamāl*], the Perfect [*Kāmil*] and the Perfecter [*Mukammil*]

Perfection [*kamāl*] is the opposite of deficiency [*naqṣ*], and the meanings of these words are well known.

The terms *kāmil* [perfect] and *mukammil* [perfecter; one who perfects] are also frequent technical terms of the Sufis. The spiritual guide is called *al-kāmil wa 'l-mukammil* [the one who is perfect and the one who perfects]. We have mentioned them above in the discussion of Beauty and Majesty.

It is necessary to explain that absolute perfection belongs to Allāh (Glory be to Him) Alone, so the human being cannot reach the extreme of absolute perfection. However beautiful or intelligent or strong he may be, the human being must grow old and die in the end.

> Every soul will taste death.
> *kullu nafsin dhā'iqatu 'l-mawt.* (3:185)

Human perfection is a relative perfection. Our master Muḥammad (Allāh bless him and give him peace) reached the ultimate limit of human perfection, for Allāh (Exalted is He) told him,

> And you are indeed of a splendid character.
> *wa inna-ka la-'alā khuluqin 'aẓīm.* (68:4)

Despite the splendor and perfection of the Muḥammadan character, Allāh (Glory be to Him and Exalted is He) also says to Muḥammad (Allāh bless him and give him peace) in the Noble Qur'ān,

> You do not guide whomever you like,
> *inna-ka lā tahdī man aḥbabta*
> but Allāh guides whomever He wills,
> *wa lākinna 'llāha yahdī man yashā'*
> and He is Best Aware of those who walk aright.
> *wa Huwa A'lamu bi'l-muhtadīn.* (28:56)

This was said at the time when the Messenger (Allāh bless him and give him peace) was longing to guide Abū Ṭālib to Islam. It is clear that guidance, in the sense of arrival, is at the disposal of Allāh Alone, for He has said (Glory be to Him),

> Thus We have inspired in you a Spirit of Our command.
> *wa ka-dhālika awḥainā ilai-ka Rūḥan min amri-nā*
> You did not know what the Book was, nor what the faith.
> *mā kunta tadrī ma 'l-Kitābu wa la 'l-īmānu*
> But We have made it a light
> *wa lākin ja'alnā-hu nūran*
> whereby We guide whom We will of Our servants.
> *nahdī bi-hi man nashā'u min 'ibādi-nā*
> You do indeed guide to a right path.
> *wa inna-ka la-tahdī ilā ṣirāṭin mustaqīm.* (42:52)

The point we are making here is that the human being in the person of the noble Prophet Muḥammad (Allāh bless him and give him peace) was commanded to convey the summons of Islam, guidance, and the truth. Likewise the prophets before him and the righteous scholars after him. "The scholars are the heirs of the prophets." While the path is the path of truth and rectitude, guidance is at the disposal of Allāh Alone.

The responsibility for spiritual direction and teaching is ancient, as ancient as the human being since it begins with Adam (peace be upon him) when he informed the angels of their names. In accordance with the duty of teaching, Allāh (Glory be to Him) commanded His angels to bow down before Adam, but that was a prostration of respect, not a prostration of worship like the prostration of Joseph's brothers before Joseph.

The Noble Qur'ān has alluded to the perfect human being,

> And when your Lord said to the angels:
> *wa idh qāla Rabbu-ka li'l-malā'ikati*
> "I am about to place a viceroy on the earth."
> *innī jā'ilun fi 'l-arḍi khalīfa.* (2:30)

Since they did not know everything, they were perplexed and:

> They said, "Will You place on it
> *qālū a-taj'alu fī-hā man yufsidu fi-hā*
> one who will do harm thereon, and will shed blood,
> *wa yasfiku 'd-dimā':*
> while we, we proclaim Your praise and sanctify You?"
> *wa naḥnu nusabbiḥu bi-ḥamdi-ka wa nuqaddisu lak.* (2:30)

Allāh (Glory be to Him) wished to make them aware of the value of the perfect human being.

> He said, "Surely I know what you do not know."
> *qāla innī a'lamu mā lā ta'lamūn.* (2:30)
>
> And He taught Adam all the names.
> *wa 'allama Ādama 'l-asmā'a kulla-hā.* (2:31)

What is meant by "the names" is not the names of the angels, but many of the secrets of which the angels had no knowledge. Adam's breast was filled with knowledge, by His saying:

> "Be," and it is.
> *kun fa-yakūn.* (2:117)

As we are told in the Qur'ān,

> Then He showed them to the angels, saying:
> *thumma 'araḍa-hum 'ala 'l-malā'ikati fa-qāla*
> "Inform Me of the names of these, if you are truthful."
> *anbi'ū-nī bi-asmā'i hā'ulā'i in kuntum ṣādiqīn.* (2:31)
>
> They said, "Glory be to You! We have no knowledge
> *qālū subḥāna-ka lā 'ilma la-nā*
> except that which You have taught us.
> *illā mā 'allamta-nā:*
> You are the All-Knowing, the All-Wise."
> *inna-ka Anta 'l-'Alīmu 'l-Ḥakīm.* (2:32)
>
> He said, "O Adam, inform them of their names."
> *qāla yā Ādamu anbi'-hum bi-asmā'i-him:*
> And when he had informed them of their names,
> *fa-lammā anba'a-hum bi-asmā'i-him*
> He said, "Did I not tell you that I know
> *qāla a-lam aqul la-kum innī a'lamu*
> the secret of the heavens and the earth?"
> *ghaiba 's-samāwāti wa 'l-arḍi*
> And I know that which you disclose
> *wa a'lamu mā tubdūna*
> and that which you have been hiding?"
> *wa mā kuntum taktumūn.* (2:33)

When the angels had been given to understand the human reality in the person of Adam whom Allāh had enveloped in virtues and perfections, He said (Glory be to Him),

> And when We said to the angels, "Bow down in prostration
> *wa idh qulnā li'l-malā'ikati 'sjudū*
> before Adam," they fell prostrate, all except Iblīs.
> *li-Ādama fa-sajadū illā Iblīs*:
> He refused and gave a display of arrogant pride,
> *abā wa 'stakbara*
> and so he came to be one of the unbelievers.
> *wa kāna mina 'l-kāfirīn*. (2:34)

Allāh has also said (Glory be to Him and Exalted is He), on the subject of David's appointment as viceroy,

> O David, We have appointed you as a viceroy in the earth;
> *yā Dāwūda innā ja'alnā-ka khalīfatan fi 'l-arḍi*
> so judge aright between humankind,
> *fa-'ḥkum baina 'n-nāsi bi'l-ḥaqqi*
> and do not follow desire.
> *wa lā tattabi'i 'l-hawā*. (38:26)

The meaning thereof is that the perfect human being is capable of directing people in accordance with his Lord's commandment.

This spiritual perfection is a permanent perfection, which carries over from one degree to another. In the view of Sufism, it begins with the lesser sainthood, then the greater, until it reaches the station of perpetuity after annihilation. This station is realized after passing through the stations we have mentioned like abstinence, repentance, and so on. If Allāh bestows this perfection on someone, he becomes qualified to provide spiritual guidance though it is a perfection that does not ascend to the perfection of the prophets. The most excellent human perfection belongs to Muḥammad (Allāh bless him and give him peace).

As we have mentioned in the discussion of Majesty and Beauty, the perfect individual [*al-kāmil*] is one who has reached the first degree of perfection. He is capable of dealing with his spiritual affairs without a director. The perfect perfecter [*al-kāmil al-mukammil*] is one who has surpassed the first degree of perfection and he is entitled to the spiritual authority to lead others to his stations. His likeness is that of the teacher who has learned from others and has the ability to teach others what he has learned. He also resembles the guide who leads those who are not familiar with the city to its lanes and alleys.

It often happens that the pupil overtakes his teacher in knowledge of his station, and the same is true of the men of Sufism. We notice that many of the leaders of the Sufi paths have reached stations higher than the stations of their shaikhs. Allāh is Best Aware of them and their affairs! These are entitled to direct people to intimate knowledge of Him (Glory be to Him). He has said (Exalted is He),

> Say, "This is my way: I call on Allāh with sure knowledge,
> *qul hādhihi sabīlī ad'ū ila 'llāhi 'alā baṣīratin*
> I and whoever follows me."
> *ana wa mani 'ttaba'a-nī.* (12:108)

> Who speaks better than one who summons to Allāh
> *wa man aḥsanu qawlan mim-man da'ā ila 'llāhi*
> and acts righteously, and says:
> *wa 'amila ṣāliḥan wa qāla*
> "I am of those who surrender"?
> *inna-nī mina 'l-muslimīn.* (41:33)

These Qur'ānic verses apply to these men who are spiritual directors, and Allāh (Glory be to Him) says of them,

> And We appointed from among them leaders
> *wa ja'alnā min-hum a'immatan*
> guiding by Our command, when they endured patiently,
> *yahdūna bi-amri-nā lammā ṣabarū*:
> and had sure faith in Our signs.
> *wa kānū bi-āyati-nā yūqinūn.* (32:24)

12. Pure Affection [*Maḥabba*]

The term *maḥabba* [pure affection] is derived from *ḥubb* [love], which is the inclination of hearts. In the view of the Sufis it differs from sexual love just as it differs from emotional love, the love of children and possessions, and the love of the self and the desires of this world. That is because our worldly love is a figurative, transitory love. Sufi love is a real love, because it is a permanent love. It is a love for the sake of Allāh, the One who never dies. It comes as a gracious favor and a gift from Allāh (Glory be to Him), so it is a spiritual state [*ḥāl*], as Shaikh 'Umar as-Suhrawardī has said. It comes through struggling with the lower self and through constant remembrance and worshipful service. It is also a spiritual station [*maqām*]. The author of *Qūt al-qulūb* [*Food of Hearts*] has written thirty pages on the subject of pure affection, which may be summarized in the following points:

1. According to the Sufis, pure affection means that Allāh (Glory be to Him) is dearer to the servant than wealth, children, and everything in this world.

2. Pure affection means that the servant's conduct is in accordance with the commandments of the Beloved (Glorious and Exalted is He). In this context, it is appropriate to cite two poetic verses by the martyr of Divine ardor [*'ishq Ilāhī*], the symbol of the path of pure affection, Rābi'a al-'Adawiyya, who says,

> You disobey God, yet you claim to love Him!
> This, by my life, is starkly in contrast.
> If your love were true, you would obey Him.
> The lover is surely obedient to the one he loves.

3. Pure affection demands constant adherence to obeying the Beloved. That is most important, because the disobedient sinner may worship his Lord, yet he may also disobey Him. The worshipful lover does not disobey the commandments of Allāh (Glory be to Him). According to Muḥammad ibn 'Alī al-Kattānī, "Pure affection is preference for the Beloved."

Just as the competitor loves to win the race, the Sufi at the station of pure affection works to gain the highest degree in this station. This pure affection has a benefit of incomparable value. If someone loves Allāh, Allāh loves him. If someone loves Allāh, he obeys Him and follows His noble Messenger, our master Muḥammad (Allāh bless him and give him peace). Allāh (Exalted is He) has said in the Sūra of the Family of 'Imrān,

> Say, "If you love Allāh, follow me; Allāh will love you."
> *qul in kuntum tuḥibbūna 'llāha fa-'ttabi'ū-nī yuḥbib-kumu 'llāhu* (3:31)

The sign of love for Him (Glory be to Him) is following the Sunna of His Prophet (Allāh bless him and give him peace), and its fruit is that Allāh (Glory be to Him) will love you. As you must realize, one of the attributes of the believers is that they love Him (Glory be to Him). In the Sūra of the Cow [*al-Baqara*], He has said (Exalted is He),

> They love them with a love like that of Allāh,
> *yuḥibbūna-hum ka-ḥubbi 'llāh*:

but those who believe are stronger in their love for Allāh.
wa 'lladhīna āmanū ashaddu ḥubban li'llāh. (2:165)

From these two Qur'ānic verses, it is clear that Allāh's affection is for the Muslims and the affection of the Muslims is for Allāh (Glory be to Him). One of the goals of Sufism is the attainment of this pure affection.

The Prophet (Allāh bless him and give him peace) once said,

A man is together with the one he loves.

That is splendid news for those who love Allāh (Glory be to Him)!

While the basic essential is the love of Allāh Alone (Glory be to Him), the pure affection of the prophets and saints reflects the pure affection of Allāh (Glory be to Him), because it is inspired by this pure affection.

As we read in the book entitled *Mu'jam muṣṭalaḥāt aṣ-ṣūfiyya* [*Glossary of the Technical Terms of Sufism*],

"Pure affection [*maḥabba*] is subdivided into ten parts. Five of them are the stations of the loving spiritual travelers: (1) familiarity [*ulfa*], (2) passion [*hawā*], (3) intimate friendship [*khulla*], (4) enamoredness [*shaghaf*], and (5) ecstasy [*wajd*]. As for the stations of the ardent lovers [*'ushshāq*], they are: (1) infatuation [*gharām*], (2) enchantment [*iftitān*], (3) rapture [*walah*], (4) bewilderment [*dahash*], and (5) annihilation [*fanā'*]."

Doctor Zakī Mubārak has discussed the subject of the stations of ardor and the states of love, on the authority of Muḥammad ibn Dāwūd, in his book *at-Taṣawwuf al-Islāmī* [*Islamic Sufism*]. "The process begins with appreciation [*istiḥsān*]; then it grows stronger and becomes fondness [*mawadda*]; then it grows stronger and becomes affection [*maḥabba*]; then it grows stronger and becomes intimate friendship [*khulla*]. Then it becomes passion [*hawā*], which becomes ardor [*'ishq*], then enthrallment [*tatayyum*], and then rapture [*walah*]." He also says, "Yearning [*shawq*] is linked to all of these states; and whenever a state intensifies, yearning intensifies.

The great shaikhs of Sufism maintain that yearning is a state that arises in the wake of affection. According to Shaikh 'Abd al-Qādir 'Īsā, in his book entitled *Ḥaqā'iq 'ani 't-taṣawwuf* [*Realities of Sufism*], "The scholars have mentioned ten stages of affection: (1) attachment [*'alāqa*], (2) desire [*irāda*], (3) fervent longing [*ṣabāba*], (4) infatuation [*gharām*], (5) fondness [*widād*], (6) enamoredness [*shaghaf*], (7) ardor [*'ishq*], (8) enthrallment [*tatayyum*], (9) servile devotion [*ta'abbud*], and (10) intimate friendship [*khulla*]."

For the Sufi, the highest of all the degrees of affection is that he loves Allāh (Glory be to Him) and Allāh loves him. As He has said (Exalted is He),

> He loves them and they love Him.
> *yuḥibbu-hum wa yuḥibbūna-hu.* (5:54)

Likewise at the station of contentment, the Sufi longs to reach the point where,

> Allāh is well pleased with them, and they are well pleased with Him.
> *raḍiya 'llāhu 'an-hum wa raḍū 'an-h.* (98:8)

Part of the Sufi's longing is that his Lord will remember him as he remembers Him, at all times, as He has said (Exalted is He),

> So remember Me, and I will remember you.
> *fa-'dhkurū-nī adhkur-kum.* (2:152)

Pure affection has been mentioned in numerous noble Qur'ānic verses as well as in the noble Prophetic traditions and the sayings of the righteous. These indicate that pure affection is not the claim of the tongue, but a practical mode of conduct. Love has signs that point to that, including the following of His commandments (Glory be to Him) and preferring His love to everything that is loved. Then the lover sees no difference between his profit and his loss the birth of his son and his death because everything belongs to Allāh and permanence belongs to Allāh Alone. What exists today will be gone tomorrow and he who does not die today will die tomorrow. It is said that one of the Sufis passed by a man who was weeping over a grave, so he asked him about the cause of his weeping. The man replied, "I have a dear one who has died." The Sufi then said, "You have wronged yourself by your love for a dear one who would die. If you loved a Dear One who will never die, you would not be tormented by His parting."

To this I would add that the purpose is not to deny the value of human sympathy on the grounds that a man will be tormented by the loss of his dear son. The intention here is to describe the state of Sufi affection, which takes possession of his heart so that it totally immerses the Sufi's feeling. It leaves him incapable of contemplating anything other than Him, for he believes that both blessing and suffering are from Allāh (Glory be to Him). The real lover does not indulge in complaining about the action of his real Beloved.

By way of analogy, note that we accept from our children, whom we love, what we absolutely refuse to accept from others. We tolerate many painful burdens of life for the sake of figurative love and worldly ardor. We tolerate many causes of displeasure for the sake of this world and its degrees. Do we not devote the years of our youth and the bloom of our life to the acquisition of credentials? Not one of us comes to his senses, except through the slap of old age on his back or his head. Death then looms with its dreadful specter, so the credentials are useless and remorse is to no avail. How is it, then, that we do not prepare by struggling with the lower self for the life everlasting, the everlasting credentials and the everlasting love? Where is this love in relation to that? This is immortal and that is dead!

The Qur'ān has clearly described the qualities of those servants whom He loves, for they are "beneficent [*muḥsinūn*]," "repentant [*tawwābūn*]," "keeping themselves clean [*mutaṭahhirūn*]," "truly devout [*muttaqīn*]," "those who are patient [*aṣ-ṣābirūn*]," "those who put their trust in Him [*al-mutawakkilīn*]," "those who are equitable [*al-muqsiṭīn*]," "those the battle for His cause in ranks [*alladhīna yuqātilūna fī sabīli-hi ṣaffan*]," and those who follow the Messenger (Allāh bless him and give him peace).

> Say, "If you love Allāh, follow me; Allāh will love you."
> *qul in kuntum tuḥibbūna 'llāha fa-'ttabi'ū-nī yuḥbib-kumu 'llāhu.* (3:31)

If someone wishes to have Allāh love him, he must adorn himself with these qualities and rid himself completely of blameworthy attributes. To prove our case, we shall cite the noble Qur'ānic verses which define the qualities of those whom He loves and the qualities of those whom He does not love. That is, the praiseworthy attributes and the blameworthy attributes. The praiseworthy attributes are the following:

> And do good. Allāh surely loves the beneficent.
> *wa aḥsinū inna 'llāha yuḥibbu 'l-muḥsinīn.* (2:195)

> Truly, Allāh loves those who repent,
> *inna 'llāha yuḥibbu 't-tawwābīna*
> and He loves those who keep themselves clean.
> *wa yuḥibbu 'l-mutaṭahhirīn.* (2:222)

He loves those who purify themselves.
yuḥibbu 'l-muṭṭahhirīn. (9:108)

He loves those who who are truly devout.
yuḥibbu 'l-muttaqīn. (3:76)

He loves those who are patient.
yuḥibbu 'ṣ-ṣābirīn. (3:146)

He loves those who put their trust in Him.
yuḥibbu 'l-mutawakkilīn. (3:159)

He loves the equitable.
inna 'llāha yuḥibbu 'l-muqsiṭīn. (5:42)

He loves those who battle for His cause in ranks.
yuḥibbu 'lladhīna yuqātilūna fī sabīli-hi ṣaffan. (61:4)

Say, "If you love Allāh, follow me; Allāh will love you."
qul in kuntum tuḥibbūna 'llāha fa-'ttabi'ū-nī yuḥbib-kumu 'llāhu. (3:31)

The following are the noble Qur'ānic verses that have been revealed on the subject of the blameworthy attributes which must be avoided by the Muslims in general, and by the Sufi in particular:

Allāh does not love those who [exceed the bounds].
inna 'llāha lā yuḥibbu 'l-mu'tadīn. (2:190)

And Allāh does not love mischief.
wa 'llāhu lā yuḥibbu 'l-fasād. (2:205)

Allāh does not love the unrighteous and the guilty.
wa 'llāhu lā yuḥibbu kulla kaffārin athīm. (2:276)

Allāh does not love the unbelievers.
fa-inna 'llāha lā yuḥibbu 'l-kāfirīn. (3:32)

Allāh does not love wrongdoers.
wa 'llāhu lā yuḥibbu 'ẓ-ẓālimīn. (3:57)

He does not love such as are proud and boastful.
lā yuḥibbu man kāna mukhtālan fakhūrā. (4:36)

He does not love one who is treacherous and sinful.
lā yuḥibbu man kāna khawwānan athīmā. (4:107)

He does not love corrupters.
lā yuḥibbu 'l-mufsidīn. (5:64)

He does not love the prodigals.
inna-hu lā yuḥibbu 'l-musrifīn. (6:141)

He does not love those who [exceed the bounds].
inna-hu lā yuḥibbu 'l-mu'tadīn. (7:55)

He does not love the treacherous.
lā yuḥibbu 'l-khā'inīn. (8:58)

He does not love the arrogant.
inna-hu lā yuḥibbu 'l-mustakbirīn. (16:23)

He does not love the wrongdoers.
inna-hu lā yuḥibbu 'ẓ-ẓālimīn. (42:40)

It is now quite clear that real affection [*maḥabba ḥaqīqiyya*], which is one of the spiritual states of Sufism, refers to a love that causes the spiritual traveler to prefer his Lord (Glory be to Him) to himself, his property and everything in his worldly life.

13. Gleams [*Lawā'iḥ*], Dawnings [*Ṭawāli'*], and Sparkles [*Lawāmi'*]

As we read in *Mu'jam muṣṭalaḥāt aṣ-ṣūfiyya* [*Glossary of the Technical Terms of Sufism*],

"These words are virtually synonymous, and they signify certain attributes of those in the initial stages of progress in the development of the heart. Gleams [*lawā'iḥ*] are like flashes of lightning that do not become visible until they have actually disappeared. Sparkles [*lawāmi'*] are brighter than gleams and they do not fade away with that same speed. Dawnings [*ṭawāli'*] are longer-lasting, have a stronger impact and a more enduring influence. They are more effective in dispelling darkness."

These are the spiritual states of the initial stages of Sufism before the rising of the sun of Divine knowledge [*ma'rifa Ilāhiyya*] in the heart of the spiritual traveler. According to Imām al-Ghazālī, in his book *al-Munqidh* [*Deliverance* (*from Error*)], "A light may become manifest in the heart of the spiritual traveler. It may then be extinguished for a while, but it will not cease to establish itself gradually until the heart of the spiritual traveler is illumined and shines as bright as day."

14. Attraction [*Jadhb*]

This term signifies the attraction [*jadhb*] by which Allāh (Exalted is He) draws a servant towards His presence. The related term *jadhba* [rapture] signifies the servant's drawing near by virtue of Allāh's providence, which means that everything has been prepared for him on Allāh's part without weary effort and exertion on his own part. If someone arrives by way of *jadhba*, he is said to be *majdhūb* [enraptured], and this may be experienced with or without a spiritual guide. The term *majdhūb* is also applied to the spiritual traveler whose Lord attracts him to His presence, without any seeking or action on his own part.

15. Receiving [*Wārid*]

This refers to all the mysterious meanings received by the heart, without deliberate intention on the servant's part. The difference between what is inwardly received and what is outwardly manifest [*bādī*] is that what is inwardly received is that which comes after what is outwardly manifest, so that it immerses the heart. Inner receiving is a Divine favor and a blessing, which the Maker (Glory be to Him) pours into the hearts of spiritual travelers.

Such is the view of the author of *al-Luma'* [Radiances], and al-Qushairī says in his *Risāla* [*Treatise*],

"Receiving is that which is received by hearts in the form of praiseworthy notions without the deliberate intention of the servant. There may be a receiving from the Truth or a receiving from knowledge. Receivings [*wāridāt*] include the receiving of joy or the receiving of sorrow; the receiving of constriction or the receiving of expansion. They may also have other meanings."

Chapter Five
Technical Terms of the Sufis

1. Spiritual exercise [*riyāḍa*]. 2. Dedicated striving [*mujāhada*]. 3. Mystic disclosure [*kashf*]. 4. Charismatic talents [*karāmāt*]. 5. Light [*nūr*]. 6. The heart [*qalb*]. 7. The self [*nafs*]. 8. Remembrance [*dhikr*]. 9. Illumination [*ishrāq*]. 10. Direct witnessing [*mushāhada*]. 11. The realm of Divinity [*Lāhūt*]. 12. The realm of Humanity [*Nāsūt*]. 13. The realm of Omnipotence [*Jabarūt*]. 14. The realm of Sovereignty [*Malakūt*]. 15. The four basic elements [*'anāṣir*]. 16. The saint [*walī*]. 17. The seeker [*murīd*]. 18. The deputy [*khalīfa*].

1,2. Spiritual Exercise [*Riyāḍa*] and Dedicated Striving [*Mujāhada*]

These terms signify relentless opposition to the passion of the lower self and its worldly desires, and the effort to curb the lower self and its cravings.

The Noble Qur'ān contains noble verses relating specifically to this opposition, including Allāh's saying (Exalted is He).

Then, as for him who was insolent
fa-ammā man ṭaghā
and preferred the life of this world,
wa āthara 'l-ḥayāta 'd-dunyā
surely Hell shall be his home.
fa-inna 'l-jaḥīma hiya 'l-māwā.
But as for him who feared to stand before his Lord,
wa ammā man khāfa maqāma Rabbi-hi
and forbade the lower self to follow passion,
wa naha 'n-nafsa 'ani 'l-hawā :
surely the Garden will be his final place of rest.
fa-inna 'l-jannata hiya 'l-māwā. (79:37–41)

They also include His saying (Exalted is He) on the subject of dedicated striving.

As for those who strive in Our cause,
wa 'lladhīna jāhadū fī-nā

> We surely guide them in Our ways.
> *la-nahdiyanna-hum subula-nā.* (29:69)

In the technical terminology of Sufism, spiritual exercise [*riyāḍa*] refers specifically to opposition to the lower self, and to its training and its purification. Dedicated striving [*mujāhada*] signifies the weaning of the lower self from the breast-feeding to which it is attached. It is well known that the lower self, when left to its natural devices, will lead its owner to the abyss and drop him into a bottomless pit from which there is no escape. Allāh (Exalted is He) has said,

> Surely the lower self is always instigating evil.
> *inna 'n-nafsa la-ammāratun bi's-sū'i.* (12:53)

The purpose of exercising the lower self is to convert it into a self that is inspiring [*mulhima*], tranquil [*muṭma'inna*], or well pleasing [*marḍiyya*]. Our method is wise training without exhaustion, weaning it from its desires. Just as a child is weaned from the mother's milk step by step, the lower self is restrained from everything unlawful and from every blameworthy attribute. Then it is adorned and embellished with praiseworthy characteristics. This transformation of the self is by no means easy to achieve. Sufi spiritual exercises may sometimes turn into practices that are reprehensible according to the Sacred Law. The spiritual traveler would gain nothing but harm from these kinds of practices if he pursued them for the sake of reputation and to show himself off as a devoutly religious and righteous man instead of perfecting them for the sake of Allāh's good pleasure (Glory be to Him).

What can be the verdict on highway robbers and those miscreants who do not refrain from lying and cheating for the sake of property and prestige or who accumulate wealth at the expense of their cheated victims? Such matters are far removed from the ordinary human being, who does not make a display of religious pretensions. What have they to do with someone who seeks the nearness of his Lord and His good pleasure?

Spiritual exercise is the curbing and weaning of the lower self. Dedicated striving is compliance with His commandments and avoidance of His prohibitions, the enjoining of what is right and proper and the forbidding of what is wrong and improper, and strong opposition to everything that is sinful, reprehensible, and unlawful. It may reach the point, in the view of Sufism, where the human being is transformed to resemble the angels. He worships none but his Lord, does nothing except what pleases Him, and adopts the characteristics of the Qur'ān.

We should also mention here that the forty-day retreat is a Sufi spiritual exercise beneficial for those who seek to achieve the goal by following the Sufi path. It is aimed at the subjugation of the lower self so that the human being may become able to control and direct it as he wishes, not as it wishes. It is like the trained horse that submits to its owner after coaching, and as chidren submit to learning their lessons after teaching and instruction. Consider how those who scale the mountains endure the exhausting agony. When their feet are firmly planted on their peaks, their agony comes to an end and they rejoice. There is no endurance and no agony after arrival.

It may be said that spiritual exercise is an heretical innovation, since the noble Prophet (Allāh bless him and give him peace) did not practice it nor did his Companions practice it. This assertion is refuted, however, by a number of considerations including the fact that the Prophet (Allāh bless him and give him peace) used to seclude himself in the cave of Ḥirā' in order to reflect on creation. That was a kind of spiritual exercise. There is also Allāh (Glory be to Him) expanding the breast of Muḥammad and purified him, for He said (Exalted is He),

> Did We not cause your breast to expand for you,
> *a-lam nashraḥ la-ka ṣadrak*
> and relieve you of your burden,
> *wa waḍa'nā 'an-ka wizrak*
> that weighed down your back?
> *alladhī anqaḍa ẓahrak*
> Did We not exalt your fame?
> *wa rafa'nā la-ka dhikrak.* (94:1–4)

The goal was thus realized for him without spiritual exercise and that is why he was given the title "the Trustworthy [*al-Amīn*]" among the tribe of Quraish. Furthermore, he was endowed with the providential care of Allāh (Glory be to Him) and His custody. The Companions' status was sufficiently enhanced by the honor of companionship with the Prophet (Allāh bless him and give him peace). Their life was adorned by sacred struggle, worshipful service, night vigil, the lofty moral standards of Islam, and good conduct in keeping with the Noble Qur'ān.

The Noble Qur'ān contains verses that stimulate the resolution of believing hearts to perform the night vigil as an act of worship for the sake of Allāh (Glory be to Him). This is practice of true devotion, dedicated striving and remembrance. They include His saying (Exalted is He) below.

Or is he who is obedient in the watches of the night,
am-man huwa qānitun ānā'a 'l-laili
bowing and standing erect, being wary of the Hereafter
sājidan wa qā'iman yaḥdharu 'l-ākhirata
and hoping for the mercy of his Lord…?
wa yarjū raḥmata Rabbih. (39:9)

They also include His sayings (Exalted is He).

Practice true devotion to Allāh,
wa 'ttaqu 'llāh:
and Allāh will teach you.
wa yu'allimu-kumu 'llāh. (2:282)

As for those who strive in Our cause,
wa 'lladhīna jāhadū fī-nā
We surely guide them in Our ways.
la-nahdiyanna-hum subula-nā. (29:69)

Their sides shun their couches,
tatajāfā junūbu-hum 'ani 'l-maḍāji'i
as they call on their Lord in fear and hope,
yad'ūna Rabba-hum khawfan wa ṭama'ā.
and spend of what We have bestowed on them.
wa mimmā razaqnā-hum yunfiqūn. (32:16)

[There are signs for] those who remember Allāh,
alladhīna yadhkurūna 'llāha
standing and sitting and on their sides,
qiyāman wa qu'ūdan wa 'alā junūbi-him
and who reflect on the creation of the heavens and the earth:
wa yatafakkarūna fī khalqi 's-samāwāti wa 'l-arḍ:
"Our Lord, You have not created this in vain. Glory be to You!
Rabba-nā mā khalaqta hādhā bāṭilā: subḥāna-ka
So guard us against the torment of the Fire."
fa-qi-nā 'adhāba 'n-nār. (3:191)

If we pondered these noble Qurānic verses, we would clearly understand the meaning of the spiritual exercise involved in keeping night vigil, that is, going with little sleep, offering supplication and hoping for response, contemplating the creation of the heavens and the earth, practicing remembrance by night and day, and observing true devotion.

While it is true that the Noble Qur'ān urges taking advantage of the good things of this world in numerous verses, it also makes plain to the human being that this world is transitory and that what is with Allāh is better and more lasting.

As we know from the Sufi experience of Imām al-Ghazālī, the prolonged practice of spiritual exercise and night vigil is strictly necessary for the tasting of knowledge. The shaikhs of Sufism have experienced the forty-day retreat in which the Sufi becomes immersed in worship with ardent yearning and his heart is enlightened by that which moves it to persistence in following this path.

The Noble Qur'ān also contains examples of spiritual exercise in the stories of the prophets, including the story of Zachariah, when he appeals to his Lord.

> Oh, give me from Your presence a successor!
> *fa-hab lī min ladun-ka waliyyā.* (19:5)

—and his Lord accepts his supplication, saying,

> O Zachariah, We bring you tidings
> *yā Zakariyyā innā nubashshiru-ka*
> of a son whose name is John.
> *bi-ghulāmini 'smu-hu Yaḥyā.* (19:7)

He then appealed to his Lord to command him to do something, as a way of giving thanks for His gracious favor.

> He said, "My Lord, appoint a sign for me."
> *qāla Rabbi 'j'al lī āya.* (3:41)

—so his Lord responded to him,

> He said, "The sign to you is that you shall not speak to people
> *qāla āyatu-ka allā tukallima 'n-nāsa*
> for three days except by signals.
> *thalāthata ayyāmin illā ramzā:*
> Remember your Lord frequently, and glorify [Him]
> *wa 'dhkur Rabba-ka kathīran wa sabbiḥ*

> in the early hours of night and morning."
> *bi 'l-'ashiyyi wa 'l-ibkār*. (3:41)

Similarly, when Allāh (Glory be to Him) commanded Moses to travel to Mount Sinai, in order to speak to Him, He said (Glory be to Him),

> And when We appointed for Moses forty nights...;
> *wa idh wā'adnā Mūsā arba'īna lailatan....* (2:51)

> And We appointed for Moses thirty nights [of solitude],
> *wa wā'adnā Mūsā thalāthīna lailatin*
> and We completed them with ten,
> *wa atmamnā-hā bi-'ashrin*
> so the appointed time of his Lord was forty nights
> *fa-tamma mīqātu Rabbi-hi arba'īna laila*. (7:142)

As these quotations indicate, the Noble Qur'ān contains evidence to support the practice of seclusion for forty days precisely.

Spiritual travelers know from experience that this seclusion contributes to training the lower self and bringing it under control, and to becoming accustomed to acts of worship performed with humility and careful attention.

3,4. Disclosure [*Kashf*] and Charismatic Talents [*Karāmāt*]

These are the fruits of progress on the path of Sufism. They are in the category of supernatural activity [*kharq al-'āda*], which means action beyond the rational limits of human capability.

If this kind of action stems from a noble Messenger as a challenge [to the unbelievers], it is a miracle [*mu'jiza*], like the revival of the dead by our master Jesus, the transforming of the staff into a serpent by our master Moses, and like the revelation of the Noble Qur'ān, which Allāh made the constant miracle of the Seal of the prophets, Allāh's Messenger Muḥammad (Allāh bless him and give him peace).

If it stems from a righteous man, without the claim of prophethood and challenge [to the unbelievers], it is in the category of disclosure and charismatic talents. If it emerges from a non-Muslim or from a sinful Muslim, it is in the category of temptation from Satan.

The difference between a miracle [*mu'jiza*] and a charismatic exploit [*karāma*] is that a miracle is a sign of the truthfulness of a prophet in his claim to prophethood, for he is commanded to make it manifest as a proof for the people. As for the righteous person endowed with charismatic talent, he endeavors to conceal it, unless he is compelled to exploit it in order to persuade those who go astray.

It is well known in Sufism that disclosure [*kashf*] is not a proof of elevated spiritual station for it may happen to a lunatic and be withheld from a righteous saint. This resembles the case of someone who acquires muscular strength through exercise and training but is of lesser status than a weak man. The fundamentally decisive factor is true devotion to Allāh and compliance with His Sacred Law.

The supernatural may occur as a precursor to prophethood, as with the splitting of Chosroes's palace on the night of the birth of the noble Messenger (Allāh bless him and give him peace). It may also be experienced by a righteous man as a sign of support when his supplication is accepted, for example.

As for the difference between knowledge of the Unseen and disclosure, knowledge of the Unseen is awareness of the veiled and hidden secret, in the past or the present or the future, whenever and however one wishes, whereas disclosure means that Allāh (Glory be to Him) removes the veil from the eye of insight when He wishes. Things become apparent, but this does not mean knowledge of the Unseen.

Since the messengers and prophets did not know the invisible, saints do not know the invisible, a fortiori. Allāh (Glory be to Him and Exalted is He) has said,

> Say, "I do not say to you that I possess the treasures of Allāh,
> *qul lā aqūlu la-kum 'indī khazā'inu 'llāhi*
> nor that I have knowledge of the Unseen;
> *wa lā a'lamu 'l-ghaiba*
> and I do not say to you, 'I am an angel.'
> *wa lā aqūlu la-kum innī malak:*
> I follow only what is inspired in me."
> *in attabi'u illā mā yūḥā ilayy.* (6:50)

> "If I had knowledge of the Unseen,
> *wa law kuntu a'lamu 'l-ghaiba*
> I should have abundance of wealth,
> *la-'stakthartu mina 'l-khairi*
> and adversity would not touch me. I am but a warner,
> *wa mā massaniya 's-sū': in ana illā nadhīrun*

and a bearer of good tidings to folk who believe."
wa bashīrun li-qawmin yu'minūn. (7:188)

Disclosure is the removal of the veil from the insight of the heart, so that it can witness secrets that Allāh (Glory be to Him) wishes to disclose. As al-Ghazālī has said in his book *al-Munqidh*, "Disclosed to me in these solitary retreats were matters impossible to count and thoroughly examine." He has also said, "From the outset of the spiritual path, travelers begin to receive disclosures and visionary experiences. In their wakefulness, they witness the angels and the spirits of the prophets from whom they hear voices and from whom they learn useful lessons."

Disclosure is recognition of the mysteries behind the veil, while charismatic talent signifies the realization of supernatural work like the acceptance of the supplication of the saints in the presence of Allāh when they plead for the healing of an invalid for the removal of a sorrow or for a blessing in sustenance. Supernatural events include the transporting of the throne of Bilqīs from a distant country in the twinkling of an eye by Allāh's leave.

In the view of the shaikhs of Sufism, the charismatic talents of the saints are an adjunct to the miracles of the Messenger (Allāh bless him and give him peace), and these charismatic talents result only from following his exemplary practice (Allāh bless him and give him peace).

Supernatural phenomena may sometimes be produced by exercising the lower self and by mental, psychological, and physical training. Such is the case of Hindu yoga which falls, as we have stated above, in the category of diabolic temptation.

According to Abū Yazīd (may Allāh bestow His mercy upon him), "Even if a man were to spread his prayer-mat on the water and rise into the air, you should not be deluded by him without seeing how you find him in relation to the [Divine] commandment and prohibition." The Muslim is someone who applies the teachings of the Sacred Law, not someone to whom things like this happen. The secrets are not disclosed to such people nor do they meet with the spirits of the prophets and the angels, like the saints of Allāh. It is clear that the master of temptation strives to use his work for material gain or reputation as seen from his signs of affectation and from the rewards he offers to attract attention to his deeds. The owner of charismatic talent strives to provide guidance for people, not to procure possessions. He does not display his talent unless urgent necessity requires him to do so.

Disclosure and charismatic talent may be conferred together on a righteous man as when it is disclosed to him that one of the seekers has been afflicted with a plague. He appeals for a remedy on his behalf and his supplication is answered.

I clearly recall an experience of this kind, which happened to my shaikh and my father. We were living in Syria during the Second World War in 1944 when I received a document from my father (may Allāh sanctify his innermost being), who was then at Biyāra, 'Irāq. He had inscribed this note in the margin in his noble handwriting, "Some days ago, I heard a voice say, 'Ibn 'Abd al-Khāliq is sick.' I have no idea whether it was a genuine or an untruthful informer. Let me know!" As a matter of fact, Ibn 'Abd al-Khāliq (who was with us as one of the Shaikh's pupils) had fallen sick with typhoid at that very same time. He was rushed to the French doctors, who isolated him and declared that his treatment would be difficult and very prolonged. To the amazement of the physicians, however, he was quick to recover completely. Here we have an example of disclosure and charismatic talent! The disclosure was awareness of the invalid's condition, despite the distance of hundreds of kilometers, while acceptance of the plea for his healing was a charismatic gift from the Lord of Truth.

The juristic and theological view of the permissibility and possibility of charismatic exploits has been expounded at length in the science of theology.

5. Light [*Nūr*]

The term *nūr* [light] is used in numerous senses. Its obvious meaning is the opposite of darkness for it signifies radiance. In the view of Sufism, it is the radiance that envelops a man's heart so that he perceives a lovely, charming radiance, a beautiful scent and a delightful flavor with a sensation that is heartfelt and spiritual, which is not susceptible of description and definition.

It occurs in the Noble Qur'ān in numerous senses.

1. It is one of the Most Beautiful Names of Allāh:

> Allāh is the Light of the heavens and the earth.
> *Allāhu nūru 's-samāwāti wa 'l-arḍ.* (24:35)

2. It is one of the names of the Noble Qur'ān and the Heavenly Books.

So believe in Allāh and His Messenger,
fa-āminū bi'llāhi wa Rasūli-hi
and in the Light which We have sent down.
wa 'n-Nūri 'lladhī anzalnā:
And Allāh is Aware of the things you do.
wa 'llāhu bi-mā ta'malūna Khabīr. (64:8)

O humankind, now has a proof from your Lord come to you,
yā ayyuha 'n-nāsu qad jā'a-kum burhānun min Rabbi-kum
and We have sent down to you a clear light.
wa anzalnā ilai-kum nūran mubīnā. (4:175)

Say, "Who revealed the Book which Moses brought,
qul man anzala 'l-Kitāba 'lladhī jā'a bi-hi Mūsā
a light and a guidance for humankind?'
nūran wa hudan li'n-nāsi. (6:91)

3. It conveys the meaning of faith [*īmān*], which is the opposite of unbelief [*kufr*]:

A Book which We have revealed to you
Kitābun anzalnā-hu ilai-ka
that you may bring forth humankind from darkness into light,
li-tukhrija 'n-nāsa mina 'ẓ-ẓulumāti ila 'n-nūri
by the permission of their Lord,
bi-idhni Rabbi-him
to the path of the Almighty, the Praiseworthy.
ilā ṣirāṭi 'l-'Azīzi 'l-Ḥamīd. (14:1)

Whereby Allāh guides him who seeks His good pleasure
yahdī bi-hi'llāhu mani 'ttaba'a riḍwāna-hu
unto paths of peace. He brings them out of darkness into light
subula 's-salāmi wa yukhriju-hum mina 'ẓ-ẓulumāti ila 'n-nūri
by His decree, and guides them to a straight path.
bi idhni hi wa yahdī him ilā ṣirāṭin mustaqīm. (5:16)

In these two noble verses, as well as in tens of other verses, it is clear that faith is a light and that unbelief is a darkness.

4. It is used in the sense of the sight of the eye,

Say, "Is the blind man equal to the one who can see,
qul hal yastawi 'l-a'mā wa 'l-baṣīr:
or is darkness equal to light?"
am hal tastawi 'ẓ-ẓulumāti wa 'n-nūr. (13:16)

5. It is used in the sense of knowledge, because it is only by knowledge that a man can distinguish between the good and the bad, whence the saying, "Knowledge is a light and ignorance is a darkness."

6. It is used in the sense of intelligence, without which the human being would be ineffective in the affairs of his life, and would not be distinguishable from other living creatures.

In *al-Falsafa al-ishrāqiyya* [*The Illuminating Philosophy*], as-Suhrawardī (of Aleppo) refers to the realm of light and the realm of darkness. He says, "The Light of lights is Allāh (Glory be to Him) for He is the source of every light." He offers this supplication in his preface, "O Self-Sustaining One, assist us with the Light, attach us firmly to the Light, and resurrect us to the Light!"

Shaikh Muḥyi 'd-Dīn ibn al-'Arabī has said in his book *Hayākil an-Nūr* [*Patterns of Light*], "Light is a Divine gift, which settles in the heart and rids it of the darkness of this fleeting world, for it leaves no room for anything but light."

According to Imām al-Ghazālī in his book *al-Munqidh*, "Sufi and spiritual knowledge is a light which Allāh casts into the heart of the Muslim."

The light that is mentioned by the masters of Sufism, like al-Ghazālī and Muḥyi'd-Dīn ibn al-'Arabī, signifies blessing, radiance, a special knowledge, discovery, and direct witnessing. It is a spiritual vision by which the spiritual travelers tread the path. Disclosure, charismatic talents, and spiritual stations become accessible to the Muslim by means of this light, which is the eye of insight. He thereby excels in his knowledge and is transformed into a different person. This light was also available to the prophets, so let us contemplate Allāh's saying (Exalted is He) to His noble Prophet Muḥammad (Allāh bless him and give him peace),

Did We not cause your breast to expand for you,
a-lam nashraḥ la-ka ṣadrak:
and relieve you of your burden, that weighed down your back?
wa waḍa'nā 'an-ka wizrak: alladhī anqaḍa ẓahrak:

Did We not exalt your fame?
wa rafa'nā la-ka dhikrak. (94:1–4)

This refers to a light which Allāh cast into the heart of the Prophet. In the story of Moses and the righteous man who recognized many of the secrets by the light of Allāh, we are told in the Noble Qur'ān,

Then they found one of Our servants,
fa-wajadā 'abdan min 'ibādi-nā
to whom We had given mercy from Us,
ātainā-hu raḥmatan min 'indi-nā
and had taught him knowledge from Our presence.
wa 'allamnā-hu min ladun-nā 'ilmā. (18:65)

This knowledge, which Allāh (Glory be to Him) casts into the servant's heart, is called a light. The Qur'ānic statement

We gave him wisdom and knowledge.
ātainā-hu ḥukman wa 'ilmā. (12:22; 21:74; 28:14)

is repeated several times, with reference to Joseph, Lot, and Moses (peace be upon them). The Noble Qur'ān contains similar references to the Divine mercy in conjunction with the word "light [*nūr*]" meaning magnanimity, generosity, knowledge, wisdom, and spiritual station. "Light" also conveys these meanings in the Sufi use of the term.

6. The Heart [*Qalb*]

If the word *qalb* [heart] were deleted from the literature of Sufism and the meetings of the Sufis, nothing would be left. It has two meanings:

1. The pine cone-shaped gland that is situated in the breast of every human being and possessor of a spirit. This is the motor of the physical body, so if it stops moving, life comes to a stop.
2. A spiritual and figurative meaning. In Sufi usage, this signifies the center of the sphere of Sufi knowledge and the core of spiritual progress. In the ethical, emotional, and psychic context, it signifies the source of inspiration for the moral and ethical senses and the tastes of ardent love.

In the books of Sufism, the term is employed in a figurative sense, meaning the center of emotional, psychic, and human feeling. In our everyday conversations, we often say things like: "My heart is inclined toward a particular color," or "My heart feels nothing but satisfaction with it," and "My heart is annoyed." These descriptions do not apply to the heart in the first sense mentioned above. In the present context, we are concerned with the particular states experienced by the heart in the second sense. From the Sufi perspective, the heart is not the pine cone-shaped gland, but a subtle essence that is the center of good and bad will. The Sufi must strive for its purification so that it becomes exclusively devoted to goodwill. This is called *tazkiyat al-qalb* [the purification of the heart], after which the heart becomes firmly committed to the love of Allāh (Glory be to Him) and a throne for His light so it does not forget His remembrance (Glory be to Him) for the twinkling of an eye.

The word *qalb* occurs in the Noble Qur'ān in more than a hundred places. It has numerous applications in the figurative sense, all of them signifying that the heart is the center of psychic feelings. While the heart is indeed like that in the real sense, it is also important in the material sense. The heart is for the body like the motor for the automobile. Were it not for the heart, the body would be nothing. In the case of the spiritual meaning, its importance is clearly expressed in the saying of the Prophet (Allāh bless him and give him peace),

> The heart of the believer is the Throne of the All-Merciful.

We are told in the Sacred Tradition [*Ḥadīth Qudsī*]:

> My earth and My heaven do not have space enough for Me, but the heart of My believing servant has space enough for Me!

The task of the Sufi spiritual traveler is to cleanse his heart, the center of the human reality, by ridding it of every flaw so that it contains nothing but the Light of his Lord (Glory be to Him). The highest point of this goal is that the heart becomes dedicated to remembrance.

As we have mentioned in the discussion of remembrance [*dhikr*] and the lower self [*nafs*], the heart that becomes accustomed to inaudible remembrance is that of someone dedicated to remembrance. He may hear the sound of his own remembrance, and the sound of his remembrance may be heard by another if that person listens to the sound of his breast. My paternal uncle, Shaikh Kāmil (may Allāh bestow His mercy upon him), the descendant of Shaikh 'Umar Ḍiyā' ad-Dīn an-Naqshbandī, used to say when he swore a solemn oath: "I swear by someone from whose breast I hear the sound 'Allāh'." I also recall that I heard him say when he was in his eighties: "I was a youngster after my father's death and I did not understand how the heart, 'a piece of flesh,' could practice remembrance by itself. Then my brother, Shaikh Najm ad-Dīn, sent for me and asked me: 'Is it true, as I have heard, that you do not believe in the remembrance of the heart?' I said politely: 'I believe in it, but I do not understand it and my heart does not feel easy about it.' He said: 'The Shaikh once called me to him while he was standing, and hugged me tight until my ear was glued to his breast. By Allāh, I could hear him saying: "Allāh, Allāh," so I moved my head away, then set it close to his breast again, and I heard the remembrance of his heart. I burst into tears at that point, and threw myself upon him. He said: 'Neither this nor that!'"

My paternal uncle also used to say: "My head used to be attracted to his breast as if by magnetism."

The matter is clear and familiar to the spiritual travelers. The heart of one of them may begin spontaneous remembrance after seven days of inaudible remembrance, while the heart of another may begin spontaneous remembrance after forty days. It all depends on the quality of the secluded retreat and the separation from everything other than Allāh (Glory be to Him).

According to the Naqshbandīs, as we have mentioned, there are five subtle centers within the inner being: (1) the heart [*al-qalb*], (2) the spirit [*ar-rūḥ*], (3) the secret [*as-sirr*], (4) the hidden [*al-khafī*], and (5) the most deeply hidden [*al-akhfā*]. The self [*an-nafs*] is a term for the subtle center pertaining to the realm of creation and matter.

The Naqshbandīs practice remembrance in a special form. After habituation therewith, the heart embarks on spontaneous remembrance, then the other subtle centers follow suit. Finally the subtle self follows. It is considered the center of the animal feeling belonging to the human being and which is always instigating evil. At this point, let me draw attention to four poetic verses from a Sufi ode by Shaikh 'Umar Ḍiyā' ad-Dīn an-Naqshbandī, the perfect spiritual guide and master of the Spiritual Path. He uttered these verses while traveling the Spiritual Path, and it is evident that he was endowed with a lofty station in Sufism. He uttered them in this connection, that is, with reference to these subtle centers and their remembrance.

By virtue of my ardent love for the Glory of the Universe,
my heart became pure and serene,
for the rust was removed by the ablution,
and the light shone forth within my breast.

Delivered from Iblīs the Accursed
were the burdens of my personal nature.
I reached the station of those who know directly,
without weariness on my part.

People washed their hands of me,
because I belonged to the party of the ardent lovers.

Whichever way I turn,
His secrets become apparent to me like the sun.
All my subtle ingredients are immersed
in the remembrance of Allāh (Glory be to Him).

This confirms what we have said about those who know directly. Perfections are realized for them without exercise and effort.

I recently read a book critical of Sufism by 'Abd ar-Raḥmān ad-Dimashqī. The points he raises include the question, "How can the heart perform remembrance?" He obviously sees the heart as nothing but this piece of flesh, but that is not how it is. Does he fail to notice that speech is nowadays is expressed by other means than the tongue, like tape-recordings, radio, and television? These are material means. If such people also deny the spiritual values, what will they say about the Qur'ānic verses that speak of hearts as hard as stone, the rust of hearts and their darknesses, and tens of other qualities attributed to the heart? Glory be to Allāh! If Allāh wishes to send someone astray, He makes him forget what he has read and learned. Was not the Noble Qur'ān sent down to the heart of Muḥammad?

For he [Gabriel] brought it down to your heart by Allāh's leave.
fa-inna-hu nazzala-hu 'alā qalbi-ka bi-idhni 'llāhi. (2:97)

It is well known that the Qur'ān is not a material object, but intelligible speech. By the same token, the heart in this context is not the piece of flesh, for the heart in this context is the reality of Muḥammad (Allāh bless him and give him peace) and the reality of his prophethood. Allāh (Exalted is He) has said,

Surely in that there is a reminder for anyone who has a heart.
inna fī dhālika la-dhikrā li-man kāna la-hu qalbun. (50:37)

If the heart in this context meant the familiar piece of flesh, we would say that every animal has a heart of this kind, but the heart in this context is the inner feeling that recognizes wisdom and good advice.

Allāh (Exalted is He) has said,

> Except one who comes to Allāh with a sound heart.
> *illā man ata 'llāha bi-qalbin salīm.* (26:89)
>
> This does Allāh print on every arrogant, disdainful heart.
> *ka-dhālika yaṭba'u 'llāhu 'alā kulli qalbi mutakabbirin jabbār.* (40:35)
>
> For if you had been harsh and hard of heart.
> *wa law kunta faẓẓan ghalīẓa 'l-qalbi.* (3:159)
>
> But blind are the hearts within the breasts.
> *wa lākin ta'ma 'l-qulūbu 'llatī fi 'ṣ-ṣudūr.* (22:46)
>
> Or are there locks upon their hearts?
> *am 'alā qulūbin aqfālu-hā.* (47:24)
>
> And hearts reached the throats.
> *wa balaghati 'l-qulūbu 'l-ḥanājira.* (33:10)
>
> It is surely from devotion of the hearts.
> *fa-inna-hā min taqwa 'l-qulūb.* (22:32)
>
> And he calls Allāh to witness as to that which is in his heart.
> *wa yushhidu 'llāha 'alā mā fī qalbi-hi.* (2:204)
>
> And he seals up his hearing and his heart.
> *wa khatama 'alā sam'i-hi wa qalbi-hi.* (45:23)
>
> And We made firm their hearts.
> *wa rabaṭnā 'alā qulūbi-him.* (18:14)
>
> And they say, "Our hearts are hardened."
> *wa qālū qulūbu-nā ghulf.* (2:88)
>
> And do not lodge in our hearts any rancor.
> *wa lā taj'al fī qulūbi-nā ghilla.* (59:10)
>
> Our Lord! Do not cause our hearts to stray.
> *Rabba-nā lā tuzigh qulūba-nā.* (3:8)
>
> For that which your hearts have earned.
> *bi-mā kasabat qulūbu-kum*: (2:225)
>
> Then your hearts were hardened.
> *thumma qasat qulūbu-kum* (2:74)

Allāh has sealed their hearts.
khatama 'llāhu 'alā qulūbi-him. (2:7)

But woe unto those whose hearts are hardened!
fa-wailun li'l-qāsiyati qulūbu-hum. (39:22)

To those whose hearts are diseased.
li'lladhīna fī qulūbi-him maraḍun. (22:53)

Allāh has set a seal upon their hearts.
wa ṭaba'a 'llāhu 'alā qulūbi-him. (9:93)

Allāh (Exalted is He) has also assigned tens of other attributes to the heart, confirming that the heart in this context is not the familiar heart in the physical body, but the heart that is the source of good and evil, and is subject to reward and punishment.

Has this writer [the critic of Sufism] not heard all these Qur'ānic verses, and in particular the noble verse,

But woe unto those whose hearts are hardened!
fa-wailun li'l-qāsiyati qulūbu-hum. (39:22)?

As a matter of fact, the response to people like him is the saying of Allāh (Exalted is He),

And he seals up his hearing and his heart.
wa khatama 'alā sam'i-hi wa qalbi-hi. (45:23)

I am amazed at someone who denies the remembrance of the heart, when he recites the sayings of Allāh (Exalted is He),

And do not obey someone whose heart We have made heedless
wa lā tuṭi' man aghfalnā qalba-hu
of Our remembrance, and who follows his own lust.
'an dhikri-nā wa 'ttaba'a hawā-hu. (18:28)

Whoever believes in Allāh, He guides his heart.
wa man yu'min bi'llāhi yahdi qalba-h. (64:11)

What is the interpretation of His saying (Exalted is He)?

For the faith has not yet entered into your hearts.
wa lammā yadkhuli 'l-īmānu fī qulūbi-kum. (49:14)

What is meant by the heart in this context? There is no doubt that faith enters the reality of the human being, and that it is experienced by him inwardly. Let us also consider His saying (Exalted is He).

> It is surely from true devotion of the hearts.
> *fa-inna-hā min taqwa 'l-qulūb.* (22:32)

This refers to the inner, spiritual entity that is trained and purified by true devotion, which rids it of envy, arrogant pride and all other blameworthy attributes. Some say it is not the heart that is the master and director of the body, but rather the brain. In any case, neither the heart not the brain should be understood in the material sense. "The heart is the subtle center that has its abode within the breast." The heart is the center of the thing, its middle and its core. It is clear to the spiritual travelers that the abode of this subtle center is the breast, and that the abode of the lower self is the face of the human being. The lower self is closer to the brain, while the heart is closer to the pine cone-shaped gland in the breast. The other subtle centers, like the spirit, the secret and the hidden, are likewise situated in the breast.

Those experienced in Sufi practices, spiritual travelers who apply its methods, are well acquainted with the location of each subtle center. They know that each color has a light which differs from that of another by color. They distinguish one subtle center from another. I shall deal with the subject, with Allāh's help, in the discussion of the Naqshbandī Spiritual Path.

The gist of our conclusion is that the heart, in the view of Sufism, is the center of these attributes mentioned by the Noble Qur'ān. The spiritual traveler must strive, through remembrance and with the help of his spiritual guide, to cleanse his heart of bad attributes and to adorn it with praiseworthy attributes. He will thereby make his heart ready to entertain the Light of his Lord, and His remembrance (Exalted is He) will become the spiritual provision of his heart. If he sticks to the Spiritual Path in remembrance and repentance, His Light (Glory be to Him) will manifest itself in his heart. If someone is deprived of this bounty, he will have no share in this light, as Allāh (Glory be to Him and Exalted is He) has said,

> And he for whom Allāh has not appointed light,
> *wa man lam yaj'ali 'llāhu la-hu nūran*
> for him there is no light.
> *fa-mā la-hu min nūr.* (24:40)

At the end of this speech of mine, let me cite this noble Qur'ānic verse:

O you who believe, practice true devotion to Allāh,
yā ayyuha 'lladhīna āmanu 'ttaqu 'llāha
and put faith in His Messenger.
wa āminū bi-Rasūli-hi
He will give you twofold of His mercy and will appoint for you
yu'ti-kum kiflaini min Raḥmati-hi wa yaj'al la-kum
a light by which to walk, and He will forgive you.
nūran tamshūna bi-hi wa yaghfir la-kum
Allāh is All-Forgiving, All-Compassionate.
wa 'llāhu Ghafūrun Raḥīm. (57:28)

(Light [*nūr*] has numerous meanings, which we have mentioned in the section devoted to it.)

* * *

Diagram showing the locations
of the five subtle centers in the body

• The self [*an-nafs*] (between eyes)

(The person's right side)	(The person's left side)
• The hidden [*al-khafī*]	• The secret [*as-sirr*]

• The most deeply hidden [*al-akhfā*]

• The spirit [*ar-rūḥ*]	• The heart [*al-qalb*]

7. The Self [*Nafs*]

The term *nafs* is commonly used in expressions [corresponding to the English reflexive pronouns ending in "-self"] like *al-insān nafsuh* [the person himself]. It sometimes means the spirit, sometimes the blood, and sometimes the passion and desire of the human being. It may also signify a willing person, who always says "Yes!" to someone who calls for him. The word *nafs* occurs in more than two hundred places in the Noble Qur'ān.

As a topic of Sufism, the self [*nafs*] is so important that it has been called the key to the door of Sufism and the very core of its purpose. The Sufi spiritual traveler strives for its enlightenment and its purification. Allāh (Glory be to Him) has referred to it in His saying,

Successful indeed is he who causes it to grow in purity,
qad aflaḥa man zakkā-hā

> and a failure indeed is he who stunts its growth.
> *wa qad khāba man dassā-hā.* (91:9,10)

—which is preceded by His saying (Glory be to Him),

> By a self and That which shaped it,
> *wa nafsin wa mā sawwāhā.*
> and inspired it with awareness of its depravity and its true devotion.
> *fa-alhama-hā fujūra-hā wa taqwā-hā.* (91:7,8)

The Sufi spiritual traveler seeks guidance in the Noble Qur'ān for the purification of his own self, by promoting the element of goodness therein and rejecting the element of evil. Allāh (Glory be to Him) has said,

> And whoever is saved from the greed of his own self,
> *wa man yūqa shuḥḥa nafsi-hi*
> such are the ones who will prosper.
> *fa-ulā'ika humu 'l-mufliḥūn.* (59:9)

The purification of the self is one of the most important disciplines of the spiritual travelers, for without it the spiritual traveler would be left in danger of falling by the wayside, and the station of sainthood would never be realized for him. After this purification comes concentration on the adornment of the inner being with praiseworthy attributes, the purpose of climbing the ladder of Sufism. But is this an easy matter? How does the human being succeed in curbing the self, and what is the fruit of this success?

The first stage begins with repentance. Then comes strict adherence to what is right and proper and to worshipful service in accordance with the teachings of the Noble Qur'ān and the Prophetic Sunna. Then comes diligent commitment to His remembrance (Glory be to Him), and opposition to selfish inclinations.

By this we mean training the self and making it accustomed to obedience, to the point where the spiritual traveler brings it to the essence of certainty, either on his own or with the help of his spiritual director. When that point is reached, nothing will adversely affect his faith. It is also incumbent upon him to avoid exaggeration and shortcoming.

The masters of Sufism have designated stages for the spiritual travelers to reach in the process of traversing this terrain. The self [*nafs*] has a particular qualification suited to each stage, based on guidance obtained from the Noble Qur'ān.

As we read in the book entitled *Mu'jam muṣṭalaḥāt aṣ-ṣūfiyya*, "The self has five levels: (1) animal [*ḥayawāniyya*], (2) domineering [*ammāra*], (3) inspired [*mulhama*], (4) censorious [*lawwāma*] and (5) tranquil [*muṭma'inna*]." According to the same source, "The self may also be rational [*nāṭiqa*], righteous [*ṣāliḥa*], wise [*ḥakīma*] and prophetic [*nabawiyya*]."

In his book *Tanwīr al-qulūb*, Shaikh Muḥammad Amīn al-Kurdī has assigned seven levels to the self: (1) domineering [*ammāra*], (2) censorious [*lawwāma*], (3) tranquil [*muṭma'inna*], (4) inspired [*mulhama*], (5) well pleased [*rāḍiya*], (6) well pleasing [*marḍiyya*], and (7) perfect [*kāmila*].

The domineering or instigating self [*an-nafs al-ammāra*] is the self that inclines to the animal side. It is called *ammāra* [domineering; instigating] because it directs its owner toward evil. This is the meaning of the noble Qur'ānic verse,

> I do not exculpate myself.
> *wa mā ubarri'u nafsī:*
> Surely the self is always instigating evil,
> *inna 'n-nafsa la-ammāratun bi's-sū'i.* (12:53)

According to some, this self is superior to the animal self, which, like grazing livestock, is interested in nothing but the stuff of this world.

The censorious self [*an-nafs al-lawwāma*] is the self that rebukes the human being when he commits a sin or intends something bad, and which goads him toward repentance. Allāh (Exalted is He) has said,

> No, I swear by the Day of Resurrection,
> *lā uqsimu bi-Yawmi 'l-Qiyāma:*
> and no, I swear by the censorious self.
> *wa lā uqsimu bi'n-nafsi'l-lawwāma.* (75:1,2)

The inspired self [*an-nafs al-mulhama*] is the self that distinguishes between profligacy and true devotion, on the basis of His saying (Exalted is He),

> By a self and That which shaped it,
> *wa nafsin wa mā sawwāhā.*
> and inspired it with awareness
> *fa-alhama-hā*

of its depravity and its true devotion.
fujūra-hā wa taqwā-hā. (91:7,8)

The self that is tranquil [*muṭma'inna*], well pleased [*rāḍiya*] and well pleasing [*marḍiyya*] is the self that is well pleased with its Lord, and with which He is well pleased, on the basis of His saying (Exalted is He).

O self now at peace,
yā ayyatuha 'n-nafsu 'l-muṭma'inna:
return unto your Lord, well pleased, well pleasing!
irji'ī ilā Rabbi-ki rāḍiyatan marḍiyya. (89:27,28)

The perfect self [*an-nafs al-kāmila*] is peculiar to the prophets and the perfect saints.

The self is one of the subtle centers of the realm of creation, supplementary to the four basic elements, for it counts as the fifth according to the philosophers of Sufism, in addition to water (moisture), earth, air, and fire (heat). The heart, the spirit, the secret, the hidden and the most deeply hidden belong to the realm of the Divine commandment. The subtle center of the self is purified by remembrance. It is the rational self according to the Naqshbandīs.

In his Ode of the Cloak [*Qaṣīdat al-burda*], the Sufi poet al-Būṣīrī (d. A.H. 696) says,

The self is like a child who grows, if you neglect him, [he continues] to suck the breast, but if you wean him he is weaned.

According to Shaikh 'Abd al-Qādir al-Jīlānī in his book *al-Ghunya*, "The danger posed by the lower self is its inclination toward boastfulness and its desire to win praise. This kind of person resembles a porter because his worshipful service amounts to nothing but the carrying of burdens, as an ostentatious display for the sake of gaining a reputation. He is likely to perish without being aware of his own condition."

Nothing is achieved without striving and righteous work. Allāh (Exalted is He) has said,

And that man has only that for which he makes an effort,
wa an laisa li'l-insāni illā mā sa'ā
and that his effort will be seen.
wa anna sa'yu-hu sawfa yurā. (53:39,40)

As for those who strive in Our cause,
wa 'lladhīna jāhadū fī-nā
We surely guide them in Our ways.
la-nahdiyanna-hum subula-nā. (29:69)

As we read in the book entitled *Futūḥ al-ghaib* [*Revelations of the Unseen*], by Shaikh 'Abd al-Qādir al-Jīlānī, "The instigating self has two states, they being happiness and joy, on the one hand, and wretchedness and torment on the other. If this world cramps a man, he becomes ungrateful, and if this world opens its doors wide for him, he drifts toward passionate desire and lustful appetites."

Allāh (Exalted is He) has said,

No indeed; the human being does exceed the proper bounds,
kallā inna 'l-insāna la-yaṭghā
in that he regards himself as self-sufficient.
an rā'-hu 'staghnā. (96:6,7)

If someone knows his own self, he knows his Lord, and if someone does not know his own self, he gives it free rein. Joseph must have known his own self, since Allāh (Glory be to Him) has quoted him as saying,

I do not exculpate myself.
wa mā ubarri'u nafsī
Surely the self is always instigating evil.
inna 'n-nafsa la-ammāratun bi's-sū'i. (12:53)

The gist of what we have mentioned is that the purification of the self is one of the basic principles of the Sufi method, in accordance with Islam.

8. Remembrance [*Dhikr*]

In the terminology of Sufism, *dhikr* means the remembrance of Allāh (Glory be to Him) and the celebration of His praise, as if by saying, "Glory be to Allāh! Praise be to Allāh! There is no god but Allāh!" It likewise applies to supplications and invocations of blessing.

The word *dhikr* occurs in the Noble Qur'ān in the sense of the ritual prayer [*ṣalāt*], and also in the sense of the Noble Qur'ān itself. Allāh (Exalted is He) has said,

O you who believe! When the call is proclaimed
yā ayyuha 'lladhīna āmanū idhā nūdiya

for the ritual prayer on the Day of Congregation,
li'ṣ-ṣalāti min yawmi 'l-jumu'ati
hasten to the remembrance of Allāh and leave trading aside.
fa-'s'aw ilā dhikri 'llāhi wa dharu 'l-bai'. (62:9)

—and what is meant here by *dhikr* [remembrance] is the ritual prayer on the Day of Congregation. He has also said (Exalted is He),

Surely We have revealed the Reminder,
innā Naḥnu nazzalna 'dh-Dhikra
and We assuredly watch over it.
wa innā la-hu la-Ḥāfiẓūn. (15:9)

—and what is meant here by *adh-Dhikr* [the Reminder] is the Noble Qur'ān.

As for *dhikr* in the sense of glorification, it occurs in a number of clear verses in the Noble Qur'ān, including among others:

So remember the Name of your Lord
wa 'dhkuri 'sma Rabbi-ka
and devote yourself to Him with intense devotion.
wa tabattal ilai-hi tabtīlā. (73:8)

Remember Allāh.
fa-'dhkuru 'llāha. (2:198)

The remembrance of Allāh is greater.
wa la-dhikru 'llāhi akbar. (29:45)

It is truly in the remembrance of Allāh
a-lā bi-dhikri 'llāhi
that hearts feel comfortably at rest.
taṭma'innu 'l-qulūb. (13:28)

Remembrance is required by the Sacred Law, as indicated by His saying (Exalted is He),

Remember your Lord often.
wa 'dhkur Rabba-ka kathīrān. (3:41)

And remember your Lord within yourself.
wa 'dhkur Rabba-ka fī nafsi-ka. (7:205)

O you who believe,
yā ayyuha 'lladhīna āmanū

> let neither your possessions nor your children distract you
> *lā tulhi-kum amwālu-kum wa lā awlādu-kum*
> from the remembrance of Allāh.
> *'an dhikri 'llāh.* (63:9)

> Remember Him as He has guided you aright.
> *wa 'dhkurū-hu ka-mā hadā-kum.* (2:198)

Remembrance does not have a specific place or a specific form. Allāh (Exalted is He) has said,

> Remember Allāh, standing, sitting, and reclining on your sides.
> *fa-'dhkuru 'llāha qiyāman wa qu'ūdan wa 'alā junūbi-kum.* (4:103)

Remembrance is not confined to the ritual prayer alone, nor is a little remembrance sufficient, for remembrance is commanded by night and by day, in private and in public, with the heart and with the tongue, and its frequent performance is required. Allāh (Exalted is He) has said,

> O you who believe, remember Allāh
> *yā ayyuha 'lladhīna āmanu 'dhkuru 'llāha*
> with frequent remembrance.
> *dhikran kathīrā.* (33:41)

> Remember your Lord often.
> *wa 'dhkur Rabba-ka kathīran.* (3:41)

> And remember your Lord within yourself,
> *wa 'dhkur Rabba-ka fī nafsi-ka.*
> humbly and with awe, without audible expression,
> *taḍarru'an wa khīfatan wa dūna 'l-jahri mina 'l-qawli*
> in the morning and the evening.
> *bi'l-ghuduwwi wa 'l-āṣāli*
> Do not be one of those who are neglectful.
> *wa lā takun mina 'l-ghāfilīn.* (7:205)

Allāh (Exalted is He) has also said,

> And he whose sight is dim to the remembrance of the All-Merciful,
> *wa man ya'shu 'an dhikri 'r-Raḥmāni*
> to him We assign a devil who becomes his comrade.
> *nuqayyiḍ la-hu shaiṭānan fa-huwa la-hu qarīn.* (43:36)

As further evidence of the obligatory nature of remembrance in it various forms, consider the threat of torment and woe for those who neglect it. Allāh (Exalted is He) has said,

> But woe unto those hearts are hardened
> *fa-wailun li'l-qāsiyati qulūbu-hum*
> against the remembrance of Allāh.
> *min dhikri 'llāh.* (39:22)

The modality of Sufi remembrance is of two kinds: remembrance with the tongue and remembrance with the heart. Some of the Sufi lineages are inclined to favor remembrance with the tongue while some are inclined to favor remembrance with the heart. Others attach importance to both forms of remembrance, maintaining that it begins with the tongue and then, after becoming a regular practice, it is transformed into remembrance with the heart.

According to the erudite scholar al-Manāwī,[1] "There are three types of remembrance: (1) the remembrance of the common folk, with the tongue, (2) the remembrance of the *élite*, with the heart, and (3) the remembrance of the *élite* of the *élite*. When the latter witness the One they remember they forsake and forget everything else. Their only wish is for the state of witnessing to last forever and that the Truth may be visible to them in every situation."

According to Imām an-Nawawī (may Allāh bestow His mercy upon him),[2] "Remembrance may be with the heart and it may be with tongue. At its best, it is performed with the heart and the tongue together, but if it is restricted to one of the two, the heart is preferable. Allāh (Exalted is He) has said,

> And do not obey someone
> *wa lā tuṭi' man*
> whose heart We have made heedless of Our remembrance.
> *aghfalnā qalba-hu 'an dhikri-nā.* (18:28)

> But woe unto those hearts are hardened
> *fa-wailun li'l-qāsiyati qulūbu-hum*
> against the remembrance of Allāh.
> *min dhikri 'llāh.* (39:22)"

1. See *Nash'at al-falsafa aṣ-ṣūfiyya wa-taṭawwuru-hā,* by Dr. 'Irfān 'Abd al-Ḥamīd.
2. *al-Luma'*, pp. 100 ff.

Preference depends on the aptitude of the practitioner of remembrance and on the guidance of the spiritual director. If the former is prone to ostentation and has a loud voice or if audible expression causes trouble for other people, there is no good in his audible remembrance. On the other hand, if his audible expression increases his enthusiasm and his ardor, it is preferable. The intelligent Muslim is guided to whichever is the better of the two [forms of remembrance].

Remembrance of Allāh is an effective treatment, tried and tested for more than fourteen hundred years. It washed hearts clean of rust and rids them of the attributes of depravity, like envy, arrogant pride, avarice, and lying. Allāh (Exalted is He) has said,

> It is truly in the remembrance of Allāh
> *a-lā bi-dhikri 'llāhi*
> that hearts feel comfortably at rest.
> *taṭma'innu 'l-qulūb*. (13:28)

The heart has rust. Just as iron becomes rusty, the heart can have spiritual rust. Allāh (Glory be to Him) has said,

> No indeed; but what they have been earning has rusted upon their hearts.
> *kallā bal rāna 'alā qulūbi-him mā kānū yaksibūn*. (83:14)

This means that evil deeds turn into spiritual rust, which becomes attached to the heart. Allāh (Glory be to Him) has said,

> And We remove whatever rancor may be in their breasts.
> *wa naza'nā mā fī ṣudūri-him min ghillin*. (7:43)

This rancor is spiritual, so we do not perceive it outwardly. It consists of malice and diseased imagination.

In his striving and his dedication to remembrance, the sole purpose of the Sufi spiritual traveler is to cleanse his heart of spiritual rust. As they have said, "The heart is like the mirror dimmed by smoke, so the remembrance of Allāh (Glory be to Him) is a polishing and a cleansing. The light of its Lord will then become manifest in it and spiritual secrets will be disclosed." This benefit is enjoyed by the spiritual traveler to the extent of his preparedness. While spiritual travelers depend on the direction of their guides for complete understanding of remembrance, it generally amounts to the declaration, "Allāh! There is no god but Allāh."

The Prophet (Allāh bless him and give him peace) once said,

> The best of what I have said—I and the prophets before me—is the statement, "There is no god but Allāh [*lā ilāha illa 'Llāh*]."

The spiritual guide may assess the condition of a disciple and then decide to teach him another remembrance like "There is no might nor any power except with Allāh [*lā ḥawla wa lā quwwata illā bi'Llāh*]," or the recitation of a Sūra from the Qur'ān.

Remembrance has various proprieties explained by the masters of intimate knowledge. The first is physical cleanliness and ritual ablution. They also include the choice of a secluded place that does not reek with the odor of ostentation. Then comes presence of the heart. The practitioner of remembrance must regard himself as present in front of his Lord. He must cultivate the most perfect attributes on a regular basis and he must not be neglectful. He must say with the fullness of his heart, "I seek Your pardon, Your good pleasure and Your nearness." The most fundamental prerequisite is repentance, whether or not he has a spiritual guide. Nothing will accrue to him except after the renunciation of every evil by means of repentance.

The emptier the place [where remembrance is performed], the more the remembrance will benefit from complete concentration. I shall examine this subject further in my discussion of the Naqshbandī Spiritual Path.

Remembrance begins with the Essence, "Allāh!"

One of the proprieties of remembrance is that the tongue should cleave to the roof of the mouth at the time of remembrance. Someone may ask himself, "What is this, and why is that?" Let me therefore describe a particular experience of mine.

I was in the fourteenth year of my life, when my Shaikh and my father (may Allāh bestow His mercy upon him) taught me the Spiritual Path. He said, "Remember Allāh with your heart and, while in the state of remembrance, fix your tongue to the roof of your mouth." I learned the lesson without asking why, firstly because of inexperience and secondly because of shyness. As for the present situation, I now recognize the wisdom of that lesson, which was aimed at binding the tongue and keeping it immobile. It is natural for the tongue to move during speech, so, if it is not stopped, it rushes into spontaneous movement. The remembrance then shifts from the heart to the tongue. The person comes to be "like spun thread that is weakened through unraveling," and nothing becomes real for the heart. Concentration is intensified by this physical act of fixing the tongue. If the practitioner of remembrance has a genuine spiritual guide, his heart will be quick to embark on remembrance and to cleansed of dirt and rust.

Another item of Sufi terminology is relevant here: namely, "the realm of creation and the realm of the [Divine] commandment," on the basis of His saying (Exalted is He):

> His is all creation and commandment.
> *a-lā la-hu 'l-khalqu wa 'l-amr:*
> Blessed be Allāh, the Lord of the Worlds!
> *tabāraka 'llāhu Rabbu 'l-'ālamīn.* (7:54)

By the realm of creation the Ṣūfis mean the realm of matter and by the realm of the commandment they mean the realm of possibilities and immaterial entities. That is a realm that comes into being through the commandment "Be!" The subtle centers that we have mentioned, namely, the heart, the spirit, the secret, the hidden and the most deeply hidden, are not tangible objects. They belong to the realm of command. They are purified one after another by the remembrance of Allāh. Then the rational self is purified since it belongs to the realm of sensory perception.

If someone begins with heart-centered remembrance, he has begun in the realm of the command. By the same token, if he begins with tongue-centered remembrance, he has begun with the realm of creation. In this case the last stage is the purification of the heart. Someone who begins with the realm of the command, meaning heart-centered remembrance, all the subtle factors and basic elements become humble and submissive because of the purification of the heart, the ruler of the body. The spiritual traveler reaches his goal. This is the significance of the saying of Shaikh Muḥammad Bahā' ad-Dīn an-Naqshband, "The first of our steps is taken at the point where others make their last stop." That is because they traverse nine stages in order to arrive at the heart, whereas we are concerned with the heart at the first of our stages.

As we have said, remembrance is performed by declaring "Allāh!" or by the negation and affirmation: "There is no god but Allāh [*lā ilāha illa 'Llāh*]."

If the remembrance "Allāh!" or "There is no god but Allāh [*lā ilāha illa 'Llāh*]" is firmly established in the self, all the members of the body engage in remembrance. That, according to the Sufis, is called "the Sultan of remembrances [*Sulṭān al-adhkār*]." When the remembrance of Allāh is heard from everything, it is called "the remembrance of everything else [*dhikr mā siwā*]."

We shall provide a more detailed account of remembrance in the section devoted to the Naqshbandī Spiritual Path. Meanwhile, the gist of what we have mentioned is that the first basic principle of Sufism is remembrance in its two forms, "Allāh!" or "There is no god but Allāh [*lā ilāha illa 'Llāh*].'

According to Imām al-Ghazālī in his book *al-Munqidh mina 'ḍ-Ḍalāl*, "It is incumbent on spiritual travelers to immerse themselves in remembrance after performing the prescribed ritual prayer and customary religious practice. Remembrance is more meritorious than recitation of the Qur'ān because remembrance trains the human being and subdues the firebrand of his willfulness. If someone has passed the test of experience, he is evidence against someone who has not been tested."

9. Illumination [*Ishrāq*]

The Sufi concept of illumination [*ishrāq*] is associated with Shaikh Shihāb ad-Dīn Yaḥyā ibn Ḥabash as-Suhrawardī, who was born in Zanjān in A.H. 549/1155 C.E. He was executed in Aleppo in A.H. 587/1191 C.E. in the time of al-Malik aẓ-Ẓāhir because he was suspected of heresy, just as al-Ḥallāj was executed in accordance with the legal opinions of religious scholars. It is said that they came to regret his execution. He is not Shaikh 'Umar as-Suhrawardī, who died in Baghdād, but they are both from the same family.

The concept of illumination [*ishrāq*] entered the realm of Sufism in the second half of the sixth century of the Hijra. It is possible for us to say that its foundation was built on Platonic philosophy or that it is the fruit of the mingling of Sufism with Platonic philosophy. According to Abu 'l-Qāsim al-Kāzarūnī (d. A.H. 1050/1610 C.E.), "Just as al-Fārābī is regarded as the renewer of peripatetic philosophy, meaning the philosophy of Aristotle, and has been called the second teacher, Shaikh Shihāb ad-Dīn as-Suhrawardī is the renewer of illuminist philosophy, the philosophy of Plato."

In defining the concept of illumination, as-Suhrawardī said, "If we depart from physical nature, and detach ourselves from the enjoyment of its pleasures, the Light of Allāh will illuminate our hearts.

It is a constant light, emanating from the Source of giving to every being and every owner of a spirit. It is called the Holy Spirit. In the language of the philosophers it is called 'the active intellect.'"

Illumination therefore means that in the case of the human being who trains his physical nature and directs his heart toward his Lord, the Light of Allāh shines from his heart like the sun.

According to some authorities,[3] "There are two paths to intimate knowledge of Allāh. The first is the path of thought and rational deduction. The second is the path of dedicated striving and spiritual exercise." The theologians follow the first path in the light of the guidance of Islam. Those who are not guided by religion on this path are the peripatetic philosophers. The Sufi community follows the second path in the light of the method of religion. Those who are not guided on this path are the illuminists.

This means that illumination [*ishrāq*] cannot be regarded as a form of Islamic Sufism, since the former is merely the pursuit of self-centered effort without guidance from the teachings of the Sacred Law.[4]

In my opinion, as-Suhrawardī, the one known as the martyr, was a brilliant Sufi Muslim, endowed with acute intelligence, extensive knowledge and strong conviction, but he was incapable of formulating his thinking in a sound pattern acceptable in terms of the Sacred Law. So he was executed as a young man in the thirty-sixth year of his life.

10. Direct Witnessing [*Mushāhada*]

According to 'Amr ibn 'Uthmān al-Makkī (may Allāh bestow His mercy upon him),[5] "Direct witnessing [*mushāhada*] is the experience in which hearts encounter the Unseen by invisible means. It is neither a form of eyewitnessing nor a form of ecstasy." He also said, "Direct witnessing [*mushāhada*] means being present and being close. It is presence in the sense of a nearness connected with the knowledge of certainty and its realities."

Those who experience direct witnessing are of three types:

1. The juniors, meaning the seekers. They witness things with the eye of consideration, or with the eye of thought.

---

3. *Ḥaqā'iq 'ani 't-taṣawwuf*, p. 182.
4. Ibid., p. 185.
5. Refer to Ḥajjī Khalīfa in his book *Kashf aẓ-ẓunūn*, and at-Tahānawī in *Kashshāf iṣṭilāḥāt al-funūn*.

2. Those in the middle range. Abū Sa'īd al-Kharrāz referred to them when he said, "Creatures are in the grip of the Lord of Truth and in His possession. When direct witnessing is complete in relation to what is between Allāh and the servant, nothing remains in the servant's innermost being, nor in his imagination, except Allāh (Exalted is He)."

3. The third type of direct witnessing is that referred to by 'Amr ibn 'Uthmān al-Makkī when he said, "The hearts of those endowed with intimate knowledge witness Allāh with a witnessing of confirmation. They witness Him in everything and they witness all entities in Him."

According to the author of *al-Luma'*,[6] "Direct witnessing is a lofty spiritual state, for it is among the signs of superabundant awareness of the realities of certainty."

According to Shaikh 'Umar as-Suhrawardī,[7] "Close presence pertains to the masters of variegation [*talwīn*], direct witnessing pertains to the masters of establishment [*tamkīn*], and disclosure [*mukāshafa*] comes between the two, until it is firmly established."

Close presence pertains to the people of knowledge; mystic disclosure pertains to the people of the eye; and direct witnessing pertains to the people of the truth, meaning the truth of certainty. Direct witnessing is vision with the eye of insight by the light of the Truth, and is experienced by the heart and the conscience. Disclosure is clarification of the thing concerned, while close presence is readiness to be with the thing concerned. Variegation and empowerment are two of the spiritual stations of Sufism. Variegation pertains to the spiritual traveler who is moving from station to station, while establishment pertains to those spiritual travelers who have arrived and settled at their destination.

11. The Realm of Divinity [*Lāhūt*]
12. The Realm of Humanity [*Nāsūt*]
13. The Realm of Omnipotence [*Jabarūt*]
14. The Realm of Sovereignty [*Malakūt*]

The realm of Divinity [*Lāhūt*] belongs to the realm of the spirit. The term *Lāhūtī* [pertaining to the Divine] is applied specifically to spiritual concerns. The subject of the science of Divinity is the Essence

6. *al-Luma'*, p. 101.
7. *'Awārif al-ma'ārif*, p. 369.

of Allāh (Glory be to Him) like the science of theology. The term *Ilāhiyyāt* is also applied to subjects of Divinity.

The realm of Humanity [*Nāsūt*] belongs to the realm of matter. The term *Nāsūt* is Syriac, derived from the word *nās* [human beings], for it is a science relating to the human being and the realm of matter. It is synonymous with *al-insāniyyāt* [the humanities].

The term *Jabarūt* [Omnipotence] is derived from *al-Jabbār* [the Omnipotent], which is one of the attributes of Allāh (Glory be to Him).

The servant has freedom of choice in the realm of Sovereignty [*Malakūt*], but in the realm of Omnipotence he is compelled to choose whatever the Lord of Truth prefers and to wish for whatever He wishes. According to Abū Ṭālib al-Makkī, "Omnipotence is the realm of Might, for it is the realm of the Divine Names and attributes." According to many, "Omnipotence is the realm of the center, which is known as the *barzakh* [isthmus], meaning that which connects Humanity and Sovereignty. It is the realm of the Unseen, while Humanity is the realm of matter, nature, and the human being."

Sovereignty [*Malakūt*] is the realm of the purified and angels [*malā'ika*].

The realm of Divinity is the realm of the Unseen, and it is linked to the Essence of Allāh (Glory be to Him) Alone.

15. The Four Basic Elements [*al-'Anāṣir al-Arba'a*]

According to the ancients, the universe consists of four basic elements: water, earth, fire, and air. Reference is made to them in the books of Sufism in the discussion of the purification of subtle centers [*laṭā'if*], especially on the Naqshbandī Sufi path. They say, "The subtle centers include the material and spiritual—or the outer and inner— existence of the human being. They are ten in number. Five of them pertain to the realm of creation, the four basic elements and the lower self [*nafs*]. The other five belong to the realm of the [Divine] command being (1) the heart [*qalb*], (2) the spirit [*rūḥ*], (3) the secret or innermost being [*sirr*], (4) that which is concealed [*khafī*], and (5) that which is most deeply hidden [*akhfā*]."

16. The Saint [*Walī*]

The term *Walī* [in the sense of "Protecting Friend"] is used as an attribute of Allāh (Glory be to Him) in the Noble Qur'ān, where it is also used [in the sense of "saintly friend"] to describe the servant. Allāh (Exalted is He) has said,

Allāh is the Protecting Friend of those who believe.
Allāhu Waliyyu 'lladhīna āmanū. (2:257)

And Allāh is the Protecting Friend of the believers.
wa 'llāhu Waliyyu 'l-mu'minīn. (3:68)

And Allāh is the Protecting Friend of the truly devout.
wa 'llāhu Waliyyu 'l-muttaqīn. (45:19)

And Allāh is sufficient as a Protecting Friend,
wa kafā bi'llāhi Waliyyan. (4:45)

Say, "Shall I choose other than Allāh as a protecting friend?"
qul a-ghaira 'llāhi attakhidhu waliyyan. (6:14)

And He befriends and protects the righteous.
wa Huwa yatawalla 'ṣ-ṣāliḥīn. (7:196)

[In the last of these Qur'ānic verses, the related verb *yatawallā* is used]. The related abstract noun *wilāya* means "safekeeping, assistance, and providential care." When used to describe the servant, the meaning of *walī* [pl. *awliyā'*] is "one who is kept safe, assisted, and dearly loved." Allāh (Exalted is He) has said,

As for the saintly friends of Allāh,
a-lā inna awliyā'a 'llāhi
surely no fear shall be upon them, nor shall they grieve.
lā khawfun 'alai-him wa lā hum yaḥzanūn. (10:62)

The Noble Qur'ān has also characterized them, for He has said (Exalted is He),

Those who believe and practice true devotion,
alladhīna āmanū wa kānū yattaqūn:
theirs are good tidings in the life of this world and in the Hereafter.
la-humu 'l-bushrā fi 'l-ḥayāti 'd-dunyā wa fi 'l-ākhira. (10:63,64)

The *walī* is therefore someone who combines faith, righteousness, and true devotion, and this is also understood from His saying (Exalted is He),

And He befriends and protects the righteous.
wa Huwa yatawalla 'ṣ-ṣāliḥīn. (7:196)

And Allāh is the Protecting Friend of the believers.

> *wa 'llāhu Waliyyu 'l-mu'minīn.* (3:68)
>
> And Allāh is the Protecting Friend of the truly devout.
> *wa 'llāhu Waliyyu 'l-muttaqīn.* (45:19)

According to the Sufi poet Mawlawi,

> The saint [*walī*] is someone endowed with intimate knowledge of Allāh, aware of His Essence and His attributes to the extent of possibility, adhering to the rules of the Sacred Law in his true devotion (with its three kinds), diligent in acts of worship, avoiding abominations.

By the three kinds of true devotion [*taqwā*], he means devout abstinence from unbelief, devout abstinence from sins, and devout abstinence from keen interest in this world.

In the customary usage of Sufism, especially the Naqshbandī tradition, the saint [*walī*] is someone who passes through the ten spiritual stations we have previously mentioned, including repentance [*tawba*], abstinence [*zuhd*] and patience [*ṣabr*]. Sainthood [*wilāya*] is subdivided into two parts: lesser sainthood and greater sainthood. He does not attain to greater sainthood except after the purification of his subtle centers [*laṭā'if*] through constant remembrance [*dhikr*].

In the view of many of the shaikhs of Sufism, prophethood [*Nubuwwa*] begins after the degrees of greater sainthood, so the saint does not reach the station of prophethood. The prophets also have their stations, like [Abraham] the Bosom Friend of Allāh [*Khalīlu 'llāh*], [Moses] the Interlocutor of Allāh [*Kalīmu 'llāh*] and [Jesus] the Spirit of Allāh [*Rūḥu 'llāh*]. The station of Muḥammad (Allāh bless him and give him peace, and may my spirit be his ransom!) is above every station of prophethood.

It may be asked, "Is the saint [*walī*] conscious of his station?" The fact of the matter is that he is not necessarily required to be aware of that!

Let me also mention something that happened when I was a young man in the prime of my life. I was urgently requested by a spiritual traveler, a disciple of my father Shaikh 'Alā' ad-Dīn (may Allāh bestow His mercy upon him), to speak with my father about his condition. His name was Faqī Muḥammad. He said, "I have not yet felt any of the blessings of the Sufi path." I duly conveyed his message to my father, who laughed and said, "He has been a saint [*walī*] for quite some time, but he does not recognize that, so give him the good news of the fact, and let him pray for blessing on your behalf!" I promptly hurried to him and gave him the good news, whereupon he was almost thunderstruck with joy.

In the view of many of those endowed with this knowledge, sainthood [*wilāya*] does not necessarily mean the attainment of disclosure [*kashf*] and charismatic talent [*karāma*]. They say, "The crucial factor is rectitude [*istiqāma*], not charismatic talent."

According to Shaikh Muḥyi 'd-Dīn ibn al-'Arabī, "Sainthood is not acquired by earnest endeavor, spiritual training and worshipful service. It is rather a gift from Allāh (Glory be to Him), the likeness of which is the likeness of the spiritual state [*ḥāl*]."

As I see it, this means that sainthood does not result from the creature's intention to perform worshipful service as a precondition of that gift. As a matter of fact, the subject of sainthood was not mentioned in this form during the period of the Prophetic mission and the first generation of Muslims. It was raised in the latter years of the second century of the Hijra. There is no doubt that the Companions were saints, and that the station of companionship is higher than the station of sainthood.

Among the earliest exponents of sainthood in the Sufi form, we may count Shaikh Muḥammad 'Alī at-Tirmidhī, who died in A.H. 296. Sainthood was likewise personified by Fuḍail ibn 'Iyāḍ (d. A.H. 187), Shaikh Ma'rūf al-Karkhī (d. A.H. 200), Shaikh Junaid (d. A.H. 297), al-Muḥāsibī (d. A.H. 243), and Dhū 'n-Nūn al-Miṣrī (d. A.H. 245). The Sufi form of sainthood was also clearly apparent in the time of Abū Yazīd al-Bisṭāmī (d. A.H. 261).

In the words of the Sacred Tradition [*Ḥadīth Qudsī*] recorded in the Ṣaḥīḥ of al-Bukhārī,

> If someone shows hostility toward a saintly friend of Mine, I exhort him to wage war [against that enemy].

17. The Seeker [*Murīd*] and the Sought [*Murād*]

Both terms are derived from the verbal noun *irāda* [seeking].

The seeker [*murīd*] is someone who is overwhelmed by the love of Allāh. He devotes himself to Him (Glory be to Him) in worshipful service and seeks His good pleasure. Allāh (Glory be to Him) has said,

> Those who have said, "Our Lord is Allāh,"

inna 'lladhīna qālū Rabbu-na 'llāhu
and then remained steadfast, to them the angels keep coming down
thumma 'staqāmū tatanazzalu 'alai-himu 'l-malā'ikatu
[to say], "Do not fear and do not grieve,
allā takhāfū wa lā taḥzanū
but hear good tidings of the Garden that you have been promised."
wa abshirū bi'l-jannati 'llatī kuntum tū'adūn. (41:30)

Those who say, "Our Lord is Allāh," and then travel straight,
inna 'lladhīna qālū Rabbu-na 'llāhu thumma 'staqāmū
no fear shall be upon them, nor shall they grieve.
fa-lā khawfun 'alai-him wa lā hum yaḥzanūn. (46:13)

He has also said (Glory be to Him) on the subject of His seekers,

And do not drive away those who call upon their Lord
wa lā taṭrudi 'lladhīna yad'ūna Rabba-hum
at morning and evening, seeking His countenance.
bi'l-ghadāti wa 'l-'ashiyyi yurīdūna wajhah. (6:52)

The one who is sought [*murād*] is the righteous penitent whom the Lord of Truth loves and whom He attracts toward Him. The term applies to all the prophets, and Ibrāhīm ibn Adham is also considered a *murād* in the view of the Sufis. It is related that he was a prince who went out hunting as a sport when a voice called out to him twice from behind the veil, "Not for this were you created and not for this have you been given authority!" He thereupon stripped off his royal garments and gave them to a herdsman who was with him in exchange for his simple clothes. He spent the rest of his life in Syria and Medina as a worshipful Sufi. A poet said of him,

Ibrāhīm Adham knows best how happy
the dervish is with his estate, so ask him!
No one appreciates the value of the shore except
one whom the flood has taken and put to the test.

The seeker [*murīd*] is one who seeks his Lord, not one who seeks his Shaikh (except in a metaphorical sense). The one who is sought [*murād*] is one who the Lord seeks.

In the book of Sufi terms, "It is incumbent upon the seeker to become detached from the desires of the self that is always instigating evil [*an-nafs al-ammāra bi's-sū'*] and to concentrate entirely on the Lord of Truth (Glory be to Him). The seeker is not truly a seeker unless his seeking is pure. His seeking is not pure unless his heart is purified of all evil attributes and adorned with comprehensive virtues. If someone is like that, Allāh (Glory be to Him) draws him near to His grace and opens for him the doors of His mercy, so he becomes one who is sought. He is thus a seeker [*murīd*] in his striving and his endeavor, and one who is sought [*murād*] in His grace and His noble generosity."

According to Shaikh 'Abd al-Qādir in his book *al-Ghunya* [*Sufficient Provision*],[8]

> The seeker [*murīd*] is made tired and weary, while the sought [*murād*] is treated gently and made comfortable.... The seeker [*murīd*] walks on his feet, while the sought [*murād*] flies through the air.... The seeker is in pursuit [*al-murīd ṭālib*], while the sought is being pursued [*al-murād maṭlūb*].... The sought [*murād*] is one who is attracted by the Lord of Truth, while the seeker [*murīd*] strives for the Lord of Truth and attains to Him through his striving.

As we read in the book entitled *Mu'jam muṣṭalaḥāt aṣ-ṣūfiyya* [*Glossary of the Technical Terms of Sufism*],

> The seeker [*murīd*] is one who is devoted to Allāh to the exclusion of theory and speculation. He is completely detached from his own view since he knows that nothing comes into existence except what Allāh wishes (Almighty and Glorious is He), not what others wish. He obliterates his own volition and wishes only for what the Lord of Truth wishes.

As we read in the book entitled *at-Ta'arruf li-madhhab ahl at-taṣawwuf* [*Familiarity with the Doctrine of the Masters of Sufism*],

> The seeker is sought, in reality, and the one who is sought is a seeker, because the seeker of Allāh (Exalted is He) does not seek except with a wish to seek received from Allāh (Almighty and Glorious is He). The only difference is that the seeker is one whose striving precedes his discoveries, while the sought is one whose discoveries precede his striving." The author then goes on to say,

8. Translator's note: For an unabridged version of this excerpt from the work of Shaikh 'Abd al-Qādir, see the Al-Baz edition of *Sufficient Provision for Seekers of the Path of Truth*, vol. 5, pp. 6–11.

> "The one who is sought is one whom the Lord of Truth attracts with the attraction of power, and to whom He discloses the spiritual states. The strength of the experience stirs him to strive for it, to focus his attention upon it, and to endure its burdens.

The proper modes of conduct for the seeker include eating very little, sleeping very little, speaking very little, seclusion, correct performance of worship, constant practice of remembrance, forsaking what does not concern him, and taking direction from a genuine spiritual guide, not from a spurious guide who is actually a highway robber.

According to some, Sufism is proper conduct [*adab*], then truthfulness [*ṣidq*] and sincere devotion [*ikhlāṣ*] to the spiritual guide [*murshid*], then rectitude [*istiqāma*] and other such virtues of religion.

It was al-Qushairī who said, "I once heard the masterful teacher Abū 'Alī ad-Daqqāq, say, 'The spiritual quest [*irāda*] is a pang of love in the core, a stinging sensation in the heart, an infatuation in the conscience, a disturbance in the inner being, and fires that blaze in the hearts." Yes, such indeed is the seeking of the seeker!

According to al-Junaid, "When Allāh (Exalted is He) wishes the seeker well, He causes him to join the Sufis and grants him the fellowship of the spiritual paupers [*fuqarā'*]." Abū Bakr ad-Daqqāq said, "The seeker does not become a seeker until the [angelic] companion of the left does not record anything against him for twenty years."

Concerning the difference between the seeker and the sought, al-Qushairī also said,

> Allāh's custom with the aspirants [*qāṣidīn*] is various. Most of them are devoted to earnest endeavors, then, after much ado, they attain to the splendor of the heights. Many of them discover at the outset the glory of the inner meanings, and they attain to what is not reached by many of the practitioners of spiritual exercises. Nevertheless, most of them resort to earnest endeavors after these companies in order to obtain fulfillment from them of what they missed by neglecting the rules of the masters of spiritual training [*riyāḍa*].

He also relates the saying of Abū Bakr ad-Daqqāq, that there is a difference here between the prophets, and he says, "Moses (peace be upon him) was a seeker, for he said,

> "My Lord! Expand my breast for me."

Rabbi 'shraḥ lī ṣadrī. (20:25)

Our own Prophet was one who is sought, for Allāh (Exalted is He) said,

Did We not cause your breast to expand for you?
a-lam nashraḥ la-ka ṣadrak. (94:1)"

They also say, "The seeker goes on his way, the one who is sought is summoned, and each attains to the goal of the quest."

18. The Deputy [*Khalīfa*]

The deputy [*khalīfa*] in the customary usage of the people of the Spiritual Path is someone who deputizes for the Shaikh and represents him in the performance of certain duties of his spiritual guide. There are several types to be distinguished:

1. The elementary type is one who represents the spiritual guide in teaching novices the regular practices of the Spritual Path such as remembrance, contemplation, seclusion, constant commitment to following the Book and the Sunna, abstinence from things that are unlawful, fulfillment of obligations and recommendations to the extent of one's ability.

2. The intermediate type is one whose subtle feelings are illumined by the refinement of the heart, the spirit, the innermost being, that which is concealed and that which is most deeply hidden, through constant practice of remembrance. He represents his spiritual guide from whom he has permission to focus with his heart on the heart of the seeker, deriving support from the spirituality of his guide. He thereby eradiates the seeker's heart with beams of light, sweeps it clean of what it contains in the form of self-centered vices and human depravities, and illumines it with the lights of Reality. The seeker comes under the control of adherence to the noble Sacred Law, becomes remote from obedience to the lower self and passion, and keeps his distance from the devil. The seeker thus becomes one of Allāh's sincerely devoted servants.

3. The third type is at the preparatory stage. He is one who represents the spiritual guide in providing direction and shedding lights, both in his presence and in his absence. If he wishes to shed lights on the hearts of absent seekers, Allāh (Exalted is He) will enable him to do so. At this stage, he receives disclosures

and spiritual instructions from his guide and these are transmitted from him to the seekers. He remains steadfast in this condition, so he is regarded as one of the righteous people who loyally follow the meaning of the Word. Such are the righteous ones to whom the Maker (Exalted is He) has pointed in many of the verses of the Wise Reminder [the Qur'ān]. The masters of this degree are among the deputies [*khulafā'*] who are qualified to educate the seekers, in the shade of the commandments of the Shaikh and spiritual guide, but only during his lifetime (not after his death).

4. The fourth type is the venerable [*muḥtaram*]. He is the seeker who follows the methods of the Spiritual Path, and attains to the degrees of annihilation [*fanā'*] and perpetuity [*baqā'*]. These are the two exalted degrees, attained by those whom Allāh (Exalted is He) has singled out with His lights, inspired with some of His secrets, and enabled to receive the Lordly emanations [*al-fuyūḍāt ar-Rabbāniyya*]. The Divine lights are constantly shining on their hearts, just as the sun shines all day long on someone who is at the horizon where it rises.

At that stage, the spiritual guide permits them [his deputies] to direct Muslims to the Truth and to the constant practice of true devotion. At that station, they are endowed with absolute guidance through the might and power of Allāh. All those degrees are explained in the traditional reports and the clear proofs, which include three dicta. First of all, one constantly adheres to worshipful obedience, and absolute avoidance of passionate desire and things that are unlawful. Secondly, one has an absence of preoccupation with this lower world and its wicked schemes. One does not neglect the remembrance of Allāh (Exalted is He), constantly performing obligatory religious duties and well-established recommendations. Thirdly, one derives benefit from those close to them from the lights of their hearts, their verbal advice, and their pleasing modes of conduct.

5. The fourth type is that individual from whom the seekers receive illumination by the lights that exist in his heart just like paper catches fire when the magnifying glass is held between it and the sun. Such expressions are used by way of analogy. Allāh verifies the truth and He guides to the right path.

It is also worth mentioning that the spiritual guide, when he authorizes a deputy [*khalīfa*] in one of the categories noted above, must define the capabilities of the deputy concerned as well as his spiritual station and his degree. This applies particularly to the deputy who is permitted to provide spiritual guidance, whether during the life of the director or thereafter, in relation to unconditional directorship. It is essential for the spiritual director to record in the text of the teaching authorization that so-and-so has attained to the station of perpetuity after annihilation [*al-baqā' ba'da 'l-fanā'*]. If he does not mention that, it means that the deputy is merely a temporary representative of the director as the latter is alive but not after.

In the Naqshbandī lineage, the living example is the diploma of Shaikh Muḥammad Bahā' ad-Dīn, the son of Shaikh 'Uthmān Sirāj ad-Dīn an-Naqshbandī, the paternal uncle of our spiritual director, Shaikh 'Alā' ad-Dīn (may Allāh bestow His mercy upon him), issued to his full brother, Shaikh 'Umar Ḍiyā' ad-Dīn (may Allāh sanctify their innermost beings). Shaikh Bahā' ad-Dīn testifies therein that his brother, Shaikh Ḍiyā' ad-Dīn, has passed through all the required stations without exception, to the point of settling in the station of perpetuity after annihilation. No one attains to the station of absolute guidance, except one endowed with enormous good fortune!

Text of the Diploma

In His Name (Glory be to Him and Exalted is He)

Praise be to Allāh, who sent down the Book to His servant, and guided the believers on the path of Truth and rightness by dispatching His noble Messenger to them. May Allāh bless our master and our patron, His beloved friend and the best of His creatures, Muḥammad, and his family and his Companions, who are the stars of guidance for those with faculties of understanding.

My father (may Allāh bestow His mercy upon him) authorized me to provide spiritual guidance [*irshād*]. If someone wishes for nearness to the emanation of Reality, and for pursuit of the Spiritual Path and the Truth of Certainty, he therefore seeks guidance from me. Each one receives what is due to him in accordance with his readiness.

One of them is my brother, Shaikh 'Umar, who has devoted a period of his life to purifying himself by performing acts of worshipful obedience under the instruction of our Shaikh, our father. He has become as distinquished among his peers as the sun is distinguished from the stars. He has traversed lofty stations and attained to the blessing of perpetuity after annihilation [*al-baqā' ba'da 'l-fanā'*]. He has deserved the honor of those who received the robe of authorization from our father and noble shaikhs. I have also authorized him to provide guidance in the Sacred Law and the Spiritual Path in conformity with the practices of the Spiritual Path confirming bonds of brotherhood, both as a blood-relationship and as a relationship in faith. He now has the right to train seekers independently in accordance with the Sacred Law of the Chief of Beings. Seekers and deputies are therefore obliged to follow his admonitions and his directions and to respect his instructions. They must be as wary of offending him as they are wary of deadly poison. If he is well pleased with someone, we shall be well pleased with that person. If he rejects someone, we shall reject that person.

The two of us are fruits of one tree, however we may be. We are from one parentage, however we may be. That is the gracious favor of Allāh, which He bestows on whom He will. Allāh is the Owner of infinite bounty. O Allāh, make him a leader for the truly devout! There is no might nor any power except with Allāh, the All-High, the Almighty. May Allāh bless our master Muḥammad, his family and his Companions, one and all. Our final supplication is that praise be given to Allāh, the Lord of All the Worlds.

Muḥammad al-'Uthmānī an-Naqshbandī
Dhū 'l-Qa'da, A.H. 1294

* * * * *

Praiseworthy Attributes and Blameworthy Attributes

The original [Kurdish] text contains a detailed account of the praiseworthy attibutes with which the Sufi adorns himself, and the blameworthy attributes of which he divests himself. In the [Arabic, and hence the English] translation, it is sufficient to enumerate them, since their meanings will be clear to the reader.

The Praiseworthy Attributes:

1. Love of what is best for people [*ḥubb al-khair li'n-nās*]. 2. Sincerity [*ikhlāṣ*]. 3. Humility [*tawāḍu'*]. 4. Generosity [*jūd*]. 5. Truthfulness [*ṣidq*]. 6. Trustworthiness [*amāna*]. 7. Contentment [*qanā'a*]. 8. Compassion [*raḥma*]. 9. Modesty and propriety [*ḥayā' wa adab*]. 10. Affection for human beings [*maḥabbat an-nās*]. 11. Courage [*shajā'a*]. 12. Reliability [*thiqa*]. 13. Tolerance [*ḥilm*]. 14. Readiness to pardon [*'afw*]. 15. Respect for family ties [*ṣilat ar-raḥim*].

16. Striving for what is good [*as-sa'y li'l-khair*]. 17. Thankfulness for blessing [*shukr an-ni'ma*]. 18. Self-denial and altruism [*nukrān adh-dhāt wa 'l-īthār*]. 19. Fidelity [*wafā'*].

The Blameworthy Attributes:

1. Envy [*ḥasad*]. 2. Ostentation and hypocrisy [*riyā' wa nifāq*]. 3. Arrogant pride, vain conceit and delusion [*kibr wa 'ujb wa ghurūr*]. 4. Miserliness [*bukhl*]. 5. Lying [*kadhib*]. 6. Betrayal of trust [*khiyānat al-amāna*]. 7. Greedy pursuit of wealth or prestige [*takālub 'ala'l-māl awi'l-jāh*]. 8. Cruelty [*qaswa*]. 9. Insolence [*waqāḥa*]. 10. Antipathy to one's fellow human beings [*karāhiyyat an-nās*]. 11. Cowardice [*jubn*]. 12. Lack of reliability [*'adam ath-thiqa*]. 13. Anger [*ghaḍab*]. 14. Vengefulness [*intiqām*]. 15. Severance of family ties [*qaṭ' ar-raḥim*]. 16. Slander [*namīma*]. 17. Ingratitude for blessing [*kufrān an-ni'ma*]. 18. Love of the self [*ḥubb adh-dhāt*].

Chapter Six
The Naqshbandī Spiritual Path
[*Ṭarīqa*]

The Spiritual Path [*tarīqa]* is a particular practice among the methods of Sufism. It is adopted by the spiritual traveler [*sālik*] for the purpose of attaining to the goal, which is the perfect faith that attains to the eye of certainty [*'ain al-yaqīn*] or the truth of certainty [*ḥaqq al-yaqīn*]. At this point, faith is not merely conventional or rational, capable of being shaken by doubt. The believer now sees with the eye of his insight, so nothing influences him. As Imām ar-Rabbānī has said in his Letters [*Maktūbāt*], "The difference between the faith of the scholars and the faith of the perfect shaikhs of Sufism is that the knowledge of the scholars is based on reasoning. The knowledge of the Sufis is acquired by discovery and experience. Whether the basis is reasoning or discovery, the goal is the application of the Muḥammadan Sacred Law [*Sharī'a*]."

In the fields of the sciences of the Sacred Law, we find that certain distinguished experts, who exercised their independent judgment, have left us with sound doctrines and methods explaining the meanings and goals of the Sacred Law of Muslims. These include Imām Mālik ibn Anas (715–795 C.E.), Abū Ḥanīfa (699–767 C.E.), Muḥammad ibn Idrīs ash-Shāfi'ī (767–820 C.E.) and Aḥmad ibn Ḥanbal (780–855 C.E.). We also find other independent experts who studied these sciences thoroughly and profoundly and who became the founders of notable schools of legal doctrine.

Likewise in the fields of the science of Sufism, we find outstanding men who marked out paths and procedures that were adopted by ardent lovers of the spirit in order to attain to perfect faith. These include Shaikh Ma'rūf al-Karkhī, Abū Yazīd al-Bisṭāmī, Dhū'n-Nūn al-Miṣrī, 'Abd al-Qādir al-Jīlānī, Aḥmad al-Badawī, Aḥmad ar-Rifā'ī, Bahā' ad-Dīn Naqshband, Shaikh 'Umar as-Suhrawardī, Abu 'l-Ḥasan ash-Shādhilī, Najm ad-Dīn al-Kubrā, Jalāl ad-Dīn ar-Rūmī, Mu'īn ad-Dīn al-Ḥasanī al-Chishtī, and Abu 'l-'Abbās at-Tījānī. There are many other men who founded particular paths for the training of the spiritual traveler, preparing him for the attainment of the destination sought. It should be noted, however, that all these practices stem from a single source. Similarly in the context of worldly affairs, we make dozens of different kinds of bread from wheat and the like, and we make numerous types of food from meat and rice. Each has a different taste from the other. The whole process leads to a single purpose, however. That is to satisfy hunger and enjoy while building and strengthening the physical body.

Consider how the Islamic schools of jurisprudence aim at clarification of the practices of worship and the rules of the Sacred Law and the Prophetic Sunna so that they may be adopted as a method for life. The Sufi paths also aim at firm establishment of perfect faith and at bringing the spiritual traveler to certain faith, the "eye of certainty." Then his heart may be tranquil, in addition to his being summoned him to apply the teachings of the Sacred Law.

The Naqshbandī Sufi Order has a special method for bringing the seeker to his goal, [just as other Sufi Orders have their special methods]. The Qādirī Spiritual Path, for instance, adopts audible remembrance [*dhikr jahrī*] as an emblem. The Mawlawi Spiritual Path is distinguished by the recitation of poems and remembrance, and by sessions of spiritual concert [*samā'*]. The Naqshbandīs have their own special litanies [*awrād*]. Despite the differences in their litanies, their practices of remembrance and their emblems, the Sufi Orders are all united in a single aim, which is intimate knowledge of Allāh (Glory be to Him), His good pleasure and nearness to Him.

They are paths defined by those endowed with intimate knowledge of Allāh, by the shaikhs who exercise independent judgment in the science of Sufism with guidance from their Lord (Glory be to Him).

> Practice true devotion to Allāh, and Allāh will teach you.
> *wa 'ttaqu 'llāh: wa yu'allimu-kumu 'llāh.* (2:282)
>
> As for those who strive in Our cause,
> *wa 'lladhīna jāhadū fī-nā*
> surely We shall guide them in Our ways.
> *la-nahdiyanna-hum subula-nā.* (29:69)

Allāh has taught them and guided them, and they are entrusted with the task of directing their pupils to these paths. For the sake of analogy, compare the physician who discovers a remedy for a sickness and describes it to his patients. These shaikhs are physicians of hearts. They have scaled the summits of hopeful expectations for the sake of intimate knowledge of Allāh, so they direct the spiritual travelers to attainment of the peaks of hopeful expectations. Without any doubt, their methods are all in keeping with the Prophetic Sunna and the example set by the righteous predecessors among the Companions and the Successors. The source of them all is the Noble Qur'ān and the Seal of the prophets, Muḥammad (Allāh bless him and give him peace).

As we have mentioned, there is no difference between the Sacred Law [*Sharī'a*] and the Spiritual Path [*ṭarīqa*], but the Sufi is devoted to remembrance and contemplation, so his heart is pure and serene. His faith increases until it becomes the eye of certainty, so he applies the Sacred Law with a heart that is filled with faith. If someone digresses from the Sacred Law, the Spiritual Path is rid of him.

After this introduction, it is time for us to offer definitive answers to the following questions:

1. What is the Naqshbandī method for attainment to the peaks of spiritual hopes?
2. How did the Naqshbandī Order begin? What is the chain [*silsila*] of its men leading up to [the author's] father [Shaikh 'Alā' ad-Dīn Bayāra] (may Allāh bestow His mercy upon him)?
3. When did this Spiritual Path come to be called "Naqshbandī"? And why?

I shall begin by quoting the sayings of the shaikhs of Sufism before embarking on the detailed response.

It was Shaikh 'Abdullāh ad-Dihlawī (d. 1230 A.H.) who said,

> The fruit of this 'Naqshbandī' Spiritual Path is the permanent attendance in the presence of the Lord of Truth (Exalted is He), the firm establishment of the Islamic doctrine as the religious doctrine of the People of the Sunna and the Community, and loyal adherence to the Sunna of the noble Prophet (Allāh bless him and give him peace).

In the book entitled *al-Ḥadīqat an-nadiyya* [*The Fruitful Garden*], by Muḥammad ibn Salmān al-Baghdādī, it is related that Shaikh Muḥammad Murād al-Uzbakī once said, "The Naqshbandī Spiritual Path is the Spiritual Path of the noble Companions. It remains true to its original source, for they have neither added to it nor subtracted from it. It is an expression signifying the permanence of worshipful servitude, both outwardly and inwardly, through the perfection of adherence to the Sunna with firm commitment. It is complete avoidance of heretical innovation and license in all states of movement and rest, in habits and transactions, together with permanence in the presence of Allāh (Exalted is He) on the path of bewilderment and total exhaustion."

In the same source, the following is related from Ibn Ḥajar al-Haitamī (909–974 A.H.).

"The lofty Spiritual Path, the one that is safe from the impurities of those who are ignorant of Sufism, is the Naqshbandī Spiritual Path."

As we read in the introduction to the book *al-Qudsiyya*, "Naqshbandī Sufism is loyal adherence to the Sunna. It is balanced and moderate and its basis is the application of the Sacred Law and the avoidance of heretical innovations." The writer of the introduction also says, "The well-balanced nature of the Naqshbandī procedure, its compliance with the Sacred Law, and the ease of the Spiritual Path all accounts for the widespread acceptance of this Spiritual Path. This applies especially to the religious scholars, for the heart of the Naqshbandī Sufi belongs to Allāh while his body belongs to the people."

As a matter of fact, the shaikhs who have described this Spiritual Path are unanimous in asserting that it is loyal adherence to the Sacred Law, and permanent commitment to remembrance, contemplation, worshipful servitude, sincere devotion, altruism, and self-denial.

With regard to the second question,

> As stated in the book entitled *Īḍāḥ aṭ-ṭarīq* [*Explanation of the Path*]: The Naqshbandīs have three means by which to attain to the summit of the quest:
>
> 1. The constant practice of remembrance.
> 2. Vigilant awareness [*murāqaba*].
> 3. Obedience to the spiritual guide.
>
> It is necessary to add that the first step is repentance, meaning the irrevocable renunciation of all bad conduct, and application of the teachings of the Qur'ān and the Prophetic Sunna.

1. Remembrance [*dhikr*]

Remembrance has two forms:

- The remembrance of "Allāh," which signifies remembrance of the Divine Essence, or remembrance of the Divine Majesty.
- The remembrance of "*Lā ilāha illa'llāh*," which signifies negation ["There is no god"] and affirmation ["except Allāh"].

It is a well-known fact that remembrance as practiced by the Naqshbandīs is remembrance concealed within the heart.

The remembrance of "Allāh" includes the following conditions: Practitioners must be in a state of ritual purity [*mutawaḍḍi'*] in a clean and quiet place, facing the *qibla* [direction of prayer]. He must appeal to Allāh (Glory be to Him) to keep him safe from the whispered temptation of the devil and the lower self. Then he must seek forgiveness from Allāh. He must also remember his spiritual guide if he has a spiritual guide. After that, he should begin the remembrance with the heart.

It is possible, however, for the practitioner to perform that remembrance in any form and at any time. Allāh (Exalted is He) has said,

> [There are signs for] those who remember Allāh,
> *alladhīna yadhkurūna 'llāha*
> standing and sitting and on their sides,
> *qiyāman wa qu'ūdan wa 'alā junūbi-him*
> and who reflect upon the creation of the heavens and the earth:
> *wa yatafakkarūna fī khalqi 's-samāwāti wa 'l-arḍ.* (3:191)

The remembrance practiced by the Naqshbandī Sufi includes the following conditions.

At the beginning, the seeker makes his tongue stick to the roof of his mouth, to prevent it from moving. The wisdom of this has already been explained. Then he remembers "Allāh" with his heart. In this context, the heart is one of the subtleties of the inner being. What is meant by it is not the pine cone-shaped gland, but it is located slightly below the left nipple. He contemplates the Sublime Glory of Allāh, not the written form of the Name "Allāh."

> There is nothing like unto Him.
> *laisa ka-mithli-hi shai'*. (42:11)

So he believes that Allāh is described by all the attributes of perfection and that He is utterly exempt from any deficiency.

It is incumbent on the practitioner to be constantly engaged in remembrance night and day without any movement of the tongue and the body until his heart begins the remembrance and he is aware of it. Then he must focus on his spirit, which is located in the other side of the breast, two finger-lengths below the right nipple. He must remember Allāh with it, until the spirit also becomes a practitioner of remembrance. Then he must focus on the subtle center of the secret entity [*sirr*], which is located two finger-lengths above the left nipple, inclining toward the breast; then on the subtle center of the hidden entity [*khafī*], which is located two finger-lengths above the right nipple, inclining toward the breast; then on the subtle center of the most deeply hidden entity [*al-akhfā*], which is located in the middle of the breast. He must then begin the remembrance.

When his subtle centers begin the remembrance, each subtle center becomes a lamp illuminated by a special light. The subtle center of the self, which is located in the forehead between the eyes, begins the remembrance. It belongs to the realm of creation, while the other subtle centers belong to the realm of the [Divine] command. The latter are immaterial subtle centers, of which only the spiritual travelers are consciously aware. (This has been mentioned previously.) After that one begins the "mold [*qālib*]," the body composed of physical elements. Every atom of his body must begin to practice remembrance and the spiritual traveler himself must be consciously aware of it.

According to Mulla Ḥāmid al-Bīsārānī, one of the Naqshbandi scholars of Sufism, "There are some among them who remember Allāh twenty-five thousand times in one day, while the least of them remember Allāh five thousand times."

From what has been stated previously, it is clear that they have assigned five stages to the remembrance of the subtle centers, which exist in the realm of the [Divine] command, and two stages to the subtle centers of the realm of creation. Remembrance therefore has seven steps. This is the meaning of Imām ar-Rabbānī's saying, "Our Spiritual Path consists of seven steps." Some of them have said, "The Spiritual Path consists of two steps," alluding to one step in the realm of the [Divine] command, and one step in the realm of creation. The persistent practice of remembrance causes the seven subtle centers, and every atom of the body to remember "Allāh." In this state, the seeker experiences comfort and refinement in his heart and his feelings. This condition is called "the Sultan of the remembrances," or "the Sultan of remembrance." It results in a state in which the practitioner comes to recognize, after his assiduous devotion to remembrance, that the whole universe remembers "Allāh." He actually hears the remembrance of "Allāh" in every atom of the universe. This remembrance is called the remembrance performed by "everything else [*mā siwā*]," in the sense that everything created remembers Allāh (Glory be to Him). This is one of the subtleties of the majestic Spiritual Path, to which Shaikh 'Umar Ḍiyā' ad-Dīn (sanctified be his innermost being) was alluding when he said, in one of his Sufi odes, "The subtle centers are all immersed in the remembrance of Allāh."

It is essential to explain that this state is the ABC of Sufism and its preface. It is one of the states of purification, that is the cleansing of the subtle centers. It is not one of the states of the annihilation [*fanā'*] of the subtle centers. Each subtle element has a special state of annihilation. After annihilation of the whole, comes survival in perpetuity [*baqā'*]. The spiritual traveler becomes aware of wondrous secrets and is endowed by his Lord with spiritual talents.

As we have mentioned, the subtle centers are transformed into radiantly illuminated lamps when they begin to practice remembrance, and they say, "The light of every subtle center is beneath the foot of one of the messengers and prophets, the masters of firm resolve." The way is opened to every spiritual traveler because of one of these subtle centers, for he bears a resemblance to the spiritual character of that Prophet. This is a relationship familiar to those endowed with intimate knowledge, and they may even recognize it after the death of its owners in their graves. The character of one person is Muḥammadan, while that of another is Jesus-like [*'Īsawī*]. If someone perceives these matters with the eye of insight, how can doubt invade his faith?

The subtle center of the heart is beneath the foot of Adam, and it is yellow.

The subtle center of the spirit is beneath the foot of two prophets, they being Noah and Abraham, and it is red.

The subtle center of the secret entity is beneath the foot of Moses, and it is white.

The subtle center of the hidden entity is beneath the foot of Jesus, and it is black. There is no mutual contradiction between the light and blackness, for blackness can be very beautiful, like the color of the eye and the eyebrows, for example.

The subtle center of the most deeply hidden entity is green, and is beneath the foot of our venerable master Muḥammad (Allāh bless him and give him peace).

If the spiritual traveler has a guide, the latter will convey his pupil from one subtle center to another, and if the light of the subtle center becomes perfect, this light will sparkle on the face of the pupil, so he and his guide will both perceive it. The subtle centers are comparable to the senses, though the senses are in the material world, while subtle centers are in the world of inner being.

After the purification of the realm of the [Divine] command, there begins the purification of the self that belongs to the realm of creation. It does not have a color of its own. Like water, it is colored by whatever enters into it, and its purification is difficult. It belongs to the realm of nature and it is basically an instigator of evil. It is the source of all wicked desires, but the remembrance of Allāh (Glory be to Him) will cleanse and train it. According to the shaikhs of Sufism, this kind of purification requires a spiritual guide, and what is meant by the spiritual guide is a worshipful devotee endowed with intimate knowledge who has undoubtedly attained to sainthood and passed through all these spiritual stations. He is a person by name, but he is actually a beam of light, angelic in constitution and Lordly in conduct. He is one of the masters of the exalted stations of perpetuity after annihilation.

It is inconceivable that such a person would ever be guilty of disloyalty to the Community of Muḥammad. It is unimaginable that his aim in providing spiritual direction would be the achievement of worldly ranks or the acquisition of material properties. It is easy for a man to follow a person who possesses these talents and attributes and to accept him as his teacher and his spiritual guide. As we have said, remembrance has two forms. The first is the remembrance of "Allāh," which we have already discussed. The second is the remembrance of "*Lā ilāha illa'llāh*," which is known as the negation ["There is no god"] and the affirmation ["except Allāh']. Most of the spiritual travelers begin with the remembrance of "Allāh," then move on to negation and the affirmation. The guide may accelerate or delay that progression, depending on his assessment of the state of the spiritual traveler.

Let us now describe the procedure of this remembrance.

> The practitioner must adopt the same manner and style that we have mentioned in connection with the remembrance of "Allāh." Then, with the tongue of the imagination, he must remember the

word "*Lā* [(There is) no…]," drawing it from beneath the navel up to the forehead. In other words, he must draw the word "*Lā*" from underneath the subtle center that is most deeply hidden, then bring it up above that subtle center, until it reaches the subtle center of the self, which is located in the forehead between the eyes. Then he must extend the word "*ilāha* [god]" from the face to the right nipple, to the side of the subtle center of the spirit and the subtle center of the hidden. Next, he must move the word "*illā* [except]" to the back of the left nipple, which is the location of the subtle center of the secret. After that, he must use his imagination to impress the word of Majesty, "Allāh," on the core of the heart, with the force of held-in breath until its impact and its intense heat appear in the rest of the body. All the corrupt parts of the body will then be scorched by that heat and all its virtuous parts will be illuminated by the light of Majesty.

After the perfecting of "*Lā ilāha illa'llāh*" with the tongue of the imagination, and in the manner we have described, one or three or more times, he must say in the state of respiration, "Muḥammadur Rasūlu'llāh [Muḥammad is Allāh's Messenger]."

Diagram showing the movement
of the internal remembrance
of the negation and the affirmation
[*Lā ilāha illa'llāh*]

• The self [*an-nafs*] (between eyes)

(The person's right side) (The person's left side)

• The hidden [*al-khafī*] • The secret [*as-sirr*]

• The most deeply hidden [*al-akhfā*]

• The spirit [*ar-rūḥ*] • The heart [*al-qalb*]

This diagram is designed to illustrate the internal remembrance of "*Lā ilāha illa'llāh* [There is no god except Allāh]." It is incumbent on the practitioner to consider the meaning, not the form of "*Lā ilāha illa'llāh*." What it signifies in his heart should be, "There is truly nothing in existence that is worthy of worship, except Allāh," for worshipful servitude is the aim of the practitioner of remembrance. By his statement "*Lā ilāha*," he should mean that everything in existence is transitory. His expression "*illa'llāh*" should signify that Allāh Alone is Everlasting.

Whether remembrance is the remembrance of "Allāh" or of "*Lā ilāha illa'llāh*," the conditions are listed below.

After performing the remembrance, the practitioner should relax for a little while, and in this state of relaxation he should say, "My God, You are my goal, Your good pleasure is what I seek, and I do not seek anything from my worship apart from Your good pleasure. I am detached from all the worlds, but I hope that You will grant me Your loving affection and intimate knowledge of You." He must contemplate with his heart without thinking about the pursuit of material interest. This vigilant awareness is called "*al-wuqūf al-qalbī* [heart-centered awareness]."

In connection with the subject of heart-centered awareness, we should mention that the Naqshbandīs have eleven maxims or aphorisms, or eleven degrees and principles. As we have stated previously, if someone does not pass through the ten spiritual stations [*maqāmāt*], he will not reach the degree of annihilation and perpetuity [*fanā' wa baqā'*]. These ten stations are: 1. Repentance [*tawba*]. 2. Reversion [*ināba*]. 3. Abstinence [*zuhd*]. 4. Pious caution [*wara'*]. 5. Contentment [*qanā'a*]. 6. Patience [*ṣabr*]. 7. Thankfulness [*shukr*]. 8. Absolute trust [*tawakkul*]. 9. Submission [*taslīm*]. 10. Good pleasure [*riḍā*].

After traversing the path of the spiritual journey, the spiritual traveler must be endowed with eleven virtuous characteristics, otherwise he will not attain to anything. Eight of these are transmitted from the venerable Shaikh 'Abd al-Khāliq al-Ghujduwānī (A.H. 575), and another three from the greatest Shaikh, Sayyid Muḥammad Bahā' ad-Dīn an-Naqshband, making a total of eleven axioms, namely:

1. Watching one's step [*an-naẓar ila'l-qadam*].
2. The journey in the homeland [*as-safar fi 'l-waṭan*].
3. Solitude in the crowd [*al-khalwa fi 'l-jalwa*].
4. Constant remembrance [*adh-dhikr ad-dā'im*].
5. Returning from remembrance [*al-'awda mina 'dh-dhikr*].
6. Alertness when breathing [*al-yaqaẓa 'inda 'n-nafas*].
7. Constant presence [*al-ḥuḍūr ad-dā'im*].
8. Preserving the effects of remembrance in the heart [*ḥifẓ āthār adh-dhikr fi 'l-qalb*].
9. Temporal awareness [*al-wuqūf az-zamānī*].

10. Numerical awareness [*al-wuqūf al-'adadī*].
11. Heart-centered awareness [*al-wuqūf al-qalbī*].

We shall explain the meanings of these axioms.

The spiritual traveler must seek gracious favor and mercy from Allāh (Glory be to Him) while turning toward heaven and observing proper conduct because Allāh (Glory be to Him) is beyond everything. He has no location and He has no above or below.

Heart-centered awareness has two prerequisites: (1) The practitioner of remembrance must try to prevent any fantastic notions from occurring to his heart. (2) If a fantastic notion does occur to his heart, he should interrupt the remembrance as if with a bridle. By striving to expel fantasies, he begins remembrance anew. This is called "*tawqīf* [interrupting; bringing to a halt]."

One of the best practices is holding one's breath at the time of remembrance, according to the wise advice of the spiritual guides. This state results in the warming of the heart and an eagerness within. It gives rise to loving affection, expels temptation, and removes the veils in front of the spiritual traveler, bit by bit.

From this it is clear that Sufism is a spiritual journey that requires knowledge and understanding of its environment.

Numerical awareness means that remembrance must be odd-numbered, in the sense that it must be performed one or three or five or seven times. Numerical awareness is a degree of progress on the Naqshbandī spiritual journey and it has an effect on the disclosure of the secrets of the Spiritual Path.

The spiritual traveler must try to remember "*Lā ilāha illa'llāh*" twenty-one times with one breath. If he does so with vigilant awareness and observance of the proprieties we have mentioned, he will obtain spiritual fruits, his heart will be cleansed, and secrets will be disclosed to his consciousness, as we have mentioned. If he does not obtain these fruits, it means that he has not fulfilled the necessary preconditions, so he must reflect in order to discover the mistake. If he has a spiritual guide, he must take his instruction to heart and act accordingly.

It is important to know that these prerequisites, like heart-centered and numerical awareness. Holding one's breath and moving the remembrance through the subtle centers become easy after regular practice. Physical exercise is difficult at the outset, but then the trainee gets used to it. It is hard for him to lift ten kilos at first, but then it becomes easy for him to lift a hundred kilos. Spiritual exercise is just like that. The fruit of physical exercise is material, whereas the fruit of worshipful servitude is the good pleasure of the Creator. Physical exercise becomes ineffective at a certain time of life, but spiritual exercise grows stronger and becomes a radiant lamp for human beings.

The fundamental fruit of this virtuous development of character is purification, just as it is in the case of the remembrance of "Allāh." In other words, it is the purification of the subtle centers. The subtle centers are purified by the remembrance of Allāh, one after the other, and light shines from them. Inasmuch as the remembrance of "*Lā ilāha illa'llāh*" passes through all the subtle centers, they shine with light all together. It begins with the heart, then the other subtle centers begin the remembrance, and a special light shines from each of them. The spiritual traveler can experience that for himself.

After having discussed the first step of the Naqshbandī Spiritual Path, remembrance, we now come to the second step:

2. Vigilant awareness [*murāqaba*]

Of all the prerequisites we have mentioned in the case of remembrance, each one is also necessary for vigilant awareness, like repentance, seeking forgiveness and so on. In order to practice vigilant awareness, the spiritual traveler should adopt an attitude of readiness, sit in a quiet place, expel fantastic notions from the heart, and turn toward the door of the Truth. He should entreat his Lord with complete humility and total ardent yearning from his inner being without the mediation of a spiritual guide or remembrance and beg Allāh to shower mercy, grace, and blessing on his heart and his inner being while illuminating his heart with the light of His countenance.

Once concentration on the Lord of Truth becomes a firmly rooted characteristic, because of assiduous devotion to this state by night and by day, the spiritual traveler attains to the condition known in Sufism as "concentration on the One who is remembered [*al-Madhkūr*], not on the remembrance [*dhikr*]." That is to say [in grammatical terms], concentration on the One referred to by the noun, He being Allāh, not on the noun remembrance.

By this, the Light of his Lord becomes manifest in his heart and direct witnessing is realized.

According to the eminent shaikhs, "Rapture [*jadhba*], attraction to the Lord of Truth, is realized by means of vigilant awareness in a manner that is quicker than remembrance." To quote another saying, "Assiduous devotion to vigilant awareness raises the vigilant traveler to the degree of spiritual ministry [*wizāra*], which is the highest of all the degrees. One of the fruits of vigilant awareness is that this vigilant spiritual traveler is obeyed in both the worldly dominion [*mulk*] and the Heavenly Dominion [*Malakūt*]. He becomes an expert in knowledge of the inner being and a commander of hearts."

If someone is characterized by vigilant awareness, he must never neglect remembrance, worship, night vigil and performance of the ritual prayers. They have also said that nearness to these righteous individuals is the cause of success and salvation. Allāh (Exalted is He) has said,

> O you who believe, practice true devotion to Allāh,
> *yā ayyuha 'lladhīna āmanu 'ttaqu 'llāha*
> and be with the truthful.
> *wa kūnū ma'a 'ṣ-ṣādiqīn*. (9:119)

Secrets are disclosed to the outstanding spiritual travelers in the state of vigilant awareness for they know and understand the rules of their journey.

This meaning of *murāqaba* is peculiar to the Naqshbandī Spiritual Path. As has previously explained, the other meaning of *murāqaba*, in the context of Sufism, is vigilant supervision of the lower self and keeping it under tight control.

3. Obedience to the spiritual guide

This means that the spiritual traveler should be a pupil to a perfect spiritual guide [*murshid*], applying his instructions with sincere devotion and propriety just like an academic pupil who receives knowledge from his professor.

According to the eminent scholars of Sufism, "This spiritual journey is very easy, and it is nearer to attainment of the goal. It is called the process of 'bonding [*rābiṭa*],' which is a term for linking the heart-centered connection with Allāh (Glory be to Him). If someone has a spiritual guide, this linkage is brought to completion by means of the heart of the spiritual guide in the following manner. The heart of the spiritual traveler becomes attached to the heart of the spiritual guide, which is undoubtedly radiant and illuminated by the Light of Allāh (Glory be to Him). Allāh (Glory be to Him) is the source of all lights. The Light of the Truth shines constantly in the heart of Muḥammad (Allāh bless him and give him peace). It is like electricity that is distributed in all directions. It is also like the river whose streams are dispersed on all sides, with each stream having dozens of farms and thousands of trees irrigated by it. In similar fashion, gracious favor is distributed like fresh water to the hearts of the ardent lovers so that the farms of their hearts may be irrigated by this gracious favor and blessing and their tasty fruits may ripen. The perfect spiritual guide obtains a share of this blessing and he distributes it to the seekers."

As we have mentioned earlier, the Sufi poet Mawlawi sent an ode to his spiritual guide, Shaikh 'Uthmān an-Naqshbandī, where he said (referring to the spiritual plantation),

> You are the farmers' irrigator,
> and you have supplied them all sufficiently.
> As for my plantation, it is complaining of thirst,
> and my fruits are complaining of dessication!
> This is unfair, so open up the streams, stream after stream,
> and irrigate my plantations!

It is necessary to explain that these links are spiritual and immaterial, imperceptible except with the eye of insight. They are not channels in which waters flow nor are they material connections.

Once bonding [*rābiṭa*] has been established and the seeker is capable of securing this connection firmly, he will derive light and blessing from it. This light will yield reflections from the subtle centers, so they will be purified one after the other. Sicknesses and diseases will be cured one after the other, for example, malicious envy, vain conceit, excessive expectation, and craving for the accumulation of material wealth, as well as all other vile spiritual diseases. Once the inner being of the spiritual traveler is purified of corruption and the light of the Truth is kindled in the subtle centers, the subtle centers begin to practice remembrance. Then the seeker will reach the state of presence and witnessing, which is the aim of the quest. With this step, his heart and his inner being achieve tranquillity, and he embarks on the stage of "the inner journey [*sair al-anfus*]," meaning progress toward the stage of annihilation [*fanā'*], in order to attain to the station of perpetuity [*baqā'*].

In the discussion of remembrance, we have indicated that the spiritual traveler should begin with heart-centered remembrance [*dhikr qalbī*] until his heart comes to practice remembrance. He should then begin to move from the remembrance of one subtle center to the remembrance of another subtle center. In this state, however, the spiritual guide should focus his attention upon him. He should focus with his heart on one of the subtle centers of the spiritual traveler and bond it with his own subtle centers. Without any doubt, the subtle center of the spiritual guide is active in remembrance and radiant with light, so it will be reflected on the subtle centers of the spiritual traveler, which in turn will also become active in remembrance and radiant with light. After concentrating for a while on one of the traveler's subtle centers, the guide should focus briefly on another of his disciple's subtle centers. If the disciple has some readiness, due to the intelligence which he is endowed, how quickly he will reach the goal and his subtle centers will be purified! The same applies to progress through all the spiritual stations, until he reaches the stage of annihilation and perpetuity.

Once he has reached this stage, he becomes independent of the spiritual guide. and he becomes perfect in the relative sense. "Absolute perfection belongs to Allāh Alone." Allāh will raise his degrees, so long as Allāh (Exalted is He) wishes to elevate his status. There are no limits to external, material knowledge, so the scholar persists in seeking knowledge in order to increase his knowledge. Likewise, the rich man seeks additional wealth. In the same manner, there is no limit to the gracious favor of Allāh. The perfect human being, the one who has reached the peak of humanity, is our master Muḥammad (Allāh bless him and give him peace). He is followed by the prophets and then the saints.

In the terminology of Sufism, when the spiritual traveler has been awarded the degree of perpetuity after annihilation, he is referred to as a perfect human being [*al-insān al-kāmil*]. This degree is like the doctorate in worldly sciences, so he becomes a teacher and a director in his profession. It is necessary to draw attention at this point to the most serious danger on the Naqshbandī Spiritual Path. This is the guide permitting his disciples to engage in bonding [*rābiṭa*] without his having attained to the degree of perpetuity after annihilation. That is a great mistake because it places him under suspicion of polytheism [*shirk*]. The guide is responsible for this. Secondly, it exposes the disciple to the sicknesses of whispered temptation and numerous other afflictions. Spiritual guidance is one thing and the authorization for bonding is something else.

Guidance [*irshād*], in the sense of "enjoining what is right and proper, and forbidding what is wrong and improper [*al-amr bi'l-ma'rūf wa 'n-nahy 'ani 'l-munkar*]," is a duty incumbent on every Muslim. Guidance relating to the Sacred Law is the duty of religious scholars. In the context of the Spiritual Path it is incumbent on the guide to cry out to his disciples saying, "I am advising you and directing you toward repentance, but I am not a perfect spiritual guide and bonding with me is not permissible for you." As an alternative, he may repeat the saying of Amīr Kulāl, the guide of Shaikh an-Naqshband, "The limits of my knowledge are drawn at this point, so you must seek another guide to teach you from here on."

Concentration does not mean that the guide must be linked to the disciple in the same physical location. The perfect guide can also concentrate on his disciple from a distant place and instill spiritual joy in his heart from afar. Local proximity is better, however, for as we have said, "Nearness to the champions of the Truth is the cause of felicity and success. The righteous and saintly man is the dear friend of Allāh, and nearness to the dear friend of Allāh is the cause of blissful happiness in the two abodes [this world and the Herafter]." It is therefore incumbent on the disciple to seek blissful happiness from his spiritual guide.

It was Shaikh 'Abdullāh ad-Dihlawī who said, "Remembrance with the tongue does not realize the aims of the spiritual traveler, as long as it has not been transformed into habitual heart-centered remembrance. Remembrance with the tongue is beneficial, nonetheless, as an immaterial, spritual step for the practitioner of remembrance if it is perfected in accordance with the prerequisites that have been mentioned."

He then went on to say, "It is incumbent on the disciple to persist in remembering Allāh standing humbly in front of the door of the Lord of Truth even when he is busy with worldly tasks." He also said, "Blessings from Allāh are raining down, but for the heart of the true believer they are accelerated."

This is called the spiritual state of "solitude in the crowd [*al-khalwa fī 'l-jalwa*]." It signifies that a person is with the Lord of Truth, not with his fellow creatures. This is the meaning of the saying, "The Sufi is present and absent (present with people in body, absent from them in spirit)." Solitude in the crowd is one of the characteristic virtues and degrees of the travelers on the Naqshbandī Spiritual Path.

As previously explained, the diseases of the heart are vices like envy and malice. The genuine Muslim is one whose heart is clean and free from these diseases, but this is a difficult matter. Otherwise the problems of human beings would already have been solved.

When the spiritual traveler has a guide, the latter is entrusted with the treatment of these diseases and with clearing them from his disciple's heart. If the spiritual traveler fulfills the well-known proprieties of remembrance, and persists in the remembrance of "*Lā ilāha illa'llāh*," the treatment of his heart-centered diseases will be easy for him. When he says "*Lā ilāha* [There is no god]," he should simultaneously imagine the expulsion of envy and without envy or anything else in his heart "*illa'llāh* [except Allāh]." He will thus experience a cleansing of his heart from envy and every other vice.

There is a type of human being who does not have certain vices like lying and arrogant pride, for instance, so he must examine his own state to find his own vices. He must use this kind of remembrance to cleanse his heart of them. He must sometimes say, confessing in his heart, "I am afflicted with these vices, so remove me from them and deliver me from them, one after the other, through the blessing of this remembrance."

This is the cleansing and purification of the heart, the illumination of the subtle centers, and the progression from one step to another. It consists of seven steps, called "the journey in the homeland [*as-safar fī 'l-waṭan*]." That is to say, the heart-centered migration from point to point, until one is completely cleansed. It is also the contemplation of the self in order to discover its diseases and their treatment. Allāh (Exalted is He) has said,

> As well as in your own selves. What, do you not see?
> *wa fī anfusi-kum a-fa-lā tubṣirūn*. (51:21)

During this stage of the journey, the Sufi must live with remembrance and abstain from everything other than the remembrance of his Lord. As they have said, "Everything other than the remembrance of Allāh (Glory be to Him) is an agony for the spirit even if it has the taste of sugar."

As we are told in the Noble Qur'ān:

> And remember Allāh frequently, for then you may prosper.
> *wa 'dhkuru 'llāha kathīran la'alla-kum tufliḥūn*. (62:10)

If someone obtains a spiritual blessing and clearly recognizes it, he must act in order to keep it safe. If it goes away, he must return to remembrance until he recovers the blesing. Then the blessing becomes a permanent state and a lasting characteristic. As we have mentioned in the definition of *lawāmi'* [sparkles],[1] the novice seeker sees rays of light in his heart, but they go away and do not become established. Then they keep recurring until they feel at home and settle in the heart.

After this, we now come to "*jadhbat al-qabūl* [the rapture of acceptance]." This is a term applied to spiritual travelers when a special state is directed toward them such that they are attracted to their Lord. The traveler thus becomes praiseworthy in the sight of his Lord. If the rapture ripens and becomes overwhelming, Divine bounties flow through the depths of his heart. The enraptured traveler can feel them, so his spirit is delighted and he rejoices. They make the traveler so happy that he loses consciousness. If this state persists, he draws near to the state of presence and annihilation. This state is called "*ḥaqīqat adh-dhikr* [the reality of remembrance]" because it represents the first stage of the bestowal of blessing. Since it is the reality of the state of presence, it is also called "*darj* (or *indirāj*) *an-nihāya fi 'l-bidāya* [experience of the final stage at the outset]." This is not attained in a day or moment. Everything has its time, its period, and its reckoning.

As for the various tasty fruits of the subtle centers, each has an act of worship, like *tahajjud* [the prayer of night vigil] and the recitation of the Noble Qur'ān. These blessings are innumerable and uncountable. In his Letters [*Maktūbāt*], Imām ar-Rabbānī has mentioned the blessings peculiar to each state according to numerous Sufi lineages. He was a spiritual guide to the Qādirī, Suhrawardī, Chishtī, and Kubrawī lineages, as well as being one of the eminent shaikhs of the Naqshbandī lineage.

It was Shaikh 'Abdullāh ad-Dihlawī who said, "The blessing of the righteous may descend like a ray of light from the sun, so that it enters the heart in a corner. It may also resemble clouds that encompass all sides of the heart. It may be like a gentle east wind, a shower of rain, a river, or like a tent of silk surrounding the whole body like the moisture that alights upon the heart."

He also said, "Ardent yearning and spiritual warmth are likely to be experienced by travelers on the Chishtī Spiritual Path, while pure serenity and brilliant illumination are likely to be experienced by travelers on the Qādirī Spiritual Path. Travelers on the

1. See p. 131 above.

Naqshbandī Spiritual Path are likely to experience absence and loss of consciousness. The Suhrawardīs have experiences like those of the Naqshbandīs."

This is but a drop from the ocean of Sufism and a bouquet of roses from a garden of song that comprises the whole earth. I have offered it with the intention of explaining a certain amount to you, not of providing a comprehensive account of the subject. In its reality, the realm of Sufism is the realm of intimate knowledge of Allāh (Glory be to Him) and that is a realm that has no end and no limit, neither in its past nor in its future.

In order to explain the technical term "*indirāj an-nihāya fi 'l-bidāya* [experience of the final stage at the outset]," we should say that, just as *indirāj* means the establishment of the reality of remembrance in the heart, as we have previously indicated, it also has another form.

In his state of concentration, the guide may transport his disciple to great spiritual stations. He may simply let him see them or he may let him stay there for a period then return him to his initial station. His aim is to encourage the disciple and urge him to work for attainment with a heart that is enthusiastic and eager.

This resembles the situation in worldly affairs when a person is invited to splendid palaces, and he is told, "If you attain to that rank, you will become the owner of these palaces." If he is one of those who desire what this world has to offer, he will then work with greater enthusiasm to obtain it.

In one of its forms, *indirāj* means that disclosure is conferred on the spiritual traveler and that certain secrets are revealed to him. For example, it may be disclosed to him if the deceased is righteous or not, even though he has not actually reached the point at which he can recognize such states with his own spiritual strength. The wisdom of that experience is that it summons him to "*al-khawf wa 'r-rajā'* [fear and hope]," and he attains to "*'ain al-yaqīn* [the eye of certainty]."

In another of its forms, it means that the disciple traverses all the stages and draws near to the destination. He thus becomes a spiritual deputy [*khalīfa*], but without being the master of blessings. This is because his inner strength falls in the shadow of the inner strength of the guide. In technical terminology, he is said to be "*fī ẓill al-murshid* [in the shadow of the spiritual guide]," or "*fī ẓill al-Quṭb* [in the shadow of the Axis]." This spiritual deputy is not aware that his strength belongs not to him but to his guide. It sometimes happens that senior shaikhs send their deputies, while in this state, on a mission of spiritual guidance.

It is clear that the foretaste of the final stage is a most important experience. People are astonished by the gifts, charismatic talents, and blessings that are bestowed on this deputy, whose focus of attention does not differ from that of his shaikh. He cures the numerous diseases of the heart, and escorts the spiritual traveler. At the same time, however, he is put to the test by the spiritual guide in order to discover his capability. Deputies may be subjected to trial and tribulation. Delusion may seize control of them and they may imagine that they have powers which they do not actually possess. If they fail to pass the test, they will not return to their original stations, but will probably be dismissed for a period of time. If they do pass the test, they will return to their stations. This process is beneficial to the disciple, if he treats it with respect and observes proper conduct. It raises his degrees of attainment and acquaints him with the highest stations. When he returns to his previous position, he will recognize that these strengths do not belong to him, but only to his spiritual guide. He needs to discover where he stands in relation to these spiritual stations, so he must engage in arduous work and constant exercise in order to attain to them.

These various forms of experiencing the final stage at the outset are dependent on the preference of the spiritual guide. That is because he is the master of the heart, its expert and its physician. He is best aware of the need of each disciple and the extent of that need.

The method of developing the subtle centers in a detailed manner is the method of Imām ar-Rabbānī. His deputies, including his son Shaikh Muḥammad Ma'ṣūm, found this task too difficult. They contented themselves with the training and development of the subtle center of the heart in the realm of the [Divine] command, and the subtle center of the self in the realm of creation. The other subtle centers, were purified, leading to the attainment of the stage of annihilation and perpetuity. Shaikh 'Abdullāh ad-Dihlawī said, "We accept the latter opinion. We therefore maintain that the Naqshbandī spiritual guide is he who chooses what he considers best and necessary for his disciple, especially in relation to those whose training is based on the method of bonding [*rābiṭa*]. When the subtle centers begin to practice remembrance, the presence of the Lord of Truth is attained. This presence is of various kinds, and eminent spiritual travelers have assigned a name to each kind that is associated with the knowledge and understanding of disciples.

"If the presence of the Lord of Truth is equivalent to the presence of creatures, inasmuch as this presence does not make you so inebriated that you forget people and they have no influence on your presence, it is called 'the remembrance of the heart [*dhikr al-qalb*].' If the presence of the Lord of Truth is predominant, this is 'the remembrance of the spirit [*dhikr ar-rūḥ*].' If this presence makes you forget yourself, but you do not forget your fellow creatures. It is 'the remembrance of the secret center [*dhikr as-sirr*].' If the presence of the Lord of Truth makes you forget both yourself and your fellow creatures, it is 'the remembrance of the hidden center [*dhikr al-khafī*].'"

What is presence and how is it experienced?

He said, "If the disciple is able to examine his heart and he recognizes that it is near to Allāh (Glory be to Him), this is presence even if it is not constant. It is clear to the spiritual traveler. Presence is seldom experienced, however, because of the disciple's preoccupation with acquiring worldly things. If his presence is in the form of 'as if you could see Him,' and it exists in every time and situation, in the time of speech and the time of silence, and during both happiness and anger. Then presence becomes an established property. This state is called 'constant consciousness [*al-wa'y ad-dā'im*],' for it is constant recollection. It is one of the fundamentals of the Naqshbandī Spiritual Path."

These efforts must be made because the spiritual traveler has been blessed with vision and witnessing with the eye of his insight. In this state, he may feel that he is witnessing with the eye of his ordinary sight, not with the eye of his insight. Presence overwhelms him and he may utter statements that seem to imply heretical belief in incarnation [*ḥulūl*] and pantheism [*ittiḥād*]. He is actually in the state of presence, so what he is says are really ecstatic utterances that spring from his mouth. He may be told, "You said such-and-such and such-and-such," but he will not believe it, like a drunkard after becoming sober.

This vision resembles the peculiar vision experienced while dreaming. The vision of Allāh is not possible with the eye of ordinary sight, so, if we hear a something contradictory from an enraptured person, we must understand that it refers to what he is feeling in himself, not in reality.

According to Shaikh 'Abdullāh ad-Dihlawī, "After this state, 'the eye of certainty [*'ain al-yaqīn*]' begins 'the awareness of togetherness [*al-murāqaba al-ma'iyya*].' Allāh has said (Glory be to Him and Exalted is He),

> And He is together with you wherever you may be.
> *wa Huwa ma'a-kum aina-mā kuntum.* (57:4)"

At this point it becomes permissible to practice remembrance with the tongue. This is the kind of close relationship that constitutes lesser sainthood, which is the first degree of the saints [*awliyā'*]. It signifies traversing the distance in the shade of the Names of Allāh, and this spiritual station is called the station of rapture [*jadhba*]. The spiritual traveler now achieves true awareness of blessed grace, throbbing of the heart, eager yearning, weeping, taste, the active affirmation of Oneness, the manifestations of the Light of the Lord of Truth, the vision of Singularity and multiplicity, and the states of intimate friendship, ardent love, loneliness, and perplexity, just as none of this is hidden from the masters of this sainthood. He also truly experiences immersion in the ocean of direct knowledge, so he is cut off from his attachments to people, he forgets everything apart from Allāh, and his heart is saved from idle notions and whispered temptation. This is realized in the stage of friendship with God. Also realized here is the annihilation of the heart, that is permanence in the state of spiritual inebriation and the expulsion of everything in his heart apart from Allāh.

In the words of one of the poets who dream of this degree,

> When I am separated from myself,
> and neither you nor I remain,
> and the only One who remains is Allāh....

This is the state of togetherness or the awareness of togetherness.

As we have previously mentioned, Allāh is near to us, and we are told in the Noble Qur'ān,

> And We are nearer to him than the jugular vein.
> *wa Naḥnu aqrabu ilai-hi min ḥabli 'l-warīd.* (50:16)

Because of the purification of his inner being, the servant is also aware of this nearness. As a matter of fact, every servant is near to Him, but the one who is pure can feel the nearness. The one who has not purified his heart is unaware of Allāh's gracious favor. Shaikh 'Abdullāh has discussed four kinds of annihilation, which he has described as follows:

1. The annihilation of creatures [*fanā' al-khalq*]. This means that the servant fears no one and hopes for no one except Allāh.

2. The annihilation of desire [*fanā' ar-raghba*]. At this point, the spiritual traveler desires nothing except nearness to Him (Glory be to Him).

3. The annihilation of the will [*fanā' al-irāda*]. He has no volition left and he is like the corpse, so he does not seek anything.

4. The annihilation of actions [*fanā' al-af'āl*]. He no longer has the power to perform any action, so he wishes for everything from his Lord. In other words, when his ability to act comes to an end, Allāh (Glory be to Him) takes charge of his actions. This is an allusion to the Sacred Tradition [*Ḥadīth Qudsī*].

> My servant continues to draw near to Me by means of supererogatory acts of worship [*nawāfil*], until I love him. Then, when I have come to love him, I am his hearing by which he hears, his sight by which he sees, and his hand with which he strikes."

As I have mentioned earlier, Naqshbandīs say that the station of sainthood [*wilāya*] is a collective term for ten spiritual stations, namely: 1. Repentance [*tawba*]. 2. Reversion [*ināba*]. 3. Abstinence [*zuhd*]. 4. Pious caution [*wara'*]. 5. Contentment [*qanā'a*]. 6. Patience [*ṣabr*]. 7. Thankfulness [*shukr*]. 8. Absolute trust [*tawakkul*]. 9. Submission [*taslīm*]. 10. Good pleasure [*riḍā*].

In the Naqshbandī Order, the station of intimacy with God and the annihilation of the heart are not enough for the Shaikh to become a spiritual guide. This can only happen after the annihilation of the self and the realization of the perfections of greater intimacy with God. Only then is he qualified for unconditional authorization to offer spiritual guidance.

In the state of annihilation of the heart, misleading notions vanish from the heart and settle in the self. In the state of annihilation of the self, the location of which is in the forehead between the eyes, there is no place left for misleading notions. These are the degrees traversed by the spiritual traveler in his journey toward Allāh (Glory be to Him), from the first of them to countless degrees that no one knows except Allāh. The spritual traveler experiences them as spheres.

These spheres include all the subtle centers, gifts, and talents.

The first is called the sphere of possibility [*imkān*] and the last is a sphere that defies definition. There are twenty spheres altogether. An expert has said about them, "When the veil is removed from the cheek of the loved one, another veil appears. Whenever a veil is removed, another veil appears."

These spheres have been discussed by Imām ar-Rabbānī in his Letters [*Maktūbāt*], and by Shaikh 'Abdullāh ad-Dihlawī in his book entitled *Īḍāḥ aṭ-Ṭarīq* [*Explanation of the Path*]. As they point out, *dā'ira* [sphere] is a spiritual term that does in fact resemble the ordinary sphere. This is clearly understood by travelers on the Naqshbandī Spiritual Path. I shall now give a brief account of the subject.

It is incumbent on the spiritual traveler, before anything else, to traverse the sphere of possibility, which covers the whole realm of creation and the [Divine] command. He then ascends by means of the purification of this realm. This involves purification of the five subtle centers as well as purification of the self, the four natural centers [earth, air, fire, and water], and the constitution of the body. If he perfects the journey through this sphere by means of purification, he will be delivered from the sphere of possibility and reach the second sphere, which is the sphere of lesser intimacy with God. He begins the journey and ascends toward the summit of the quest in the shade of the [Divine] Names and attributes. This is the point of entry into the real experience of annihilation, and "rapture [*jadhba*]" is one of its fruits.

After the ascension from the previous sphere, by way of the journey in the shade of Allāh's Names, what follows is entry into greater intimacy with God, which is essentially peculiar to the prophets (blessing and peace be upon them). The attainment of their noble Companions to this sphere is due to their loyal following. If someone attains to this sphere, he has passed through the station of "annihilation of the self [*fanā' an-nafs*]."

I must emphasize that annihilation of the self and annihilation of the heart are different from purification the self and purification of the heart. Purification belongs to the initial stage and it is merely a cleansing of the heart. Annihilation of the subtle centers, on the other hand, is a very high station and an ultimate degree.

Greater intimacy with God has three spheres and a single arc, meaning three circles and one semicircle. The spiritual traveler should be aware of this and must pass through them one after the other with every effort of strength and virility just like the worldly traveler on a mountain path or a desert trail. The traveler himself must know where he is!

The journey on this path is completed in the shade of the Names and attributes. The fruits that the spiritual traveler obtains from this sphere are real annihilation, the reality of Islam, expansion of the breast, the station of constant thankfulness and good pleasure, and deliverance from blameworthy characteristics.

The Sphere of the Highest Intimacy with God [*al-Wilāyat al-'Ulyā*]

This is the sphere of the Supreme Court of the angels and the spirits, and it is accessible to the righteous by means of strict compliance with religious guidelines of behavior.

Imām ar-Rabbānī explained that precisely. He said, "The entire life of the human being would not be enough for a single step of progress in this domain were it not for the providence of Allāh." With reference to this subject, he drew attention to His saying (Exalted is He),

> The angels and the Spirit ascend to Him in a Day
> *ta'ruju 'l-malā'ikatu wa 'r-rūḥu ilai-hi*
> of which the span is fifty thousand years.
> *fī yawmin kāna miqdāru-hu khamsīna alfa sana.* (70:4)

Ascension to this degree is impossible without help from Allāh (Glory be to Him). One of its fruits is the light obtained by the spiritual traveler. He recalls the time he devoted to the "Sultan of the remembrances," and the light he then received. But how does this new light compare with that one? This is indeed a splendid and exalted station.

Since this intimacy belongs essentially to the Supreme Court, the spiritual traveler acquires a relationship with the spirits and the angels. He perceives the secrets that are among the fruits of the secret subtle center, and the most deeply hidden subtle center. May the lords of felicity enjoy their felicity! Then begins the journey in the sphere of the perfections of prophethood. In this sphere he receives the manifestation of the Essence without the covering of the Names and the attributes.

Imām ar-Rabbānī says, "Progress here by a single step is superior to the stations of high office since presence is realized without hesitation or palpitation of the heart. The refreshing coolness of certainty is realized, something beyond the reach of the spiritual state and the spiritual station. The sciences of the Sacred Law are also revealed here to the spiritual traveler. This is a station basically peculiar to the prophets and it is inherited by the saints through loyal adherence to their exemplary path."

I shall now quote some excerpts from the writing of Shaikh 'Abdullāh ad-Dihlawī, in his book entitled *Īḍāḥ aṭ-Ṭarīq* [*Explanation of the Path*], concentrating on some of the most important aspects of this subject.

> The other spheres are a journey in the perfections, since perfection after perfection is received by the great men of Sufism. Examples include:
>
> The sphere of the perfection of messengership [*Risāla*].
> The sphere of the perfection of the masters
> of firm resolve [*ulū 'l'azm*].
> The sphere of the reality of the Ka'ba.
> The sphere of the reality of the Qur'ān.
> The sphere of the reality of the ritual prayer [*ṣalāt*].
> The sphere of pure worshipful servitude [*'ubūdiyya*].
>
> The journey on foot comes to a halt at this point and the visionary journey begins. The spiritual traveler sees these stations with the eye of insight. With this eye they behold the 'sphere of bosom friendship [*dāirat al-khilliyya*],' which is the station of our master Abraham, the Bosom Friend of Allāh [*Khalīlu 'llāh*]. The other prophets are his followers in this station.
>
> Follow the religion of Abraham, as one by nature upright.
> *ani 'ttabi' millata Ibrāhīma ḥanīfā.* (16:123)
>
> As one says in ritual prayer,
>
> O Allāh, bless Muḥammad and the family of Muḥammad,
> *Allāhumma ṣalli 'alā Muḥammadin wa 'alā āli*
> *Muḥammadin*
> as You have blessed Abraham and the family of Abraham
> *kamā ṣallaita 'alā Ibrāhīma wa 'alā āli Ibrāhīm.*
>
> The expression 'as You have blessed...' signifies the continuity [of the Prophetic model]. This sphere is called 'the Abrahamic reality [*al-ḥaqīqat al-Ibrāhīmiyya*].'

Then comes the sphere of 'pure Essential affection [*al-maḥabbat aṣ-ṣirfat adh-Dhātiyya*],' which becomes apparent to the most distinguished spiritual travelers. From its center emerges the Mosaic reality, for it is the sphere of 'the reality of Moses [*ḥaqīqat Mūsā*].' Next comes the sphere of 'the married couple of lovingness and belovedness [*al-muḥibbiyya wa 'l-maḥbūbiyyat al-mutazawwijatain*],' which is the sphere of the Muḥammadan reality. It is a truly majestic sphere.

Then comes the sphere of 'pure Essential belovedness [*al-maḥbūbiyyat aṣ-ṣirfat adh-Dhātiyya*],' which is the Aḥmadan reality. Next comes the sphere of 'pure love [*al-ḥubb aṣ-ṣirf*],' followed by the 'indefinable [*al-lā-ta'yīniyya*],' which is the sphere that no one reaches by the journey on foot, but only by way of the visionary journey.

The spiritual traveler may sometimes be blessed with a station defined as 'accompaniment [*taba'iyya*],' which is a technical term of the Sufis. It means that the holder of the station (or the blessing) takes his beloved friend by 'accompaniment' to a station that does not belong to his loved one. Since the latter is a follower and not a station-holder, he is treated with respect in this station in appreciation of his host like in worldly affairs and relationships. The basis of this is the love of Abū Bakr (may Allāh be well pleased with him) for our master Muḥammad (Allāh bless him and give him peace). He said (Allāh bless him and give him peace),

> Allāh has never poured anything into my breast, without my having poured it into the breast of Abū Bakr.

Shaikh 'Abdullāh ad-Dihlawī also said, on another subject,

> The three degrees of sainthood are "the lesser [*aṣ-ṣughrā*], the greater [*al-kubrā*] and the highest [*al-a'lā*]." The three perfections are those of prophethood, of messengership, and of the masters of firm resolve. The seven realities are: (1) the reality of the Ka'ba, (2) the Qur'ān, (3) ritual prayer, (4) the Abrahamic, (5) the Mosaic, (6) the Muḥammadan, and (7) the Aḥmadan. Then come the spheres of pure affection and that which is indefinable. They are not reached by everyone who travels by following paths. Some attain to sainthood of the heart, yet may not pass beyond the sphere of possibility. Some attain to greater intimacy and a

few of them attain to the highest intimacy. Very few of them attain to the three perfections. Where is he who attains to the seven realities and their highest height?!

The Eleven Axioms of the Naqshbandī Spiritual Path

The Naqshbandī Spiritual Path is based on the practical application of eleven Sufi axioms and principles derived from the experience of the shaikhs of the Spiritual Path. Eight of them have been transmitted from Shaikh ʻAbd al-Khāliq al-Ghujduwānī (A.H. 575), and the other three from the Greatest Shaikh, Muḥammad Bahā' ad-Dīn an-Naqshband (A.H. 717–791).

It is well-known that the Naqshbandī Order is based on heart-centered remembrance [*adh-dhikr al-qalbī*]. Remembrance is the contemplation of Allāh's Name (Exalted is He) until the heart and the whole body begin to practice remembrance. Its fruit is the cleansing of the heart from depravities and the constant preservation of the state of presence [*ḥuḍūr*]. Its real aim is contact with the One who is remembered [*al-Madhkūr*] and nearness to the Lord of Truth. Remembrance is a means to nearness. When the Light of Allāh becomes manifest in the heart and presence is realized, remembrance ceases since the One who is remembered is present. As we have said, this nearness is not the nearness of person to person nor is it the nearness of the body to the Essence of Allāh (Glory be to Him). It is rather the nearness of the inner being to the Light of Allāh (Glory be to Him).This nearness is perceived with the eye of the heart, not with the eye of the head. That is to say, with insight, not with sight.

As we have also said, the likeness of that is the vision experienced while in the state of dreaming. With what eye does the dreamer see? That is how we approach the inner content of our souls.

These are the eleven axioms:

1. Alertness when breathing [*al-yaqaẓa ʻinda 'n-nafas*].
2. Watching one's step [*an-naẓar ila'l-qadam*].
3. The journey in the homeland [*as-safar fi 'l-waṭan*].
4. Solitude in the crowd [*al-khalwa fi 'l-jalwa*].
5. Constant remembrance [*adh-dhikr ad-dā'im*].
6. Returning from remembrance to the Essence [*al-ʻawda mina 'dh-dhikr ila 'dh-dhāt*].

7. Guarding the heart against fits of heedlessness and idle notions [*ḥirāsat al-qalb min al-ghafalāt wa 'l-khawāṭir*]; in other words, Constant presence [*al-ḥuḍūr ad-dā'im*].
8. Preserving the effects of remembrance in the heart [*ḥifẓ āthār adh-dhikr fī 'l-qalb*].
9. Temporal awareness [*al-wuqūf az-zamānī*].
10. Numerical awareness [*al-wuqūf al-'adadī*].
11. Heart-centered awareness [*al-wuqūf al-qalbī*].

1. Alertness when breathing [*al-yaqaẓa 'inda 'n-nafas*] (in Persian: *hūsh dar dam*)

This means preserving the breath from heedlessness during its inhalation, its exhalation, and the interval between the two. That the servant's heart is present with Allāh in all breaths in case that his imaginings are not lavished on worldly matters.

According to an-Naqshband, "Since the work of the spiritual traveler is connected with his breathing, he must recognize whether his breath is moving with present awareness or with heedlessness. This is so that he will remain in the state of remembrance and his attention will not be lavished on the past or the future in the state of heedlessness."

According to Shaikh 'Ubaidullāh al-Aḥrār (A.H. 809–895), one of the great shaikhs of the Naqshbandī lineage, "The most important work in the Naqshbandī Spiritual Path is vigilant awareness of the breath so that it is not exhaled in heedlessness. If someone does not think about it, he is said to have 'lost his breath.'"

According to Shaikh Sa'd ad-Dīn al-Kāshgharī, Shaikh 'Ubaidullāh's contemporary, "The meaning of alertness when breathing is that the spiritual traveler must not be heedless from breath to breath, that he must breathe with present awareness, and that his breath must not be devoid of the Truth."

In short, according to the men of the Naqshbandī Spiritual Path, this axiom signifies alertness, attentiveness, and thoughtfulness when breathing, and it is one of the degrees of the Spiritual Path. If the spiritual traveler wastes a breath, it is as if he has committed a sin because the wasting of breath is harmful to him.

2. Watching one's step [*an-naẓar ila'l-qadam*] (in Persian: *naẓar bar qadam*)

According to some, the meaning of this is as follows, "While the Sufi is walking on the Path, his gaze must be focused on his footsteps, so that his feelings and his mind do not become dispersed in many directions. His mind and his thinking are with Allāh and he is not deluded by the beauty and pleasure of this world. This is a praiseworthy action." According to Imām ar-Rabbānī, however, "'Watching one's step' is the state of 'the journey in the homeland [*as-safar fi 'l-waṭan*].'" They are a pair of spiritual concepts.

Before he journeys from one station to a higher station, the spiritual traveler must examine this station with the eye of insight before taking a step with his spiritual foot. As we have noted in the discussion of the spheres, the journey on foot leads to the end of the stations of the realities. The last of them is the reality of ritual prayer, where the visionary journey begins.

According to Imām ar-Rabbānī, "The visionary journey, like the exploration of the journey on foot, is made for the purpose of ascending the spiritual stations. Before he takes a step toward the new station, the traveler must make sure that he is setting his foot on the right spot. This verification of the new station is called 'watching one's step.' It therefore resembles the state of 'the journey in the homeland,' because watching one's step means traveling from station to station, which has the same meaning as the journey in the homeland. After the stage of the journey on foot, the spiritual traveler embarks on the stage of the visionary journey in which he sees the greatest stations with the vision of insight alone."

According to Fakhr ad-Dīn al-Kāshifī, in the *Rashaḥāt* [*Beads of Dew*], "'Watching one's step' refers to the progress of the traveler on the path of Sufism for the purpose of ascending to the stations of spirituality and passing beyond the knot of egoism." He is the author of an important book, entitled *al-Uṣūl an-Naqshbandiyya* [*Naqshbandī Principles*], preserved in the National Library of France.

3. The journey in the homeland [*as-safar fi 'l-waṭan*] (in Persian: *safar dar waṭan*)

This has several meanings:

• The first meaning: We have no doubt that making a journey, in the ordinary sense, is a valuable means of gaining experience and expanding consciousness. Traveling on the earth gives rise to keen interest in the products of creation, and directs the perceptive faculties of the human being toward the Might and Glory of his Creator.

Making a journey is an incentive to reflection and Allāh (Glory be to Him) has applauded those who reflect upon the creation of the heavens and the earth. He has linked them together with those who practice remembrance, for He has said (Glory be to Him),

> [There are signs for] those who remember Allāh,
> *alladhīna yadhkurūna 'llāha*
> standing and sitting and on their sides,
> *qiyāman wa qu'ūdan wa 'alā junūbi-him*
> and who reflect upon the creation of the heavens and the earth.
> *wa yatafakkarūna fī khalqi 's-samāwāti wa 'l-arḍ.* (3:191)

He has also commended those who travel [*as-sā'iḥūn*] on the earth,[1] and He has linked them together with those who repent and practice worshipful service, for He has said (Glory be to Him),

> Those who are penitent, those who are worshipful,
> *at-tā'ibūna 'l-'ābidūna 'l-*
> those who praise [the Lord], those who travel, those who bow down,
> *ḥāmidūna 's-sā'iḥūna 'r-rāki'ūna 's-*
> those who fall prostrate, those who enjoin what is right and fair
> *sājidūna 'l-āmirūna bi'l-ma'rūfi*
> and who forbid what is wrong and unfair,
> *wa'n-nāhūna 'ani 'l-munkari*
> and those who keep the limits of Allāh.
> *wa'l-ḥāfiẓūna li-ḥudūdi 'llāh.* (9:112)

He has also mentioned women travelers [*sā'iḥāt*], in His saying (Glory be to Him),

> It may happen that his Lord, if he divorces you,
> *'asā Rabbu-hu in ṭallaqa-kunna an yubdi*
> will give him in your stead wives better than you,
> *la-hu azwājan khairan min-kunna*
> submissive, believing, pious,
> *muslimātin mu'minātin qānitātin*
> penitent, worshipful, travelers, widows, and maids.
> *tā'ibātin 'ābidātin sā'iḥātin thayyibātin wa abkārā.* (66:5)

1. Translator's note: The usual meaning of the Arabic word *sā'iḥūn* (and its feminine counterpart *sā'iḥāt*) is "travelers, those who travel." In the context of these particular Qur'ānic verses, however, many traditional commentators have interpreted them as meaning "those who fast."

The Noble Qur'ān contains a special solicitude for those who travel on the earth. Sometimes it warns of the chastisement in store for those who are guilty of transgression on the earth, and sometimes it points to the changes and upheavals that occur in the affairs of life. In four verses of the Noble Qur'ān, Allāh says (Glory be to Him),

> So have they not traveled on the earth?
> *a-fa-lam yasīrū fi 'l-arḍi.* (12:109; 22:46; 40:82; 47:10)

—in three verses,

> Say, "Travel on the earth."
> *qul sīrū fi 'l-arḍi.* (6:11; 27:69; 29:20)

—and in two verses,

> And have they not traveled on the earth?
> *a-wa lam yasīrū fi 'l-arḍi.* (30:9; 35:44)

These Qur'ānic verses encourage the Muslims to travel and wander about on the earth for the sake of increasing their faith in Allāh (Glory be to Him). This must surely mean that this Naqshbandī Sufi principle represents the Qur'ānic standard of Islamic morality!

• The second meaning is the search for the appropriate spiritual guide. The great shaikhs have advised the seekers to travel in search for a perfect guide and they have added that the spiritual traveler must obey the guide in everything he commands him to do. The journey of our master, Khālid an-Naqshbandī, took him from 'Irāq to Syria and the Ḥijāz, from the Ḥijāz to Kurdistān, and from there to Īrān, Afghānistān, Kābul, and Qandahār, until he reached the venerable Shaikh 'Abdullāh ad-Dihlawī and found what he sought in the presence of this perfect guide. This journey exemplifies important Sufi journeys. Another example is the journey of Imām al-Ghazālī in search of a spiritual guide from Ṭūs to Baghdād, and from there to Syria and the Ḥijāz.

• The third meaning is the spiritual meaning for Naqshbandīs. According to the Naqshbandīs, the spiritual meaning of this axiom represents the traveler's endeavor to migrate from vile human attributes to the virtuous angelic attributes. This is a journey from the realm of creatures [*khalq*] to the realm of the Truth [*Ḥaqq*]. It is moving away from the delusions of this world and drawing near to the Master of the two abodes [this world and the Hereafter]. It is a journey from one state and station to a finer and loftier state and station.

4. Solitude in the crowd [*al-khalwa fi 'l-jalwa*] (in Persian: *khalwat dar anjuman*)

This means that the servant's body is with his fellow creatures, while his heart is with his Lord.

There are two kinds of solitude.

• Material solitude. This signifies the spiritual traveler's withdrawal into an isolated corner in order to devote himself to worship and contemplation. This helps the traveler to control his feelings and enables him to concentrate on his heart and become preoccupied with the state of his heart. As is well-known, the more he is able to deactivate the external attributes, the more the internal attributes increase in vigor and effectiveness. He thereby draws near in fine style to the realm of Sovereignty [*Malakūt*].

• Solitude of the heart. In this second kind of solitude, the spiritual traveler never neglects the remembrance of his Lord. Even when he is together with people, busily engaged in earning a livelihood and going to and fro, his heart remains active in remembrance and he does not forget his Lord. Allāh (Exalted is He) has said,

> Men whom neither commerce nor trade diverts
> *rijālun lā tulhī-him tijāratun wa lā bai'un*
> from the remembrance of Allāh.
> *'an dhikri 'llāhi.* (24:37)

The reference here is to the second meaning.

According to Shaikh Muḥammad Amīn al-Kurdī, "The majority of the great scholars of Sufism consider it best for the spiritual traveler to stay close to people, working to earn lawful sustenance after becoming established and making progress on his spiritual course."

According to Shaikh Abū Sa'īd al-Kharrāz (d. A.H. 279), "The perfect Sufi is not someone from whom all kinds of charismatic marvels emanate. The perfect Sufi is one who sits among his fellow creatures, buys and sells with them, marries, mingles with people, and does not forget his Lord for a single instant."

As the saying goes, "The Sufi is present, absent." In other words, he is outwardly and physically present with his fellow creatures, but absent from them inwardly where the heart is concerned.

According to Imām ar-Rabbānī, "Seclusion in the crowd is a branch of the journey in the homeland. When the journey in the homeland becomes easy, he must also travel in the seclusion of the homeland in the very midst of the crowd. Completing the outer journey does not lead to the region of the inward."

He also said, "This task is difficult at the outset, but it very soon becomes easy.... This talent is bestowed on the novices in our Spiritual Path. In the other Paths, however, it is only conferred on those who have reached the final stage. That is because it is obtained in the inner journey. It is the beginning of the Naqshbandī Spiritual Path, where the outer journey coincides with the inner journey. Travelers on the other Paths must complete the outer journey, then embark on the inner journey."

For the sake of clarification, I should explain that the outer journey is a journey in the realm of matter and the realm of creation. The inner journey, it is the process of traversing the internal, heart-centered stations, which are also called the subtle centers belonging to the realm of the [Divine] command. The secrets and lights revealed outside of the heart belong to the realm of creation, meaning the outer realm.

I used to hear my father say (sanctified be his innermost being), "Many of the righteous go to the marketplace where they enter the gatherings without being recognized by the people there. They do so in order to be specially favored by the mercy of Allāh (Glory be to Him). Since His mercy descends on all the people, but it only reaches those who are not heedless. The people in the marketplace are heedless. This is what is meant by seclusion in the crowd."

The manifestation of these attributes and the ability to realize these actions are some of the talents of those spiritual travelers who have mastered these degrees through their dedication to remembrance, worshipful servitude, truthfulness, and earnest endeavor.

5. Constant remembrance [*adh-dhikr ad-dā'im*] (in Persian: *yād kard*)

This refers to remembrance in the general sense, which includes remembrance of the Name of Majesty, contemplation, ritual prayer, recitation of the Noble Qur'ān, and supplication. It is the basis of Sufi practice and it most commonly signifies remembrance of the Name of Majesty ("Allāh") and contemplation.

Remembrance may be performed audibly [*jahrān*] and it may be performed inaudibly [*sirrān*]. Naqshbandī spiritual training relies on inaudible remembrance, which has two forms: (1) the remembrance of "Allāh" (Almighty and Glorious is He), and (2) "*Lā ilāha illa 'llāh*," which is called the negation ["There is no god"] and the affirmation ["except Allāh"].

In the words of the noble Prophetic tradition,

> The finest expression uttered by me and by the prophets before me is, "*Lā ilāha illa 'llāh* [There is no god except Allāh]."

This Spiritual Path used to be called *aṭ-Ṭarīqat al-Khwājiyya* after the name of its great spiritual guide, known as Khwāja 'Abd al-Khāliq Ghujduwānī. He established and propagated inaudible remembrance in the Naqshbandī Spiritual Path. He was the first to provide the wise advice that we are in the process of explaining. Audible remembrance continued to be practiced by spiritual travelers alongside hidden remembrance until the time of Shaikh Muḥammad Bahā' ad-Dīn an-Naqshband, the chieftain of the Naqshbandī Spiritual Path. He decided that heart-centered remembrance is the only proper method. He added three other counsels to the axioms of al-Ghujduwānī: temporal awareness [*al-wuqūf az-zamānī*], numerical awareness [*al-wuqūf al-'adadī*], and heart-centered awareness [*al-wuqūf al-qalbī*], so there came to be eleven axioms or counsels.

In this context, what is meant by remembrance is the constant practice of remembrance and recollection. The advantage of heart-centered remembrance is that it does not need sound or pronunciation with the tongue, so the spiritual traveler can practice remembrance even in the midst of work. Verbal remembrance, on the other hand, is impractical in the state of work, especially in conversation with people.

This heart-centered remembrance demands constant practice until the spiritual traveler truly experiences constant presence with the One who is remembered, He being Allāh (Glory be to Him). Its aim is this presence. Only then does the spiritual traveler perceive, with his inner feeling and the eye of his insight, that he is present before his Lord. He sees the blessings, for this is the state of witnessing.

As we have mentioned, some remember Allāh twenty-five thousand times in one day. In the case of novices, remembrance must be performed at least five thousand times. After reaching the stage of presence, the number is no longer significant, and the same applies to verbal remembrance. That is because the One who is remembered, He being Allāh, has enveloped his heart, and the spiritual traveler has traversed the stations.

6. Returning from remembrance to the Essence [*al-'awda mina 'dh-dhikr ila 'dh-dhāt*] (in Persian: *bāz gasht*)

This means the return of the practitioner of remembrance from "*Lā ilāha illa 'llāh*" (the negation ["There is no god"] and affirmation ["except Allāh"])—after releasing his breath—to expressing this noble sentence with the tongue or the heart, "My God, You are my aim and Your good pleasure is what I seek." That is for the purpose of expelling all imaginings from his heart so that the existence of the whole of creation disappears from his sight.

7. Guarding the heart against fits of heedlessness and idle notions [*ḥirāsat al-qalb min al-ghafalāt wa 'l-khawāṭir*]; or constant presence [*al-ḥuḍūr ad-dā'im*] (in Persian: *nigāh dāsht*)

This means that the seeker must keep his heart safe from the intrusion of distracting notions even for an instant. If something occurs to his heart, whether it be true or false, he must halt his remembrance until he has finished expelling the distracting notions and then begin the remembrance anew.

As we read in the book entitled *Manāhij as-sair* [*Procedures of the Journey*], by Sayyid Abū'l-Ḥasan Zaid al-Mujaddidī al-Fārūqī, "The meaning of this pause is that the spiritual traveler must preserve the fruits of the blessings he receives through constant remembrance, or preserve the degree of presence and witnessing, which he receives through his steadfast commitment to remembrance. He must not permit the intrusion of distractions into his heart."

In the book entitled *Rashaḥāt 'Ain al-Ḥayāt* [*Dew Drops from the Source of Life*], Fakhr ad-Dīn 'Alī al-Kāshifī quotes from Sa'd ad-Dīn al-Kāshgharī, "It is incumbent on the spiritual traveler to devote one, two or three hours daily, according to his ability, to the practice of controlling his mental and heart-centered thinking so that nothing invades his heart and nothing remains in his heart except Allāh (Glory be to Him)."

According to some authorities, the pause is peculiar to the remembrance of negation and affirmation ("*Lā ilāha illa 'llāh*") and it is made for the purpose of fixing and confining the meaning of the remembrance in the heart so that the meaning of "*Lā ilāha illa 'llāh*" remains intact. If he cannot observe this practice, he will not experience heart-centered presence.

This effort is obviously aimed at the preservation of constant presence. That is because presence of heart and keeping the heart safe from all notions and imaginings are among the most important objectives of Sufism. All would-be Sufis must cultivate them since they constitute one of the degrees of Sufism. The shaikhs have many sayings and wise counsels to offer on this subject. The point is not that no notion should ever pass through the heart, but that none should settle therein. They should be like the leaves that pass quickly over flowing water and do not come to a standstill.

In the book entitled *al-Ḥadā'iq al-wardiyya* [*The Rose Gardens*], by Sayyid 'Abd al-Majīd al-Khānī, the following saying is attributed to 'Alī ad-Dīn al-'Aṭṭār, "It is hard and troublesome to keep notions and imaginings from intruding into the heart, but you must work at expelling them and preventing their survival." He also said, "I guarded my heart for twenty years against notions and imaginings, yet they still invaded my heart after all this length of time, but they did not settle there."

8. Witnessing [*mushāhada*] (in Persian: *yād dāsht*)

This means pure concentration on witnessing the lights of the Essence. It is also called the eye of certainty [*'ain al-yaqīn*].

According to Shaikh Muḥammad Amīn al-Kurdī, "It is a metonym for the heart's presence with Allāh (Exalted is He) constantly in every condition without affectation and without strenuous exertion. Such presence is really no easy matter except after traversing the stations of rapture [*jadhba*] and covering the stages of the spiritual journey."

He also said, "The truth is that it is attainable only after perfect annihilation [*fanā'*] and complete perpetuity [*baqā'*]. Witnessing or "*yād dāsht*" [in Persian] is the fruit of the spiritual traveler's work and it signifies the state of the seeker after the attainment of his goal. It may also be the fruit of remembrance, vigilant awareness, or the assistance of the spiritual guide. The traveler reaches it after surmounting all obstacles."

According to Shaikh 'Ubaidullāh al-Aḥrār, "This axiom signifies witnessing the Truth with Essential love. It is a presence in which there is no absence. Love envelops the spiritual traveler in a permanent form. It is also called "*yād kard*" [in Persian], which is the constant practice of remembrance, and "*rujū*' [returning]," in the sense that the traveler returns to his heart after any pause in remembrance. After this return he says, 'My God, You are my aim and Your good pleasure is what I seek.' Pausing signifies the preservation of this state without remembering anything." Witnessing is therefore the constant preservation of this state and the safeguarding of presence.

The three axioms added by Shaikh an-Naqshband to the eight principles discussed above are detailed below.

9. Temporal awareness [*al-wuqūf az-zamānī*]

This is heart-centered reckoning. It means that the spiritual traveler is required to consider his personal state after every two or three hours. If it has been in the state of presence with Allāh (Exalted is He), he must give thanks to Allāh (Exalted is He) for this enabling grace. If it has been in the state of heedlessness, he must seek His forgiveness and repent.

As we read in the book entitled *Rashaḥāt* [*Beads of Dew*], Shaikh Bahā' ad-Dīn an-Naqshband once said, "Temporal awareness means that the spiritual traveler must be conscious of his state, recognizing whether it is worthy of thankfulness or whether it calls for apology. If it is good, he should thank Allāh for it, and if it is not, he should apologize."

According to Mawlānā Ya'qūb Charkhī, one of the eminent disciples of Shaikh an-Naqshband, "Shaikh Muḥammad Bahā' ad-Dīn an-Naqshband used to advise the spiritual traveler to seek forgiveness if he was afflicted by the state of constriction [*qabḍ*], and to give thanks to Allāh (Glory be to Him) if Allāh had blessed him with the state of expansion [*basṭ*]." Temporal awareness is therefore vigilant awareness of the two states of constriction and expansion. It should also be understood that the basis of the state of expansion is alertness, whereas the basis of the state of constriction is heedlessness.

10. Numerical awareness [*al-wuqūf al-'adadī*]

This is the careful observance of the odd number of repetitions—three or five, for instance—of the negation and affirmation "*Lā ilāha illa 'llāh* [There is no god except Allāh]." There are some who can perform the remembrance twenty-one times with a single breath. The spiritual traveler must remain consciously alert by holding his breath for the odd-numbered remembrance. This is remembrance with the heart and the inner being. Counting is also with the heart and the inner being, not with the tongue. This awareness yields a great spiritual fruit. It has been experienced by shaikhs and disciples, making it one of the fundamental tenets of the Spiritual Path.

According to Shaikh 'Abd ar-Raḥmān al-Jāmī (A.H. 817–898), in his work *ar-Risālat an-Nūriyya* [*The Luminous Treatise*],[2] "The wisdom of numerical awareness is the spiritual traveler's conscious recognition of when and how many times he must perform the remembrance in order to obtain its fruit. If he reaches twenty-one times, but does not notice the spiritual fruit, this is a clear sign of failure to fulfill its prerequisites. He must pay vigilant attention to the number in order to recognize whether or not he will receive the blessing. If he has not received the blessing from twenty-one repetitions, he must discover the secret of what is lacking in his work."

According to Shaikh an-Naqshband, "The aim of this numerical awareness is control of the spiritual traveler's thinking so that his mind does not wander and go from here to there."

According to 'Alā' ad-Dīn al-'Aṭṭār, "What is important to obtaining the fruit is not the frequency of remembrance. What is important is the alertness and vigilance with which it is performed. This is realized through temporal and numerical awareness."

11. Heart-centered awareness [*al-wuqūf al-qalbī*]

According to Shaikh 'Abdullāh ad-Dihlawī, "This signifies the spiritual traveler's attention to the state of his heart, by exerting his vigilance and the effort to recognize whether or not he is truly practicing remembrance. He must concentrate with his heart on His Essence (Glory be to Him), not on what the heart imagines nor on the Name."

Heart-centered awareness is therefore the safeguarding of the heart, to ensure that it remembers Allāh constantly and never forgets Him. The aim of remembrance is the One who is remembered, not the wording. The spiritual traveler waits for the blessing turning toward heaven. It is true that Allāh (Glory be to Him) is everywhere while heaven in human terms is the center of exaltation and blessing.

According to Shaikh Muḥammad Bahā' ad-Dīn Naqshband, "Heart-centered awareness is superior to temporal awareness and numerical awareness. Despite the importance of these two for the acquisition of blessings, their omission does not affect the progress of

2. Shaikh 'Abd ar-Raḥmān al-Jāmī is the author of *Nafaḥāt al-Uns*. His treatise *ar-Risālat an-Nūriyya* is preserved in Cairo.

the Sufi. Heart-centered awareness is strictly necessary, however, for if the spiritual traveler loses it when practicing remembrance, and his remembrance becomes the mere movement of the tongue or the heart, without conscious alertness, he will not acquire anything at all."

The Naqshbandī Chain of Transmission [*Silsila*]

The Naqshbandī Spiritual Path [*ṭarīqa*] ascends link by link, until it reaches our most noble Prophet, our master Muḥammad (Allāh bless him and give him peace). It has three chains of transmission:

• The first chain of transmission [*silsila*] is connected to the Household [of the Prophet (Allāh bless him and give him peace)], and it is called the Golden Chain. Its links are the following:

1. The most noble Messenger, our master Muḥammad (Allāh bless him and give him peace).
2. Imām ʻAlī (peace be upon him).
3. Imām al-Ḥusain (peace be upon him).
4. Imām Zain al-ʻĀbidīn (peace be upon him).
5. Imām al-Bāqir (peace be upon him).
6. Imām Jaʻfar aṣ-Ṣādiq.
7. Imām Mūsā al-Kāẓim.
8. Imām ar-Riḍā.
9. Shaikh Maʻrūf al-Karkhī.
10. Sarī as-Saqaṭī.
11. Junaid al-Baghdādī.
12. Shaikh Abū ʻAlī ar-Rūdbārī.
13. Abū ʻUthmān al-Maghribī.
14. Abu'l-Qāsim al-Jurjānī.
15. Shaikh Abū ʻAlī al-Fārmadī.

All three chains share the connection with Shaikh Abū ʻAlī al-Fārmadī, who has absolute authorization from both sides, and two chains share an earlier connection with Shaikh Maʻrūf.

• The second chain of transmission:

1. The most noble Messenger, our master Muḥammad (Allāh bless him and give him peace).
2. Imām ʻAlī (peace be upon him).
3. Shaikh Ḥasan al-Baṣrī.
4. Shaikh Dāwūd aṭ-Ṭā'ī.
5. Shaikh Maʻrūf al-Karkhī.

Shaikh Ma'rūf received authority from the two chains just as Imām Ja'far aṣ-Ṣādiq received authority from his paternal grandfather, Imām 'Alī, and also from his mother's father, our master Abū Bakr aṣ-Ṣiddīq.

In his beautiful handwriting, the elegant calligrapher Sayyid Ṭāhir al-Hāshimī inscribed for me the chains of transmission of the Naqshbandī Order, and these are printed in this book. I shall write them in the form that is customary in the seal, which is a term for a rite of remembrance [*dhikr*] at daybreak and at sunset, performed by the circles of the Naqshbandī spiritual travelers. They remember death first of all, and visualize the spiritual guide. Then they chant the invocations of blessing and say, with a specified number of repetitions.

> There is no might nor any power except with Allāh,
> the All-High, the Almighty.
> *lā ḥawla wa lā quwwata illā bi'llāhi 'l-'Aliyyi 'l-'Aẓīm.*
> O Everlasting One, You are the Everlasting One!
> *yā Bāqī Anta 'l-Bāqī.*

Then they recite the Qur'ān and offer the likeness of its reward to the spirit of their guide, to the guide of their guide, and so on, concluding with the Prophet (Allāh bless him and give him peace). At this time, the candles are extinguished and they lower their eyes, to prevent random notions from invading their hearts and for the sake of concentration. Everything mentioned here has a known quantity. The spiritual guide participates with them and may focus with his heart on the heart of the disciples, providing them with bounties. This is called directing attention [*tawajjuh*]. He may sometimes appoint one of his deputies to perform *tawajjuh*. This is a sign of the deputy's attainment to the level of guidance and instruction, though it is only the beginning of the Spiritual Path.

Benefit may be derived from the spiritual guide if he is genuine, even without his actual presence. He may provide his disciple with benefit that the disciple could not obtain by himself even if he worked for ten long years. As I have previously stressed, these facts are related on the basis of some familiarity with the sources of the books of Sufism, though I have no direct knowledge of them. Nevertheless, I do enjoy the honor of having received instruction in the Spiritual Path from my father, Shaikh 'Alā' ad-Dīn. Even though I have not been endowed with his charismatic talents, I am fortunate to be both his physical son and his spiritual son and I consider myself his disciple. May Allāh accept from me this loyalty, which is loyalty to the Sunna of the most noble Messenger, our master Muḥammad (Allāh bless him and give him peace)!

• This is the chain of transmission of the Naqshbandī Spiritual Path, which I received from my father and my spiritual guide:

1. Shaikh Muḥammad 'Alā' ad-Dīn an-Naqshbandī.
2. Shaikh 'Umar Ḍiyā' ad-Dīn an-Naqshbandī.
3. Shaikh Bahā' ad-Dīn an-Naqshbandī.
4. Shaikh 'Uthmān Sirāj ad-Dīn an-Naqshbandī.
5. Shaikh Mawlānā Khālid an-Naqshbandī.
6. Shaikh 'Abdullāh ad-Dihlawī.
7. Shams ad-Dīn Ḥabībullāh Jān Jānān.
8. Sayyid Nūr Muḥammad al-Bada'ūnī.
9. Sayyid Muḥammad Saif ad-Dīn.
10. Shaikh Muḥammad Ma'ṣūm.
11. (Imām ar-Rabbānī, Shaikh Aḥmad al-Fārūqī al-Mujaddid.)
12. Shaikh Muḥammad al-Bāqī.
13. Muḥammad Khwājagī Amkanī.
14. Darwīsh Muḥammad.
15. Shaikh Muḥammad al-Qāḍī az-Zāhid.
16. Shaikh 'Ubaidullāh al-Aḥrār.
17. Shaikh Ya'qūb Charkhī.
18. Shaikh 'Alā' ad-Dīn al-'Aṭṭār.
19. (Shaikh Muḥammad Bahā' ad-Dīn an-Naqshband.)
20. Shaikh Sayyid Kulāl.
21. Shaikh Muḥammad Baba Sammāsī.
22. Shaikh 'Alī ar-Rāmitanī.
23. Shaikh Maḥmūd Anjīr Faghnawī.
24. Shaikh 'Ārif Riwgarī.
25. (Shaikh 'Abd al-Khāliq al-Ghujduwānī.)
26. Yūsuf al-Hamadānī.
27. Abū 'Alī al-Fārmadī.
28. Abū'l-Ḥasan al-Kharaqānī.
29. Abū Yazīd al-Bisṭāmī.
30. Our master Ja'far aṣ-Ṣādiq.
31. Qāsim ibn Muḥammad ibn Abī Bakr aṣ-Ṣiddīq.
32. Sulaimān al-Fārisī.
33. Our master Abū Bakr aṣ-Ṣiddīq.
34. Our master, our beloved friend and our intercessor, Muḥammad (Allāh bless him and give him peace).

When was this Spiritual Path called "Naqshbandī" and why?

It has become clear to us in our study that the Naqshbandī Spiritual Path is a complete and perfect observance of the true Islamic religion and the pure Sunna [exemplary practice of the Prophet (Allāh bless him and give him peace)]. It is well known that some of the Companions (may Allāh be well pleased with them all) were distinguished from the others in constant dedication to remembrance, worship, and the sacred struggle, but the honor of companionship is loftier and more beautiful, and that is why they were all called the Companions. As for those Successors [*Tābi'ūn*] who showed an inclination toward Sufi isolation in their time, their case is similar, for the title "Successors" continued to be the most notable designation applied to them all. Then, in the middle of the second Hijrī century, they gradually ceased to be referred to as Successors. The terms "ascetic [*zāhid*]" and worshipper [*'ābid*]" began to be used instead when describing the worshipful sages who chose the life of isolation and secluded retreat.

In the latter part of the second Hijrī century, the term "Sufi" was applied for the first time to those devout worshippers who were not deceived by the illusions of this world and who remained steadfast in absolute servitude to Allāh (Glory be to Him) just as the preeminent Companions and Successors had been.

After this research, there can be no doubt that the wearing of wool [*ṣūf*] is consistent with this disposition. That this way of life is the reason for the application of the name "Sufi" to those devout worshippers who withdrew into the isolated corner of retreat.

When Rābi'a al-'Adawiyya, the martyr of ardent Sufi love, was in the throes of death, she said to one of her female companions, "When I die, you must bathe me and shroud me in this cloak of mine, which is made of wool."

As we read in the book entitled *Tadhkirat al-awliyā'* [*Memento of the Saints*], by Farīd ad-Dīn al-'Aṭṭār, "Al-Ḥasan al-Baṣrī would not start preaching until Rābi'a al-'Adawiyya was present. He used to say, 'The blessing of my sermon comes from this old woman who covers herself with wool.'" Just consider that this Sufi woman used to wear wool in a place like Baṣra, which is extremely hot!

Where this early period is concerned, I wish to emphasize certain points. The term Spiritual Path [*Ṭarīqa*] was nonexistent and unknown, and the distinctive titles in common use were "the Companions" and "the Successors," just as the term *madhhab* [school of Islamic jurisprudence] was nonexistent and unknown. When these terms eventually came into use, they were qualified by the names of their leaders and their great founders. But for Abū Ḥanīfa and ash-Shāfi'ī, there would have been no Ḥanafī and Shāfi'ī schools of jurisprudence. But for 'Abd al-Qādir al-Jīlānī and Bahā' ad-Dīn an-Naqshband, there would have been no Qādirī and Naqshbandī Spiritual Paths.

According to the masters of the Naqshbandī Spiritual Path, their Path was originally called "*aṭ-Ṭarīqat aṣ-Ṣiddīqiyya*" after Abū Bakr aṣ-Ṣiddīq (may Allāh be well pleased with him). Then it came to be called "*aṭ-Ṭarīqat aṭ-Ṭaifūriyya*," after Abū Yazīd al-Bisṭāmī, whose first name was Ṭaifūr.

That does not mean that Abū Bakr and 'Alī named a particular school. The point is that the chain of transmission from guide to guide leads to our master Abū Bakr or 'Alī (may Allāh be well pleased with them). It may mean that we follow the example set by our master Abū Bakr aṣ-Ṣiddiq, after the death of the Messenger (Allāh bless him and give him peace). The Prophet (Allāh bless him and give him peace) once said,

> Allāh has never poured anything into my breast without my having poured it into the breast of Abū Bakr.

This is not about something material, but about spiritual love, true knowledge, and wisdom. These are secrets that give rise to blissful happiness. In the science of Sufism, this state is called *ḍimniyya* [inclusiveness], for the spiritual station essentially belongs to another person, but that person is able to include someone else and share this blessing with him.

Our Spiritual Path was eventually called "*aṭ-Ṭarīqat an-Naqshbandiyya*," in relation to Bahā' ad-Dīn Naqshband.

Since the time of Naqshband, this Spiritual Path has also been called by the names of the most famous men, including 'Ubaidullāh al-Aḥrār, Imām ar-Rabbānī al-Mujaddid, and Mawlānā Khālid an-Naqshbandī. (Notice that not one of them omitted the name "an-Naqshband"!) It has thus been referred to as [*aṭ-Ṭarīqat*] al-Aḥrāriyya, al-Mujaddidiyya and al-Khālidiyya, but an-Naqshbandiyya is still its proper name. None of those others claimed to have reached a station higher than that of Bahā' ad-Dīn Naqshband, just as no one has yet claimed to have reached the station of Shaikh 'Abd al-Qādir al-Jīlānī.

We shall now conclude this account of the Naqshbandī Spiritual Path with a brief biography of this great man, Bahā' ad-Dīn Naqshband.

The Life of Bahā' ad-Dīn an-Naqshband

This is a brief biography of Shaikh Bahā' ad-Dīn Muḥammad ibn Muḥammad ibn Muḥammad, widely known as an-Naqshband, and surnamed Muḥammad al-Bukhārī.

He was born (sanctified be his innermost being) in the sacred month of Muḥarram A.H. 717, in the village of Qaṣr-i Hinduwān, which was later called Qaṣr-i 'Ārifān a few miles from Bukhāra. According to some sources, he was a Sayyid Ḥusainī [descendent of the blessed Prophet's grandson al-Ḥusain], and his great-grandfather was Muḥammad Jalāl ad-Dīn Rūmī.

He was the disciple of Khwāja Muḥammad Baba as-Sammāsī, the Shaikh of the Spiritual Path of the Masters of Wisdom [*Khwājagān*]. (As we have noted earlier, this Spiritual Path used to be called *Ṭarīqat-i Khwājagān*.) Khwāja Muḥammad Baba as-Sammāsī died in A.H. 755.

Together with a number of his disciples, as-Sammāsī once stayed as a guest in Qaṣr-i Hinduwān, the native village of Muḥammad Bahā' ad-Dīn, who was barely three days old at the time. The child's grandfather embraced him and carried him to Shaikh as-Sammāsī, who was delighted by him and said, "This child is a son of mine!" He gave his disciples the good news that this child would become a leader for his own time. His grandfather wished to provide him with Sufi training, so he found him a wife when he was eighteen years old and took him to Sammās in the same year, to enter the service of the great sage, Shaikh Muḥammad as-Sammāsī, from whom he received the Spiritual Path.

After Shaikh as-Sammāsī's death in A.H. 755, his grandfather took him to Samarqand to look for a righteous man capable of training him. Then the two of them went to Amīr Kulāl, Shaikh as-Sammāsī's deputy. He received the Spiritual Path from him and embarked on the spiritual journey. Amīr Kulāl told him that the venerable Shaikh Muḥammad as-Sammāsī had bequeathed him to him, and had said to him, "You must spare no effort in training my son, Muḥammad Bahā' ad-Dīn, nor in treating him kindly!" Bahā' ad-Dīn thus embarked on the practice of remembrance and contemplation by training the heart and purifying the self.

His aptitude was above the ordinary, so he used to cover a month's distance in a single day, and a year's distance in a few days. Sayyid Amīr Kulāl assembled his disciples one day, and said to Muḥammad Bahā' ad-Dīn in front of them, "I have fulfilled the bequest of my guide, Khwāja as-Sammāsī, where your training is concerned, and I have spared no effort in training you." Then he placed his hand on his breast and said, "I have suckled you with everything that my breast contained, so my nipple is dry. You have thus been enabled to extract your heart from the husk of humanity and to deliver it from the lower self and the devil. You have become a splendid man and I have appointed you to my own position, but your aspiration seeks the highest height. This marks the end of my ability to train you and I hereby permit you to look for a man who is better qualified than I am. Perhaps he will raise you up to a higher station." As I have previously mentioned, there are some disciples who advance beyond their shaikhs, like Shaikh an-Naqshband in relation to his guide, Sayyid Amīr Kulāl.

After leaving Sayyid Amīr Kulāl, he spent seven years with Mawlānā 'Ārif ad-Dīkkarānī, a companion of Kulāl and one of his deputies. He then spent twelve years with a Turkish Shaikh called Khalīl Ata, for he was ardently devoted to worshipful servitude and the spiritual journey. In addition to pursuing the spiritual journey, Bahā' ad-Dīn used to frequent the company of scholars versed in the Sacred Law, especially for the purpose of studying the Prophetic Sunna.

He performed the Pilgrimage [Ḥajj] on two occasions, and on one of his journeys he went to Herāt, where he was received with respect by the king, Mu'izz ad-Dīn. He went on many journeys, traveling to Samarqand, Simnān, Rewartūn, Merv, Ṭūs, Mashhad, Taibād, Qizil Ribāṭ and Kish. Shaikh Muḥammad Bahā' ad-Dīn an-Naqshband died on a Monday night, the 3rd of Rabī' al-Awwal A.H. 791. He was buried in his orchard in the place he had designated. His followers built a huge dome over his grave, which is still a site of visitation. He had trained tens of thousands of disciples, some of whom attained to the degree of unconditional authorization and experienced the degrees of perpetuity after annihilation.

By the grace of his blessings, his deputies and representatives were able to bring their disciples to their goals. One of them was Khwāja Muḥammad Pārsā, born in Bukhārā in A.H. 749 and who died in Balkh in A.H. 865. He left dozens of literary works, including *al-Qudsiyya*, which is a book containing the sayings of Shaikh an-Naqshband. He was succeeded by his son, Abū 'n-Naṣr Pārsā, one of the great shaikhs of the Naqshbandī Order.

Of the outstanding figures of the Naqshbandī Order who are links in our chain of transmission, one is Shaikh Muḥammad ibn Muḥammad, widely known as 'Alā' ad-Dīn al-'Aṭṭār. He trained hundreds of disciples and enabled them to reach the peaks of their goals. The book entitled *al-Ḥadā'iq al-wardiyya* [*The Rose Gardens*] contains the names of dozens of his disciples and reports of dozens of his deputies. It states that he had deputies "like the stars in the sky."

In the book entitled *al-Qudsiyya*, printed and edited by Sayyid Aḥmad Ṭāhir al-'Irāqī, there is an index of the manuscripts relating to the Naqshbandī Order. It is also adorned with a picture of the mausoleum of an-Naqshband. According to a Danish orientalist who was in Bukhāra from 1896 to 1899, "Bahā' ad-Dīn's mausoleum is in a corner of an orchard filled with many mulberry and apricot trees. Its two sides form a mosque and it is a site of frequent visitation."

According to another nineteenth-century orientalist, a Hungarian called Arminius Vambery, "Many people are constantly flocking to his mausoleum, even from China. The inhabitants of Bukhāra make a habit of visiting it every Wednesday and some of them spend the whole night praying there. Beside the tower there is a mosque and a dervish convent."

As we read in the book entitled *al-Ḥadā'iq al-wardiyya* [*The Rose Gardens*], "When Bahā' ad-Dīn died, he was buried in his orchard, and a dome and a mosque were promptly constructed beside his tomb. Kings and aristocrats made considerable financial contributions to the pious endowment established for the upkeep of his mausoleum."

According to the editor of *al-Qudsiyya*, "As well as *ar-Risāla al-Qudsiyya*, several other treatises of Bahā' ad-Dīn Naqshband can be found in the world's libraries like *al-Awrād al-Bahiyya*, *Awrād aṣ-Ṣaghīr* and *al-Awrād al-Bahā'iyya*. The latter has a commentary attached, as has *Risālat al-Wāridāt* found in the Aya Sophia library [in Istanbul] along with the book entitled *Dalīl al-'Āshiqīn and Risālat al-ḥayāt*."

The word "an-Naqshband"

Many people are curious about the meaning of this word, which is [the noun] Naqshband, not [the adjective] Naqshbandī. It is a Persian word meaning *nāqish* [engraving tool], which is used for carving in stone and wood. The term *naqqāsh* is applied to someone who sculpts by hand. The word *naqsh* is Arabic, and it occurs in the saying, "Teaching the young is like carving [*naqsh*] in stone."

It has been said that his ancestors were sculptors, but that is not correct. Had it been true, Bahā' ad-Dīn's name would have been Naqshbandī, not Naqshband. Throughout the whole course of his life, he engaged in no work other than the Sufi profession, so the meaning is someone who concentrates on spiritual concerns. In other words, Bahā' ad-Dīn was the sculptor of hearts. He fixed the engraving of "Allāh" in his own heart and the hearts of his disciples. His purpose was clearly to work for the One who is remembered so that He would be in his heart.

In the words of the Naqshbandī poet,

O comrade on the Path of an-Naqshband!
Earnestly engrave remembrance of the Truth within your heart!

Some have said that Naqshband is a village in Bukhāra, and Bahā' ad-Dīn was one of its inhabitants. This is not correct, however, since no village with that name exists, and his life is well-known and clearly documented. If there had been a village with that name, he would have been called an-Naqshbandī, not an-Naqshband. The fact is that he promoted silent remembrance for the sake of keeping the One who is remembered permanently in the heart, and engraving Him in the inner being.

His names include Muḥammad Bahā' ad-Dīn al-Uwaisī al-Bukhārī. This shows that he came from Bukhāra, but what is the meaning of "al-Uwaisī"? According to the author of the book entitled *Ta'rīkh at-taṣawwuf fī Kurdistān*, who quotes from *Ta'rīkh as-Sulaimāniyya* by Amīn Zakī, "He was called an Uwaisī because his character in Sufism was the character of Uwais al-Qaranī."

As a matter of fact, the title "al-Uwaisī" is given to those shaikhs who gained access to the path of shaikhs who died before their own time or whom they did not meet in the flesh. They received their training from them through spiritual, not physical, contact just as our master Uwais al-Qaranī was deprived of the benefit of meeting with the Messenger (Allāh bless him and give him peace), yet he was endowed with his spirituality and his blessings.

As he said when describing his spiritual journey, an-Naqshband received his spiritual training from the spirituality of Khwāja 'Abd al-Khāliq al-Ghujduwānī. Amīr Kulāl acknowledged that he had brought him to a particular station, to the extent of his ability, and that he was then raised to this great station by the spirituality of Shaikh al-Ghujduwānī, who died many years before Bahā' ad-Dīn. On this basis he was "Uwaisī by disposition [*mashrab*]," and that is why he is called "Bahā' ad-Dīn al-Uwaisī." That also explains why it is said that Bahā' ad-Dīn an-Naqshband's chain of transmission [*silsila*] is linked to the Prophet (Allāh bless him and give him peace) by way of only ten shaikhs. Between Bahā' ad-Dīn and al-Ghujduwānī, the chain includes Amīr Kulāl, as-Sammāsī, 'Alī ar-Rāmitanī, Maḥmūd Anjīr Faghnawī and 'Ārif Riwgarī. It was the spirituality of al-Ghujduwānī that trained Bahā' ad-Dīn an-Naqshband so he is considered his direct guide.

This Uwaisī station was not peculiar to him. It was also attained by Shaikh Ḥasan al-Kharaqānī, who died in A.H. 475. It is widely known Ḥasan was trained by the spirituality of Bāyazīd al-Bisṭāmī, who died in A.H. 261. It is also widely known that al-Bisṭāmī received his training from Imām Ja'far aṣ-Ṣādiq, who died in A.H. 148. (According to some, there are two individuals with the name Bāyazīd, one of whom lived in the time of Imām Ja'far.)

My intention here is simply to explain the meaning of "Uwaisī," without obscuring the fact that all of these great shaikhs were devoted to Allāh (Glory be to Him), for He is Present in every place and He is the Guide of His servant.

> Practice true devotion to Allāh and Allāh will teach you.
> *wa 'ttaqu 'llāh: wa yu'allimu-kumu 'llāh.* (2:282)

If someone has a great spiritual guide like Amīr Kulāl and he says, "I have given you all that I possess, and I have extracted you from the human mold," this is a reference to the station of perpetuity after annihilation. He can then move away from that guide. Allāh (Glory be to Him) is Capable of commanding the spirituality of a righteous man to conduct the training of others.

One of the great shaikhs guided by an-Naqshband is Khwāja Ya'qūb al-Charkhī (d. A.H. 851). He is one of the knights of the path of right guidance and spiritual directorship and he enabled hundreds of spiritual travelers to reach their goals.

To obtain a clear understanding of these Sufi topics, it is enough to study the sayings of Bahā' ad-Dīn an-Naqshband concerning the signs and secrets of the Spiritual Path. If someone wishes to study the Naqshbandī Spiritual Path and its great shaikhs, he ought to study these books:

1. *al-Qudsiyya* [*Holiness*]. This contains the sayings of Bahā' ad-Dīn an-Naqshband. It has been published in Persian by Sayyid Aḥmad Ṭāhir al-'Irāqī, and it includes references to many other sources.

2. Other treatises by Shaikh Bahā' ad-Dīn an-Naqshband.

3. *The Maktūbāt* [*Letters*] *of Imām ar-Rabbānī*. This is a splendid book.

4. *Nafaḥāt al-uns* [*Breaths of Divine Intimacy*] by Mulla Jāmī.

5. *Rashaḥāt-i 'ain al-ḥayāt* [*Beads of Dew from the Source of Life*] by Fakhr ad-Dīn Kāshifī.

6. *Anīs aṭ-ṭālibīn wa 'ūddat as-sālikīn* [*The Close Friend of the Seekers and the Preparation of the Spiritual Travelers*].

7. *al-Ḥadīqat an-nadiyya fī ādāb aṭ-ṭarīqat an-Naqshbandiyya* [*The Fruitful Garden, concerning the Proprieties of the Naqshbandī Spiritual Path*] by Muḥammad ibn Sulaimān al-Baghdādī. (Printed in Cairo.)

8. *Ḥabīb as-sair* [*The Friend of the Journey*].

9. *Manāhij as-sair* [*The Procedures of the Journey*] by Abū 'l-Ḥasan al-Mujaddidī. (Printed in Delhi, 1957.)

10. *al-Mawāhib as-sarmadiyya fī manāqib an-Naqshbandiyya* [*The Everlasting Gifts, concerning the Marvelous Talents of the Naqshbandī Order*] by Shaikh Muḥammad Amīn al-Kurdī.

11. *Tanwīr al-qulūb fī mu'āmala 'allām al-ghuyūb* [*The Enlightenment of Hearts, concerning the Conduct of the Expert in Mysteries*] by Shaikh Muḥammad Amīn al-Kurdī.

12. *al-Ḥadā'iq al-wardiyya fī ijlā' an-Naqshbandiyya* [*The Rose Gardens, concerning the Clarification of the Naqshbandī Order*] by 'Abd al-Majīd al-Khānī.

13. *al-Anwār al-qudsiyya min manāqib as-sādāt an-Naqshbandiyya* [*The Holy Lights; some of the Marvelous Talents of the Naqshbandī Leaders*] by Muḥammad ar-Rakhāwī. (The same as the book entitled *al-Ḥadā'iq*.)

14. *Asrār at-tawḥīd fī maqāmāt ash-Shaikh Abī's-Sa'īd* [*The Secrets of the Affirmation of Oneness, concerning the Spiritual Stations of Shaikh Abū's-Sa'īd*].

15. *Riyāḍ al-mushtāqīn* [*The Gardens of the Ardently Yearning*] by Mulla Ḥāmid al-Bīsārānī, the deputy of Shaikh 'Uthmān Sirāj ad-Dīn an-Naqshbandī. (Manuscript.)

According to the author of the Introduction to the book entitled *al-Qudsiyya* [*Holiness*], "It is unfortunate that what has been written about the Naqshbandī lineage is mostly stored in Europe and America. A young orientalist, M. Molé, has made considerable research into the Naqshbandī lineage, and an article containing his findings was published in the *Revue des Études Islamiques*, Paris, 1963."

I have drawn attention to these books so that modern writers may be encouraged to take advantage of these references. I recommend *al-Qudsiyya* as a most important source. The same applies to the other works referred to in this book.

Sources

1. The Noble Qur'ān.
2. *Studies in Islamic Mysticism* : R.A. Nicholson.
3. *Alfāẓ aṣ-ṣūfiyya* [*Terms of Sufism*]: Ḥasan Muḥammad ash-Sharqāwī.
4. *al-Anwār al-qudsiyya fī manāqib as-sādāt an-Naqshbandiyya* [*Holy Lights of the Marvelous Talents of the Naqshbandī Leaders*]: Muḥammad ar-Rakhāwī.
5. *al-Anwār al-qudsiyya fī ma'rifat al-qawā'id aṣ-ṣūfiyya* [*Holy Lights of Knowledge concerning Sufi Principles*]: Imām 'Abd al-Wahhāb ash-Sha'rawānī.
6. *Īḍāḥ aṭ-ṭarīq* [*Explanation of the Path*]: Shāh 'Abdullāh ad-Dihlawī. (Manuscript).
7. *Īqāẓ al-himam wa sharḥ al-ḥikam* [*Awakening of Aspirations and Commentary on Wise Sayings*]: Aḥmad ibn Muḥammad ibn 'Ajība.
8. *Baina 't-taṣawwuf wa 'l-ḥayāt* [*Between Sufism and Life*]: 'Abd al-Bārī an-Nadawī.
9. *History of Philosophy in Islam* : J. DeBoer.
10. *at-Taṣawwuf al-Islāmī* [*Islamic Sufism*]: Dr. Zakī Mubārak.
11. *at-Taṣawwuf al-Islāmī* [*Islamic Sufism*]: Dr. 'Abd ar-Raḥmān Badawī.
12. *at-Taṣawwuf wa Farīd ad-Dīn al-'Aṭṭār* [*Sufism and Farīd ad-Dīn al-'Aṭṭār*]: Dr. 'Abd al-Wahhāb 'Azzām.
13. *at-Taṣawwuf 'inda 'l-Mustashriqīn* [*Sufism according to the Orientalists*]: Dr. Muḥammad ash-Sharbāṣī.
14. *at-Taṣawwuf* [*Sufism*]: Abū 'Abd ar-Raḥmān as-Sulamī.
15. *Tadhkirat al-awliyā'* [*Memoirs of the Saints*]: Farīd ad-Dīn al-'Aṭṭār.
16. *at-Ta'arruf li-madhhab ahl at-taṣawwuf* [*Inquiry into the Tenets of the Sufis*]: al-Kalābādhī.
17. *Tafsīr "Rūḥ al-bayān" li'l-Bursawī* [*Commentary on al-Bursawī's "Spirit of Explanation"*]—and other commentaries.
18. *Tanwīr al-qulūb* [*The Enlightenment of Hearts*]: Muḥammad Amīn al-Kurdī.
19. *Ḥaqā'iq 'an at-taṣawwuf* [*Realities of Sufism*]: 'Abd al-Qādir 'Īsā.
20. *Dirāsāt fī 'l-falasafat ad-dīniyya wa 'ṣ-ṣūfiyya* [*Studies in Religious

and Sufi Philosophy]: Dr. ʻAbd al-Qādir Maḥmūd.
21. *Dā'irat al-ma'ārif al-Islamiyya* [*The Encyclopaedia of Islam*]: Biography of Ibrāhīm Zalī and his friends.
22. *ar-Risālat al-Qushairiyya* [*Qushairi's Treatise*]: ʻAbd al-Karīm ibn Hawāzin al-Qushairī.
23. *Risāla ṭibb al-qulūb* [*Treatise on "Medicine of the Hearts"*]: Shaikh ʻAlā' ad-Dīn ʻUmar an-Naqshbandī.
24. *Rasā'il Ibn al-ʻArabī* [*Treatises of Ibn al-ʻArabī*]: Shaikh Muḥyi'd-Dīn ibn al-ʻArabī.
25. *Riyāḍ al-mushtāqīn* : [*Gardens of the Ardently Yearning*]: Mulla Ḥāmid al-Bīsārānī. (Manuscript).
26. *Sharḥ al-Ḥikam al-ʻaṭā'iyya* [*Commentary on al-Ḥikam al-ʻAṭā'iyya*]: Muḥammad ibn Ibrāhīm an-Nafarī.
27. *Shaṭaḥāt aṣ-ṣūfiyya* [*Ecstatic Utterances of the Ṣūfis*]: ʻAbd ar-Raḥmān Badawī.
28. *Ṣaḥīḥ Muslim* : Imām Muslim's collection of noble Prophetic Traditions.
29. *Ṣaḥīḥ al-Bukhārī* : Imām al-Bukhārī's collection of noble Prophetic Traditions.
30. *aṭ-Ṭabaqāt al-kubrā* [*The Esteemed Generations*]: Imām ash-Shaʻrānī.
31. *ʻAwārif al-maʻārif* [*Bounties of Divine Knowledge*]: Shaikh ʻUmar as-Suhrawardī
32. *al-Ghunya* [*Sufficient Provision*]: Shaikh ʻAbd al-Qādir al-Jīlānī.
33. *al-Futuḥāt al-Makkiyya* [*The Meccan Revelations*]: Shaikh Muḥyi'd-Dīn ibn al-ʻArabī.
34. *Fuṣūṣ al-ḥikam* [*Bezels of Wisdom*]: Shaikh Muḥyi'd-Dīn ibn al-ʻArabī.
35. *al-Falsafat al-akhlāqiyyat al-Aflāṭūniyya* [*Plotinian Moral Philosophy*]: Dr. Nājī at-Takrītī.
36. *al-Falsafat aṣ-ṣūfiyya fi 'l-Islam* [*Sufi Philosophy in Islam*]: Dr. ʻAbd al-Qādir Maḥmūd.
37. *al-Falsafat al-ʻIlmiyya wa uslūb at-taḥqīq* [*Scientific Philosophy and the Method of Verification*]: Filīsīn Shāleh. (Persian).
38. *al-Fatḥ ar-rabbānī* [*The Sublime Revelation*]: Shaikh ʻAbd al-Qādir al-Jīlānī.
39. *al-Fatḥ ar-rabbānī* [*The Sublime Revelation*]: Shaikh ʻAbd al-Ghanī an-Nāblusī.
40. *al-Fihrist* [*The Index*]: Ibn an-Nadīm.
41. *Qūt al-qulūb* [*Nourishment of Hearts*]: Abū Ṭālib al-Makkī.
42. *al-Qudsiyya* [*Holiness*]: Sayings of Bahā' ad-Dīn an-Naqshband.

43. *Qawānīn ḥikam al-ishrāq* [*Rules of the Wisdom of Illumination*]: Jamāl ad-Dīn Muḥammad Abū'l-Mawāhib.
44. *al-Luma'* [*Beams of Light*]: Abū Naṣr as-Sarrāj.
45. *Muqaddimat Ibn Khaldūn* [*Ibn Khaldūn's Introduction*].
46. *al-Madkhal ilā 't-taṣawwuf al-Islāmī* [*Introduction to Islamic Sufism*]: Muḥammad Abu'l-Faiḍ al-Manūfī.
47. *Madārij as-Sālikīn* [*Stages of Spiritual Travelers*]: Ibn Qayyim al-Jawziyya.
48. *al-Murshid ilā āyāt al-Qur'ān al-Karīm* [*Guide to the Verses of the Noble Qur'ān*]: Muḥammad Fāris ar-Rāzī.
49. *Mirṣād al-'ibād min al-mabda' ila 'l-ma'ād* [*Observation Post of the Servants from the Outset to the Final Destination*]: Shaikh Najm ad-Dīn ar-Rāzī.
50. *al-Mu'jam aṣ-ṣūfī* [*Sufi Lexicon*]: Dr. Sū'ād al-Ḥakīm.
51. *Mu'jam muṣṭalaḥāt aṣ-ṣūfiyya* [*Lexicon of the Technical Terms of Sufism*]: Dr. 'Abd al-Mun'im al-Khafnī.
52. *Maktūbāt al-Imām ar-Rabbānī* [*Letters of Imām ar-Rabbānī*]: Shaikh Aḥmad al-Fārūqī.
53. *al-Munqidh min aḍ-ḍalāl* [*Savior from Error*]: Imām Muḥammad al-Ghazālī.
54. *Manāzil as-sā'irīn* [*Stages of the Travelers*]: Shaikh Imām al-Harawī.
55. *al-Mawāhib as-sarmadiyya fī manāqib as-sādāt an-Naqshbandiyya* [*Everlasting Gifts concerning the Marvelous Talents of the Naqshbandī Order*]: Muḥammad Amīn al-Kurdī.
56. *Nash'at al-Falsafat aṣ-ṣūfiyya wa taṭawwuru-hā* [*The Origin of Sufi Philosophy and its Development*]: Dr. 'Irfān 'Abd al-Ḥamīd Fattāḥ.
57. *Nash'at al-Falsafat aṣ-ṣūfiyya* [*The Origin of Sufi Philosophy*]: Dr. Ibrāhīm Basyūnī.
58. *Na't al-Bidāyāt wa taṣwīf an-nihāyāt* [*Account of the Beginnings and Description of the Final Stages*]: Muḥammad Fāḍil ibn Māmīn.
59. *Nūr an-Nāẓirīn* [*The Light of the Viewers*]: Mulla Muḥammad Bākī. (Manuscript).
60. *al-Waṣāyā* [*Bequests*]: Shaikh Muḥyi'd-Dīn ibn al-'Arabī.
61. My personal memoirs.

In addition to the above, reference has been made to approximately fifty other books, lexicons, and dictionaries.

Naqshbandi Khanaqha Complex, Biyara, Kurdistan, Iraq

Khanaqha Courtyard — Ablution fountain

Mausoleum and Mosque complex to the right

Naqshbandi Mosque complex

Mausoleum Interior - Graves of Wives of the Shaykhs

Mausoleum Interior

Mausoleum Interior —Grave of Shaikh Muhammad Ma‘sum Naqshbandi (ra) - Far right

Mausoleum Exterior Sign - Graves of:
* Shaikh Umar Diya ad-Din an-Naqshbandi,
* Shaikh Najam ad-Din an-Naqshbandi,
* Shaikh Muhammad Ala ad-Din an-Naqshbandi

Shaikh Amin Ala ad-Din an-Naqshbandi, Author, *Sufism: A Wayfarer's Guide to the Naqshbandi Way*

NFIE Mawlid 1994 Chicago—(from Left to Right) Bahauddin Baha (Justice Supreme Court Kabul),Shaykh Muhammad Masum Naqshbandi (RA), Muhammad Ali, Ahmed Mirza M.D